the new

HOLLY CLEGG

trim&TERRIFIC

Cookbook

the new

HOLLY CLEGG
trim&TERRIFIC
Cookbook

by Holly Clegg

Photography by David Humphreys

RUNNING PRESS
PHILADELPHIA · LONDON

Library of Congress Cataloging-in-Publication Number 2005929943
ISBN-13: 978-0-7624-2599-0
ISBN-10: 0-7624-2599-7

Cover and interior design by Amanda Richmond
Edited by Diana C. von Glahn
Photography assistance: Wes Kroninger
Typography: Berkeley and Trade Gothic

This book may be ordered by mail from the publisher.
Please include $2.50 for postage and handling.
But try your bookstore first!

Running Press Book Publishers
125 South Twenty-second Street
Philadelphia, Pennsylvania 19103-4399

Visit us on the web!
www.runningpress.com

Dishes pictured on cover: Orange Glazed Carrots, Chicken Fajita Pizza, Glazed Salmon, Chocolate Chip, Peanut
Butter, and Holiday Cookies, Cranberry-Pineapple and Tropical Muffins, Chicken and Black Bean Enchiladas, and
Greek Chicken Salad Bowl.

Also by Holly Clegg*:
Home Entertaining the Easy Way
Meals on the Move: Rush Hour Recipes
Eating Well Through Cancer: Easy Recipes & Recommendations During and After Treatment
* To order these books, call 1-800-88HOLLY or visit her website at www.hollyclegg.com

Table of Contents

Acknowledgments

I take this opportunity to acknowledge the special people in my life. My children, truly my #1 accomplishment, you continually make me so proud. Todd, my oldest child, an Associate at Onex Corporation, a private equity firm, your role has changed in my eyes from taste tester to advisor. I know you think I stalk you with my constant New York trips, but I really am there to work! I cherish our New York times together, dining experiences, and phone chats. My daughter, Courtney, a senior at George Washington University in journalism, your skills and talents in and out of the kitchen have made you invaluable to me. From editing, to chauffeuring, to recipe testing, we share a special bond no matter where you are. I feel such gratification knowing all those times I made you travel with me, bribed you to cook, and took you on television, actually had a positive impact on your life and your upcoming career. Haley, my eighteen year old, you will always be my baby. Your infectious smile and upbeat attitude bring me joy. Having you at home this year has been a treasured time. We share a mutual passion for food, eating, and cooking. You have tested recipes, whipped up desserts for friends, and helped me edit head- notes with your witty expertise, as you too, have tasted every recipe. Robert, my stepson, thanks for the kitchen breaks, as you are the one person I trust on the grill. To Elvis, my dachshund, who sometimes is more company than I want in my office. And of course, I saved the best for last: eternal gratitude to my husband and best friend, Mike, who makes everything worthwhile because we share it together. Your support continues unconditionally, your advice is always right on, and we still have fun after twenty-six years.

To my incredible parents, Ruth and Jerry, who are the best parents a child can ask for. You continue to listen enthusiastically to every word I say whenever I call (which is often). Thank you for encouraging me to reach for the stars and be the best I can be! Mae Mae, my invaluable in-town mother and #1 babysitter, you continually give us love and attend to our every need, including granddog sitting. NaNa and Papa, you are the godparents to all my children and have supported me since I first moved to Baton Rouge. Aunt Garney, I admire your energetic personality and spunk! My sister, Ilene, my best friend, confidant, critic, and most importantly, my daily phone call. Your advice and guidance is endless, except in the kitchen where I take over. Pam, my Clegg sis and cooking sidekick, we share it all from fun, fashion, phone calls, and recipes. I especially thank you for helping me prepare all the recipes for these photographs. You are the best kitchen "queen" I could ever ask for. True love and champagne cheers! And big thanks to the rest of the clan: Bart (for keeping those hormones straight), Jim (putting up with all my Boulder visits), Cannon (my Mississippi connection), Michael and Kim (the wine connoisseurs), and Chuck (Finky) and Barbara.

To my long time Baton Rouge friends, you know who you are as I am not getting new ones . . . Francine and Doll, Louann and Ronnie, Karen and Anthony, Gail and Louis, Lynell and Jeff, Mary and Rob, Gracie and Bill, Lisa and Dale, Louise, Melanie, and our neighbor friends for 20 years—the Cliffords (my kids' second family), the Sligars, and the Mocklers, for fun, friendship and always food. My college friends— Amy (for all my fabulous jewelry), Jolie, Les, Lila, Missy and all those I visit throughout my travels—I love picking up the phone or popping in and realizing the unique bond we have is still there after all these years . . . and I am still cooking! To Gerald, the best coauthor. Writing my cancer book with you was a truly rewarding endeavor and I'm proud to share it with the finest oncologist I know! To Renate, who would have thought my London Cordon Bleu stay would end up with a loving, caring relationship of almost thiry years? To Marcia, Selma and Joyce (just ate), my mother's friends, who instilled in me my passion for cooking. I still nag them for recipes. Baton Rouge, you are my home, and have put me on the national map with your incredible local and loyal support.

Thanks to the Diane Allen & Associates: Al (my mentor), Diane (my buddy), and Nancy for keeping me straight! Thanks to the Louisiana Sweet Potato Commission for having me all these years as the national spokesperson for Louisiana Yams, a role I enjoy so much. To Baton Rouge Coca-Cola Bottling Company, thanks for the great dream kitchen make over promotion that started with you, Gary, Melanie, Darin, Bob, and Kelly—we are a hard working, exciting and enthusiastic team. Dublin & Associates, I enjoy our opportunities together. Sybil, I love it when our paths cross.

Thanks to my beauty dream team: Burly, Mary, and Missy. A big thanks to Marlene, for typing my recipes faster than I could proof them. Tami Hancock from Hancock Nutrition thanks for the excellent job with the nutritional analysis. I know and I do always count on you. Thanks to Freddie Strange, for our great working relationship with my self- published books.

A big thanks to Carlos, Senior Counselor of Dezenhall Resources, for your confidence in me and for making me your top choice.

Carlo DeVito was instrumental in publishing the first edition of this book with his first enthusiastic phone call. Now, Jon Anderson, Running Press' Publisher, is the talented, creative leader I will eagerly follow. I look forward to working with you for many years (and you know the deal—you can't leave!!!). Diana von Glahn, my editor, your optimistic smile and good-hearted nature has been an asset to this book, from lending a helping hand in the kitchen, improving the manuscript, and having your heart and soul in my book to make it be the best ever! Bill Jones, for your dedicated design leadership, and Amanda Richmond, your creativity and insightfulness turned our vision of this book into reality. Seta, thanks for getting the word out there—I appreciate your effort.

David Humphreys, the photography is incredible!! I appreciate the many hats you wear, from your tireless effort shooting the photos to your resourceful and ingenious food styling, but most importantly, for making me laugh. Wes, your talent is appreciated in so many ways, my guaranteed smile in the photos, your set up or touch up…always ready and available for our needs.

To my Kitchen Dream Team: All the food photographed in the book was prepared in my kitchen, photographed, and then we all ate it, so thank goodness it was "Trim & Terrific." I could have never accomplished this daunting task of endurance cooking without my illustrious gang: Pam, the Prez, who kept the kitchen going, prepared more recipes than I can count, and opened our champagne nightly . . . and willingly made the official daily grocery run; Haley, my daughter who led the baking efforts and made all the kid's recipes with her friend, Macon, both ready to prepare whatever was needed, run errands, and maybe even wash a dish; Mae Mae, who did the job nobody wanted, cleaning up and washing dishes so there was always a clean measuring cup or white plate; my niece Shannon, who cheerfully agreed to chop, help, or accept whatever cooking chore at the time with her sweet smile; Robert, for running all sorts of errands; Diana, my editor, who flew in from Philadelphia to join the kitchen team, whether assisting, chopping, or styling, you were a joy and asset to have around—we hated to see you leave; and Gracie, you fit right in with your errand running, and willingness to hit the kitchen with both feet. Francine, you even made it by on crutches to get in on the action. And a big thanks to Biff for keeping me supplied in fish for the photo shoot. This team made standing on our feet for hours and hours in the kitchen more fun than you could imagine!!!

Last but not least, a Super Size Thank You to all my Trim & Terrific cookbook users through the years. I treasure all the emails, letters, and phone calls letting me know how my books have made a difference in your kitchen and influenced your lifestyle. Now, hit the kitchen and start cooking "Trim & Terrific."

Holly B. Clegg

A Note on the Recipes

- For all recipes that call for margarine, an equal amount of butter may be substituted.

- The nutritional analysis provided for each recipe is based on the larger portion size listed.

- Although most of the recipes in this book have diabetic exchanges, not all recipes are appropriate for diabetics. Follow your doctor's recommendations.

- Unless otherwise stated, all eggs used should be large.

- Unless otherwise stated, onions and lemons should be medium-sized.

- Many of the recipes suggest using non-stick pots, pans, and baking sheets. I always like the added protection of spraying my cookware and bakeware with non-stick cooking spray.

A guide to the symbols:

VEGETARIAN RECIPE

FREEZER-FRIENDLY RECIPE

Introduction

"I don't have time to cook and I don't want to eat bland tasting diet food!"

If you love to eat, have limited time to cook, and prefer a healthier lifestyle, you opened the right book. I am the author of the *"Trim & Terrific"* cookbook series known for "user friendly" 30-minute recipes. I HATE DIETS and don't plan to give up ANY food, but I prefer a more health-conscious way of life. So, I am using my expertise to show today's busy person how to create menus using favorite and classic recipes prepared with a healthier twist. Good food choices and good food habits can be made daily. With my goal and philosophy in mind and a passion for food, this book, *The New Holly Clegg Trim & Terrific Cookbook,* offers cooking solutions for the everyday person. This book contains all of your favorite recipes, answers frequently asked culinary questions, contains a dictionary of terms and ingredients, menus for every occasion and has the nutritional analysis as well as the diabetic exchange for every recipe. *The New Holly Clegg Trim & Terrific Cookbook is* an invaluable resource of recipes and information, and will guide you to a healthy lifestyle in today's fast-paced life.

This compilation of 500 palate-pleasing recipes, including favorites from the past, updated versions of familiar recipes, and newly developed recipes, will spark your taste buds. Today's food emphasizes bold flavors, ethnic ingredients, and intensified flavors. These are all represented in recipes throughout *The New Holly Clegg Trim & Terrific Cookbook.*

As a mother of three children, I understand the importance of spending time in the kitchen with your children. Cooking is a valuable teaching experience for children to learn to follow directions, read in sequence, and understand measurements. And the satisfied smile on a child's face after the completion of a recipe, makes cooking a worthwhile experience. For these beginning cooks, my *Cooking with Kids* section contains creative and fun food ideas and easy recipes. Best of all, many of these simple recipes are family favorites that any age will enjoy time and time again.

With my workable recipes, a prepared pantry, and a basic knowledge of cooking terms, you will never look at cooking as a chore. I have devoted the last section of my book, *Back to the Basics,* to relieving kitchen stress by including how to stock a pantry, techniques, tips, kitchen vocabulary, and menu planning. *The New Holly*

Clegg Trim & Terrific Cookbook also includes recipes for effortless entertaining. Plus, the menus in the back of the book will guide you through any occasion. Throughout the book, the recipes include *Quick Tips* and *Food Facts* that provide helpful hints and additional information about each recipe.

Each recipe comes with a nutritional analysis and a diabetic exchange. However, keep in mind that the portion size of some recipes may not be appropriate for diabetic diets. For these particular recipes, cut them to whatever size is needed. Remember, always follow your doctor's recommendations if you're watching your diet.

All the recipes in the book are personally tested by me (and my family!), which makes them mother cooked and kid approved. My family benefited from my testing, as there was always an abundance of food, sometimes a multitude of entrees and desserts. Most importantly, these quick-cooking recipes, made with familiar ingredients, emphasize good nutrition and family fun. Having a well-stocked kitchen, learning to use herbs and spices to infuse flavor, and using lower fat substitutes can make a difference in healthier meal preparation.

Whether you are preparing comfort food for your family or fine dining to impress guests, all the recipes in the book are healthier, delicious, and of course, easy. Consider this book your guide to everyday cooking for the busy person. Let's hit the kitchen and start cooking!

Holly B. Clegg

Glazed Brie

Appetizers

Roasted Red Bell Pepper Dip 🥕

Simple to make, this creamy red dip goes great with veggies or pita crisps. For pizzazz, serve in hollowed-out red or green bell peppers.

MAKES 3 CUPS OR 12 (¼-CUP) SERVINGS

1 (10-ounce) jar roasted red bell peppers, drained
1 tablespoon olive oil
1 (16-ounce) container reduced-fat cottage cheese
½ teaspoon minced garlic
1 tablespoon lemon juice
Dash hot pepper sauce
Salt and pepper to taste

Place the peppers, oil, cottage cheese, garlic, lemon juice, hot pepper sauce, and salt and pepper to taste in food processor; blend until very smooth.

Nutritional information per serving

Calories 34, Protein (g) 5, Carbohydrate (g) 2, Fat (g) trace, Calories from Fat (%) 10, Saturated Fat (g) 0, Dietary Fiber (g) 0, Cholesterol (mg) 2, Sodium (mg) 248, Diabetic Exchanges: 1 very lean meat

Black Bean Dip 🥕

This nutritious dip, full of fiber and protein, will be popular with guests. The sour cream and green onion slices complement this snappy dip.

MAKES 9 (¼-CUP) SERVINGS

1 onion, chopped
1 (15-ounce) can black beans, rinsed and drained (slightly chopped)
1 cup salsa
1 cup shredded reduced-fat Cheddar cheese, divided
⅓ cup fat-free sour cream
½ cup sliced green onions (scallions)

In a medium non-stick saucepan, sauté the onion until tender. Add the black beans, salsa, and ⅔ cup cheese, cooking over low heat until the cheese is melted. Pour into a serving dish; sprinkle with the remaining ⅓ cup cheese, the sour cream, and the green onion slices. Serve with chips.

Nutritional information per serving

Calories 90, Protein (g) 6, Carbohydrate (g) 11, Fat (g) 2, Calories from Fat (%) 23, Saturated Fat (g) 2, Dietary Fiber (g) 3, Cholesterol (mg) 7, Sodium (mg) 392, Diabetic Exchanges: 1 very lean meat, 0.5 starch

Spinach Dip

This is the ultimate spinach dip, and it tastes great with crackers or fresh veggies. This dip is best when made a day ahead.

MAKES 12 (¼-CUP) SERVINGS

1 (10-ounce) package frozen chopped spinach, thawed and squeezed dry
½ cup light mayonnaise
1 cup nonfat plain yogurt
1 teaspoon seasoned salt
½ teaspoon dried dill weed leaves
Juice of ½ lemon
½ cup chopped parsley
½ cup chopped green onions (scallions)

Blend all ingredients in a medium-sized bowl. Refrigerate.

Nutritional information per serving

Calories 54, Protein (g) 2, Carbohydrate (g) 4, Fat (g) 3, Calories from Fat (%) 56, Saturated Fat (g) 1, Dietary Fiber (g) 1, Cholesterol (mg) 4, Sodium (mg) 231, Diabetic Exchanges: 1 vegetable, 0.5 fat

Spinach Dip

Guacamole 🥕

Avocado has many health benefits. Since it is made up of monounsaturated fat, which is con-sidred a "good fat," you can enjoy this favorite without guilt. This is my most requested recipe for classic guacamole.

MAKES 8 (3-TABLESPOON) SERVINGS

1 large avocado, peeled, pitted, and mashed
Salt and pepper to taste
1 clove garlic, minced
¼ teaspoon chili powder
1 teaspoon lemon juice
2 teaspoons minced onion
¼ cup nonfat plain yogurt

Mash the avocado in a small bowl, and season with the salt, pepper, garlic, chili powder, and lemon juice. Stir in the onion. Cover with the yogurt to keep the mixture from darkening. Refrigerate until serving. Just before serving, stir well.

Nutritional information per serving
Calories 56, Protein (g) 1, Carbohydrate (g) 3, Fat (g) 5, Calories from Fat (%) 72, Saturated Fat (g) 1, Dietary Fiber (g) 2, Cholesterol (mg) 0, Sodium (mg) 10, Diabetic Exchanges: 1 fat

Wasabi Guacamole 🥕

Asian cuisine influences this classic guacamole. This palate-pleasing dip can be served with seared tuna or grilled fish. Wasabi can be found in the Asian section of grocery stores.

MAKES 10 TO 12 SERVINGS

2 cups mashed avocado
⅓ cup finely diced red onion
2 tablespoons finely diced, seeded serrano pepper
2 tablespoons lime juice
2 teaspoons prepared wasabi
Salt to taste

In a large bowl, mix together the avocado, onion, pepper, lime juice, wasabi, and salt. Serve with chips, veggies, or as a condiment.

Nutritional information per serving
Calories 65, Protein (g) 1, Carbohydrate (g) 4, Fat (g) 6, Calories from Fat (%) 74, Saturated Fat (g) 1, Dietary Fiber (g) 2, Cholesterol (mg) 0, Sodium (mg) 7, Diabetic Exchanges: 1 veg-etable, 1 fat

QUICK TIP:

To pit and peel an avocado, hold the avocado in one hand. Run a sharp knife lengthwise around the avo-cado, turning only the avocado, not the knife. Twist the two halves apart. Using the sharp edge of your knife, make a quick downward stroke into the pit, twist, and remove it. Cut each avocado half length-wise in two, and then peel away the skin or scoop out the avocado with a spoon.

Tex-Mex Dip

This popular and addictive spread feeds a crowd, and is easily doubled. It is an attention grabber at any party.

MAKES 15 TO 20 SERVINGS

1 cup fat-free sour cream
½ cup low fat mayonnaise
1 (1¼-ounce) package taco seasoning mix
1 (16-ounce) can fat-free refried beans
1 large tomato, chopped
1 bunch green onions (scallions), chopped
1 (3½-ounce) can pitted ripe olives, drained and chopped
1 cup shredded reduced-fat sharp Cheddar cheese

In a small bowl, combine the sour cream, mayonnaise, and taco seasoning.

To assemble, spread the refried beans on a large shallow serving plate; then spread the sour cream taco mixture over the beans. Sprinkle with the tomato, green onions, and olives. Top with the shredded Cheddar cheese. Refrigerate until serving.

Nutritional information per serving

Calories 83, Protein (g) 4, Carbohydrate (g) 9, Fat (g) 4, Calories from Fat (%) 39, Saturated Fat (g) 1, Dietary Fiber (g) 1, Cholesterol (mg) 5, Sodium (mg) 389, Diabetic Exchanges: 0.5 very lean meat, 0.5 starch, 0.5 fat

Corn Dip

These simple ingredients create a dip that is zesty and appealing, garnering tons of compliments and recipe requests.

MAKES 16 (¼-CUP) SERVINGS

2 (11-ounce) cans Mexi-corn, drained
1 (4-ounce) can chopped green chilies, drained
1 (4-ounce) can chopped jalapeño peppers, drained
5 green onions (scallions), chopped
1 cup shredded reduced-fat Cheddar cheese
1 cup fat-free sour cream

In a large bowl, mix together the Mexi-corn, green chilies, jalapeño peppers, green onions, cheese, and sour cream. Refrigerate until serving.

Nutritional information per serving

Calories 64, Protein (g) 4, Carbohydrate (g) 9, Fat (g) 1, Calories from Fat (%) 19, Saturated Fat (g) 1, Dietary Fiber (g) 1, Cholesterol (mg) 4, Sodium (mg) 359, Diabetic Exchanges: 0.5 very lean meat, 0.5 starch

Shrimp Rémoulade

Serve this creamy and flavorful rémoulade on a bed of lettuce as a light meal or with crackers as a dip.

MAKES 8 (¼-CUP) SERVINGS

2 pounds cooked, peeled shrimp
¼ cup light mayonnaise
2 tablespoons horseradish
2 tablespoons grainy, deli style, or country Dijon mustard
2 tablespoons Dijon mustard
1 tablespoon lemon juice
⅓ cup chopped fresh parsley
1 bunch green onions (scallions), chopped
Salt and pepper to taste

In a large bowl, mix together the mayonnaise, horseradish, grainy mustard, Dijon mustard, lemon juice, parsley, and green onions. Add the shrimp and season with salt and pepper to taste. Refrigerate until serving.

Nutritional information per serving
Calories 148, Protein (g) 24, Carbohydrate (g) 2, Fat (g) 4, Calories from Fat (%) 24, Saturated Fat (g) 1, Dietary Fiber (g) 1, Cholesterol (mg) 224, Sodium (mg) 483, Diabetic Exchanges: 3.5 very lean meat

Shrimp Spread

This versatile and easy recipe can serve as a dip or as stuffing for celery or tomatoes.

MAKES 16 SERVINGS

1 pound cooked, peeled shrimp, coarsely chopped
1 (8-ounce) package reduced-fat cream cheese, softened
¼ cup light mayonnaise
1 bunch green onions (scallions), thinly chopped
1 tablespoon chopped parsley
1 tablespoon lemon juice
1 teaspoon Worcestershire sauce
¼ teaspoon hot pepper sauce
Salt and pepper to taste

Combine all ingredients except shrimp in a bowl and mix well. Add the shrimp and refrigerate until serving.

Nutritional information per serving
Calories 78, Protein (g) 8, Carbohydrate (g) 1, Fat (g) 5, Calories from Fat (%) 54, Saturated Fat (g) 2, Dietary Fiber (g) 0, Cholesterol (mg) 67, Sodium (mg) 159, Diabetic Exchanges: 1 very lean meat, 1 fat

QUICK TIP:

To speed up ripening avocados, place in a brown paper bag overnight, or cook at medium power in the microwave for 30 seconds. Let sit for 10 minutes before using.

Shrimp, Avocado, and Artichoke Dip

Shrimp, Avocado, and Artichoke Dip

Even though this recipe uses only three main ingredients, you shouldn't underestimate its bold taste. If you're not a seafood fan, leave out the shrimp for an equally satisfying appetizer.

MAKES 16 SERVINGS

1 pound peeled medium shrimp

1 tablespoon margarine

Salt and pepper to taste

2 tablespoons lemon juice

2 (14-ounce) cans quartered artichoke hearts, drained

2 avocados, peeled, pitted, and cubed

3 tablespoons capers, drained

2 bunches green onions (scallions), chopped

½ cup grainy mustard

¼ cup ketchup

In a small non-stick pan, sauté the shrimp in the margarine for 5 to 7 minutes or until done. Season to taste. Remove from heat and stir in the lemon juice. Transfer to a bowl and refrigerate for 15 minutes or until chilled.

In a separate bowl, combine the artichoke hearts, avocado, capers, green onion, and cooled shrimp. In a small bowl, mix together the mustard and ketchup, and carefully toss with the shrimp mixture. Refrigerate until serving.

Nutritional information per serving

Calories 86, Protein (g) 6, Carbohydrate (g) 6, Fat (g) 5, Calories from Fat (%) 48, Saturated Fat (g) 1, Dietary Fiber (g) 2, Cholesterol (mg) 40, Sodium (mg) 36, Diabetic Exchanges: 0.5 very lean meat, 1 vegetable, 1 fat

Shrimp Southwestern Pizza Dip

Southwestern-flavored shrimp and seasonings are the key ingredients in this attractive, layered, crowd-pleasing dip. For the black bean dip, you can also use two cans of black beans, drained and mashed, mixed with a little salsa.

MAKES 10 TO 12 SERVINGS

1 pound small peeled shrimp
1 teaspoon chili powder
1 teaspoon ground cumin
1 (16-ounce) jar black bean dip
½ (8-ounce) package fat-free cream cheese
½ cup fat-free sour cream
1 (1¼-ounce) package taco seasoning mix
1 (16-ounce) jar chunky salsa
½ cup chopped green onions (scallions)
1 cup shredded reduced-fat Monterey Jack cheese or
   Cheddar cheese or mixture

In a medium non-stick skillet, cook the shrimp for 5 minutes or until done. Drain and mix with the chili powder and cumin. Set aside.

Spread the black bean dip to cover the bottom of a 10-inch platter. In a small bowl, mix together the cream cheese, sour cream, and taco seasoning mix until creamy. Carefully spread the cream cheese mixture over the bean layer. Cover with the salsa. Sprinkle with the cooked shrimp, green onions, and shredded cheese. Refrigerate until serving.

Nutritional information per serving

Calories 153, Protein (g) 13, Carbohydrate (g) 13, Fat (g) 4, Calories from Fat (%) 27, Saturated Fat (g) 2, Dietary Fiber (g) 2, Cholesterol (mg) 66, Sodium (mg) 746, Diabetic Exchanges: 1.5 lean meat, 1 starch

QUICK TIP:

To sneak soy protein into your recipes, use half cream cheese and half silken tofu.

Shrimp Cocktail Spread

Shrimp Cocktail Spread

This new take on the classic recipe uses all the same ingredients but in a layered, colorful presentation. I make this festive recipe during the holidays. It can also be made ahead of time.

MAKES 8 (¼-CUP) SERVINGS

2 (8-ounce) packages fat-free cream cheese, softened
1 tablespoon Worcestershire sauce
½ teaspoon minced garlic
½ teaspoon hot pepper sauce
1 (12-ounce) bottle cocktail sauce
½ cup chopped green onions (scallions)
2 cups cooked, peeled small shrimp
2 tablespoons minced parsley

In a large bowl, blend the cream cheese, Worcestershire sauce, garlic, and hot pepper sauce until creamy. Spread on the bottom of a 9-inch serving plate. Cover the cream cheese mixture with the cocktail sauce, and sprinkle with the green onions, shrimp, and parsley. Refrigerate until serving.

Nutritional information per serving

Calories 122, Protein (g) 15, Carbohydrate (g) 13, Fat (g) 1, Calories from Fat (%) 5, Saturated Fat (g) 0, Dietary Fiber (g) 1, Cholesterol (mg) 60, Sodium (mg) 877, Diabetic Exchanges: 2 very lean meat, 1 other carbohydrate

Tortilla Shrimp Bites ❄

Serve this southwestern-style recipe with salsa for a great party food. Make ahead and freeze, if desired, in zipper-lock bags.

MAKES 25 (2-PIECE) SERVINGS

1 (8-ounce) package reduced-fat cream cheese, softened
2 tablespoons light mayonnaise
½ cup chopped green onions (scallions)
1 (4-ounce) can chopped green chilies, drained
½ teaspoon chili powder
½ teaspoon garlic powder
Salt and pepper to taste
½ cup coarsely chopped cooked, peeled shrimp
10 (6- to 8-inch) tortillas
Salsa

In a medium bowl, blend the cream cheese and mayonnaise. Add the green onion, chilies, chili powder, garlic powder, salt, pepper, and shrimp, mixing well. Place about ⅛ cup of the filling on one end of a tortilla and roll up, jelly-roll style. Place the rolled tortillas, seam side down, on a tray or baking sheet. Refrigerate until ready to serve, up to several days. Cut each tortilla into 5 pieces before serving. Serve with salsa.

Nutritional information per serving

Calories 65, Protein (g) 2, Carbohydrate (g) 8, Fat (g) 2, Calories from Fat (%) 34, Saturated Fat (g) 1, Dietary Fiber (g) 1, Cholesterol (mg) 11, Sodium (mg) 176, Diabetic Exchanges: 0.5 starch, 0.5 fat

Spinach Artichoke Dip

This simple and cheesy spinach dip is full of great flavors and won't add to your waistline.

MAKES 10 SERVINGS

½ teaspoon minced garlic
1 onion, chopped
2 tablespoons all-purpose flour
1 (12-ounce) can evaporated skimmed milk
2 (10-ounce) boxes frozen chopped spinach, thawed and squeezed dry
4 ounces reduced-fat Monterey Jack cheese, cubed
1 (14-ounce) can quartered artichoke hearts, drained
Salt and pepper to taste
Dash Worcestershire sauce

In a non-stick pot, sauté the garlic and onion until very tender. Add the flour. Gradually stir in the milk, heating until thickened. Add the spinach and cheese, stirring until the cheese is melted. Stir in the artichoke hearts. Season with the salt, pepper, and Worcestershire sauce to taste. Serve hot.

Nutritional information per serving

Calories 97, Protein (g) 9, Carbohydrate (g) 11, Fat (g) 2, Calories from Fat (%) 21, Saturated Fat (g) 1, Dietary Fiber (g) 2, Cholesterol (mg) 7, Sodium (mg) 228, Diabetic Exchanges: 0.5 very lean meat, 0.5 skim milk, 1 vegetable

Zesty Cucumber Dip 🥕

It amazes me how many compliments I get every time I prepare this simple dip. Sometimes, I substitute diced avocado for the cucumber—fabulous!

MAKES 16 (2-TABLESPOON) SERVINGS

1 cup nonfat plain yogurt
1 (.7-ounce) package Italian dressing mix
1 tomato, seeded and chopped
½ cucumber, seeded, peeled, and chopped
3 green onions (scallions), chopped
1 tablespoon lemon juice

In a medium bowl, mix together the yogurt and dressing mix until well combined. Stir in the tomato, cucumber, green onions, and lemon juice. Refrigerate until ready to serve. Serve with chips.

Nutritional information per serving

Calories 16, Protein (g) 1, Carbohydrate (g) 3, Fat (g) 0, Calories from Fat (%) 0, Saturated Fat (g) 0, Dietary Fiber (g) 0, Cholesterol (mg) 0, Sodium (mg) 144, Diabetic Exchanges: Free

Hummus 🥕

Serve this simply prepared and full-flavored Greek dip with toasted pita bread.

MAKES 8 (¼-CUP) SERVINGS

2 (15-ounce) cans garbanzo beans, rinsed and drained
1 teaspoon minced garlic
1 tablespoon tamari
¼ cup lemon juice
1 tablespoon sesame oil
Salt and cayenne to taste

Place the garbanzo beans, garlic, tamari, lemon juice, sesame oil, salt, and cayenne in a food processor or blender and purée. Serve as a dip or sauce.

Nutritional information per serving

Calories 112, Protein (g) 5, Carbohydrate (g) 16, Fat (g) 3, Calories from Fat (%) 24, Saturated Fat (g) 0, Dietary Fiber (g) 4, Cholesterol (mg) 0, Sodium (mg) 420, Diabetic Exchanges: 0.5 very lean meat, 1 starch

FOOD FACT:

Hummus is a classic Middle Eastern spread made with ground garbanzo beans (chickpeas). Garbanzo beans provide healthy soluble fiber, complex carbohydrates, protein, potassium, iron, and zinc.

Salsa with Tortilla Chips

I can't tell you how many times I've made this quick salsa (using canned tomatoes). It is always a party favorite.

MAKES 2 CUPS

3 green onions (scallions), chopped
2 cloves garlic, minced
1 (28-ounce) can chopped tomatoes, drained
2 tablespoons finely chopped jalapeño pepper
¼ cup chopped fresh cilantro
1 teaspoon dried oregano leaves
¼ teaspoon ground cumin

In a small bowl, combine the green onion, garlic, tomatoes, jalapeño pepper, cilantro, oregano, and cumin. Serve with homemade Tortilla Chips (see recipe at right) or as a topping for chicken or fish.

TORTILLA CHIPS

These make a great snack. For a variation, sprinkle with your favorite seasonings.

MAKES 12 SERVINGS

12 (6- to 8-inch) whole wheat or white flour tortillas
Water

Preheat the oven to 425°F.

Brush each tortilla with water. Cut each tortilla into eight wedges, and place on a non-stick baking sheet. Bake for 3 minutes, turn, and continue baking 3 minutes longer, or until crisp.

Repeat until all the tortillas have been baked.

Nutritional information per serving
Calories 111, Protein (g) 3, Carbohydrate (g) 20, Fat (g) 2, Calories from Fat (%) 16, Saturated Fat (g) 1, Dietary Fiber (g) 2, Cholesterol (mg) 0, Sodium (mg) 224, Diabetic Exchanges: 1 starch, 1 vegetable

QUICK TIP:

Cilantro has a distinctive flavor and is available year-round. Choose bunches that have bright, even-colored leaves with no sign of wilting. Store in a plastic bag up to 1 week.

Fiesta Salsa

This blast of colors creates a favorite in my home. It takes only minutes to prepare and is devoured even faster! My family requests this salsa so often, and there's never any left. Perfect to serve on holidays.

MAKES 14 ($\frac{1}{4}$-CUP) SERVINGS

2 avocados, peeled, pitted, and chopped

1 pint cherry tomatoes, quartered, or grape tomatoes, halved

1 cup frozen corn, thawed

1 (4-ounce) can chopped green chilies, drained

1 bunch green onions (scallions), chopped

3 tablespoons lime juice

½ teaspoon sugar

Salt and pepper to taste

In a large bowl, carefully toss together the avocados, tomatoes, corn, green chilies, green onions, lime juice, sugar, salt, and pepper.

Nutritional information per serving

Calories 67, Protein (g) 1, Carbohydrate (g) 7, Fat (g) 5, Calories from Fat (%) 55, Saturated Fat (g) 1, Dietary Fiber (g) 2, Cholesterol (mg) 0, Sodium (mg) 19, Diabetic Exchanges: 1.5 vegetable, 1 fat

Fiesta Salsa

Fruit Dip 🥕

All ages will grab fresh fruit to dunk into this fabulous dip, with its burst of orange and abundance of flavor.

MAKES 8 (¼-CUP) SERVINGS

2 (8-ounce) containers nonfat lemon yogurt
¼ cup blanched almonds, chopped and toasted
1 teaspoon grated orange rind
2 tablespoons orange liqueur or orange juice

In a small bowl, combine the yogurt, almonds, orange rind, and orange liqueur, and mix well. Refrigerate at least 1 hour before serving to blend the flavors.

Nutritional information per serving
Calories 84, Protein (g) 4, Carbohydrate (g) 12, Fat (g) 2, Calories from Fat (%) 18, Saturated Fat (g) 0, Dietary Fiber (g) 0, Cholesterol (mg) 1, Sodium (mg) 40, Diabetic Exchanges: 1 skim milk

Sweet Cheese Ball 🥕 ❄

The seasoned cream cheese mixed with the dried fruit makes this an unforgettable cheese ball. Serve with sweet crackers, gingersnaps, or apple slices. This makes a big ball, so divide in half if you desire. It freezes well.

MAKES 32 (2-TABLESPOON) SERVINGS

1 (8-ounce) package fat-free cream cheese, softened
1 (8-ounce) package reduced-fat cream cheese, softened
1 teaspoon seasoned salt
2 tablespoons finely chopped onion
1 cup shredded reduced-fat Cheddar cheese
1 cup chopped dates
1 cup golden raisins
1 cup dried cranberries
½ cup chopped pecans, toasted

In a large bowl, mix the cream cheeses, seasoned salt, and onion. Stir in the Cheddar cheese, dates, raisins, cranberries, and pecans, mixing well. Mold into a ball, and refrigerate until serving.

Nutritional information per serving
Calories 89, Protein (g) 3, Carbohydrate (g) 12, Fat (g) 4, Calories from Fat (%) 35, Saturated Fat (g) 2, Dietary Fiber (g) 1, Cholesterol (mg) 8, Sodium (mg) 131, Diabetic Exchanges: 1 fruit, 1 fat

QUICK TIP:

For a variation, use dried cherries or other dried fruits in the cheeseball.

Hamburger Dip ❄

Men always gravitate to this easy, five-ingredient, hearty and satisfying dip. During football season, this recipe is requested often in my house. My son even called for the recipe from college! Serve with chips.

MAKES 20 (¼-CUP) SERVINGS

1 pound ground sirloin
1 onion, chopped
½ pound mushrooms, sliced
1 (16-ounce) jar salsa
1 (8-ounce) package reduced-fat Monterey Jack cheese, cut into chunks

In a heavy, medium-sized, non-stick pot, cook the sirloin, onion, and mushroom over medium heat for 5 to 7 minutes until the meat is well browned. Drain off excess liquid.

Add the salsa and cheese, stirring over medium heat until the cheese is melted. Serve hot.

Nutritional information per serving

Calories 72, Protein (g) 8, Carbohydrate (g) 2, Fat (g) 3, Calories from Fat (%) 41, Saturated Fat (g) 2, Dietary Fiber (g) 0, Cholesterol (mg) 18, Sodium (mg) 190, Diabetic Exchanges: 1 lean meat

Mexican Bean Dip ✏ ❄

This dip is so versatile, it can be used as stuffing for burritos.

MAKES 10 (¼-CUP) SERVINGS

½ cup chopped onion
1 tablespoon margarine
1 (16-ounce) can fat-free refried beans
½ cup shredded reduced-fat Cheddar cheese
1 (11-ounce) can Mexi-corn, drained
½ teaspoon minced garlic
3 tablespoons taco sauce
1 bunch green onions (scallions), chopped

In a medium non-stick pot, sauté the chopped onion in margarine over medium heat until tender. Stir in the beans, cheese, and corn, stirring until the cheese is melted. Add the garlic and taco sauce.

Pour into a serving bowl or chafing dish. Top with the green onion slices. Serve warm.

Nutritional information per serving

Calories 88, Protein (g) 5, Carbohydrate (g) 12, Fat (g) 2, Calories from Fat (%) 22, Saturated Fat (g) 1, Dietary Fiber (g) 3, Cholesterol (mg) 3, Sodium (mg) 377, Diabetic Exchanges: 0.5 very lean meat, 1 starch

Oyster Rockefeller Dip ❄

Oysters, spinach, and a variety of seasonings team together to create a dip that everyone will love. And there's no fuss filling oyster shells!

MAKES 14 (¼-CUP) SERVINGS

2 (10-ounce) packages chopped spinach

3 dozen oysters, drained (reserve liquid)

1 bunch parsley, stems removed

1 bunch green onions (scallions), cut into 1-inch pieces

4 stalks celery, cut into pieces

4 tablespoons margarine

3 tablespoons Worcestershire sauce

½ cup Italian bread crumbs

2 tablespoons lemon juice

1 tablespoon anchovy paste, optional

¼ cup grated Parmesan cheese

½ cup evaporated skimmed milk

¼ cup oyster liquid

3 tablespoons anisette or Pernod, optional

Cook the spinach according to package directions; drain very well and set aside.

Broil the oysters on a non-stick baking sheet until the oysters begin to curl. Cut into bite-size pieces; set aside.

Purée the parsley, green onions, and celery in a food processor. In a large non-stick pot, melt the margarine, and sauté the puréed mixture until the veggies are very tender. Add the cooked spinach, stirring until mixed. Stir in the Worcestershire sauce, bread crumbs, lemon juice, anchovy paste, Parmesan cheese, skimmed milk, and oyster liquid, stirring until heated. Add the anisette and chopped oysters, mixing well. Serve hot.

Nutritional information per serving

Calories 100, Protein (g) 5, Carbohydrate (g) 10, Fat (g) 5, Calories from Fat (%) 42, Saturated Fat (g) 1, Dietary Fiber (g) 2, Cholesterol (mg) 11, Sodium (mg) 260, Diabetic Exchanges: 0.5 very lean meat, 0.5 starch, 1 fat

Crawfish Dip ❄

Create a Southern favorite with these staple ingredients wherever you live. If there is any leftover, serve it over rice or pastry shells for another great meal.

MAKES 16 (¼-CUP) SERVINGS

¼ cup margarine
¼ cup all-purpose flour
½ teaspoon minced garlic
1 bunch green onions (scallions), chopped
1 small onion, chopped
1 (10¾-ounce) can 98% fat-free cream of mushroom soup
1 (10-ounce) can diced tomatoes and green chilies
1 teaspoon Worcestershire sauce
Salt and pepper to taste
1 pound crawfish tails, rinsed and drained

In a non-stick pot, melt the margarine, then add the flour, mixing well. Add the garlic, green onions, and onion, sautéing over medium heat until tender, stirring constantly to prevent sticking. Add the mushroom soup and the chopped tomatoes and green chilies; mix well. Season with the salt and pepper to taste. Gently stir in the crawfish tails. Cook over medium heat until dip is thoroughly heated, about 3 minutes. Serve hot.

Nutritional information per serving
Calories 74, Protein (g) 5, Carbohydrate (g) 5, Fat (g) 4, Calories from Fat (%) 45, Saturated Fat (g) 1, Dietary Fiber (g) 1, Cholesterol (mg) 38, Sodium (mg) 263, Diabetic Exchanges: 1 lean meat, 1 vegetable

Black-Eyed Pea Dip 🥕 ❄

Black-eyes peas, tomatoes, and cheese make this traditional New Year's Day dip appealing any time of year. Prepare it as a dip or as a veggie side dish.

MAKES 20 (¼-CUP) SERVINGS

1 onion, chopped
⅓ cup chopped green bell pepper
1 tablespoon chopped jalapeño peppers
2 (15-ounce) cans black-eyed peas, drained
3 tablespoons all-purpose flour
1 (10-ounce) can diced tomatoes and green chilies
4 ounces reduced-fat Monterey Jack cheese, shredded

In a non-stick pot, sauté the onion, green pepper, and jalapeño over medium-low heat until tender, about 5 minutes. Add the black-eyed peas, and stir in the flour. Gradually add the tomatoes and chilies and the cheese, stirring until melted and heated thoroughly. Serve hot.

Nutritional information per serving
Calories 57, Protein (g) 4, Carbohydrate (g) 8, Fat (g) 1, Calories from Fat (%) 17, Saturated Fat (g) 1, Dietary Fiber (g) 1, Cholesterol (mg) 3, Sodium (mg) 177, Diabetic Exchanges: 0.5 very lean meat, 0.5 starch

Sweet-and-Spicy Chicken Strips ❄

These sweet-and-spicy glazed strips make an easy dinner dish or great pickups as appetizers.

MAKES 24 SERVINGS

1 cup picante sauce
¼ cup honey
½ teaspoon ground ginger
1½ pounds skinless, boneless chicken breasts, cut into strips

Preheat the oven to 400°F.

In a medium bowl, mix the picante sauce, honey, and ginger. Toss the chicken strips with the picante sauce mixture. Place in a non-stick shallow baking pan. Bake for 40 to 50 minutes, or until glazed and done, turning and brushing often with sauce during the last 30 minutes. Serve.

Nutritional information per serving

Calories 45, Protein (g) 7, Carbohydrate (g) 4, Fat (g) trace, Calories from Fat (%) 7, Saturated Fat (g) 0, Dietary Fiber (g) 0, Cholesterol (mg) 16, Sodium (mg) 89, Diabetic Exchanges: 1 very lean meat

Sweet and Spicy Chicken Strips

Caponata

Eggplant, onions, peppers, and tomatoes are the foundation of this great Italian dip. Serve with pita chips.

MAKES 48 (¼-CUP) SERVINGS

2 medium eggplants

2 onions, chopped

1½ cups thickly sliced celery

2 green bell peppers, seeded and cut into 1-inch chunks

2 garlic cloves, minced

⅓ cup red wine vinegar

2 (14½-ounce) cans Italian stewed tomatoes
  with their juice

2 tablespoons sugar

2 tablespoons dried basil leaves

3 tablespoons tomato paste

½ cup chopped parsley

1 teaspoon pepper

¼ cup sliced stuffed green olives

Cut the unpeeled eggplants into 1-inch cubes.

Heat a large non-stick pot over medium-low heat, and add the eggplant and onion, sautéing until lightly golden. Add the celery, green pepper, garlic, vinegar, tomatoes, sugar, basil, tomato paste, parsley, pepper, and green olives to the pot, and stir gently but thoroughly. Simmer, covered, for 30 minutes, stirring occasionally.

Remove the lid, and simmer about 10 minutes more, or until thick. Cool and refrigerate. Serve chilled or at room temperature.

Nutritional information per serving

Calories 20, Protein (g) 1, Carbohydrate (g) 5, Fat (g) 0, Calories from Fat (%) 8, Saturated Fat (g) 0, Dietary Fiber (g) 1, Cholesterol (mg) 0, Sodium (mg) 71, Diabetic Exchanges: 1 vegetable

Marinated Shrimp

The marinade in this recipe infuses the shrimp with bold flavors. This recipe is great for gatherings because it can be served with toothpicks.

MAKES 10 SERVINGS

¼ cup olive oil
½ teaspoon minced garlic
1 tablespoon dry mustard
½ cup lemon juice
Salt and pepper to taste
1 tablespoon red wine vinegar
1 bay leaf
Dash cayenne pepper
2 tablespoons chopped fresh parsley
1 small red onion, thinly sliced
2 tablespoons capers, drained
2 pounds cooked shrimp, peeled

In a bowl, combine the oil, garlic, dry mustard, lemon juice, salt, pepper, vinegar, bay leaf, and cayenne pepper; mix well. Stir in the parsley, red onion, and capers. Add the shrimp, tossing until well coated. Refrigerate for 2 hours or overnight.

Drain the marinade, remove the bay leaf, and serve the shrimp with the onion, parsley, and capers.

Nutritional information per serving
Calories 94, Protein (g) 19, Carbohydrate (g) 1, Fat (g) 1, Calories from Fat (%) 10, Saturated Fat (g) 0, Dietary Fiber (g) 0, Cholesterol (mg) 177, Sodium (mg) 255, Diabetic Exchanges: 3 very lean meat

Marinated Crab Fingers

A pinch of sugar adds a little something extra to this vinaigrette. Be sure to make this ahead of time, since the longer it sits, the better it gets.

MAKES 16 SERVINGS

½ cup balsamic vinegar
¼ cup Worcestershire sauce
2 tablespoons olive oil
¼ cup lemon juice
2 tablespoons minced garlic
½ teaspoon pepper
1 teaspoon dried basil leaves
1 teaspoon sugar
2 pounds crab fingers

In a large bowl, mix the vinegar, Worcestershire sauce, olive oil, lemon juice, garlic, pepper, basil, and sugar. Add the crab fingers. Refrigerate for several hours or overnight.

Lay the mixture on leaf lettuce to serve.

Nutritional information per serving
Calories 71, Protein (g) 14, Carbohydrate (g) 1, Fat (g) 1, Calories from Fat (%) 9, Saturated Fat (g) 0, Dietary Fiber (g) 0, Cholesterol (mg) 61, Sodium (mg) 58, Diabetic Exchanges: 2 very lean meat

Incredible Crabmeat Dip

This recipe uses fresh crabmeat and makes a dip like none other. To cut the cost, sometimes I mix in 1 pound cooked small shrimp instead of 1 pound white crabmeat.

MAKES 25 SERVINGS FOR A COCKTAIL PARTY

½ cup light mayonnaise
1 bunch green onions (scallions), chopped
¼ cup finely chopped onion
1 tablespoon lemon juice
1 tablespoon Worcestershire sauce
Dash hot pepper sauce
Salt and pepper to taste
2 pounds lump crabmeat
1 pound white crabmeat

In a large bowl, combine the mayonnaise, green onions, onion, lemon juice, Worcestershire sauce, hot sauce, salt, and pepper. Pick through the crabmeat and remove any shells; then carefully fold in the crabmeat. Transfer to a 6-cup mold coated with non-stick cooking spray. Refrigerate until set.

Nutritional information per serving
Calories 80, Protein (g) 11, Carbohydrate (g) 1, Fat (g) 3, Calories from Fat (%) 39, Saturated Fat (g) 1, Dietary Fiber (g) 0, Cholesterol (mg) 55, Sodium (mg) 205, Diabetic Exchanges: 1.5 very lean meat

Caviar Mold

A great way to serve caviar to a crowd, this mold also makes the perfect brunch appetizer served with miniature rye bread slices or crackers.

MAKES 15 TO 20 SERVINGS

1 package unflavored gelatin
¼ cup water
2 hard-cooked eggs, chopped
4 hard-cooked eggs, whites only, chopped
1 (8-ounce) container French onion dip
⅓ cup light mayonnaise
¼ cup finely chopped onion
1 tablespoon Worcestershire sauce
3 tablespoons lemon juice
⅛ teaspoon cayenne pepper
½ teaspoon hot pepper sauce
1 (4-ounce) jar lumpfish black caviar

Stir the gelatin into the water until dissolved. Gently mix in the chopped eggs and egg whites, French onion dip, mayonnaise, onion, Worcestershire sauce, lemon juice, cayenne pepper, and hot pepper sauce.

Rinse the caviar in a strainer until the water runs clear, and drain well. Add to the gelatin mixture, pour into a 1-quart mold coated with non-stick cooking spray, and refrigerate two hours or until set.

Nutritional information per serving
Calories 37, Protein (g) 2, Carbohydrate (g) 1, Fat (g) 3, Calories from Fat (%) 64, Saturated Fat (g) 1, Dietary Fiber (g) 0, Cholesterol (mg) 40, Sodium (mg) 127, Diabetic Exchanges: 0.5 fat

Smoked Salmon Tortilla Pinwheels

Smoked Salmon Tortilla Pinwheels ❄

For an outstanding presentation, arrange these pinwheels cut-side up on a serving platter.

MAKES 4 TO 5 DOZEN PINWHEELS

1 (5-ounce) package reduced-fat garlic-and-herb spreadable cheese
1 (8-ounce) package reduced-fat cream cheese, softened
¼ cup chopped red onion
¼ cup capers, drained
1 tablespoon lemon juice
4 ounces smoked salmon
8 (6- to 8-inch) tortillas

Cut salmon into pieces. In a mixing bowl, blend together both cheeses until creamy. Stir in the red onion, capers, lemon juice, and smoked salmon. Divide and spread the filling to cover each tortilla; then roll up jelly-roll style. Place seam down on a tray, and secure each roll with a toothpick. Refrigerate until well chilled. Cut each roll into pinwheels about ⅜-inch thick. Serve with toothpicks.

Nutritional information per 2 pieces
Calories 57, Protein (g) 3, Carbohydrate (g) 6, Fat (g) 3, Calories from Fat (%) 42, Saturated Fat (g) 2, Dietary Fiber (g) 0, Cholesterol (mg) 9, Sodium (mg) 233, Diabetic Exchanges: 0.5 starch, 0.5 fat

Salmon Mousse with Dill Sauce

This is a great party recipe when you want to serve a mold. The Dill Sauce gives it an extra kick. Serve with crackers.

MAKES 10 SERVINGS

2 envelopes unflavored gelatin
¼ cup cold water
½ cup boiling water
½ cup nonfat plain yogurt
1 tablespoon lemon juice
1 tablespoon grated onion
½ teaspoon hot pepper sauce
½ teaspoon paprika
Salt and pepper to taste
1 (14.75-ounce) can red salmon, drained, skin discarded, and bones picked
2 tablespoons capers, drained
½ cup evaporated skimmed milk, chilled
Dill Sauce (recipe follows)

In a small bowl, soften the gelatin in the cold water. Add the boiling water, and stir until the gelatin is dissolved; let cool. Add the yogurt, lemon juice, onion, hot pepper sauce, paprika, salt, and pepper; mix well. Refrigerate until the mixture is the consistency of unbeaten egg whites. Add the salmon and capers, mixing well.

In a chilled mixing bowl, beat the cold evaporated milk at high speed until stiff peaks form. Fold into the salmon mixture. Pour into a 6-cup mold coated with non-stick cooking spray. Refrigerate two hours or until set.

Unmold and cover with Dill Sauce (see recipe below), or serve the Dill Sauce on the side in a bowl.

DILL SAUCE

1 cup nonfat plain yogurt
¼ teaspoon sugar
2 tablespoons lemon juice
1 tablespoon grated onion
Salt and pepper to taste
1 tablespoon dried dill weed leaves
½ cup grated, peeled, and seeded cucumber

In a small bowl, mix the yogurt, sugar, lemon juice, onion, salt, pepper, dill weed, and cucumber. Stir and refrigerate.

Nutritional information per serving
Calories 104, Protein (g) 13, Carbohydrate (g) 5, Fat (g) 3, Calories from Fat (%) 28, Saturated Fat (g) 1, Dietary Fiber (g) 0, Cholesterol (mg) 20, Sodium (mg) 324, Diabetic Exchanges: 1 lean meat, 0.5 skim milk

FOOD FACT:

Farmed salmon is a good source of heart-healthy omega 3 fatty acids and high-quality protein.

Cold Poached Salmon with Dill Dijon Sauce

For an appetizer or for dinner—poached salmon is a winner anytime. The Dill Dijon Sauce is so good, you could eat it with a spoon or serve it with other fish dishes.

MAKES 10 SERVINGS

2 cups water
1 cup dry white wine
1 carrot, diced
1 stalk celery, chopped
1 onion, sliced
½ tablespoon black peppercorns
1 (2-pound) fresh salmon fillet
Dill Dijon Sauce (recipe follows)

In a large poacher or pan, combine water, wine, carrot, celery, onion, and peppercorns. Bring to a boil. Lower heat, cover, and cook for 15 minutes.

Add the salmon fillet. Cover and cook over low heat until the salmon is done, approximately 15 to 20 minutes. Cool the salmon in its stock.

When cool, remove the salmon from its stock and remove the skin from the salmon; chill for several hours or overnight.

Serve with Dill Dijon Sauce (see recipe at right).

DILL DIJON SAUCE

1 cup nonfat plain yogurt
1½ tablespoons white vinegar
1½ tablespoons Dijon mustard
3 tablespoons light brown sugar
2 teaspoons dried dill weed leaves

In a small bowl, mix the yogurt, vinegar, mustard, brown sugar, and dill weed together. Refrigerate before serving; it's best if refrigerated overnight.

Nutritional information per serving
Calories 164, Protein (g) 20, Carbohydrate (g) 11, Fat (g) 3, Calories from Fat (%) 18, Saturated Fat (g) 1, Dietary Fiber (g) 1, Cholesterol (mg) 48, Sodium (mg) 146, Diabetic Exchanges: 2.5 very lean meat, 0.5 starch

Seafood-Stuffed Mushrooms

Seafood and a touch of sherry enhance stuffed mushrooms. Even though they can be time-consuming, you can make these ahead of time and refrigerate until you're ready to serve.

MAKES 36 MUSHROOMS

36 fresh medium mushrooms

1 onion, chopped

½ bunch green onions (scallions), chopped

¼ cup chopped green bell pepper

1 cup bread crumbs

½ teaspoon white pepper

¼ teaspoon cayenne pepper, optional

½ teaspoon garlic powder

Salt and pepper to taste

1 pound crawfish tails, rinsed and drained, or cooked shrimp

2 tablespoons olive oil

1 tablespoon sherry

Preheat the oven to 350°F.

Wash the mushrooms and remove the stems; chop the stems, and set aside both the mushrooms and the stems.

In a large non-stick skillet, sauté the onion, green onions, green bell pepper, and mushroom stems until tender. Add the bread crumbs, white pepper, cayenne pepper, garlic powder, salt, pepper, and crawfish tails. Mix together and cook over low heat for 5 minutes, stirring occasionally. Add the olive oil and sherry, and remove from heat.

Place the mushrooms in a metal colander over a pot of boiling water. Cover with a lid. Cook the mushrooms for about 5 minutes. Remove from heat and submerge in ice water. Drain and lay on a non-stick baking sheet. Stuff the mushrooms with the filling; then bake for 15 minutes or until heated.

Nutritional information per serving

Calories 36, Protein (g) 3, Carbohydrate (g) 3, Fat (g) 1, Calories from Fat (%) 27, Saturated Fat (g) 0, Dietary Fiber (g) 0, Cholesterol (mg) 7, Sodium (mg) 38, Diabetic Exchanges: 1 vegetable

Portabella Mushrooms Stuffed with Goat Cheese and Roasted Red Peppers

The rich, hearty flavor of portabella mushrooms combined with goat cheese and roasted peppers makes this a tasteful choice. Cut in fourths for pickups, or serve whole as a first course.

MAKES 16 SERVINGS

2 ounces goat cheese, softened
4 large portabella mushroom caps
1 (10-ounce) jar roasted red bell peppers, drained
1 tablespoon olive oil
Salt and freshly ground pepper to taste

Preheat the oven to 350°F.

Place the mushrooms fan side up on a non-stick baking sheet. Spread $\frac{1}{4}$ of the goat cheese on top of each mushroom cap. Cover the cheese with a layer of roasted red peppers. Drizzle the top of the mushrooms with olive oil, and season with salt and freshly ground pepper.

Roast for 15 minutes, or until the cheese begins to melt, cut into fourths and serve immediately.

Nutritional information per serving

Calories 32, Protein (g) 1, Carbohydrate (g) 2, Fat (g) 2, Calories from Fat (%) 60, Saturated Fat (g) 1, Dietary Fiber (g) 0, Cholesterol (mg) 4, Sodium (mg) 84, Diabetic Exchanges: 0.5 fat

QUICK TIP:

Roasted red peppers in jars are a quick, convenient, and sometimes less expensive substitution for roasting fresh red peppers.

Portabella Mushrooms Stuffed with
Goat Cheese and Roasted Red Peppers

Spinach Balls with Jezebel Sauce

You can freeze these spinach balls on a baking sheet before baking them. Once frozen, transfer them to zipper-lock bags and store in the freezer. Take them directly from the freezer to bake in the oven. I've made these spinach balls for years, and they are always popular with the Jezebel Sauce, which adds a real bite.

MAKES 48 BALLS

2 (10-ounce) packages frozen chopped spinach, cooked and well drained
2 cups herb bread stuffing mix
1 cup finely chopped onion
½ cup grated Romano cheese
1½ teaspoons garlic powder
1 teaspoon dried thyme leaves
⅛ teaspoon pepper
2 eggs
4 egg whites
Jezebel Sauce (recipe follows)

Preheat the oven to 350°F.

In a large bowl, combine the spinach, stuffing mix, onion, cheese, garlic powder, thyme, pepper, eggs, and egg whites; mix well. Form into ¾-inch balls, and place on a non-stick baking sheet. Bake for 20 minutes.

Serve with Jezebel Sauce (see recipe at right).

JEZEBEL SAUCE

MAKES 2 CUPS SAUCE

½ cup apricot preserves
1 (10-ounce) jar apple jelly
2 tablespoons dry mustard
2 tablespoons prepared horseradish
1 teaspoon pepper

In a small bowl, mix together the apricot preserves, apple jelly, dry mustard, horseradish, and pepper.

Nutritional information per 1 ball and 2 teaspoons sauce
Calories 51, Protein (g) 2, Carbohydrate (g) 9, Fat (g) 1, Calories from Fat (%) 14, Saturated Fat (g) 0, Dietary Fiber (g) 1, Cholesterol (mg) 10, Sodium (mg) 68, Diabetic Exchanges: 0.5 other carbohydrate

QUICK TIP:

Jezebel Sauce, which is named after history's sweet-and-spicy vixen, is also great served over reduced-fat cream cheese on crackers.

Mini Taco Cups

This easy-to-make appetizer is the perfect pickup or snack for all ages. The chipotle salsa gives the meat a smoky flavor. If you can't find chipotle salsa, add chipotle seasoning, which can be found in the spice section of your grocery.

MAKES 24 SERVINGS

24 won ton wrappers
1 pound ground sirloin
1 teaspoon ground cumin
1 teaspoon chili powder
⅔ cup chipotle salsa, divided in half
1 cup shredded reduced-fat Cheddar cheese

Preheat the oven to 425°F.

Press the won ton wrappers into non-stick mini-muffin cups. Cook the meat in a non-stick skillet until browned; then drain off excess liquid. Stir in the cumin, chili powder, and ⅓ cup salsa. Spoon the beef mixture into the won ton cups. Top with the remaining salsa and the cheese. Bake about 8 minutes, or until the won tons are golden brown. Serve immediately with additional salsa, if desired.

Nutritional information per serving

Calories 61, Protein (g) 6, Carbohydrate (g) 5, Fat (g) 2, Calories from Fat (%) 28, Saturated Fat (g) 1, Dietary Fiber (g) 0, Cholesterol (mg) 13, Sodium (mg) 78, Diabetic Exchanges: 1 very lean meat, 0.5 starch

Mini Taco Cups

Artichoke Bites

Quick to make, these bites have a ton of flavor! Make ahead and refrigerate until ready to bake.

MAKES 48 BITES

2 (14-ounce) cans artichoke hearts, drained and finely chopped
1 (4-ounce) can chopped green chilies, drained
½ cup grated Parmesan cheese
¼ cup light mayonnaise
¼ cup Dijon mustard
1 (.65-ounce) package cheese garlic or Italian dressing mix
Dash hot pepper sauce
6 English muffins, cut in half

Preheat the oven to 350°F.

In a small bowl, combine the artichoke hearts, green chilies, Parmesan cheese, mayonnaise, Dijon mustard, dressing mix, and hot pepper sauce, mixing well. Divide the mixture on top of each of the split muffin halves, and place on a non-stick baking sheet. Bake for 30 minutes, or until lightly browned.

Cut each half into four pieces, and serve immediately.

Nutritional information per 2 pieces
Calories 64, Protein (g) 2, Carbohydrate (g) 9, Fat (g) 2, Calories from Fat (%) 25, Saturated Fat (g) 1, Dietary Fiber (g) 1, Cholesterol (mg) 3, Sodium (mg) 362, Diabetic Exchanges: 0.5 starch

Artichoke Dip

This incredibly simple dip satisfies even the most sophisticated taste buds. I am always asked for the recipe. Serve with veggies or crackers.

MAKES 12 (2-TABLESPOON) SERVINGS

½ cup fat-free sour cream
½ cup light mayonnaise
1 (.7-ounce) package cheesy Italian or Italian dressing mix
1 (14-ounce) can artichoke hearts, drained and finely chopped

In a medium bowl, mix the sour cream, mayonnaise, Italian dressing mix, and artichoke hearts together. Refrigerate until serving.

Nutritional information per serving
Calories 57, Protein (g) 1, Carbohydrate (g) 6, Fat (g) 3, Calories from Fat (%) 52, Saturated Fat (g) 1, Dietary Fiber (g) 0, Cholesterol (mg) 4, Sodium (mg) 26, Diabetic Exchanges: 0.5 starch, 0.5 fat

Artichoke Squares

These tasty squares—filled with peppers, mushrooms, and cheese—can be served hot, at room temperature, or even out of the refrigerator. Be sure to cover when reheating. For a snack or a tasty appetizer, these squares will become a favorite standby.

MAKES 30 SQUARES

1 cup chopped onion
1 cup chopped red bell pepper
1 cup chopped green bell pepper
1 cup sliced mushrooms
1 teaspoon minced garlic
2 (14-ounce) cans artichoke hearts, drained, rinsed, and chopped
3 egg whites, slightly beaten
2 eggs, slightly beaten
1 teaspoon dried oregano leaves
1 teaspoon dried basil leaves
¼ teaspoon cayenne pepper
½ cup Italian bread crumbs
¾ cup shredded reduced-fat sharp Cheddar cheese
¼ cup grated Parmesan cheese

Preheat the oven to 350°F.

In a medium non-stick pan, sauté the onion, red pepper, green pepper, mushroom, and garlic over medium heat until the vegetables are tender. Transfer the sautéed vegetables into a large bowl, and add the chopped artichokes, egg whites, eggs, oregano, basil, cayenne pepper, bread crumbs, Cheddar cheese, and Parmesan cheese, stirring until well combined.

Pour the mixture into a 2-quart oblong dish coated with nonstick cooking spray. Bake for 30 minutes, or until the mixture is set and the top is light brown.

Cut into squares before serving. Serve immediately.

Nutritional information per serving
Calories 37, Protein (g) 3, Carbohydrate (g) 4, Fat (g) 1, Calories from Fat (%) 28, Saturated Fat (g) 1, Dietary Fiber (g) 1, Cholesterol (mg) 16, Sodium (mg) 119, Diabetic Exchanges: 1 vegetable

Hearty Stuffed Artichokes

Add meat to artichoke stuffing and, voila! You've just made a bold and satisfying appetizer. My kids didn't believe I made these myself, as they look and taste like fancy restaurant quality—but better. I think you'll agree.

MAKES 9 TO 12 SERVINGS

1 onion, chopped
1 teaspoon minced garlic
1 pound ground sirloin
1½ cups Italian bread crumbs
¼ cup grated Romano cheese
2 teaspoons dried basil leaves
2 tablespoons lemon juice
¼ cup olive oil
3 whole artichokes
Sliced lemons, optional

In a large non-stick pan, sauté the onion, garlic, and sirloin until the meat is browned. Drain any excess fat; remove from heat. Add the bread crumbs, cheese, basil, lemon juice, and olive oil, mixing well. Set aside.

Trim the stems off the artichokes with a sharp knife. With scissors, snip off the pointed tops of the leaves. Holding the artichokes firmly with one hand, turn the leaves down and pound them on a flat surface to force open the leaves. Turn the leaves up, and rinse quickly under cold running water. Shake to remove excess moisture. With your fingers, open the leaves more to make room for the stuffing. Stuff the reserved mixture into the spaces inside the open leaves. Top each artichoke with sliced lemon if desired.

Place the artichokes in a large pot with 1 inch lightly salted water. Bring to a boil; lower heat, cover, and cook about 1 hour, or until leaves pull off easily and are tender on the inside. Watch to be sure there is always water in the pot, and add more water as needed. Serve immediately.

Nutritional information per serving

Calories 168, Protein (g) 11, Carbohydrate (g) 16, Fat (g) 7, Calories from Fat (%) 37, Saturated Fat (g) 2, Dietary Fiber (g) 3, Cholesterol (mg) 22, Sodium (mg) 290, Diabetic Exchanges: 1 very lean meat, 1 starch, 1 fat

Artichoke and
Red Pepper Pizza

*Start with a prepared crust and add these
gourmet ingredients for a real winner. Also
makes a good light lunch.*

MAKES 12 SLICES

1 (10-ounce) can refrigerated pizza crust dough
5 cloves garlic
2 tablespoons olive oil
2 red bell peppers, seeded and cut into ¼-inch strips
1 teaspoon dried basil leaves
1 (2.5-ounce) jar sliced mushrooms, drained
1 (14-ounce) can artichoke hearts, drained and chopped
1½ cups shredded part-skim Mozzarella cheese

Preheat the oven to 425°F.

Coat a 12-inch non-stick pizza pan with non-stick cooking spray. Unroll the dough and place in the prepared pan, starting at the center and pressing out with your hands. Bake for 5 to 8 minutes, or until light golden brown.

In a food processor, mince the garlic and add the olive oil, blending well. Spread the garlic mixture over the partially baked crust.

In a medium non-stick skillet, sauté the red pepper strips until crisp-tender, about 5 minutes. Layer the pepper strips, basil, mushroom slices, and artichokes over the garlic mixture; top with the cheese. Bake for 10 minutes, or until the crust is golden brown and the cheese is melted. Cut into small slices before serving.

Nutritional information per serving

Calories 134, Protein (g) 6, Carbohydrate (g) 15, Fat (g) 5, Calories from Fat (%) 36, Saturated Fat (g) 2, Dietary Fiber (g) 1, Cholesterol (mg) 8, Sodium (mg) 304, Diabetic Exchanges: 0.5 lean meat, 1 starch, 0.5 fat

QUICK TIP:

Rub a halved garlic clove on top of the pizza crust to add lots of flavor with little effort.

Spinach-and-Cheese Tortilla Pizza

Everyday ingredients make this pizza a great pickup, or serve a single tortilla for lunch with a bowl of soup or salad.

MAKES 12 SLICES

2 large (10-inch) flour tortillas
2 tablespoons fat-free sour cream
1 (10-ounce) package frozen chopped spinach, thawed and squeezed dry
1 large tomato, chopped
Salt and pepper to taste
½ cup shredded reduced-fat Monterey Jack cheese
¼ cup thinly chopped green onions (scallions)

Preheat the oven to 450°F.

Place the tortillas on a non-stick baking sheet. Bake for 3 minutes, or until golden brown. Remove from the oven, and reduce the temperature to 350°F.

Spread the sour cream evenly over the tortillas. Top with spinach, tomato, salt, and pepper to taste. Next, sprinkle evenly with the Monterey Jack cheese. Bake for 5 minutes more, or until the cheese is melted. Sprinkle with the green onion. Cut each tortilla into four slices, and serve immediately.

Nutritional information per serving

Calories 65, Protein (g) 3, Carbohydrate (g) 9, Fat (g) 2, Calories from Fat (%) 25, Saturated Fat (g) 1, Dietary Fiber (g) 1, Cholesterol (mg) 3, Sodium (mg) 108, Diabetic Exchanges: 0.5 starch

Asparagus and Brie Pizza

Brie and asparagus team up to create a pizza of simple elegance. Substitute broccoli or your favorite veggie for asparagus, if desired.

MAKES 12 SLICES

12 thin asparagus spears, tips only

1 red bell pepper, seeded and thinly sliced, or 1 roasted red bell pepper cut into strips

1 teaspoon minced garlic

1 (10-ounce) can refrigerated pizza crust dough, or 1 (16-ounce) Boboli prepared crust

½ teaspoon dried basil leaves

½ teaspoon dried oregano leaves

Salt and pepper to taste

3½ ounces Brie, rind removed, thinly sliced

Preheat the oven to 425°F.

Fill a small saucepan with water, and bring to a boil. Cook the asparagus tips in the boiling water until tender, about 4 minutes. Drain and set aside.

Heat a non-stick skillet over medium heat, and sauté the red pepper until tender, about 4 minutes or microwave on high for about 2 minutes. Stir in the garlic.

Coat a 12-inch non-stick pizza pan with non-stick cooking spray. Unroll the dough and place in the prepared pan, starting at the center and pressing out with your hands. Bake for 5 minutes. Remove from heat, and sprinkle the crust with the basil, oregano, salt, and pepper; then evenly distribute the red pepper, Brie, and asparagus over the crust. Bake for 8 to 10 minutes more. Slice and serve immediately.

Nutritional information per serving

Calories 96, Protein (g) 4, Carbohydrate (g) 13, Fat (g) 3, Calories from Fat (%) 30, Saturated Fat (g) 1, Dietary Fiber (g) 1, Cholesterol (mg) 8, Sodium (mg) 210, Diabetic Exchanges: 1 starch, 0.5 fat

Glazed Brie

Nuts, sugar, and coffee liquer over hot, oozing brie call for a splurge! It's worth every bite. Keep ingredients handy to whip up this crowd pleaser at a moment's notice.

MAKES 20 SERVINGS

¼ cup walnuts or pecans, chopped
¼ cup coffee liqueur
3 tablespoons light brown sugar
½ teaspoon vanilla extract
1 (14-ounce) round Brie cheese
Assorted crackers
Assorted sliced fruit (apples, pears)

Preheat the oven to 325°F.

In a small non-stick saucepan, sauté the walnuts until golden brown, about 3 minutes, stirring. Stir in the liqueur, brown sugar, and vanilla, cooking until the brown sugar is melted; set aside. Watch carefully, as it cooks quickly.

Remove the top rind of the Brie. Place the Brie in a shallow non-stick baking dish. Top with the walnut mixture. Bake for 8 to 10 minutes, or until the Brie is soft and heated through. Serve immediately with assorted crackers and fruit slices.

Nutritional information per serving

Calories 96, Protein (g) 4, Carbohydrate (g) 4, Fat (g) 6, Calories from Fat (%) 60, Saturated Fat (g) 4, Dietary Fiber (g) 0, Cholesterol (mg) 20, Sodium (mg) 126, Diabetic Exchanges: 0.5 high-fat meat, 0.5 other carbohydrate, 0.5 fat

FOOD FACT:

Brie is a cream-colored, buttery-soft cheese that should be perfectly ripe for the best flavor—it oozes at the peak of ripeness. Brie from France is considered the best.

Glazed Brie

Tropical and Cranberry-Pineapple Muffins

Breads, Muffins, and Brunch

Beer Bread

This effortless bread can replace your usual home-made loaf. Its four ingredients include everyone's favorite—beer!

MAKES 16 SLICES

3 cups self-rising flour
⅓ cup sugar
1 (12-ounce) can light beer (room temperature)
2 tablespoons margarine, melted

Preheat the oven to 350°F. Coat a 9 x 5 x 3-inch non-stick loaf pan with non-stick cooking spray.

In a large bowl, combine the flour, sugar, beer, and margarine, mixing until just moistened. Pour the batter into the loaf pan. Bake for 50 minutes, or until golden brown. Serve warm.

Nutritional information per serving

Calories 110, Protein (g) 2, Carbohydrate (g) 21, Fat (g) 1, Calories from Fat (%) 11, Saturated Fat (g) 0, Dietary Fiber (g) 0, Cholesterol (mg) 0, Sodium (mg) 287, Diabetic Exchanges: 1.5 starch

QUICK TIP:

For a whole wheat version of this bread, use the following ingredients, but follow the same cooking instructions listed above.
  2 cups self-rising flour
  1 cup whole wheat flour
  4 tablespoons honey
  1 teaspoon baking powder
  1 (12-ounce) can light beer (room temperature)
  2 tablespoons margarine, melted

Herbed French Bread

Dried seasonings take this French bread to a new level.

MAKES 6 TO 8 SERVINGS

3 tablespoons margarine, melted
1 teaspoon finely chopped parsley
½ teaspoon Worcestershire sauce
¼ teaspoon dried oregano leaves
¼ teaspoon dried basil leaves
¼ teaspoon garlic powder
1 (8-ounce) loaf French bread, split in half lengthwise

Preheat the oven to 350°F.

In a small bowl, combine the margarine, parsley, Worcestershire sauce, oregano, basil, and garlic powder, stirring well. Lightly brush each half of the bread with the margarine mixture. Wrap in foil and bake for 10 minutes, or until the bread is crispy on the outside. Slice and serve.

Nutritional information per serving

Calories 117, Protein (g) 3, Carbohydrate (g) 15 Fat (g) 5, Calories from Fat (%) 40, Saturated Fat (g) 1, Dietary Fiber (g) 1, Cholesterol (mg) 0, Sodium (mg) 226, Diabetic Exchanges: 1 starch, 1 fat

Italian Puffs

Italian Puffs

My kids love these melt-in-your-mouth rolls and will even make them for me. For lower fat puffs, or if desired, leave out the Cheddar cheese. They'll still melt in your mouth.

MAKES 8 PUFFS

1 (8-ounce) can reduced-fat crescent dinner rolls

3 ounces reduced-fat Cheddar cheese, cut into
  ¾-inch cubes

2 tablespoons fat-free Italian dressing

3 tablespoons sesame seeds

3 tablespoons grated Parmesan cheese

Preheat the oven to 375°F.

Separate the crescent dough into eight triangles. Place a cheese cube on the wide end of each triangle. Fold both corners on the wide side over the cheese, and roll to the opposite point, completely covering the cheese, sealing well.

Pour the dressing in a small bowl. On a small plate, combine the sesame seeds and Parmesan cheese. Dip each roll in the dressing, and then roll in the sesame seed/ cheese mixture. Place the rolls on a non-stick baking sheet or muffin tins coated with non-stick cooking spray. Bake for 12 to 15 minutes, or until the rolls are golden. Serve immediately.

Nutritional information per serving

Calories 166, Protein (g) 7, Carbohydrate (g) 13, Fat (g) 9, Calories from Fat (%) 51, Saturated Fat (g) 3, Dietary Fiber (g) 0, Cholesterol (mg) 8, Sodium (mg) 400, Diabetic Exchanges: 0.5 lean meat, 1 starch, 1 fat

Biscuits

Here's a great recipe when you have the urge for homemade biscuits. Best served hot.

MAKES 8 SERVINGS

1 cup all-purpose flour
1½ teaspoons baking powder
⅛ teaspoon baking soda
⅛ teaspoon salt
2 tablespoons margarine
½ cup nonfat plain yogurt
1 teaspoon honey

Preheat the oven to 425°F.

In a medium bowl, combine the flour, baking powder, baking soda, and salt; cut in the margarine with a pastry blender or fork until the mixture resembles coarse meal. Add the yogurt and honey, stirring just until the dry ingredients are moistened.

Turn the dough onto a floured surface and knead four times. Roll the dough to ½-inch thickness; cut with a cutter about 2½ inches wide. Place on an ungreased baking sheet. Bake for 10 minutes, or until golden. Serve hot.

Nutritional information per serving

Calories 94, Protein (g) 3, Carbohydrate (g) 14, Fat (g) 3, Calories from Fat (%) 29, Saturated Fat (g) 1, Dietary Fiber (g) 0, Cholesterol (mg) 0, Sodium (mg) 193, Diabetic Exchanges: 1 starch, 0.5 fat

Mexican Brunch Biscuit Bake

This recipe is perfect for an eggless breakfast, a great snack, or a terrific bread with dinner.

MAKES 8 TO 10 SERVINGS

1 (12-ounce) can buttermilk biscuits (10 count)
1 (6-ounce) can buttermilk biscuits (5 count)
1 (16-ounce) jar chunky salsa
1 bunch green onions (scallions), chopped
1 cup shredded reduced-fat Monterey Jack cheese

Preheat the oven to 350°F. Coat a 13 x 9 x 2-inch non-stick baking pan with non-stick cooking spray.

Separate the biscuits, and cut each into quarters. In a large mixing bowl, toss the biscuits with the salsa, green onions, and cheese. Transfer the mixture into the prepared pan. Bake, uncovered, for 30 minutes, or until the middle is fully cooked. Serve hot from the oven.

Nutritional information per serving

Calories 150, Protein (g) 6, Carbohydrate (g) 21, Fat (g) 3, Calories from Fat (%) 22, Saturated Fat (g) 1, Dietary Fiber (g) 1, Cholesterol (mg) 6, Sodium (mg) 643, Diabetic Exchanges: 0.5 lean meat, 1.5 starch

Pull-Apart Biscuit Bake 🥕 ❄

There's little time involved in this dish that's sure to be a family favorite.

MAKES 6 TO 8 SERVINGS

2 tablespoons margarine, melted
1½ teaspoons dried dill weed leaves
1½ teaspoons poppy seeds
⅓ cup grated Parmesan cheese
2 (10-ounce) cans refrigerated buttermilk biscuits

Preheat the oven to 400°F.

   Pour the melted margarine into a 9-inch non-stick round pan coated with non-stick cooking spray. In a zipper-lock plastic bag, combine the dill weed, poppy seeds, and Parmesan cheese. Cut each biscuit into two pieces; add the biscuit pieces to the bag, and shake to coat. Arrange the coated biscuit pieces in the prepared pan; sprinkle with any remaining mixture. Bake for 15 minutes, or until golden. Serve hot.

Nutritional information per serving

Calories 214, Protein (g) 6, Carbohydrate (g) 33, Fat (g) 7, Calories from Fat (%) 28, Saturated Fat (g) 1, Dietary Fiber (g) 1, Cholesterol (mg) 3, Sodium (mg) 709, Diabetic Exchanges: 2 starch, 1 fat

Herbed Biscuits 🥕 ❄

Hard to believe these incredible herby rolls begin with packaged biscuit dough. Prepare ahead, refrigerate covered, and bring up to room temperature before baking.

MAKES 4 TO 6 SERVINGS

3 tablespoons margarine
1 (10-ounce) can refrigerated biscuits
2 cloves garlic, minced
1 teaspoon dried basil leaves
½ teaspoon dried oregano leaves
2 tablespoons grated Parmesan cheese
1 tablespoon sesame seeds
1 tablespoon chopped parsley

Preheat the oven to 400°F.

   Melt the margarine in a 9-inch non-stick round pan in the oven. Separate the biscuits, and cut each into four pieces. Stir the garlic, basil, oregano, cheese, sesame seeds, and parsley into the margarine in the pan. Arrange the pieces of biscuits next to one another in the margarine. Bake for 15 minutes, or until the tops are brown. Immediately invert the biscuits onto a platter and serve.

Nutritional information per serving

Calories 183, Protein (g) 4, Carbohydrate (g) 22, Fat (g) 9, Calories from Fat (%) 42, Saturated Fat (g) 1, Dietary Fiber (g) 1, Cholesterol (mg) 2, Sodium (mg) 505, Diabetic Exchanges: 1.5 starch, 1.5 fat

Yam Biscuits

Whip up these nutritious and delicious biscuits with pantry ingredients. Make different sizes of biscuits to match their intended use. I've served these at parties with a meat tray.

MAKES 20 TO 24 BISCUITS

1 (15-ounce) can sweet potatoes (yams), drained and mashed
4 cups biscuit baking mix
½ teaspoon ground cinnamon
¾ cup skim milk
3 tablespoons margarine, softened

Preheat the oven to 450°F.

In a mixing bowl, mix the mashed yams with the baking mix and cinnamon. Add the milk and margarine to the mixture, stirring until blended. Roll on a floured surface to 1-inch thickness. Cut with a 2-inch cutter or glass, and place on an ungreased baking sheet. Bake for 10 to 12 minutes, or until golden brown. Serve hot.

Nutritional information per serving

Calories 115, Protein (g) 2, Carbohydrate (g) 17, Fat (g) 4, Calories from Fat (%) 35, Saturated Fat (g) 1, Dietary Fiber (g) 1, Cholesterol (mg) 0, Sodium (mg) 286, Diabetic Exchanges: 1 starch, 1 fat

Yam Biscuits

Cranberry Orange Scones

There's no need to pick up scones at a coffee shop when, in no time at all, you can whip these up for a quick, wonderful morning treat.

MAKES 10 SCONES

2 cups all-purpose flour
¼ cup sugar
2 teaspoons baking powder
½ teaspoon baking soda
1 teaspoon grated orange rind
3 tablespoons chilled margarine, cut into small pieces
1 cup nonfat plain yogurt
⅓ cup dried cranberries

Preheat the oven to 400°F.

In a large bowl, combine the flour, sugar, baking powder, baking soda, and orange rind; cut in the margarine with a pastry blender until the mixture resembles coarse meal. Add the yogurt to the dry ingredients, stirring just until the ingredients are mixed. Stir in the cranberries. The dough will be sticky.

Turn the dough onto a floured surface and knead with floured hands several times, or until the dough can be rolled. Roll dough into a circle about 8 inches in diameter, and cut into rounds with a 2-inch biscuit cutter or glass. Place on a non-stick baking sheet, and bake for 15 minutes, or until golden brown.

Nutritional information per serving

Calories 167, Protein (g) 4, Carbohydrate (g) 29, Fat (g) 4, Calories from Fat (%) 20, Saturated Fat (g) 1, Dietary Fiber (g) 1, Cholesterol (mg) 0, Sodium (mg) 220, Diabetic Exchanges: 1.5 starch, 0.5 fruit, 0.5 fat

Lemon Berry Bread 🥕 ❄

The lemon syrup soaks through this luscious bread, enhancing the flavor, and making it a lemon lover's favorite.

MAKES 16 SERVINGS

⅓ cup canola oil

⅔ cup plus ½ cup sugar, divided

2 tablespoons lemon extract

1 egg

2 egg whites

1½ cups all-purpose flour

1 teaspoon baking powder

½ cup skim milk

1 cup fresh blueberries

2 tablespoons grated lemon rind

½ cup lemon juice

Preheat the oven to 350°F. Coat a 9 x 5 x 3-inch non-stick loaf pan with non-stick cooking spray.

In a large bowl, mix the oil, ⅔ cup sugar, lemon extract, egg, and egg whites. In a separate, small bowl, combine the flour with the baking powder. Add the flour mixture to the sugar mixture alternately with the milk, stirring just until blended. Fold in the blueberries and lemon rind.

Pour the batter into the prepared pan. Bake for 40 to 50 minutes, or until a wooden toothpick inserted in the center comes out clean.

Immediately poke holes at 1-inch intervals on the top of the bread. In a small saucepan over medium heat or in a microwave oven, combine the remaining ½ cup sugar and the lemon juice, heating until the sugar is dissolved. Pour over the bread. Cool, and slice to serve.

Nutritional information per serving

Calories 161, Protein (g) 2, Carbohydrate (g) 26, Fat (g) 5, Calories from Fat (%) 28, Saturated Fat (g) 0, Dietary Fiber (g) 1, Cholesterol (mg) 13, Sodium (mg) 46, Diabetic Exchanges: 1.5 starch, 0.5 other carbohydrate, 1 fat

QUICK TIP:

You can also use frozen blueberries in this recipe. If you do, do not thaw before using, or the berries will become too mushy.

Lemon Berry Bread

Cranberry Orange Bread

This is a great holiday bread! Substitute dried cranberries for fresh, and throw in some toasted pecans, if desired. This bread freezes well.

MAKES 16 SLICES

2 cups all-purpose flour
1½ teaspoons baking powder
½ teaspoon baking soda
1 cup sugar
¼ cup canola oil
¾ cup orange juice
1 egg, beaten
1 tablespoon grated orange rind
½ teaspoon almond extract
1½ cups cranberries, coarsely chopped

Preheat the oven to 350°F. Coat a 9 x 5 x 3-inch non-stick loaf pan with non-stick cooking spray.

In a large bowl, combine the flour, baking powder, baking soda, and sugar. In a small bowl, combine the oil, orange juice, egg, orange rind, and almond extract. Add the wet mixture to the dry ingredients, stirring just until the dry ingredients are moistened. Fold in the cranberries. Pour the batter into the prepared pan. Bake for 45 to 50 minutes, or until a toothpick inserted in the center comes out clean. Cool in the pan.

Nutritional information per serving
Calories 152, Protein (g) 2, Carbohydrate (g) 27, Fat (g) 4, Calories from Fat (%) 23, Saturated Fat (g) 0, Dietary Fiber (g) 1, Cholesterol (mg) 13, Sodium (mg) 90, Diabetic Exchanges: 1 starch, 1 other carbohydrate, 0.5 fat

Easy Cranberry Yam Bread

Cream cheese gives this incredible, yet easy, bread a rich flavor packed with the natural sweetness of yams and a burst of cranberries. Toss in some walnuts for added flavor and crunch.

MAKES 16 SLICES

1 (8-ounce) package reduced-fat cream cheese, softened
1 cup sugar
1 (15-ounce) can sweet potatoes (yams), drained and mashed
2 eggs
1½ cups biscuit baking mix
1 teaspoon ground cinnamon
½ teaspoon ground nutmeg
1 cup dried cranberries, or 1 cup chopped fresh cranberries

Preheat the oven to 350°F. Coat a 9 x 5 x 3-inch non-stick loaf pan with non-stick cooking spray.

In a large mixing bowl, beat the cream cheese and sugar until light and fluffy. Beat in the sweet potatoes and eggs. Stir in the biscuit mix, cinnamon, nutmeg, and cranberries until just blended. Transfer to the prepared pan. Bake for 45 minutes to 1 hour, or until a toothpick inserted in the center comes out clean. Cool in the pan for 15 minutes before serving.

Nutritional information per serving
Calories 189, Protein (g) 4, Carbohydrate (g) 31, Fat (g) 6, Calories from Fat (%) 26, Saturated Fat (g) 3, Dietary Fiber (g) 1, Cholesterol (mg) 37, Sodium (mg) 231, Diabetic Exchanges: 1.5 starch, 0.5 fruit, 1 fat

Banana Cranberry Bread ✐ ❄

Use overripe bananas with tart cranberries for this wonderful bread. Take advantage of the cranberry season to add color to everyday banana bread.

MAKES 16 SLICES

2 bananas
¼ cup sugar
½ cup light brown sugar
¼ cup canola oil
2 eggs
1 teaspoon vanilla extract
1 cup all-purpose flour
¼ teaspoon baking soda
½ teaspoon baking powder
¼ cup buttermilk
1 cup dried cranberries, or 1 cup chopped fresh
   cranberries
1 teaspoon grated orange rind

Preheat the oven to 350°F. Coat a 9 x 5 x 3-inch non-stick loaf pan with non-stick cooking spray.

In a large bowl, beat the bananas until puréed. Add the sugar, brown sugar, canola oil, eggs, and vanilla, and continue beating until creamy. In a small bowl combine the flour, baking soda, and baking powder. Stir the flour mixture alternately with the buttermilk into the banana mixture, beginning and ending with the flour, mixing only until combined. Stir in the dried cranberries and orange rind.

Pour the batter into the prepared pan. Bake for 40 to 45 minutes, or until a toothpick inserted in the center comes out clean. Cool in the pan.

Nutritional information per serving
Calories 144, Protein (g) 2, Carbohydrate (g) 25, Fat (g) 4, Calories from Fat (%) 26, Saturated Fat (g) 1, Dietary Fiber (g) 1, Cholesterol (mg) 27, Sodium (mg) 50, Diabetic Exchanges: 1 starch, 0.5 fruit, 0.5 fat

QUICK TIP:

Coat only the bottoms of loaf pans for fruit breads. The ungreased sides allow the batter to cling while rising during baking, helping to form a gently rounded top.

Zucchini Bread 🥕 ❄️

This bread resembles carrot bread and is packed with flavor and texture. I sometimes substitute golden raisins for dark raisins.

MAKES 16 SLICES

¾ cup whole wheat flour
¾ cup all-purpose flour
½ teaspoon baking soda
½ teaspoon baking powder
1 teaspoon ground cinnamon
2 egg whites
⅓ cup sugar
⅓ cup light brown sugar
⅓ cup canola oil
1 teaspoon vanilla extract
1 cup shredded zucchini, unpeeled
½ cup crushed pineapple
⅓ cup raisins
⅓ cup pecans, toasted, optional

Preheat the oven to 350°F. Coat a 9 x 5 x 3-inch non-stick loaf pan with non-stick cooking spray.

In a large bowl, mix the whole wheat flour, flour, baking soda, baking powder, and cinnamon. Add the egg whites, sugars, oil, and vanilla. Mix thoroughly. Fold in the zucchini, pineapple, raisins, and pecans. Pour the batter into the prepared loaf pan.

Bake for 40 to 45 minutes, or until a toothpick inserted in the center comes out clean. Cool in the pan.

Nutritional information per serving

Calories 133, Protein (g) 2, Carbohydrate (g) 21, Fat (g) 5, Calories from Fat (%) 31, Saturated Fat (g) 0, Dietary Fiber (g) 1, Cholesterol (mg) 0, Sodium (mg) 66, Diabetic Exchanges: 1 starch, 0.5 fruit, 1 fat

QUICK TIP:

Don't fret—a large, lengthwise crack in the center is characteristic of quick breads.

Chocolate Zucchini Bread

The unique combination of chocolate and zucchini produces an exceptionally moist, tasty bread with a carrot cake texture.

MAKES 16 SLICES

1½ cups all-purpose flour
¼ cup cocoa
1 teaspoon baking soda
1 teaspoon ground cinnamon
¼ teaspoon baking powder
1 cup sugar
2 large eggs
⅓ cup canola oil
1 teaspoon vanilla extract
2 cups shredded zucchini

Preheat oven to 350°F. Coat a 9 x 5 x 3-inch non-stick loaf pan coated with non-stick cooking spray.

In a bowl, mix the flour, cocoa, baking soda, cinnamon, and baking powder; set aside. In a medium bowl, mix the sugar, eggs, oil, and vanilla until well blended. Stir in the zucchini. Add dry ingredients to the wet ingredients and stir until just moistened. Pour the batter into the pan. Bake for 45 to 55 minutes, or until a toothpick inserted in the center comes out clean. Cool in the pan.

Nutrition information per serving

Calories 150, Protein (g) 3, Carbohydrate (g) 23, Fat (g) 6, Calories from Fat (%) 33, Saturated Fat (g) 1, Dietary Fiber (g) 1, Cholesterol (mg) 26, Sodium (mg) 94, Diabetic Exchanges: 1 starch, 0.5 other carbohydrate, 1 fat

QUICK TIP:

Cocoa is a great way to enjoy chocolate without the saturated fat in solid chocolate.

Mango Bread

Magnificent mangoes make up this hard-to-beat quick bread. If you've never experienced mangoes, here's an ideal recipe to try.

MAKES 16 SLICES

¼ cup margarine

¾ cup sugar

1 egg, lightly beaten

1 cup puréed mango (about 2 medium)

1 teaspoon vanilla extract

2 tablespoons lime juice

1½ cups all-purpose flour

1½ teaspoons baking powder

½ teaspoon baking soda

½ teaspoon ground cinnamon

½ cup chopped walnuts, toasted

Preheat the oven to 350°F. Coat a 9 x 5 x 3-inch non-stick loaf pan with non-stick cooking spray.

In a large mixing bowl, cream the margarine and sugar, beating well. Add the egg, mango, vanilla, and lime juice. In a separate large bowl, combine the flour, baking powder, baking soda, and cinnamon. Add the mango mixture to the flour mixture, stirring just until the dry ingredients are moistened. Stir in the walnuts. Pour the batter into the prepared loaf pan.

Bake for 40 minutes, or until a toothpick inserted in the center comes out clean. Cool in the pan for 10 minutes before serving.

Nutritional information per serving

Calories 152, Protein (g) 2, Carbohydrate (g) 24, Fat (g) 6, Calories from Fat (%) 33, Saturated Fat (g) 1, Dietary Fiber (g) 1, Cholesterol (mg) 13, Sodium (mg) 123, Diabetic Exchanges: 1 starch, 0.5 fruit, 1 fat

QUICK TIP:

When buying mangoes, look for a yellowish outer skin tinged with red, which is a sign of ripeness. If you can't find ripe mangoes, papayas will work just as well.

Mango Bread

Apricot Bread 🥕 ❄️

Munching on this sweet citrus bread with tart apricots is as good as eating cake. My tasters immediately demanded the recipe.

MAKES 16 SLICES

1 cup diced dried apricots
1 egg
1 cup sugar
2 tablespoons margarine, melted
2 cups all-purpose flour
1 tablespoon baking powder
¼ teaspoon baking soda
¾ cup orange juice

Preheat the oven to 350°F.

Coat a 9 x 5 x 3-inch non-stick loaf pan with non-stick cooking spray.

Pour boiling water over the apricots to cover, and let stand 5 minutes. Drain apricots, discard water, and set aside.

In a mixing bowl, beat the egg and sugar. Add the margarine. In a separate large bowl, combine the flour, baking powder, and baking soda. Add the flour mixture alternately with the orange juice to the sugar mixture. Stir in the drained apricots. Pour the batter into the prepared pan. Bake for 50 minutes to 1 hour, or until a toothpick inserted in the center comes out clean. Cool in the pan.

Nutritional information per serving
Calories 152, Protein (g) 2, Carbohydrate (g) 32, Fat (g) 2, Calories from Fat (%) 11, Saturated Fat (g) 0, Dietary Fiber (g) 1, Cholesterol (mg) 13, Sodium (mg) 133, Diabetic Exchanges: 1.5 starch, 0.5 fruit

Banana Chip Bread 🥕 ❄️

In the mood for banana bread with flair? Add your favorite types of morsels. For a basic old-fashioned banana bread, leave the morsels out. Toss in some nuts, if desired, which I always do…especially walnuts.

MAKES 16 SLICES

1¾ cups all-purpose flour
1 teaspoon baking soda
½ teaspoon ground cinnamon
1 cup sugar
2 eggs
1½ cups mashed bananas (2 to 3 bananas)
¼ cup canola oil
¼ cup skim milk
½ cup butterscotch, chocolate or peanut butter chips

Preheat oven to 350°F. Coat a 9 x 5 x 3-inch non-stick loaf pan with non-stick cooking spray. Combine the flour, baking soda, and cinnamon in a bowl; set aside. In a mixing bowl, combine the sugar, eggs, mashed bananas, and oil, blending well. Add the flour mixture alternately with the milk to the banana mixture, mixing only until combined. Stir in the chips. Pour into the prepared loaf pan. Bake for 45 to 50 minutes or until a toothpick inserted in the center comes out clean. Cool in pan.

Nutrition information per serving
Calories 197, Protein (g) 2, Carbohydrate (g) 32, Fat (g) 6, Calories from Fat (%) 29, Saturated Fat (g) 2, Dietary Fiber (g) 1, Cholesterol (mg) 26, Sodium (mg) 95, Diabetic Exchanges: 1 starch, 1 other carbohydrate, 1 fat

Cinnamon Crescents

Save a trip to the bakery—in just a few minutes you can prepare these easy, melt-in-your-mouth jumbo crescents. My kids like to leave out the pecans, and I like to add raisins—either way, they are outstanding!

MAKES 8 CRESCENTS

¼ cup light brown sugar
¼ cup chopped pecans
1 teaspoon ground cinnamon
2 cups biscuit baking mix
1 tablespoon sugar
½ cup cold water
3 tablespoons margarine, softened
Glaze (recipe follows)

Preheat the oven to 425°F.

In a small bowl, combine the brown sugar, pecans, and cinnamon; set aside. In a separate, large bowl, mix the baking mix, sugar, and water until a soft dough forms; beat vigorously for 30 seconds. Roll the mixture into a ball with hands dusted with baking mix so the dough will not stick. Knead 1 minute. Pat or roll the dough into a 10- to 12-inch circle. Spread with the margarine and sprinkle the brown sugar mixture, and cut into eight wedges. Roll up, beginning at wide edges, to point.

Place the crescents on an ungreased baking sheet; shape into a semicircle. Bake for 10 minutes, or until golden brown. Cool slightly on the baking sheet; drizzle with the glaze (see recipe at right).

GLAZE

½ cup confectioners' sugar
1 tablespoon margarine, softened
¼ teaspoon vanilla extract
1 tablespoon water

In a small bowl, mix the confectioners' sugar, margarine, vanilla, and water with a fork, adding more water as needed, until blended and smooth.

Nutritional information per serving

Calories 261, Protein (g) 3, Carbohydrate (g) 35, Fat (g) 13, Calories from Fat (%) 44, Saturated Fat (g) 2, Dietary Fiber (g) 1, Cholesterol (mg) 0, Sodium (mg) 447, Diabetic Exchanges: 2 starch, 0.5 other carbohydrate, 2 fat

Cranberry Pineapple Muffins 🥕 ❄️

* See photo on page 71
Cranberry, pineapple, and pecans, with a touch of cinnamon, make this a popular muffin. Dried cranberries will substitute for fresh cranberries.

MAKES 12 MUFFINS

1 cup all-purpose flour
½ cup whole wheat flour
½ cup quick-cooking oatmeal
¼ cup plus 1 tablespoon sugar, divided
2 teaspoons baking powder
½ teaspoon plus ¼ teaspoon ground cinnamon, divided
¼ cup margarine
1 egg, beaten
1 cup skim milk
1 cup fresh or dried cranberries, coarsely chopped
½ cup unsweetened crushed pineapple, drained
½ cup chopped pecans, optional

Preheat the oven to 400°F. Line a muffin pan with paper cups, or coat it with non-stick cooking spray.

In a large bowl, combine the flour, whole wheat flour, oatmeal, ¼ cup sugar, baking powder, ½ teaspoon cinnamon, and margarine with a pastry blender or fork until the mixture resembles coarse crumbs. In a separate small bowl, combine the beaten egg and the milk; add to the dry ingredients, stirring just until moistened. Gently fold in the cranberries, pineapple, and pecans. Spoon the batter into the prepared pan, filling the cups three-quarters full.

Combine 1 tablespoon sugar and ¼ teaspoon cinnamon; sprinkle evenly over the remaining muffin batter. Bake for 20 to 25 minutes, or until golden brown. Remove immediately from the pan, and cool on a wire rack.

Nutritional information per serving
Calories 143, Protein (g) 4, Carbohydrate (g) 22, Fat (g) 5, Calories from Fat (%) 29, Saturated Fat (g) 1, Dietary Fiber (g) 2, Cholesterol (mg) 18, Sodium (mg) 142, Diabetic Exchanges: 1.5 starch, 1 fat

QUICK TIP:

When chopping raisins or dried fruit, coat the knife blade with nonstick cooking spray to prevent sticking.

Chunky Whole Wheat Apple Muffins

Apple, pecans, and raisins enliven this moist, yummy muffin.

MAKES 12 MUFFINS

1½ cups all-purpose flour, divided
½ cup peeled, chopped baking apples
½ cup whole wheat flour
⅓ cup light brown sugar
1½ teaspoons baking powder
½ teaspoon ground cinnamon
¼ teaspoon salt
½ cup skim milk
3 tablespoons canola oil
2 egg whites, lightly beaten
⅓ cup chopped pecans
⅓ cup golden raisins

Preheat the oven to 400°F. Line a muffin pan with paper cups or coat with a non-stick cooking spray.

In a small bowl, combine ½ cup flour and the apples, tossing to coat. Set aside.

In a large bowl, combine the remaining 1 cup flour, whole wheat flour, brown sugar, baking powder, cinnamon, and salt; make a well in the center of the mixture.

In a small bowl, combine the milk, oil, and egg whites; stir well. Add the milk mixture, apple mixture, pecans, and raisins to the flour mixture, stirring just until the dry ingredients are moistened. Spoon the batter into the prepared pan, filling two-thirds full.

Bake for 20 minutes, or until golden brown. Cool in pan.

Nutritional information per serving

Calories 173, Protein (g) 4, Carbohydrate (g) 27, Fat (g) 6, Calories from Fat (%) 31, Saturated Fat (g) 1, Dietary Fiber (g) 2, Cholesterol (mg) 0, Sodium (mg) 127, Diabetic Exchanges: 1.5 starch, 0.5 fruit, 1 fat

Lemon Raspberry Muffins

Raspberries and lemon pair for a very enticing muffin.

MAKES 12 TO 16 MUFFINS

2 cups all-purpose flour
⅔ cup sugar
1 tablespoon baking powder
1 cup skim milk
⅓ cup canola oil
1 teaspoon lemon extract
1 egg
2 egg whites
1½ cups fresh or frozen raspberries (if frozen, no syrup)
1 teaspoon grated lemon rind

Preheat the oven to 425°F. Line a muffin pan with paper cups or coat with non-stick cooking spray.

In a large bowl, combine the flour, sugar, and baking powder, mixing well. In a small bowl, combine the milk, oil, lemon extract, egg, and egg whites, blending well. Add to the dry ingredients, stirring just until the ingredients are moistened. Carefully fold in the raspberries and lemon rind. Fill the prepared pan three-quarters full with batter.

Bake for 18 to 23 minutes, or until golden brown. Cool 5 minutes; remove from the pan.

Nutritional information per serving
Calories 148, Protein (g) 3, Carbohydrate (g) 23, Fat (g) 5, Calories from Fat (%) 31, Saturated Fat (g) 0, Dietary Fiber (g) 1, Cholesterol (mg) 14, Sodium (mg) 111, Diabetic Exchanges: 1.5 starch, 1 fat

Tropical Muffins

Tropical paradise in a muffin. If desired, use whole wheat flour.

MAKES 12 MUFFINS

2 cups all-purpose flour
⅓ cup light brown sugar
2 teaspoons baking powder
½ teaspoon baking soda
1 cup nonfat plain yogurt
2 egg whites
¼ cup canola oil
2 teaspoons coconut extract
1 cup crushed pineapple, well drained

Preheat the oven to 400°F. Line a muffin pan with paper cups or coat with non-stick cooking spray.

In a large bowl, combine the flour, brown sugar, baking powder, and baking soda. In another bowl, mix together the yogurt, egg whites, oil, and coconut extract. Mix this into the flour mixture, stirring until just blended. Fold in the drained pineapple. Spoon the batter into the prepared pan, filling three-quarters full.

Bake for 20 to 25 minutes, or until golden. Cool in the pan.

Nutritional information per serving
Calories 167, Protein (g) 4, Carbohydrate (g) 27, Fat (g) 5, Calories from Fat (%) 26, Saturated Fat (g) 0, Dietary Fiber (g) 1, Cholesterol (mg) 0, Sodium (mg) 163, Diabetic Exchanges: 1.5 starch, 0.5 fruit, 1 fat

Cranberry Pineapple Muffins and Tropical Muffins

Bran Muffins

This batter keeps in the refrigerator for several weeks in a covered plastic or glass container, so you can serve hot muffins in very little time. This quickie is my favorite bran muffin.

MAKES 24 MUFFINS

4 cups raisin bran cereal
1 cup sugar
2½ cups all-purpose flour
2½ teaspoons baking soda
2 teaspoons ground cinnamon
2 eggs, beaten
⅓ cup canola oil
2 cups buttermilk

Preheat the oven to 400°F. Line muffin pans with paper cups, or coat with non-stick cooking spray.

In a large bowl, mix the cereal, sugar, flour, baking soda, and cinnamon together. Add the eggs, oil, and buttermilk, stirring with a spoon until well combined. Fill each muffin cup two-thirds full.

Bake for 15 minutes, or until a toothpick inserted in the center of a muffin comes out clean. Cool and remove to wire rack.

Nutritional information per serving

Calories 152, Protein (g) 3, Carbohydrate (g) 27, Fat (g) 4, Calories from Fat (%) 23, Saturated Fat (g) 1, Dietary Fiber (g) 2, Cholesterol (mg) 18, Sodium (mg) 217, Diabetic Exchanges: 2 starch, 0.5 fat

Surprise Corn Bread 🥕❄️

This fulfilling, fabulous corn bread begins with convenience items, so it's a simple indulgence. Corn bread is perfect with chili and barbecued meats.

MAKES 12 TO 16 SERVINGS

2 (8-ounce) packages corn muffin mix
2 eggs
⅔ cup skim milk
1 cup picante sauce
1 cup shredded reduced-fat Cheddar cheese

Preheat the oven to 400°F. Coat a 9 x 9 x 2-inch non-stick square pan with non-stick cooking spray.

In a bowl, mix together the corn muffin mix, eggs, and milk, stirring well. Spread half the batter into the prepared pan, and top with the picante sauce and cheese. Carefully spread the remaining batter on top.

Bake for 20 minutes, or until golden brown. Cut into squares, and serve warm.

Nutritional information per serving

Calories 146, Protein (g) 4, Carbohydrate (g) 23, Fat (g) 4, Calories from Fat (%) 26, Saturated Fat (g) 2, Dietary Fiber (g) 0, Cholesterol (mg) 30, Sodium (mg) 357, Diabetic Exchanges: 1.5 starch, 0.5 fat

Cheesy Corn Muffins 🥕❄️

This deluxe cornmeal muffin goes really well with barbecue. For a quick pickup, make in miniature muffin tins (makes about 4 dozen miniature muffins).

MAKES 18 MUFFINS

1 cup chopped onion
1 (8½-ounce) can cream-style corn
1 cup shredded reduced-fat sharp Cheddar cheese
⅔ cup fat-free sour cream
2 tablespoons canola oil
2 egg whites
1 tablespoon sugar
1½ cups self-rising cornmeal mix

Preheat the oven to 400°F. Coat muffin tins with a non-stick cooking spray.

In a non-stick pan, sauté the onion over low heat until tender. In a large bowl, combine the onion with the corn, cheese, sour cream, oil, egg whites, and sugar. Add the cornmeal, and blend well. Fill the muffin tins three-quarters full, and bake for 20 to 25 minutes, or until done. Remove the muffins, and cool on a wire rack.

Nutritional information per serving

Calories 108, Protein (g) 4, Carbohydrate (g) 15, Fat (g) 3, Calories from Fat (%) 27, Saturated Fat (g) 1, Dietary Fiber (g) 1, Cholesterol (mg) 3, Sodium (mg) 292, Diabetic Exchanges: 1 starch, 0.5 fat

Bread Pudding Florentine

An outstanding brunch recipe that is one of my personal favorites, this can be made the night before and popped into the oven to cook in the morning. It's great for a group.

MAKES 10 TO 12 SERVINGS

5 eggs
4 egg whites
3 cups skim milk
¼ cup Dijon mustard
1 (16-ounce) loaf day-old French bread,
    cut into 1-inch slices
½ pound mushrooms, sliced
1 teaspoon minced garlic
1 onion, chopped
2 (10-ounce) boxes frozen chopped spinach, thawed
    and squeezed dry
1 tablespoon all-purpose flour
Salt and pepper to taste
1½ cups shredded reduced-fat Swiss cheese, divided

Coat a 13 x 9 x 2-inch non-stick pan with non-stick cooking spray.

In a large mixing bowl, beat the eggs and egg whites with the milk and mustard. Set aside.

Place half the bread slices in the prepared pan. In a non-stick skillet, sauté the mushrooms, garlic, and onion until tender. Add the spinach and flour, stirring to mix well. Season with salt and pepper to taste. Spread the mixture over the bread layer. Sprinkle with 1 cup of the cheese. Top with the remaining bread. Sprinkle with the remaining ½ cup of the cheese. Pour the egg mixture over the casserole, and refrigerate 2 hours or overnight.

Bake at 350°F for 40 to 50 minutes, or until puffed and golden. Serve immediately.

Nutritional information per serving

Calories 230, Protein (g) 15, Carbohydrate (g) 27, Fat (g) 6, Calories from Fat (%) 24, Saturated Fat (g) 3, Dietary Fiber (g) 3, Cholesterol (mg) 97, Sodium (mg) 552, Diabetic Exchanges: 1.5 lean meat, 1.5 starch, 1 vegetable

Bread Pudding Florentine

Crabmeat Egg Casserole

This makes a crowd-pleasing brunch, especially for crabmeat fans. Any seafood, or ham, may be used instead of crabmeat.

MAKES 10 SERVINGS

6 slices white or whole wheat bread
1½ cups water
1 onion, chopped
½ cup chopped green bell pepper
½ cup chopped celery
2 cloves garlic, minced
2 cups shredded reduced-fat sharp Cheddar cheese
1 (8-ounce) can sliced water chestnuts, drained
1 pound lump crabmeat, picked for shells
1 egg
2 egg whites
½ cup light mayonnaise
Salt and pepper to taste
Several dashes hot pepper sauce

Preheat the oven to 350°F. Coat a 2- to 3-quart oblong baking dish with non-stick cooking spray.

Place the bread in a large bowl with the water. Let stand 15 minutes.

In a medium non-stick skillet, sauté the onion, green pepper, celery, and garlic until tender. Add the shredded cheese to the bread-and-water mixture, stirring together. Carefully stir in the sautéed vegetables, water chestnuts, and crabmeat.

In a medium mixing bowl, beat the egg, egg whites, mayonnaise, salt, pepper, and hot pepper sauce. Combine with the crabmeat mixture, mixing well, and transfer to the prepared dish. Bake for 30 to 40 minutes, or until the filling is set.

Nutritional information per serving
Calories 223, Protein (g) 20, Carbohydrate (g) 13, Fat (g) 10, Calories from Fat (%) 40, Saturated Fat (g) 4, Dietary Fiber (g) 2, Cholesterol (mg) 72, Sodium (mg) 521, Diabetic Exchanges: 2.5 lean meat, 0.5 starch, 1 vegetable

Egg and Green Chile Casserole

This Southwestern egg dish cuts easily into squares. The sliced tomato topping makes this delicious casserole appealing to the eye.

MAKES 12 SERVINGS

1 (8-ounce) package reduced-fat Monterey Jack cheese, shredded
1 cup shredded reduced-fat Cheddar cheese
2 (4-ounce) cans chopped green chiles, drained
1 bunch green onions (scallions), chopped
5 eggs
7 egg whites
3 tablespoons nonfat plain yogurt
1 tomato, thinly sliced

Coat a 2- to 3-quart oblong glass baking dish with non-stick cooking spray.

Combine cheeses, green chiles, and green onions; spread on the bottom of the dish. Beat the eggs and egg whites together with the yogurt. Pour over the cheeses, making a space with a fork so the eggs will go through to the bottom. Refrigerate overnight.

Place in a cold oven, and bake for 15 minutes at 350°F. Add sliced tomatoes along the top of the casserole, and continue baking for 15 to 20 minutes longer, or until done. Serve immediately.

Nutritional information per serving

Calories 132, Protein (g) 13, Carbohydrate (g) 3, Fat (g) 7, Calories from Fat (%) 51, Saturated Fat (g) 4, Dietary Fiber (g) 1, Cholesterol (mg) 104, Sodium (mg) 312, Diabetic Exchanges: 2 lean meat

Tex-Mex Eggs

An open-faced omelet with tortillas, Southwestern seasonings, and cheese, this is a great choice for brunch. Serve with salsa for an additional Tex-Mex touch.

MAKES 4 SERVINGS

5 (6-inch) flour or corn tortillas
1 bunch green onions (scallions), finely chopped
1 red bell pepper, seeded and chopped
2 tablespoons chopped pickled jalapeño pepper
¼ cup finely chopped fresh cilantro
2 eggs
6 egg whites
¼ cup skim milk
1 teaspoon ground cumin
Salt and pepper to taste
⅓ cup shredded reduced-fat sharp Cheddar cheese

Preheat the oven to 500°F.

Dip the tortillas into water, drain, and place on a non-stick baking sheet coated with non-stick cooking spray. Bake for 4 minutes, turn, and bake for 2 minutes longer, or until crisp; set aside.

In a large non-stick skillet, sauté the green onions, red pepper, and jalapeño over medium-high heat until tender. Stir in cilantro and set aside.

In a large bowl, mix the eggs, egg whites, milk, cumin, salt, and pepper. Crumble the crisp tortillas into the egg mixture; let stand for 5 minutes.

Pour the egg mixture into a non-stick skillet over medium heat. As the mixture begins to cook, gently lift the edges with a spatula and tilt the pan to allow the uncooked portions to flow underneath. When the eggs are almost set, spoon the vegetable mixture over the top, combining with the eggs. Sprinkle with the cheese, and continue cooking until the eggs are done and the cheese is melted. Serve immediately.

Nutritional information per serving

Calories 223, Protein (g) 16, Carbohydrate (g) 30, Fat (g) 4, Calories from Fat (%) 18, Saturated Fat (g) 2, Dietary Fiber (g) 2, Cholesterol (mg) 112, Sodium (mg) 516, Diabetic Exchanges: 2 very lean meat, 1.5 starch, 1 vegetable

Quick Cheese Grits

Cheese grits are hard to beat, especially with this simple recipe.

MAKES 8 TO 10 SERVINGS

4 cups water

1 cup skim milk

½ teaspoon salt

1½ cups quick grits

4 ounces reduced-fat pasteurized processed
   cheese spread

6 ounces reduced-fat sharp Cheddar cheese,
   shredded

2 tablespoons margarine

1 tablespoon Worcestershire sauce

¼ teaspoon garlic powder

¼ teaspoon cayenne pepper

In a saucepan, bring the water, milk, and salt to a boil. Add the grits, reduce heat, and cook about 5 minutes, stirring occasionally. Add the cheeses, margarine, Worcestershire sauce, garlic powder, and cayenne pepper. Stir until the margarine and cheeses have melted. Serve immediately.

Nutritional information per serving

Calories 191, Protein (g) 10, Carbohydrate (g) 22, Fat (g) 7, Calories from Fat (%) 33, Saturated Fat (g) 3, Dietary Fiber (g) 0, Cholesterol (mg) 14, Sodium (mg) 462, Diabetic Exchanges: 1 lean meat, 1.5 starch, 0.5 fat

QUICK TIP:

For heartier grits, sauté 2 cups each: onion, green bell pepper, and Canadian bacon, and add to cooked grits along with chopped tomatoes and cheese. It's a great way to start a busy day.

Steak Creole
with Cheese Grits ❄

Ever heard of grillades and grits? This unbelievably flavored dish is served at a true Southern brunch, and it also makes a good light evening meal. See recipe for Quick Cheese Grits, on page 79.

MAKES 6 SERVINGS

3 pounds lean, boneless top round steak

¼ teaspoon pepper

¼ cup all-purpose flour

1 onion, thickly sliced

2 green bell peppers, seeded and sliced

1 tablespoon minced garlic

2 cups canned beef broth

1 (15-ounce) can tomato sauce

1 teaspoon light brown sugar

1 tablespoon Worcestershire sauce

1 teaspoon dried basil leaves

1 teaspoon dried thyme leaves

1 teaspoon dried oregano leaves

Trim any fat from the steak. Season the steak with the pepper, and dredge it in the flour, shaking off any excess. In a large non-stick skillet, brown the steak over medium-high heat for 5 to 7 minutes on each side. Remove the steak from the skillet and set aside.

Add the onion and bell pepper to the skillet, and cook over moderate heat, stirring occasionally, about 5 minutes. Stir in the garlic, beef broth, tomato sauce, brown sugar, Worcestershire sauce, basil, thyme, and oregano; bring to a boil. Return the steak to the skillet, and baste with the sauce. Cover and cook over medium-low heat for 1½ to 2 hours, or until the steak is very tender, stirring occasionally. Serve with Quick Cheese Grits (see page 79).

Nutritional information per serving

Calories 381, Protein (g) 57, Carbohydrate (g) 16, Fat (g) 8, Calories from Fat (%) 21, Saturated Fat (g) 3, Dietary Fiber (g) 2, Cholesterol (mg) 141, Sodium (mg) 861, Diabetic Exchanges: 6 very lean meat, 0.5 starch, 1.5 vegetable

Steak Creole with Cheese Grits

Hot Fruit Casserole

I love serving this dish at a brunch when good fresh fruit is unavailable. Next time you have to bring a luncheon dish, volunteer with this simple, fabulous recipe, which requires little effort with a terrific outcome.

MAKES 10 TO 12 SERVINGS

1 (20-ounce) can pineapple chunks in their own juice
2 (16-ounce) packages frozen sliced peaches
1 (16-ounce) can pitted tart red cherries, drained
4 bananas, peeled and sliced
2 tablespoons lemon juice
⅔ cup light brown sugar
1 cup vanilla wafer crumbs
4 tablespoons margarine, cut up
⅓ cup crème de banana liqueur

Preheat the oven to 350°F.

In a bowl, mix together the pineapple chunks, peaches, and cherries. Sprinkle the bananas with the lemon juice, add to the other fruit. Transfer half the combined fruit to a 3-quart casserole dish. Sprinkle with half the brown sugar, half the vanilla wafer crumbs, half the margarine, and half the crème de banana. Cover with the remaining fruit liqueur and top with the remaining brown sugar, vanilla wafer crumbs, margarine, and crème de banana liqueur.

Bake for 35 to 45 minutes, or until the fruit is bubbly. Serve hot.

Nutritional information per serving

Calories 258, Protein (g) 3, Carbohydrate (g) 49, Fat (g) 6, Calories from Fat (%) 20, Saturated Fat (g) 1, Dietary Fiber (g) 3, Cholesterol (mg) 1, Sodium (mg) 86, Diabetic Exchanges: 2 fruit, 1 other carbohydrate, 1 fat

Hot Fruit Casserole

Basic Pancakes

For a fun and tasty variation, add 1 cup chopped bananas, blueberries, or even chocolate chips.

MAKES 10 TO 12 PANCAKES

1¼ cups all-purpose flour
2 teaspoons baking powder
2 tablespoons sugar
Dash salt
1¼ cups skim milk
1 teaspoon vanilla extract
1 tablespoon canola oil

In a bowl, combine the flour, baking powder, sugar, and salt. Add the milk, vanilla, and oil. Stir only until combined; the batter will be lumpy.

Pour the batter into a heated pan, and cook on one side until bubbles appear on top and the bottom is brown, about 2 to 4 minutes. Flip and cook on other side until browned. Serve with a light syrup.

Nutritional information per serving

Calories 76, Protein (g) 2, Carbohydrate (g) 14, Fat (g) 1, Calories from Fat (%) 16, Saturated Fat (g) 0, Dietary Fiber (g) 0, Cholesterol (mg) 0, Sodium (mg) 95, Diabetic Exchanges: 1 starch

Baked French Toast ✐

Here's a great recipe to serve a group—especially for kids. Add ½ cup orange juice and/or a little grated orange rind to the egg mixture for a wonderful orange flavor.

MAKES 8 SERVINGS

1 cup light maple syrup
1 (16-ounce) loaf French bread
2 eggs
2 egg whites
2 tablespoons sugar
1½ cups skim milk
1 tablespoon vanilla extract
½ teaspoon ground cinnamon

Coat a 3-quart oblong baking dish with non-stick cooking spray. Pour the maple syrup into the dish. Slice the French bread into 2-inch slices, and place over the syrup.

In another bowl, beat the eggs, egg whites, sugar, skim milk, vanilla, and cinnamon until well blended. Pour the egg mixture over the bread, pressing the bread to soak up the liquid. Cover with plastic wrap and refrigerate overnight, or leave at room temperature for 30 minutes before baking.

Preheat the oven to 350°F.

Bake for 40 to 45 minutes, or until golden brown. Serve immediately.

Nutritional information per serving

Calories 261, Protein (g) 9, Carbohydrate (g) 47, Fat (g) 3, Calories from Fat (%) 11, Saturated Fat (g) 1, Dietary Fiber (g) 2, Cholesterol (mg) 54, Sodium (mg) 444, Diabetic Exchanges: 0.5 very lean meat, 2 starch, 1 other carbohydrate

Cereal Mixture ✐

This crunchy mixture with a peanut butter flavor is great for a quick morning pickup or a snack any time of day.

MAKES 6 (½-CUP) SERVINGS

3 tablespoons honey
3 tablespoons margarine
3 tablespoons reduced-fat peanut butter
3 cups cereal (assorted crispy wheat, corn, bran cereal squares)

Preheat the oven to 175°F.

In a microwave oven on high power, combine the honey, margarine, and peanut butter for 30 seconds to one minute, stirring occasionally until smooth. Toss with the cereal, coating well. Spread on a non-stick baking sheet, and bake for 90 minutes.

Nutritional information per serving

Calories 194, Protein (g) 4, Carbohydrate (g) 28, Fat (g) 9, Calories from Fat (%) 38, Saturated Fat (g) 1, Dietary Fiber (g) 3, Cholesterol (mg) 0, Sodium (mg) 283, Diabetic Exchanges: 1.5 starch, 1 other carbohydrate, 1.5 fat

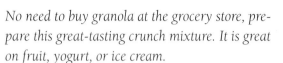

Snack Mix

This sweet-and-salty mix is always addictive!

MAKES 20 (½-CUP) SERVINGS

3 tablespoons sesame oil
3 tablespoons honey
1 tablespoon low sodium soy sauce
½ teaspoon garlic powder
½ teaspoon onion powder
4 cups honey-nut toasted rice and corn cereal squares
6 cups mini-pretzels
1 cup soy nuts
1 cup dry roasted peanuts
1 cup candy-coated chocolate pieces
1 cup raisins, optional

Preheat the oven to 250°F.

In a small bowl, whisk together the sesame oil, honey, soy sauce, garlic powder, and onion powder. In a large bowl, toss together the cereal squares, pretzels, soy nuts, and peanuts. Drizzle the oil mixture over the cereal mixture, tossing gently to coat. Scatter the mixture on a foil-lined jelly roll pan, and bake for 25 minutes, stirring often to prevent too much browning. Turn off the oven and let the cereal stay in the oven for 1 hour to continue crisping. When cool, toss with the chocolate candies and raisins. Store in an airtight container for up to one week.

Nutritional information per serving
Calories 221, Protein (g) 6, Carbohydrate (g) 30, Fat (g) 9, Calories from Fat (%) 36, Saturated Fat (g) 2, Dietary Fiber (g) 2, Cholesterol (mg) 1, Sodium (mg) 309, Diabetic Exchanges: 1 starch, 1 other carbohydrate, 1.5 fat

Granola

No need to buy granola at the grocery store, prepare this great-tasting crunch mixture. It is great on fruit, yogurt, or ice cream.

MAKES 16 (½-CUP) SERVINGS

4 cups old-fashioned oatmeal
½ cup wheat bran
2 tablespoons nonfat dry milk
1 teaspoon ground cinnamon
½ cup sunflower seeds
½ cup pumpkin seeds
⅔ cup honey
2 tablespoons molasses
½ cup dried cranberries
1 cup dried mixed fruit bits

Preheat the oven to 300°F. Line a baking sheet with heavy foil.

Mix together the oatmeal, bran, dry milk, cinnamon, sunflower seeds, and pumpkin seeds; spread on the lined pan. In a small bowl, mix together the honey and molasses. Pour the honey mixture over the cereal, stirring and tossing until well coated.

Bake for 30 to 35 minutes, stirring every 15 minutes and cooking until mixture is golden brown. Let cool, and toss with the cranberries and dried mixed fruit. Store in a sealed container or zipper-lock bag.

Nutritional information per serving
Calories 214, Protein (g) 6, Carbohydrate (g) 38, Fat (g) 6, Calories from Fat (%) 22, Saturated Fat (g) 1, Dietary Fiber (g) 4, Cholesterol (mg) 0, Sodium (mg) 10, Diabetic Exchanges: 1 starch, 0.5 fruit, 1 other carbohydrate, 1 fat

Chicken Tortilla Soup

Soups and Stews

Vichyssoise 🥕

This cold potato soup is always a good standby, mild enough for children but sophisticated enough for adults. For a light meal, serve in chilled mugs with a sandwich.

MAKES 8 SERVINGS

1 tablespoon margarine
1 onion, chopped
3 baking potatoes, peeled and diced
2 (16-ounce) cans fat-free chicken or vegetable broth
1 (12-ounce) can evaporated skim milk
1 cup skim milk
½ cup fat-free sour cream
Salt and pepper to taste
Green onions (scallions), chopped, for garnish

In a large non-stick pot, melt the margarine; add the onion and sauté until tender, about 3 minutes. Add the potatoes, chicken broth, and evaporated milk. Bring to a boil, lower the heat, and simmer until potato pieces are tender, about 15 minutes.

Transfer the mixture to a food processor or blender, and purée. Whisk in the skim milk and sour cream. Season with the salt and pepper. Refrigerate, covered, and serve chilled with green onions on top.

Nutritional information per serving
Calories 131, Protein (g) 9, Carbohydrate (g) 22, Fat (g) 2, Calories from Fat (%) 10, Saturated Fat (g) 0, Dietary Fiber (g) 2, Cholesterol (mg) 2, Sodium (mg) 411, Diabetic Exchanges: 1 starch, 0.5 skim milk

White Gazpacho 🥕

Here's the perfect summer soup that includes all the fresh veggies of the season. The longer it's refrigerated, the better it becomes. Serve chilled.

MAKES 7 SERVINGS

2 cups buttermilk
2 cups fat-free sour cream
3 tablespoons lime juice
½ cup finely chopped green bell pepper
½ cup finely chopped red bell pepper, optional
2 cups peeled, seeded, and finely chopped cucumbers
½ cup chopped green onions (scallions)
2 cups finely chopped tomato
1 cup fat-free canned vegetable (or chicken) broth
Salt and pepper to taste

In a large bowl, combine the buttermilk, sour cream, and lime juice. Add the green and red pepper, cucumber, green onion, tomato, chicken broth, salt, and pepper. Refrigerate until well chilled. Serve chilled.

Nutritional information per serving
Calories 133, Protein (g) 8, Carbohydrate (g) 22, Fat (g) 1, Calories from Fat (%) 6, Saturated Fat (g) 0, Dietary Fiber (g) 1, Cholesterol (mg) 2, Sodium (mg) 226, Diabetic Exchanges: 0.5 starch, 0.5 skim milk, 1.5 vegetable

QUICK TIP:

Substitute vegetable broth for chicken broth for a vegetarian treat.

Gazpacho with Shrimp

Gazpacho with Shrimp

This terrific chilled tomato-based soup adds shrimp for a twist. For classic gazpacho, leave out the shrimp. Make this meal ahead of time to give the flavors time to blend.

MAKES 8 SERVINGS

6 cups tomato juice

2 tablespoons red wine vinegar

1 tablespoon minced garlic

1 cup finely chopped green bell pepper

½ cup finely chopped red bell pepper

1½ cups finely chopped tomato

½ cup chopped onion

1 cup chopped green onions (scallions)

1 teaspoon dried basil leaves

1 teaspoon dried oregano leaves

Dash hot pepper sauce

Salt and pepper to taste

1 pound small cooked, peeled shrimp

In a large bowl, mix together the tomato juice, vinegar, and garlic.

In another bowl, combine the green pepper, red pepper, tomato, onion, and green onion. Add half the vegetable mixture to the tomato juice mixture. Place the remaining half of the vegetable mixture in a food processor, and process until smooth. Add to the tomato juice mixture. Stir in the basil, oregano, hot sauce, salt, pepper, and shrimp. Cover and refrigerate overnight, or until well chilled. Serve chilled.

Nutritional information per serving

Calories 121, Protein (g) 14, Carbohydrate (g) 13, Fat (g) 1, Calories from Fat (%) 6, Saturated Fat (g) 0, Dietary Fiber (g) 3, Cholesterol (mg) 111, Sodium (mg) 779, Diabetic Exchanges: 2 very lean meat, 3 vegetable

Cucumber and Avocado Soup

A refreshing cold soup with a twist. The delightful combination of cucumber and avocado makes this a recipe you won't want to miss.

MAKES 4 SERVINGS

3 cups cucumber, peeled and diced
2 cups buttermilk
½ cup chopped avocado, divided
¼ cup chopped red onion, divided
½ teaspoon chopped fresh basil leaves, divided
Salt and pepper to taste
1 teaspoon lime juice
½ cup seeded chopped tomatoes
4 tablespoons nonfat plain yogurt

In a blender, combine the cucumber and buttermilk. Add ¼ cup avocado, half the red onion, and half the basil. Blend until very smooth. Season with salt and pepper. Cover and refrigerate until chilled, about 1 hour.

In a small bowl, mix the remaining avocado, onion, and basil, the lime juice, and the tomato. Ladle the cucumber soup into bowls. Dollop each with 1 tablespoon yogurt; top with the tomato mixture. Refrigerate until serving.

Nutritional information per serving
Calories 109, Protein (g) 6, Carbohydrate (g) 13, Fat (g) 4, Calories from Fat (%) 33, Saturated Fat (g) 1, Dietary Fiber (g) 2, Cholesterol (mg) 5, Sodium (mg) 146, Diabetic Exchanges: 0.5 skim milk, 1 vegetable, 0.5 fat

Strawberry Soup

A fruit smoothie in a bowl! This cold soup is nice to serve at a ladies' luncheon on a hot day. It is also high in fiber and flavor.

MAKES 5 SERVINGS

1 quart strawberries, hulled
Juice of 1 orange
3 tablespoons confectioners' sugar
1 (12-ounce) can peach nectar
1½ cups nonfat plain yogurt

In a food processor, combine the strawberries and orange juice, blending until smooth. Add the sugar. Gradually add the peach nectar, blending well. Add the yogurt, blending until mixed. Refrigerate until serving.

Nutritional information per serving
Calories 141, Protein (g) 5, Carbohydrate (g) 30, Fat (g) 1, Calories from Fat (%) 4, Saturated Fat (g) 0, Dietary Fiber (g) 3, Cholesterol (mg) 1, Sodium (mg) 63, Diabetic Exchanges: 1.5 fruit, 0.5 skim milk

QUICK TIP:

To quickly de-seed a cucumber, cut it in half and run the pointed end of a teaspoon down the center, scooping out the seeds. English cucumbers are virtually seedless.

Peach Soup

This is an exceptional cold soup that is easy to make. For a social gathering, serve the soup in a punch bowl and use punch cups.

MAKES 10 SERVINGS

1½ pounds fresh peaches, peeled, pitted, and sliced, or 1 (28-ounce) can sliced peaches, drained
2 cups nonfat plain yogurt
1 cup fresh orange juice
1 cup pineapple juice
1 tablespoon lemon juice
2 tablespoons sugar
1 tablespoon almond extract

Pureé the peaches in a food processor until smooth. Add the yogurt, orange juice, pineapple juice, lemon juice, sugar, and almond extract, blending until smooth. Refrigerate until serving.

Nutritional information per serving

Calories 92, Protein (g) 3, Carbohydrate (g) 18, Fat (g) 0, Calories from Fat (%) 0, Saturated Fat (g) 0, Dietary Fiber (g) 1, Cholesterol (mg) 1, Sodium (mg) 38, Diabetic Exchanges: 1 fruit

Peach Soup

Seafood Gumbo ❄

The browned flour substitutes for a roux, so you have the nutty flavor without the fat. I always make tons of gumbo and freeze it in containers. Adding fresh fish to the mix for extra flavor makes for a variety of seafood.

MAKES 12 SERVINGS

¾ cup all-purpose flour

1 tablespoon minced garlic

2 onions, chopped

2 green bell peppers, seeded and chopped

2 stalks celery, chopped

2 tablespoons chopped parsley

9 cups water

1 (14½-ounce) can diced tomatoes with juices

3 bay leaves

Juice of half a lemon

1 teaspoon dried thyme leaves

¼ teaspoon cayenne pepper

4 whole cloves

1 pint claw crabmeat

2 pounds small to medium shrimp, peeled

2 pounds trout, cut into pieces, optional

Salt and pepper to taste

1 cup chopped green onions (scallions)

Preheat the oven to 400°F.

Place the flour on a baking sheet, and bake for 20 to 30 minutes, stirring every 7 minutes, or until the flour is brown (the color of pecan shells). This process also works well in a toaster oven. Set aside.

In a large non-stick pan, sauté the garlic, onions, green peppers, celery, and parsley until tender. Gradually add the browned flour (the roux), stirring constantly. Gradually add the water, tomatoes, bay leaves, lemon juice, thyme, cayenne pepper and cloves. Bring to a boil; lower the heat and cook for 20 minutes.

Add the crabmeat, shrimp, and trout, cooking for another 20 minutes, or until all the seafood is done. Add salt and pepper. Discard the bay leaves and cloves before serving; sprinkle with the green onions and serve over rice.

Nutritional information per serving

Calories 214, Protein (g) 31, Carbohydrate (g) 13, Fat (g) 4, Calories from Fat (%) 15, Saturated Fat (g) 1, Dietary Fiber (g) 2, Cholesterol (mg) 149, Sodium (mg) 254, Diabetic Exchanges: 4 very lean meat, 0.5 starch, 1.5 vegetable

FOOD FACT:

A roux is a mixture of flour and fat that is used to flavor and thicken gumbo. The roux turns a deep brown golden color after cooking slowly over low heat.

Chicken and Sausage Gumbo ❄

If you're not in a location with plentiful seafood, chicken and sausage gumbo is the answer. This thicker gumbo is a very popular dinner in my house. The browned flour replaces the traditional roux as a thickening and flavor agent.

MAKES 10 TO 12 SERVINGS

⅔ cup all-purpose flour
2 onions, chopped
1 teaspoon minced garlic
2 green bell peppers, seeded and chopped
2 stalks celery, chopped
10 cups water
1 (14½-ounce) can chopped tomatoes, with their juice
3 to 4 pounds skinless, boneless chicken breasts,
  cut into pieces
½ teaspoon dried thyme leaves
¼ teaspoon cayenne pepper
1 pound reduced-fat sausage, sliced into ¼-inch pieces
1 bunch green onions (scallions), chopped
1 tablespoon Worcestershire sauce

Preheat the oven to 400°F.

Place the flour on a baking sheet, and bake for 20 to 30 minutes, stirring every 7 minutes, or until the flour is brown (the color of pecan shells). This process works well in a toaster oven. Set aside.

In a large, heavy non-stick pot, sauté garlic, green peppers, and celery until tender. Add the browned flour (the roux), stirring constantly. Gradually add the water, tomatoes, chicken, thyme, and cayenne pepper. Bring to a boil, lower the heat, and simmer for 45 minutes to 1 hour, or until the chicken is tender.

While the gumbo is cooking, brown the sausage in a skillet or heat in the microwave oven. Add the sausage, green onions, and Worcestershire sauce to the gumbo, cooking 10 more minutes. Skim any fat from the surface of the gumbo. Serve over rice.

Nutritional information per serving
Calories 226, Protein (g) 33, Carbohydrate (g) 16, Fat (g) 3, Calories from Fat (%) 11, Saturated Fat (g) 1, Dietary Fiber (g) 2, Cholesterol (mg) 79, Sodium (mg) 464, Diabetic Exchanges: 4 very lean meat, 0.5 starch, 1.5 vegetable

QUICK TIP:

When thickening stews and soups with flour, prevent lumps by mixing the flour thoroughly in a cold liquid before adding it to the boiling mixture. To prevent a starchy flavor, heat the thickened liquid to boiling.

SOUPS & STEWS

SOUPS AND STEWS | 93

Easy Crab Soup

I have prepared this simple, incredible soup at our governor's mansion many times.

MAKES 4 SERVINGS

1 onion, finely chopped
2 tablespoons margarine
1 (14½-ounce) can fat-free chicken broth
½ cup water
1 (12-ounce) can evaporated skimmed milk
1 pound lump crabmeat, pick for shells
3 green onion stems (scallions), finely chopped

In a large pot, sauté the onion in the margarine until tender. Add the broth and water. Simmer for 10 minutes over low heat. Add the milk. Stir well, and fold in the crabmeat. Garnish with the green onion slices. Serve immediately.

Nutritional information per serving

Calories 274, Protein (g) 35, Carbohydrate (g) 17, Fat (g) 7, Calories from Fat (%) 24, Saturated Fat (g) 1, Dietary Fiber (g) 1, Cholesterol (mg) 90, Sodium (mg) 889, Diabetic Exchanges: 4 very lean meat, 1 skim milk, 1 vegetable

Salmon Bisque

When you have leftover salmon, use it to create this soup that will turn salmon lover's heads. It adds gourmet appeal to your table with little effort. Don't let bisque intimidate you, as it is just a thick, creamy soup.

MAKES 6 TO 8 SERVINGS

2 tablespoons margarine or butter
1 bunch green onions (scallions), chopped
½ teaspoon minced garlic
⅓ cup all-purpose flour
4 cups skim milk
2 tablespoons tomato paste
½ pound fresh salmon fillet, cooked, skin removed, and flaked
1 teaspoon dried dill weed leaves
Salt and white pepper to taste
2 tablespoons dry sherry, optional

In large pot, melt margarine and stir in green onions and garlic, cooking until tender. Blend in flour, stirring for one minute. Gradually, stirring constantly, add the milk and bring to a boil, about 10 minutes stirring until mixture starts to thicken. Whisk in tomato paste, cooking for a few minutes. Add flaked salmon, dill weed, and salt and pepper to taste. Stir in sherry and serve.

Nutrition information per serving

Calories 134, Protein (g) 11, Carbohydrate (g) 13, Fat (g) 4, Calories from Fat (%) 27, Saturated Fat (g) 1, Dietary Fiber (g) 1, Cholesterol (mg) 17, Sodium (mg) 120, Diabetic Exchanges 1 lean meat, 0.5 starch, 0.5 skim milk

Broccoli Soup

Broccoli and cheese join together for this wonderful creamy soup that will attract all ages. Two (10-ounce) packages of frozen chopped broccoli may be used instead of fresh.

MAKES 6 TO 8 SERVINGS

4 cups fresh broccoli florets
¼ cup water
1 onion, chopped
⅔ cup all-purpose flour
1½ cups skim milk
2 (14½-ounce) cans vegetable broth or fat-free
  chicken broth
1 cup shredded reduced-fat Monterey Jack cheese
Salt and pepper to taste
⅛ teaspoon dried thyme leaves

Cook the broccoli in a microwave dish in the water, covered, for 8 to 10 minutes, or until tender. Drain and set aside.

In a large non-stick pot, sauté the onion over medium heat until softened, about 3 to 5 minutes. In a small bowl, mix together the flour and milk. Stir the flour and milk mixture into the onion. Gradually add the vegetable broth and the broccoli. Stir to combine. Cook over medium heat until the mixture comes to a boil, stirring constantly, for about 5 minutes, or until thickened.

Transfer the soup to a food processor or blender, purée the soup, and return to the pot over low heat. Add the cheese, salt, pepper, and thyme, cooking until heated through and the cheese is melted. Serve immediately.

Nutritional information per serving
Calories 121, Protein (g) 9, Carbohydrate (g) 15, Fat (g) 3, Calories from Fat (%) 24, Saturated Fat (g) 2, Dietary Fiber (g) 2, Cholesterol (mg) 9, Sodium (mg) 576, Diabetic Exchanges: 0.5 lean meat, 0.5 starch, 1.5 vegetable

Three Bean Soup

Create your own high fiber bean soup with your favorite beans instead of buying packaged soup mixes at the store. You can add ham or sausage for extra flavor when sautéing.

MAKES 10 SERVINGS

1 cup dried red kidney beans
1 cup dried Great Northern beans
1 cup dried black beans
1 cup chopped onion
1 green bell pepper, seeded and chopped
1 tablespoon minced garlic
1½ cups diced peeled carrots
8 cups water
2 (10-ounce) cans diced tomatoes and green chilies
1 (15-ounce) can tomato sauce
1½ teaspoons dried oregano leaves
1 teaspoon dried thyme leaves
2 bay leaves
Salt and pepper to taste

Rinse the red kidney, Great Northern, and black beans, picking out any bad beans. Place in a large pot with water to cover; soak overnight. Drain and rinse the beans.

In a large non-stick pot, sauté the onion, green pepper, garlic, and carrots over medium-high heat for 3 to 5 minutes, or until tender. Add the beans, water, tomatoes and green chilies, tomato sauce, oregano, thyme, and bay leaves; bring to a boil. Cover, reduce the heat, and continue cooking for 2 hours, or until the beans are tender. Remove and discard the bay leaf. Season with the salt and pepper. Serve.

Nutritional information per serving

Calories 232, Protein (g) 14, Carbohydrate (g) 44, Fat (g) 1, Calories from Fat (%) 3, Saturated Fat (g) 0, Dietary Fiber (g) 13, Cholesterol (mg) 0, Sodium (mg) 480, Diabetic Exchanges: 1 very lean meat, 2.5 starch, 2 vegetable

Black Bean Soup

Try serving this black bean soup Cuban style: thick soup over rice with chopped onion on top.

MAKES 6 TO 8 SERVINGS

1 (1-pound) package dried black beans
1½ cups chopped onion
1 teaspoon minced garlic
½ cup chopped green bell pepper
½ cup chopped celery
4 ounces lean ham, chopped
8 cups water
1 teaspoon Worcestershire sauce
1 teaspoon sugar
1 teaspoon ground cumin
4 bay leaves
Salt and pepper to taste

Rinse and sort the beans; then soak the beans overnight in water.

Drain and rinse the beans. In a large non-stick pot, sauté the onion, garlic, green pepper, celery, and ham over medium-low heat until tender, about 5 minutes. Add the beans, water, Worcestershire sauce, sugar, cumin, and bay leaves. Cook over low heat for 2 hours, or until the beans are tender, adding water if needed. Season with salt and pepper. Discard the bay leaves before serving.

Nutritional information per serving

Calories 244, Protein (g) 17, Carbohydrate (g) 40, Fat (g) 2, Calories from Fat (%) 8, Saturated Fat (g) 1, Dietary Fiber (g) 10, Cholesterol (mg) 13, Sodium (mg) 27, Diabetic Exchanges: 1.5 very lean, 2.5 starch, 1 vegetable

Black Bean Soup

Chicken Tortilla Soup ❄

This simple Southwestern one-pot meal will quickly become a family favorite. We make extra tortilla strips to serve with salsa for a terrific snack.

MAKES 4 TO 6 SERVINGS

1 cup chopped red onion

½ cup chopped red or green bell pepper

1 teaspoon minced garlic

1 (4-ounce) can chopped green chilies, drained

8 cups fat-free canned chicken broth

2 cups chopped cooked skinless chicken breast

1 cup frozen corn, thawed

¼ cup chopped fresh cilantro, optional

2 tablespoons lime juice

1 teaspoon ground cumin

1 teaspoon chili powder

4 (6- to 8-inch) flour tortillas, cut into ¼-inch strips

1 cup shredded reduced-fat Monterey Jack cheese

In a large, heavy non-stick pot, sauté the onion, bell pepper, and garlic over medium heat until tender, about 7 minutes. Add the chilies, chicken broth, chicken, corn, cilantro, lime juice, cumin, and chili powder. Simmer, uncovered, for 10 minutes.

While the soup is cooking, preheat the oven to 350°F.

Place the tortilla strips on a baking sheet. Bake for 10 to 15 minutes, or until crisp. Spoon the soup into bowls; top with the tortilla strips and cheese.

Nutritional information per serving

Calories 254, Protein (g) 27, Carbohydrate (g) 25, Fat (g) 5, Calories from Fat (%) 19, Saturated Fat (g) 3, Dietary Fiber (g) 3, Cholesterol (mg) 50, Sodium (mg) 1,230, Diabetic Exchanges: 3 very lean meat, 1.5 starch, 1 vegetable

Chicken Tortilla Soup

Chicken, Barley, and Bowtie Soup

My kids love chicken soup, and the barley and pasta turn this family favorite into a heartier version.

MAKES 8 TO 10 SERVINGS

1½ pounds skinless, boneless chicken breasts, cut
  into 1-inch pieces
1 cup chopped celery
1 cup chopped onion
2 cups thinly sliced peeled carrots
1 bay leaf
8 cups water
4 cups fat-free canned chicken or vegetable broth
½ cup pearl barley
Salt and pepper to taste
½ teaspoon dried basil leaves
1 (8-ounce) package bowtie pasta

Place the chicken, celery, onion, carrots, and bay leaf in a large pot filled with the water and broth. Bring to a boil, and add the barley. Reduce the heat, cover, and cook until the chicken and barley are done, about 30 minutes. Season with the salt and pepper, and add the basil. Meanwhile, cook the pasta according to the package directions, omitting oil and salt. Drain. Add the pasta to the chicken soup, and remove the bay leaf.

Nutritional information per serving
Calories 219, Protein (g) 21, Carbohydrate (g) 30, Fat (g) 1, Calories from Fat (%) 6, Saturated Fat (g) 0, Dietary Fiber (g) 3, Cholesterol (mg) 39, Sodium (mg) 315, Diabetic Exchanges: 2 very lean meat, 1.5 starch, 1 vegetable

Corn Soup

It's hard to believe this easy and luscious soup is not full of heavy cream.

MAKES 8 SERVINGS

1 onion, chopped
1 green bell pepper, seeded and chopped
½ teaspoon minced garlic
1 (16-ounce) bag frozen sweet corn
1 (8½-ounce) can cream-style corn
1 (10-ounce) can diced tomatoes and green chilies
1 (14½-ounce) can fat-free chicken (or vegetable) broth
1 tablespoon Worcestershire sauce
Salt and pepper to taste
2 cups skim milk
⅓ cup all-purpose flour
Chopped green onions (scallions), optional

In a non-stick pot, sauté the onion, green pepper, and garlic over medium-high heat until tender, about 5 minutes. Add the frozen corn, cream-style corn, diced tomatoes and green chilies, chicken broth, Worcestershire sauce, salt, and pepper. In a separate bowl, blend together the milk and flour. Gradually stir into the corn mixture. Bring to a boil, lower heat, and cook until the soup thickens, about 15 minutes. Garnish with green onions.

Nutritional information per serving
Calories 134, Protein (g) 6, Carbohydrate (g) 29, Fat (g) 1, Calories from Fat (%) 5, Saturated Fat (g) 0, Dietary Fiber (g) 3, Cholesterol (mg) 1, Sodium (mg) 424, Diabetic Exchanges: 1.5 starch, 1 vegetable

Spicy Corn and Squash Chowder

When the garden was abundant with squash, I mixed squash with some of my other favorite ingredients, and the outcome was this very tasty chowder. This recipe will appeal to you even if you're not a squash fan.

MAKES 4 SERVINGS

1 pound yellow squash, thinly sliced

Salt and pepper to taste

1 cup water

1 onion, finely chopped

½ cup chopped green bell pepper

½ teaspoon minced garlic

1 large tomato, chopped

1 (15-ounce) can cream-style corn

1 (4-ounce) can diced green chilies, drained

1 (12-ounce) can evaporated skimmed milk

2 slices reduced-fat American cheese, cut into 1-inch pieces

In a medium pot, cook the squash with the salt and pepper in the water, covered, over medium-high heat until the squash is tender, 5 to 7 minutes. Drain and set aside.

In a non-stick pot, sauté the onion and green pepper over medium heat until tender, about 5 minutes. Add the garlic and tomato, and sauté for 2 minutes. Stir in the corn, green chilies, squash (breaking up with a fork), and evaporated milk. Bring to a boil, reduce the heat, and add the cheese; stir until the cheese is melted, and serve.

Nutritional information per serving

Calories 236, Protein (g) 14, Carbohydrate (g) 43, Fat (g) 2, Calories from Fat (%) 8, Saturated Fat (g) 1, Dietary Fiber (g) 6, Cholesterol (mg) 11, Sodium (mg) 660, Diabetic Exchanges: 1 starch, 1 skim milk, 3 vegetable

Shrimp, White Bean, and Pasta Soup ❄

SOUPS & STEWS

Canadian bacon gives this delicious soup a burst of flavor that enhances the shrimp, beans, and pasta. This soup freezes well. If it is too thick when reheating, add more water or chicken broth.

MAKES 8 SERVINGS

¼ cup chopped Canadian bacon
1 onion, chopped
1 green bell pepper, seeded and chopped
1 teaspoon minced garlic
1½ pounds medium shrimp, peeled
8½ cups water
1 (8-ounce) can tomato sauce
2 (15½-ounce) cans Great Northern beans, drained and rinsed
1½ cups rotini pasta
Salt and pepper to taste
1 bunch green onions (scallions), chopped

In a large non-stick pot, cook the bacon over medium heat until lightly browned, about 3 minutes. Add the onion, green pepper, and garlic, and sauté until the vegetables are tender, about 5 minutes. Add the shrimp, water, tomato sauce, and beans. Bring to a boil, and add the pasta, cooking until the shrimp and pasta are done.

Add the salt, pepper, and green onions; heat for 1 minute, and serve.

Nutritional information per serving

Calories 231, Protein (g) 20, Carbohydrate (g) 4, Fat (g) 1, Calories from Fat (%) 5, Saturated Fat (g) 0, Dietary Fiber (g) 5, Cholesterol (mg) 103, Sodium (mg) 437, Diabetic Exchanges: 2 very lean meat, 2 starch, 1 vegetable

Easy Shrimp and Corn Soup ❄

This great-tasting soup, so easy to prepare, was noted by Cooking Light *magazine as one of the best recipes they tested. They couldn't believe it wasn't full of calories and fat!*

MAKES 8 SERVINGS

1 onion, chopped

1 teaspoon minced garlic

1 green bell pepper, seeded and chopped

1 (8-ounce) package fat-free cream cheese, softened

2 (15-ounce) cans cream-style corn

2 (10-ounce) cans cream of shrimp soup or corn chowder
  soup or combination

2 cups skim milk

1 (10-ounce) can diced tomatoes and green chilies

1 pound medium shrimp, peeled

Chopped green onions (scallions), for garnish

In a large, heavy non-stick pot, sauté the onion, garlic, and green pepper until tender, about 5 minutes. Stir in the cream cheese. Add the corn, soup, milk, tomatoes and green chilies, and shrimp. Bring to a boil, reduce heat, and cook until the shrimp are done, about 10 minutes.

Serve with green onions. When reheating the soup, if it's too thick, add more milk.

Nutritional information per serving
Calories 230, Protein (g) 18, Carbohydrate (g) 33, Fat (g) 4, Calories from Fat (%) 15, Saturated Fat (g) 2, Dietary Fiber (g) 2, Cholesterol (mg) 81, Sodium (mg) 1,289, Diabetic Exchanges: 1 lean meat, 1.5 starch, 0.5 skim milk, 1 vegetable

Shrimp, Corn, and Sweet Potato Soup ❄

These wonderful ingredients blend to make a savory, satisfying soup. This soup is perfect for cool nights.

MAKES 12 SERVINGS

1 red onion, chopped

½ cup chopped celery

½ teaspoon minced garlic

1 green bell pepper, seeded and chopped

2 cups diced peeled sweet potato (yam)

1 (16-ounce) bag frozen corn

1 (15-ounce) can cream-style corn

1 (10-ounce) can chopped tomatoes and green chilies

1 (6-ounce) can tomato paste

4 cups fat-free canned chicken broth

1½ pounds peeled medium shrimp

Salt and pepper to taste

Chopped green onions (scallions), optional

In a large non-stick pot, sauté the onion, celery, garlic, and green pepper until tender. Add the sweet potato, corn, tomatoes and green chilies, tomato paste, and broth; bring the mixture to a boil.

Add the shrimp, bring to a boil, reduce heat and continue cooking until the shrimp are done, about 10 minutes. Season with salt and pepper; garnish with the green onions, if desired, and serve.

Nutritional information per serving

Calories 153, Protein (g) 13, Carbohydrate (g) 26, Fat (g) 1, Calories from Fat (%) 6, Saturated Fat (g) 0, Dietary Fiber (g) 4, Cholesterol (mg) 81, Sodium (mg) 513, Diabetic Exchanges: 1 very lean meat, 1.5 starch, 1 vegetable

Shrimp, Corn, and Sweet Potato Soup

Double Potato Bisque

Sweet potatoes and potatoes make a mild, smooth, intensely flavored soup. The sweet potato adds nutrition and color.

MAKES 4 TO 6 SERVINGS

1 large sweet potato (yam), peeled and cut into
  ½-inch cubes
1 large baking potato, peeled and cut into ½-inch cubes
1 onion, chopped
½ teaspoon minced garlic
1 (14½-ounce) can vegetable broth
1 teaspoon dried thyme leaves
⅛ teaspoon cayenne pepper
1 (12-ounce) can evaporated skimmed milk
Salt and pepper to taste
Green onion stems (scallions), optional

In a large pot, combine the sweet potato, potato, onion, garlic, and vegetable broth; bring to a boil. Reduce the heat and simmer, covered, for 15 minutes, or until the potatoes are tender.

Pour the mixture into a food processor and blend until smooth; return to the pot. Add the thyme, cayenne, and evaporated milk, and cook over a low heat just until heated through.

Season with the salt and pepper. Garnish with the green onion. Serve.

Nutritional information per serving

Calories 115, Protein (g) 7, Carbohydrate (g) 23, Fat (g) 0, Calories from Fat (%) 0, Saturated Fat (g) 0, Dietary Fiber (g) 2, Cholesterol (mg) 2, Sodium (mg) 386, Diabetic Exchanges: 1 starch, 0.5 skim milk

QUICK TIP:

Purchase already-peeled shrimp in your seafood market or grocery to avoid the hassle of peeling them yourself.

Creamy Potato Soup

Potato soup is a popular request. You would think this rich soup is a no-no where healthy eating is concerned, but it's completely painless to eat. For the deluxe version, top with shredded reduced-fat Cheddar cheese and a dollop of fat-free sour cream.

MAKES 8 SERVINGS

1 tablespoon margarine

1 cup chopped onion

½ teaspoon minced garlic

3 tablespoons all-purpose flour

2 (16-ounce) cans fat-free chicken broth

4 cups peeled diced potatoes (about 3 large)

Salt and pepper to taste

1 cup liquid nondairy creamer

Chopped parsley or sliced green onions (scallions),
  for garnish

Melt the margarine in a large pot over medium heat, and sauté the onion and garlic in the margarine until tender, about 5 minutes. Lower the heat and add the flour, stirring until smooth.

Gradually add the broth, stirring constantly. Add the potato. Bring to a boil; cover, reduce the heat, and simmer for 20 minutes, stirring occasionally, or until the potato chunks are tender.

Transfer the mixture to a blender or food processor, and blend until smooth, in batches if necessary. Return to the pot. Add salt and pepper, stir in the nondairy creamer, and heat thoroughly. Garnish with the parsley or green onions, and serve.

Nutritional information per serving

Calories 136, Protein (g) 4, Carbohydrate (g) 22, Fat (g) 4, Calories from Fat (%) 26, Saturated Fat (g) 1, Dietary Fiber (g) 2, Cholesterol (mg) 0, Sodium (mg) 349, Diabetic Exchanges: 1.5 starch, 0.5 fat

Cream of Spinach and Brie Soup

Though a tad high in fat, this is a great way to enjoy spinach. You can accompany this rich, velvety soup with lower-fat side dishes or even reduce the amount of Brie.

MAKES 6 SERVINGS

½ cup chopped onion
⅓ cup all-purpose flour
2 cups skim milk
2 cups fat-free canned chicken broth
8 ounces Brie cheese, rind removed, cubed
2 cups fresh baby spinach, washed, stemmed, and chopped
Salt and pepper to taste

In a non-stick pot, sauté the onion until soft. Stir in the flour for 30 seconds. Gradually stir in the milk and chicken broth. Bring to a boil, stirring constantly until thickened, about 10 minutes.

Lower the heat and add the Brie, stirring until melted. Add the spinach, salt, and pepper, stirring until the spinach is wilted. Serve.

Nutritional information per serving
Calories 192, Protein (g) 13, Carbohydrate (g) 11, Fat (g) 11, Calories from Fat (%) 50, Saturated Fat (g) 7, Dietary Fiber (g) 1, Cholesterol (mg) 39, Sodium (mg) 495, Diabetic Exchanges: 1.5 high-fat meat, 0.5 starch

Pumpkin Soup

This quick soup is especially perfect in the fall.

MAKES 6 SERVINGS

½ cup finely chopped onion
½ teaspoon minced garlic
1 (15-ounce) can solid-pack pumpkin
2 (14½-ounce) cans fat-free chicken broth
½ cup skim milk
½ teaspoon hot sauce
Salt and pepper to taste
Fat-free sour cream, for garnish

In a non-stick pot, sauté the onion and garlic over medium heat until tender, about 5 minutes. Add the pumpkin, and gradually add the chicken broth and milk. Add the hot sauce, and season with the salt and pepper. Cook until heated through, about 5 minutes. Serve with a dollop of sour cream.

Nutritional information per serving
Calories 45, Protein (g) 4, Carbohydrate (g) 8, Fat (g) 0, Calories from Fat (%) 0, Saturated Fat (g) 0, Dietary Fiber (g) 3, Cholesterol (mg) 0, Sodium (mg) 391, Diabetic Exchanges: 0.5 starch

Southwestern Vegetable Soup

You'll really enjoy this veggie soup with a Southwestern flair.

MAKES 6 SERVINGS

1 cup chopped onion

1 teaspoon minced garlic

2 cups peeled and sliced carrots

1 pound red potatoes, peeled and cut into small chunks

2 (14½-ounce) cans vegetable broth

1 (15-ounce) can tomato sauce

1½ cups mild salsa

2 teaspoons dried oregano leaves

2 teaspoons ground cumin

1 (10-ounce) package frozen corn

½ cup sliced green onions (scallions)

½ cup shredded reduced-fat Monterey Jack cheese

In a large non-stick pot, sauté the onion and garlic over medium heat until tender, 3 to 5 minutes. Add the carrot, potato, vegetable broth, tomato sauce, salsa, oregano, cumin, and corn. Bring the mixture to a boil, lower the heat, and simmer for 20 minutes, or until the carrot and potato chunks are tender. When serving, sprinkle each bowl with the green onion and cheese.

Nutritional information per serving

Calories 221, Protein (g) 9, Carbohydrate (g) 40, Fat (g) 3, Calories from Fat (%) 12, Saturated Fat (g) 1, Dietary Fiber (g) 5, Cholesterol (mg) 5, Sodium (mg) 1,363, Diabetic Exchanges: 1.5 starch, 3 vegetable

Split Pea Soup

Split pea fans—this easy, high-fiber recipe is meant for you.

MAKES 6 SERVINGS

5 slices center-cut bacon, cut into pieces

1 onion, chopped

½ cup chopped celery

2 cups dried split peas

4 cups water

4 cups fat-free canned chicken broth

1 bay leaf

2 cups sliced carrots

1 potato, peeled and diced

Salt and pepper to taste

½ teaspoon dried thyme leaves

In a large pot, sauté the bacon, onion, and celery until tender. Add the peas, water, chicken broth, bay leaf, carrot, potato, salt, pepper, and thyme. Bring the soup to a boil, lower the heat, and cook, covered, for 1½ to 2 hours, or until the peas are very soft. Stir occasionally.

If the soup gets too thick, thin with additional broth or water. Remove the bay leaf before serving.

Nutritional information per serving

Calories 355, Protein (g) 21, Carbohydrate (g) 52, Fat (g) 9, Calories from Fat (%) 21, Saturated Fat (g) 3, Dietary Fiber (g) 19, Cholesterol (mg) 9, Sodium (mg) 539, Diabetic Exchanges: 2 very lean meat, 3 starch, 1 vegetable, 1 fat

Italian Soup

Rich in flavor and packed full of nutritious ingredients, you will make this soup often as winter weather arrives.

MAKES 10 TO 12 SERVINGS

1 (5-ounce) package Canadian bacon,
  chopped into pieces
½ teaspoon minced garlic
1 large onion, sliced
⅔ cup peeled, chopped carrots
2 zucchini, sliced
1 (28-ounce) can chopped tomatoes with juice
½ cup red wine
Salt and pepper to taste
½ teaspoon dried oregano leaves
4 (10¾-ounce) cans beef consommé
1½ cups water
1 (15-ounce) can red kidney beans, drained and rinsed
2 cups chopped cabbage
1 cup chopped fresh baby spinach
1 cup shell macaroni
1 teaspoon dried basil leaves

In a large non-stick pot, cook the Canadian bacon over medium heat until brown, about 3 minutes. Stir in the garlic, onion, carrot, zucchini, tomatoes, red wine, salt, pepper, oregano, beef consommé, water, kidney beans, cabbage, and spinach. Bring to a boil, lower the heat, and cook for 10 minutes.

Add the macaroni and basil, and continue cooking for 20 minutes, or until the macaroni is done. Serve.

Nutritional information per serving

Calories 144, Protein (g) 12, Carbohydrate (g) 21, Fat (g) 1, Calories from Fat (%) 7, Saturated Fat (g) 0, Dietary Fiber (g) 5, Cholesterol (mg) 6, Sodium (mg) 902, Diabetic Exchanges: 1 very lean meat, 1 starch, 1.5 vegetable

QUICK TIP:

Unlike whole peas, split peas don't need soaking before being cooked. Smoked sausage, ham, or bacon are ideal flavor partners for split peas.

Beefy Vegetable and Barley Soup ❄

This veggie-packed soup is perfect on a cold night. Instead of frozen veggies, clean out the refrigerator and toss in whatever veggies you have.

MAKES 6 TO 8 SERVINGS

2 pounds lean round steak, 2 inches thick
1 onion, chopped
3 stalks celery, chopped
1 bay leaf
2 tablespoons chopped parsley
2 cups water, divided
1 (46-ounce) container low-sodium cocktail vegetable juice or salsa
1 (14-ounce) can beef broth
1 red potato, peeled and cut into small cubes
½ cup barley
1 large carrot, peeled and sliced
1 (16-ounce) package frozen mixed vegetables

Cut the meat into 1-inch cubes. In a large, heavy non-stick pot, cook the meat over medium-high heat until browned, stirring often. Add the onion, celery, bay leaf, parsley, and water. Bring to a boil, lower heat, and simmer, covered, for 45 minutes.

Add the vegetable juice, broth, potato, and barley. Return to a boil, lower the heat, and cover, cooking for 30 minutes.

Add the carrot and mixed vegetables, cover, and continue to cook over low heat for 30 minutes, or until the meat is tender and the barley is done. Remove the bay leaf before serving.

Nutritional information per serving
Calories 278, Protein (g) 31, Carbohydrate (g) 28, Fat (g) 5, Calories from Fat (%) 15, Saturated Fat (g) 2, Dietary Fiber (g) 5, Chol um (mg) 533, Diabetic Exchanges: 3 lean meat, 1 starch, 3 vegetable

Beefy Vegetable and Barley Soup

Wild Rice Soup ❄

This hearty, great-tasting soup can be the answer to using leftover chicken or holiday turkey.

MAKES 4 TO 6 SERVINGS

½ cup chopped onion
½ cup peeled and finely chopped carrots
½ cup all-purpose flour
3 cups fat-free canned chicken broth
1 (6-ounce) package long-grain and wild rice mix
1 cup chopped cooked chicken or turkey
3 tablespoons sherry

In a large non-stick pot, sauté the onion and carrot over medium heat until tender, about 5 minutes. Stir in the flour. Gradually add the broth, and bring to a boil, stirring constantly.

Meanwhile, prepare the rice according to the package directions, omitting any oil and salt. Add the cooked rice and cooked chicken to the broth mixture, and simmer 5 minutes. Add the sherry. If the soup gets too thick, add more chicken broth or water. Boil 1 minute, and serve.

Nutritional information per serving

Calories 217, Protein (g) 13, Carbohydrate (g) 33, Fat (g) 3, Calories from Fat (%) 13, Saturated Fat (g) 1, Dietary Fiber (g) 1, Cholesterol (mg) 19, Sodium (mg) 754, Diabetic Exchanges: 1 very lean meat, 2 starch

Artichoke Soup 🥕 ❄

Throw all the ingredients in the blender, heat, and serve with a smile. Everyone will think you spent hours in the kitchen to prepare this simple and creamy soup.

MAKES 6 TO 8 SERVINGS

3 (14-ounce) cans artichoke hearts, drained
3 (10¾-ounce) cans 98% fat-free cream of mushroom soup
1 cup skim milk
2 cups fat-free canned chicken broth
½ cup dry white wine
Dash cayenne pepper

Place the artichokes in a food processor, and purée. Add the mushroom soup, milk, broth, white wine, and cayenne pepper. Blend until well combined. Transfer to a pot, and warm over low heat to serve.

Nutritional information per serving

Calories 122, Protein (g) 5, Carbohydrate (g) 17, Fat (g) 3, Calories from Fat (%) 21, Saturated Fat (g) 1, Dietary Fiber (g) 1, Cholesterol (mg) 5, Sodium (mg) 1,201, Diabetic Exchanges: 0.5 starch, 1.5 vegetable, 0.5 fat

Onion Soup

Onion Soup

Onion soup is one of my personal favorites, and I prefer this version to the high-fat recipes I've tried. The soup is full-flavored without being heavy.

MAKES 8 SERVINGS

1 tablespoon margarine

3 large onions (about 2 pounds), halved and thinly sliced

1 teaspoon sugar

3 tablespoons all-purpose flour

2 cups water

2 (14½-ounce) cans beef broth

1 (10½-ounce) can beef consommé

1 teaspoon Worcestershire sauce

2 tablespoons Cognac, optional

8 (½-inch-thick) slices French bread, toasted

1 cup shredded part-skim mozzarella cheese

In a large non-stick pot, melt the margarine over medium heat. Add the onion, and cook, stirring frequently, for 20 minutes, or until golden. Add the sugar, and
stir well. Add the flour, stirring constantly for 1 minute. Gradually add the water, broth, and consommé. Bring to a boil; cover, reduce the heat, and simmer for 30 minutes.

Stir in the Worcestershire sauce and Cognac, if desired. Preheat the broiler. Place eight ovenproof soup bowls on a baking sheet, and fill with the soup. Top each with a slice of French bread. Sprinkle the cheese evenly over the bread. Broil several minutes, or until the cheese melts.

Nutritional information per serving

Calories 181, Protein (g) 10, Carbohydrate (g) 26, Fat (g) 4, Calories from Fat (%) 22, Saturated Fat (g) 2, Dietary Fiber (g) 3, Cholesterol (mg) 8, Sodium (mg) 735, Diabetic Exchanges: 0.5 lean meat, 1 starch, 2 vegetable

Quick Vegetarian Chili 🥕

If you can work a can opener and accept compliments graciously, you can prepare this impressive, hearty chili. Serve with shredded Monterey Jack cheese, if desired.

MAKES 8 SERVINGS

2 cups salsa
1 (28-ounce) can diced tomatoes, with juice
1 (15-ounce) can pinto beans, drained and rinsed
1 (15-ounce) can red kidney beans, drained and rinsed
1 (19-ounce) can garbanzo beans, drained and rinsed
1 green bell pepper, seeded and chopped
½ teaspoon minced garlic
1 onion, chopped
2 medium zucchini, halved lengthwise and thinly sliced
2 tablespoons chili powder
½ teaspoon ground cumin
1 teaspoon dried oregano leaves
½ teaspoon sugar

Combine all ingredients in a large pot. Heat to boiling. Reduce the heat and simmer, covered, for 40 minutes, stirring occasionally.

Nutritional information per serving
Calories 207, Protein (g) 9, Carbohydrate (g) 36, Fat (g) 2, Calories from Fat (%) 7, Saturated Fat (g) 0, Dietary Fiber (g) 11, Cholesterol (mg) 0, Sodium (mg) 924, Diabetic Exchanges: 1 very lean meat, 1.5 starch, 3 vegetable

Speedy Chili ❄

The chipotle salsa gives this excellent, easy-to-make chili a rich, smoky flavor that's hard to beat. If desired, serve with shredded reduced fat cheddar cheese and chopped red onions.

MAKES 6 TO 8 SERVINGS

2 pounds ground sirloin
1 teaspoon minced garlic
1 tablespoon chili powder
1 teaspoon ground cumin
1 (16-ounce) jar chipotle chunky salsa
1 (16-ounce) package frozen whole-kernel corn
2 (14½-ounce) cans seasoned beef broth with onion
1 (15-ounce) can red kidney beans, rinsed and drained, optional

In a large pot, brown the meat and garlic over medium high heat until done. Drain any excess liquid. Add the chili powder, cumin, salsa, corn, beef broth, and beans. Bring the mixture to a boil, reduce the heat, and cook for 15 minutes.

Nutritional information per serving
Calories 212, Protein (g) 26, Carbohydrate (g) 14, Fat (g) 6, Calories from Fat (%) 24, Saturated Fat (g) 2, Dietary Fiber (g) 2, Cholesterol (mg) 60, Sodium (mg) 794, Diabetic Exchanges: 3 lean meat, 1 starch

QUICK TIP:

Chipotle peppers are actually dried, smoked jalapeño chilies with a mild, smoky flavor. With chipotle salsa, you can enjoy the flavor without working with the peppers.

White Chicken Chili

To add diversity to your chili, try this amazing dish using chicken, beans, and tomatoes with a hint of cumin and oregano.

MAKES 8 SERVINGS

1 tablespoon olive oil

2 pounds skinless, boneless chicken breasts, diced

1 onion, chopped

1 teaspoon minced garlic

2 (14½-ounce) cans chopped tomatoes, with juice

2 (14½-ounce) cans fat-free chicken broth

2 (4-ounce) cans chopped green chilies

1 teaspoon dried oregano leaves

½ teaspoon ground cumin

2 (11-ounce) cans cannellini beans, drained

3 tablespoons fresh lime juice

¼ teaspoon pepper

½ cup shredded reduced-fat Monterey Jack cheese

In a large non-stick pot, add olive oil, and cook the chicken over medium high heat until done, stirring. Remove the chicken from the pan; set aside.

Add the onion and garlic to the pan, and sauté until tender. Stir in the tomatoes, chicken broth, green chilies, oregano, and cumin, and add the chicken. Bring to a boil, reduce the heat, and simmer for 20 minutes.

Add the beans, and cook until heated, about 5 minutes. Add the lime juice and pepper. Spoon into bowls, and serve topped with the cheese.

Nutritional information per serving

Calories 264, Protein (g) 34, Carbohydrate (g) 20, Fat (g) 5, Calories from Fat (%) 16, Saturated Fat (g) 1, Dietary Fiber (g) 6, Cholesterol (mg) 70, Sodium (mg) 797, Diabetic Exchanges: 4 very lean meat, 0.5 starch, 2 vegetable

White Chicken Chili

Southwestern Shrimp and Black Bean Chili

SOUPS & STEWS

A wonderful blend of flavors produces this very easy recipe that includes all my favorites: black beans, corn, and shrimp. This chili is not only very flavorful but also high in fiber and low in fat.

MAKES 4 TO 6 SERVINGS

1 green bell pepper, seeded and chopped

1 red bell pepper, seeded and chopped

1 large onion, chopped

1 cup peeled, shredded carrots

1 tablespoon finely chopped pickled jalapeño pepper

½ teaspoon minced garlic

1 tablespoon chili powder

1½ teaspoons dried cumin

1 (14½-ounce) can chopped tomatoes, with juice

1 (16-ounce) can black beans, drained and rinsed

½ cup water

1 pound medium shrimp, peeled

1 (10-ounce) package frozen corn

In a large non-stick pot, sauté the green and red peppers, onion, carrot, jalapeño pepper, and garlic until tender, about 6 to 8 minutes. Stir in the chili powder, cumin, tomatoes, black beans, water, and shrimp; bring to a boil. Reduce the heat, and cook for 5 to 10 minutes, or until the shrimp are pink. Add the corn, and continue cooking 5 minutes longer.

Nutritional information per serving

Calories 205, Protein (g) 17, Carbohydrate (g) 32, Fat (g) 2, Calories from Fat (%) 8, Saturated Fat (g) 0, Dietary Fiber (g) 9, Cholesterol (mg) 90, Sodium (mg) 436, Diabetic Exchanges: 2 very lean meat, 1 starch, 3 vegetable

Meatball Stew ❄

If you enjoy meatballs, this stew with a tomato gravy laced with rice and peas proves to be a hearty one-dish meal. Add more broth or water if the stew is too thick for your taste.

MAKES 6 SERVINGS

2 pounds ground sirloin

2 egg whites, lightly beaten

⅓ cup bread crumbs

1 onion, finely chopped

1 tablespoon minced garlic

Salt and pepper to taste

1 teaspoon dried basil leaves

1 teaspoon dried thyme leaves

1 green bell pepper, seeded and chopped

2 (14½-ounce) cans chopped tomatoes, with juice

1 (15-ounce) can tomato sauce

2 cups canned beef broth

⅔ cup long-grain rice

1 (10-ounce) package frozen green peas

Preheat the broiler.

In a bowl, combine the meat, egg whites, bread crumbs, onion, garlic, salt, pepper, basil, and thyme. Shape into 30 balls about 1½ inches in diameter. Place the meatballs on a baking sheet coated with nonstick cooking spray. Broil in the oven for 4 to 5 minutes; then turn the meatballs and continue broiling for 4 minutes longer, or until done. Remove from the broiler, and set aside.

In a large non-stick pot, sauté the green pepper over medium heat until tender, about 5 minutes. Add the tomatoes, tomato sauce, and beef broth. Bring to a boil, and add the meatballs. Mix in the rice; cover, reduce the heat, and continue cooking for 20 minutes, or until the rice is done. Stir in the peas, cover, and continue cooking for 10 minutes, or until the peas are tender. Serve.

Nutritional information per serving
Calories 391, Protein (g) 40, Carbohydrate (g) 42, Fat (g) 8, Calories from Fat (%) 18, Saturated Fat (g) 3, Dietary Fiber (g) 7, Cholesterol (mg) 80, Sodium (mg) 1,115, Diabetic Exchanges: 4 lean meat, 2 starch, 3 vegetable

Southwestern Pork Stew

Pork, yams, and corn make this an eye-catching, easy one-dish meal that will be repeated often at family dinners.

MAKES 8 SERVINGS

1¾ pounds pork tenderloin, trimmed of fat
  and cut into 1-inch cubes
¼ cup all-purpose flour
1 cup chopped red onion
2 cups fat-free canned chicken broth
1 (10-ounce) can chopped tomatoes and green chilies
1¼ pounds sweet potatoes (yams), peeled and cut
  into 1-inch cubes
1 teaspoon chili powder
½ teaspoon ground cumin
1 (4-ounce) can diced green chilies, drained
1 (16-ounce) package frozen corn
Salt and pepper to taste

Toss the pork with the flour to coat. In a large non-stick pot, brown the pork over medium heat, about 5 to 7 minutes. Add the onion, and cook until tender. Add the remaining ingredients and bring to a boil.

Lower the heat, and simmer until the potato cubes are tender and the pork is done, approximately 45 minutes. If the stew gets too thick, add more chicken broth. Add the salt and pepper to taste.

Nutritional information per serving

Calories 275, Protein (g) 25, Carbohydrate (g) 37, Fat (g) 4, Calories from Fat (%) 13, Saturated Fat (g) 1, Dietary Fiber (g) 5, Cholesterol (mg) 64, Sodium (mg) 429, Diabetic Exchanges: 3 very lean meat, 2 starch, 1 vegetable

Southwestern Pork Stew

Quick Beef Stew ❄

Everyone needs a basic recipe for this old-time classic.

MAKES 6 SERVINGS

2 pounds lean boneless top round steak, trimmed of fat
  and cut into 1-inch cubes
⅓ cup all-purpose flour
2 cups sliced carrots (1-inch slices)
1¾ pounds red potatoes, peeled and cubed
1 large onion, sliced
½ pound fresh mushrooms, quartered
½ teaspoon minced garlic
¼ cup chopped parsley
½ teaspoon dried thyme leaves
Salt and pepper to taste
1 (14½-ounce) can beef broth
1 cup light beer

Combine the meat and flour in a plastic bag; close the bag, and shake.

In a large non-stick pot, cook the meat over high heat until browned, about 8 minutes, stirring often. Add the remaining ingredients and cover. Cook about 1 hour, or until the meat is tender and the vegetables are done.

Nutritional information per serving

Calories 391, Protein (g) 42, Carbohydrate (g) 39, Fat (g) 6, Calories from Fat (%) 14, Saturated Fat (g) 2, Dietary Fiber (g) 5, Cholesterol (mg) 94, Sodium (mg) 397, Diabetic Exchanges: 4 very lean meat, 2 starch, 2 vegetable

Quick Beef Stew

Salad Niçoise

Salads

Caesar Salad

*Enjoy this guilt-free recipe for classic
Caesar Salad.*

MAKES 6 SERVINGS

1 head romaine lettuce, torn into pieces
2 tablespoons grated Parmesan cheese
1 teaspoon coarsely ground black pepper
2 tablespoons lemon juice
1 teaspoon Worcestershire sauce
2 tablespoons red wine vinegar
½ teaspoon dry mustard
½ teaspoon garlic powder
⅓ cup nonfat plain yogurt
1 cup croutons, optional

In a large bowl, combine the lettuce, cheese, and
pepper. In a separate bowl, combine the lemon
juice, Worcestershire sauce, vinegar, dry mustard, and garlic powder; blend well. Add the
yogurt, and stir well. Add the dressing to the lettuce mixture, and toss gently to coat. If you'd
like, add croutons to the lettuce mixture, and
toss gently. Serve immediately.

Nutritional information per serving
*Calories 40, Protein (g) 4, Carbohydrate (g) 5, Fat (g) 1, Calories from
Fat (%) 20, Saturated Fat (g) 0, Dietary Fiber (g) 2, Cholesterol (mg) 2,
Sodium (mg) 68, Diabetic Exchanges: 1 vegetable*

QUICK TIP:

For an easy way to incorporate soy protein into your
diet, sprinkle soy nuts on your favorite salad for
great taste and extra crunch.

Spinach Salad

*Brown sugar and balsamic vinegar join together
for a spicy, sweet and tart dressing on a salad
packed with flavors and textures.*

MAKES 6 SERVINGS

1 (12-ounce) bag fresh spinach, washed, stemmed,
   and torn into pieces
½ cup sliced green onions (scallions)
1 (8-ounce) can sliced water chestnuts, drained
½ cup shredded reduced-fat Monterey Jack cheese
3 tablespoons light brown sugar
⅓ cup fat-free canned chicken broth
3 tablespoons balsamic vinegar
2 dashes hot pepper sauce
1 (11-ounce) can mandarin orange slices, drained

Combine the spinach, green onion, water chestnuts, and cheese. Toss well and set aside.

In a small saucepan combine the brown sugar,
chicken broth, vinegar, and hot pepper sauce.
Stir well, and bring to a boil. Remove from the
heat, and stir in the mandarin orange slices.

Pour the dressing over the spinach mixture.
Toss gently. Serve immediately.

Nutritional information per serving
*Calories 102, Protein (g) 5, Carbohydrate (g) 18, Fat (g) 2, Calories
from Fat (%) 17, Saturated Fat (g) 1, Dietary Fiber (g) 3, Cholesterol
(mg) 5, Sodium (mg) 150, Diabetic Exchanges: 0.5 lean meat, 1.5
vegetable, 0.5 other carbohydrate*

SALADS

Raspberry Spinach Salad

Raspberry Spinach Salad

With its subtly sweet dressing paired with fresh fruit and nuts, this outstanding salad has a fantastic flavor. Strawberries can be substituted for raspberries.

MAKES 8 SERVINGS

3 tablespoons raspberry wine vinegar

3 tablespoons raspberry jam

¼ cup canola oil

8 cups fresh spinach, washed, stemmed, and torn into pieces

¼ cup coarsely chopped macadamia nuts

1 cup fresh raspberries

3 kiwis, peeled and sliced

Whisk the vinegar and jam in a small bowl or blend in a food processor or blender. Add the oil in a thin stream, blending well; set aside.

Carefully toss the fresh spinach, nuts, raspberries, and kiwis with the dressing. Serve immediately.

Nutritional information per serving

Calories 145, Protein (g) 2, Carbohydrate (g) 13, Fat (g) 10, Calories from Fat (%) 61, Saturated Fat (g) 1, Dietary Fiber (g) 3, Cholesterol (mg) 0, Sodium (mg) 26, Diabetic Exchanges: 0.5 fruit, 0.5 other carbohydrate, 2 fat

Mixed Greens with Citrus Vinaigrette and Sugared Pecans

Tangy citrus and toasted pecans combine with a light vinaigrette to make this a flavorful yet light salad.

SALADS

MAKES 6 SERVINGS

2 teaspoons olive oil
¼ cup chopped pecans
1 teaspoon sugar
⅛ teaspoon cayenne pepper
9 cups mixed salad greens
½ cup Citrus Vinaigrette (recipe follows)
2 cups fresh orange sections

Heat the oil in a non-stick skillet over medium heat; add the pecans. Sprinkle with the sugar and cayenne; sauté 2 minutes, or until the pecans begin to brown. Remove from heat and let cool.

In a large bowl, combine the greens and Citrus Vinaigrette (see recipe at right); toss gently. Toss with the oranges and pecans, and serve immediately.

CITRUS VINAIGRETTE

½ cup orange juice
2 tablespoons lemon juice
2 tablespoons olive oil
1 tablespoon low-sodium soy sauce
1 tablespoon Dijon mustard
1 tablespoon honey

Place the orange juice, lemon juice, olive oil, soy sauce, mustard, and honey in a blender; process until smooth.

Nutritional information per serving
Calories 125, Protein (g) 3, Carbohydrate (g) 14, Fat (g) 8, Calories from Fat (%) 51, Saturated Fat (g) 1, Dietary Fiber (g) 4, Cholesterol (mg) 0, Sodium (mg) 84, Diabetic Exchanges: 1 fruit, 1.5 fat

FOOD FACT:

Mixed greens are often referred to as "mesclun," a derivative of a Latin word that means "mixture." The key to a good mesclun is a balance of colors, flavors, and textures.

Mixed Green Salad with Cranberries and Sunflower Seeds

Savory, sweet, and crunchy—this sensational salad is chock-full of simple ingredients.

MAKES 8 SERVINGS

6 cups mixed greens
½ cup dried cranberries
¼ cup shredded carrot
½ cup sliced green onions (scallions)
¼ cup raspberry wine vinegar
2 tablespoons red wine vinegar
2 tablespoons olive oil
2 tablespoons honey
2 tablespoons sunflower seeds

Place the greens in a large bowl. Add the cranberries and carrot.

In a small bowl, whisk the green onion, raspberry wine vinegar, red wine vinegar, olive oil, and honey.

Just before serving, pour over the greens mixture, and toss. Sprinkle with the sunflower seeds, and serve.

Nutritional information per serving

Calories 96, Protein (g) 1, Carbohydrate (g) 13, Fat (g) 5, Calories from Fat (%) 43, Saturated Fat (g) 1, Dietary Fiber (g) 2, Cholesterol (mg) 0, Sodium (mg) 14, Diabetic Exchanges: 0.5 fruit, 0.5 other carbohydrate, 1 fat

Mixed Green Salad with Cranberries and Sunflower Seeds

Green Salad with Oriental Vinaigrette

This is the perfect salad to complement any Chinese- or Asian-style dish. The chow mein noodles substitute as the croutons.

MAKES 4 SERVINGS

2 tablespoons honey
1 teaspoon sugar
1 tablespoon low-sodium soy sauce
¼ cup rice wine vinegar
1 teaspoon minced garlic
2 tablespoons olive oil
4 cups mixed greens
¼ cup sliced green onions (scallions)
Chow mein noodles, optional

In the bowl of a food processor, combine the honey, sugar, soy sauce, vinegar, garlic, and oil. Pulse until mixed.

In a separate bowl, combine the mixed greens with the green onion, and toss with the dressing. Top with the chow mein noodles, if desired, and serve.

Nutritional information per serving
Calories 118, Protein (g) 1, Carbohydrate (g) 14, Fat (g) 7, Calories from Fat (%) 50, Saturated Fat (g) 1, Dietary Fiber (g) 1, Cholesterol (mg) 0, Sodium (mg) 114, Diabetic Exchanges: 1 other carbohydrate, 1.5 fat

Orange Almond Mixed Green Salad

Simple enough for the family, oranges and almonds make it fancy enough to please guests.

MAKES 4 SERVINGS

3 tablespoons canola oil
¼ cup red wine vinegar
1 tablespoon lemon juice
2 tablespoons sugar
½ teaspoon salt
½ teaspoon dry mustard
1 (11-ounce) can mandarin orange segments, drained
¼ cup slivered almonds, toasted
1 head red leaf or butter lettuce, washed and torn into pieces

Combine the oil, vinegar, lemon juice, sugar, salt, and dry mustard together in a jar with a lid. Shake, and refrigerate until ready to use.

Toss the mandarin oranges and almonds with the lettuce. Before serving, pour the dressing over the salad, tossing gently.

Nutritional information per serving
Calories 188, Protein (g) 2, Carbohydrate (g) 16, Fat (g) 14, Calories from Fat (%) 63, Saturated Fat (g) 1, Dietary Fiber (g) 2, Cholesterol (mg) 0, Sodium (mg) 297, Diabetic Exchanges: 0.5 fruit, 0.5 other carbohydrate, 3 fat

Asian-Style Coleslaw

By purchasing already chopped cabbage and shredded carrots, this coleslaw is a flash to make. The garlic chili sauce gives the slaw some kick, while the peanuts add crunch.

MAKES 8 TO 10 SERVINGS

8 cups shredded cabbage (combination green and
   red cabbage)
1 cup shredded carrots
1 cup red onion, thinly sliced in rings, halved
1 tablespoon garlic chili sauce
2 tablespoons lime juice
⅓ cup rice wine vinegar
2 tablespoons light brown sugar
3 tablespoons peanut or olive oil
⅓ cup peanuts

In a large bowl, mix the cabbage, carrots, and red onion.

In a small bowl, whisk together the garlic chili sauce, lime juice, vinegar, brown sugar, and peanut oil. Toss the dressing with the cabbage mixture. Add the peanuts, mixing well. Refrigerate until serving.

Nutritional information per serving
Calories 102, Protein (g) 2, Carbohydrate (g) 10, Fat (g) 7, Calories from Fat (%) 54, Saturated Fat (g) 1,Dietary Fiber (g) 2, Cholesterol (mg) 0, Sodium (mg) 0, Diabetic Exchanges: 2 vegetable, 1.5 fat

Oriental Cabbage Salad

Picking up a bag of shredded red cabbage makes this a simple salad to prepare, with plenty of flavor and texture.

MAKES 4 TO 6 SERVINGS

3 cups shredded red cabbage
1 bunch green onions (scallions), chopped
¼ cup slivered almonds, toasted
1 (3-ounce) package Oriental ramen noodle soup
   (with seasoning packet)
1 tablespoon canola oil
¼ cup red wine vinegar
1 tablespoon sugar
Salt and pepper to taste

Combine the cabbage, green onions, and almonds in a large bowl. Coarsely break up the dry soup noodles, and stir into the cabbage mixture.

In a small bowl, mix the oil, seasoning packet, vinegar, sugar, salt, and pepper. Pour over the salad, and toss. Cover with plastic wrap, and refrigerate for 2 hours; serve chilled.

Nutritional information per serving
Calories 136, Protein (g) 3, Carbohydrate (g) 16, Fat (g) 7, Calories from Fat (%) 45, Saturated Fat (g) 1, Dietary Fiber (g) 2, Cholesterol (mg) 0, Sodium (mg) 171, Diabetic Exchanges: 1 starch, 1 fat

Cucumber and Tomato Salad

This simple summer salad is especially good when cucumbers and tomatoes are straight from the garden. Feta adds a nice Mediterranean touch.

MAKES 6 (^{1}/$_2$-CUP) SERVINGS

2 cucumbers, peeled and thinly sliced
1 cup chopped tomato
½ cup sliced red onion
¼ cup crumbled Feta cheese
½ teaspoon minced garlic
⅓ cup white vinegar
½ teaspoon sugar
2 tablespoons olive oil
Salt and pepper to taste

In a bowl, combine the cucumber, tomato, onion, and Feta.

In a small bowl, whisk together the garlic, vinegar, sugar, oil, salt, and pepper. Toss with the cucumber mixture. Refrigerate until serving.

Nutritional information per serving

Calories 81, Protein (g) 2, Carbohydrate (g) 6, Fat (g) 6, Calories from Fat (%) 65, Saturated Fat (g) 2, Dietary Fiber (g) 1, Cholesterol (mg) 6, Sodium (mg) 74, Diabetic Exchanges: 1 vegetable, 1 fat

Black-Eyed Pea and Rice Salad

Black-eyed peas and rice team up for a salad full of fiber and flavor.

MAKES 14 TO 16 SERVINGS

1 (6-ounce) box long-grain and wild rice mix
2 cups cooked white rice
½ cup chopped red onion
¼ cup finely sliced green onions (scallions)
1 red bell pepper, seeded and finely chopped
1 green bell pepper, seeded and finely chopped
¼ cup chopped fresh parsley
½ teaspoon minced garlic
2 (15-ounce) cans black-eyed peas, rinsed and drained
¼ cup olive oil
⅓ cup red wine vinegar
1 tablespoon Dijon mustard
2 jalapeño peppers, seeded and finely chopped
Salt and pepper to taste

Cook the rice mix according to the directions on the package, omitting margarine; cool. Combine with the white rice, onion, green onion, bell peppers, parsley, garlic, and black-eyed peas.

In a small bowl, combine the olive oil, red wine vinegar, mustard, jalapeño pepper, salt, and pepper. Toss with the rice mixture, and refrigerate until serving.

Nutritional information per serving

Calories 142, Protein (g) 4, Carbohydrate (g) 23, Fat (g) 4, Calories from Fat (%) 23, Saturated Fat (g) 0, Dietary Fiber (g) 2, Cholesterol (mg) 0, Sodium (mg) 280, Diabetic Exchanges: 1.5 starch, 0.5 fat

Seven-Layer Salad

When you need a make-ahead salad for a crowd, I recommend this great layered salad.

MAKES 8 TO 10 SERVINGS

½ cup fat-free sour cream

½ cup buttermilk

½ cup crumbled Feta cheese

1 teaspoon sugar

¼ teaspoon dried dill weed leaves

½ teaspoon dried basil leaves

⅛ teaspoon ground white pepper

1 (9-ounce) package spinach tortellini

6 cups fresh baby spinach leaves or torn romaine lettuce

½ pound fresh mushrooms, sliced

2 Roma (plum) tomatoes, chopped

4 green onions (scallions), chopped

2½ ounces sliced Canadian bacon, pan-cooked and cut into pieces

To make the dressing, blend the sour cream, buttermilk, feta cheese, sugar, dill weed, basil, and pepper in a food processor until smooth.

Cook the tortellini according to the package directions, omitting any oil and salt. Drain and rinse in cold water.

In a 3-quart oblong dish, layer the spinach leaves, tortellini, mushrooms, tomatoes, and green onions. Pour the dressing over the salad, spreading to cover. Do not toss. Sprinkle with the bacon. Cover and chill at least 2 hours to blend the flavors.

Nutritional information per serving

Calories 112, Protein (g) 7, Carbohydrate (g) 12, Fat (g) 4, Calories from Fat (%) 33, Saturated Fat (g) 2, Dietary Fiber (g) 1, Cholesterol (mg) 44, Sodium (mg) 248, Diabetic Exchanges: 0.5 lean meat, 0.5 starch, 1 vegetable

QUICK TIP:

If you don't have Canadian bacon, substituting lean ham will work fine.

Black Bean and Corn Salad

A blaze of color with simple ingredients creates this outstanding combination that will be popular on anyone's plate. A repeat recipe, for sure!

MAKES 6 SERVINGS

1 (15-ounce) can black beans, drained and rinsed
1 (11-ounce) can golden sweet corn, drained
1 tomato, chopped
¼ cup fresh chopped cilantro
2 tablespoons chopped red onion
3 tablespoons lemon juice
2 tablespoons olive oil
Salt and pepper to taste

Combine all ingredients in a large bowl.

This salad is best refrigerated until it's ready to be served, but it can be served immediately.

Nutritional information per serving

Calories 138, Protein (g) 5, Carbohydrate (g) 18, Fat (g) 6, Calories from Fat (%) 35, Saturated Fat (g) 1, Dietary Fiber (g) 5, Cholesterol (mg) 0, Sodium (mg) 285, Diabetic Exchanges: 0.5 very lean meat, 1 starch, 1 fat

Black Bean and Corn Salad

Corn Salad

A medley of ingredients marinated in a light vinaigrette makes this a colorful, flavorful salad.

MAKES 6 SERVINGS

2 (11-ounce) cans white shoepeg corn, drained
1 (2-ounce) jar diced pimiento, drained
½ cup chopped green bell pepper
½ cup chopped red onion
½ cup chopped celery
¼ cup sugar
2 tablespoons olive oil
¼ cup vinegar (white or red)
Salt and pepper to taste

Combine all ingredients in a large bowl. Refrigerate until serving.

Nutritional information per serving

Calories 167, Protein (g) 2, Carbohydrate (g) 28, Fat (g) 5, Calories from Fat (%) 27, Saturated Fat (g) 1, Dietary Fiber (g) 2, Cholesterol (mg) 0, Sodium (mg) 230, Diabetic Exchanges: 1.5 starch, 0.5 other carbohydrate, 1 tat

FOOD FACT:

Store tomatoes at room temperature, stem side up. Never refrigerate them, because refrigeration destroys texture and flavor.

Macaroni, Tomato, and Corn Salad

This terrific make-ahead salad includes pasta and fresh summer specialties.

MAKES 8 TO 10 SERVINGS

1 (8-ounce) package elbow macaroni
1 cup chopped tomato
1 cup thinly chopped green onions (scallions)
1 cup coarsely-chopped, peeled cucumber
1 cup corn (frozen, fresh, or canned)
1 teaspoon dried basil leaves
⅓ cup nonfat plain yogurt
2 tablespoons light mayonnaise
1½ tablespoons lime juice
1 teaspoon minced garlic
Salt and pepper to taste

Cook the macaroni according to the package directions, drain, and transfer to a large bowl. Add the tomato, green onion, cucumber, and corn.

In a separate bowl, blend the basil, yogurt, mayonnaise, lime juice, and garlic. Toss the dressing with the macaroni mixture, mixing well. Season with the salt and pepper. Cover and refrigerate until ready to serve, or serve immediately.

Nutritional information per serving

Calories 124, Protein (g) 4, Carbohydrate (g) 24, Fat (g) 2, Calories from Fat (%) 11, Saturated Fat (g) 0, Dietary Fiber (g) 2, Cholesterol (mg) 1, Sodium (mg) 36, Diabetic Exchanges: 1.5 starch

Sweet-and-Sour Broccoli Salad 🥕

The subtly sweet dressing mixed with veggies and fruit makes this salad a most requested recipe, delicious with every bite.

MAKES 6 SERVINGS

4 cups broccoli florets, cut into small pieces
½ cup sliced green onions (scallions)
2 cups red or green grapes or combination
1 head red tip lettuce, torn into pieces
1 tablespoon margarine
¼ cup slivered almonds
½ cup red wine vinegar
¼ cup sugar
2 tablespoons low-sodium soy sauce
1 tablespoon olive oil

In a large bowl, combine the broccoli, green onion, grapes, and lettuce; set aside.

In a small non-stick skillet, melt the margarine. Add the almonds and sauté until light brown; set aside.

In a small bowl, whisk together the red wine vinegar, sugar, soy sauce, and olive oil. Pour over the broccoli mixture, and toss. Stir in the almonds. Serve immediately, or refrigerate until ready to serve.

Nutritional information per serving

Calories 163, Protein (g) 3, Carbohydrate (g) 25, Fat (g) 7, Calories from Fat (%) 36, Saturated Fat (g) 1, Dietary Fiber (g) 3, Cholesterol (mg) 0, Sodium (mg) 170, Diabetic Exchanges: 1 fruit, 0.5 other carbohydrate, 1.5 fat

Marinated Green Beans 🥕

Sweet-and-spicy marinated green beans are good at room temperature or chilled. This recipe works well for a party buffet. For a twist, toss in some Feta.

MAKES 8 TO 10 SERVINGS

2 pounds fresh green beans, trimmed
¼ cup chopped red onion
2 cups cherry tomato halves
3 tablespoons balsamic vinegar
2 teaspoons Dijon mustard
2 teaspoons sugar
2 tablespoons olive oil
Salt and pepper to taste

Cook or steam the green beans in a little water in the microwave or on the stove until crisp-tender. Drain. Add the red onion and tomato.

In a small bowl, mix together the vinegar, mustard, sugar, olive oil, salt, and pepper, and toss with the green bean mixture. Serve, or refrigerate until serving.

Nutritional information per serving

Calories 71, Protein (g) 2, Carbohydrate (g) 10, Fat (g) 3, Calories from Fat (%) 36, Saturated Fat (g) 0, Dietary Fiber (g) 4, Cholesterol (mg) 0, Sodium (mg) 29, Diabetic Exchanges: 2 vegetable, 0.5 fat

Loaded
Couscous Salad

Couscous is such a quick side dish to prepare. The fresh veggies combined with the tart cranberries, toasted pine nuts, and goat cheese make this a simple yet sophisticated choice.

MAKES 16 (½-CUP) SERVINGS

½ cup orange juice

1½ cups water

2 cups plain couscous

1 cup dried cranberries

1 cup peeled and cubed cucumber

¼ cup chopped parsley

½ cup chopped green onions (scallions)

1 tablespoon Dijon mustard

2 tablespoons distilled vinegar (or whatever is on hand)

2 tablespoons honey

1 clove garlic, minced

½ cup crumbled goat cheese

¼ cup pine nuts, toasted

Salt and pepper to taste

In a saucepan, bring the orange juice and water to a boil. Stir in the couscous, cover; remove from heat and let stand for 5 to 7 minutes. Transfer to a large bowl, and fluff with a fork. Add the cranberries, cucumber, parsley, and green onion, mixing well.

In a small bowl, whisk together the mustard, vinegar, honey, and garlic. Pour the dressing over the couscous, mixing well, and stir in the goat cheese and pine nuts, carefully tossing together. Add the salt and pepper to taste. Serve at room temperature or chilled.

Nutritional information per serving

Calories 166, Protein (g) 5, Carbohydrate (g) 30, Fat (g) 3, Calories from Fat (%) 15, Saturated Fat (g) 1, Dietary Fiber (g) 1, Cholesterol (mg) 4, Sodium (mg) 39, Diabetic Exchanges: 1.5 starch, 0.5 fruit

QUICK TIP:

Pine nuts have a high fat content and can therefore turn rancid quickly. They are best stored airtight in the refrigerator, where they can be kept for up to 3 months.

Mediterranean Couscous Salad

Mediterranean ingredients added to the couscous make a light, fluffy and mildly flavored salad. If you haven't had couscous, you should know that it is very quick and easy to cook.

MAKES 6 TO 8 SERVINGS

2 cups fat-free canned chicken broth
½ teaspoon minced garlic
1⅓ cups couscous
½ cup chopped green onions (scallions)
⅓ cup chopped parsley
2 cups chopped peeled cucumber
3 tablespoons chopped fresh mint leaves or 1 tablespoon dried mint
1 (15-ounce) can cannellini beans, rinsed and drained
1 cup chopped tomato
½ cup roasted red bell peppers or pimentos from a jar, cut into pieces
⅓ cup sliced kalamata olives
¼ cup lemon juice
2 tablespoons olive oil
1½ teaspoons paprika
½ cup crumbled Feta, optional
Salt and pepper to taste

In a saucepan, bring the chicken broth and garlic to a boil. Add the couscous; stir, remove from heat, and cover for 7 minutes. Fluff with a fork, and transfer to a large bowl. Add the green onion, parsley, cucumber, mint, beans, tomato, roasted pepper, and olives, mixing well.

In a small bowl, mix together the lemon juice, olive oil, and paprika, and toss with the couscous mixture. Add the Feta, if desired. Season with the salt and pepper to taste. Serve immediately, or refrigerate.

Nutritional information per serving

Calories 244, Protein (g) 8, Carbohydrate (g) 39, Fat (g) 6, Calories from Fat (%) 22, Saturated Fat (g) 1, Dietary Fiber (g) 4, Cholesterol (mg) 0, Sodium (mg) 373, Diabetic Exchanges: 2.5 starch, 1 fat

Mediterranean Couscous Salad

Potato Salad

This light, marinated potato salad is an easy alternative to traditional potato salad, since you don't need to peel the potatoes.

MAKES 6 TO 8 SERVINGS

2 pounds red potatoes
¼ cup chopped parsley
¼ cup chopped green onions (scallions)
½ teaspoon minced garlic
¼ teaspoon dry mustard
1 teaspoon sugar
1 teaspoon Worcestershire sauce
¼ cup olive oil
¼ cup tarragon vinegar
Salt and pepper to taste

Place the potatoes with skins on in a pot filled with enough water to cover, and boil until the potatoes are tender when pricked with a fork, about 30 minutes. Let cool, then cut into chunks. Transfer to a bowl, and sprinkle with parsley and green onions.

In a small bowl, combine the garlic, dry mustard, sugar, Worcestershire sauce, olive oil, and vinegar, mixing well. Pour over the potatoes, tossing gently. Season with the salt and pepper. Let stand at least 4 hours to marinate, stirring every hour. Serve at room temperature.

Nutritional information per serving
Calories 144, Protein (g) 3, Carbohydrate (g) 21, Fat (g) 7, Calories from Fat (%) 38, Saturated Fat (g) 1, Dietary Fiber (g) 3, Cholesterol (mg) 0, Sodium (mg) 9, Diabetic Exchanges: 1.5 starch, 1 fat

Waldorf Pasta Salad

Here's a wonderful way to include apples in a salad, mixed with pasta, pecans, and celery in a tangy, sweet, creamy dressing.

MAKES 4 TO 6 SERVINGS

1 (8-ounce) package rotini (spiral) pasta
½ cup fat-free sour cream
2 tablespoons light mayonnaise
¼ cup lime juice
2 tablespoons sugar
⅓ cup chopped pecans, toasted
1 cup chopped celery
1 green apple, cored and chopped
2 medium red apples, cored and chopped
½ cup chopped green onions (scallions)

Cook the pasta according to the package directions, omitting any oil and salt. Rinse with cold water; drain. In small bowl, stir together the sour cream, mayonnaise, lime juice, and sugar; set aside.

Just before serving, in a large bowl, toss together the pasta, pecans, celery, green and red apples, and green onion. Drizzle with the dressing, and toss gently to coat. Serve immediately or refrigerate.

Nutritional information per serving
Calories 291, Protein (g) 7, Carbohydrate (g) 51, Fat (g) 7, Calories from Fat (%) 21, Saturated Fat (g) 1, Dietary Fiber (g) 5, Cholesterol (mg) 2, Sodium (mg) 78, Diabetic Exchanges: 2 starch, 1 fruit, 0.5 other carbohydrate, 1 fat

Marinated Crabmeat Salad

Make the marinated mixture ahead, and toss with the lettuce before serving. For added nutrition, throw in some carrots or veggies.

MAKES 6 TO 8 SERVINGS

¼ cup olive oil

3 tablespoons distilled or wine vinegar

Salt to taste

½ teaspoon pepper

¼ teaspoon dry mustard

⅛ teaspoon dried thyme leaves

¼ teaspoon dried basil leaves

2 tablespoons chopped fresh parsley

1 large red onion, chopped

2 tablespoons lime juice

1 pound lump or white crabmeat, picked for shells

1 head lettuce, washed and torn into bite-size pieces

In a small bowl, combine the olive oil, vinegar, salt, pepper, mustard, thyme, basil, parsley, onion, and lime juice; mix well. Add the crabmeat, tossing gently. Cover with plastic wrap, and refrigerate at least 4 hours. Stir occasionally.

Before serving, gently toss the crabmeat and marinade with the lettuce.

Nutritional information per serving
Calories 144, Protein (g) 14, Carbohydrate (g) 5, Fat (g) 8, Calories from Fat (%) 48, Saturated Fat (g) 1, Dietary Fiber (g) 2, Cholesterol (mg) 43, Sodium (mg) 222, Diabetic Exchanges: 2 very lean meat, 1 vegetable, 1 fat

FOOD FACT:

The greener the lettuce, the more nutrition it contains.

Pasta Salad with Herb Dijon Vinaigrette

Pasta Salad with Herb Dijon Vinaigrette

A variety of veggies, Romano cheese, and an unbeatable dressing combine to make the perfect pasta salad—one I make over and over.

MAKES 10 SERVINGS

2 cups snow peas
1 bunch broccoli, florets only
1 (12-ounce) package colored pasta
1 (6-ounce) package tri-colored stuffed tortellini
½ pound mushroom halves
1 cup cherry tomato halves
1 red bell pepper, seeded and cut into strips
⅓ cup grated Romano cheese
Herb Dijon Vinaigrette (recipe follows)

Cook the snow peas and broccoli in the microwave until crisp-tender. Drain and set aside.

Cook the pasta and tortellini according to the package directions, omitting any oil and salt. Drain and set aside.

In a large bowl, combine the snow peas, broccoli, pasta, tortellini, mushrooms, tomatoes, red pepper, and cheese. Toss with Herb Dijon Vinaigrette (see recipe at right).

HERB DIJON VINAIGRETTE

1 bunch green onions (scallions), chopped
½ cup red wine vinegar
⅓ cup olive oil
2 tablespoons chopped parsley
3 cloves garlic, minced
2 teaspoons dried basil
1 teaspoon dried dill weed leaves
½ teaspoon dried oregano leaves
Salt and pepper to taste
½ teaspoon sugar
1½ teaspoons Dijon mustard

In a small bowl, combine the green onions, red wine vinegar, olive oil, parsley, garlic, basil, dill weed, oregano, salt, pepper, sugar, and mustard, mixing well. Pour over the pasta salad. Refrigerate until serving.

Nutritional information per serving

Calories 286, Protein (g) 10, Carbohydrate (g) 41, Fat (g) 10, Calories from Fat (%) 30, Saturated Fat (g) 2, Dietary Fiber (g) 3, Cholesterol (mg) 12, Sodium (mg) 101, Diabetic Exchanges: 2 starch, 2 vegetable, 2 fat

FOOD FACT:

Dijon mustard is from Dijon, France, and known for its clean, sharp flavor. Always use the type of mustard that is called for in a recipe, or you could end up with a completely different flavor than was intended.

Italian Pasta Salad

Pasta plus Italian ingredients and a light Dijon vinaigrette make this simple salad simply satisfying.

MAKES 8 TO 10 SERVINGS

8 ounces ziti pasta
4 ounces tri-colored rotini (spiral) pasta
1 green bell pepper, seeded and chopped
1 red bell pepper, seeded and chopped
½ cup chopped celery
2 teaspoons capers, drained
⅓ cup thinly chopped green onions (scallions)
2 Roma (plum) tomatoes, chopped
½ cup red wine vinegar
¼ cup water
1 tablespoon olive oil
1 teaspoon dried basil leaves
1 teaspoon dried oregano leaves
½ teaspoon minced garlic
1 tablespoon Dijon mustard
¼ cup grated Parmesan cheese

In a large saucepan, cook both the pastas together according to the package directions, omitting any oil and salt. Rinse, drain, and place in a large bowl. Add the green pepper, red pepper, celery, capers, green onion, and tomatoes.

In a small bowl, combine the vinegar, water, oil, basil, oregano, garlic, mustard, and Parmesan cheese, mixing well. Pour over the pasta mixture, and toss well. Refrigerate until serving.

Nutritional information per serving
Calories 168, Protein (g) 6, Carbohydrate (g) 30, Fat (g) 3, Calories from Fat (%) 15, Saturated Fat (g) 1, Dietary Fiber (g) 2, Cholesterol (mg) 2, Sodium (mg) 110, Diabetic Exchanges: 2 starch

QUICK TIP:

For pasta in a cold salad, drain and rinse with cold water.

Marinated Pasta and Veggies

The sweet, zesty dressing gives this attractive marinated salad a memorable flavor.

MAKES 8 TO 10 SERVINGS

1 (8-ounce) package tubular pasta
1 (15-ounce) can whole-kernel corn, drained
1 (15-ounce) can garbanzo beans, drained and rinsed
2 cups peeled, sliced cucumber
2 tablespoons capers, drained
1 cup chopped tomatoes
½ cup chopped red onion
⅓ cup cider or white vinegar
¼ cup lemon juice
1 tablespoon Dijon mustard
3 tablespoons sugar
2 tablespoons olive oil

Cook the pasta according to the package direc

In a large bowl, mix together the pasta, corn, beans, cucumber, capers, tomatoes, and onion.

In a small bowl, whisk together the vinegar, lemon juice, Dijon mustard, sugar, and oil until well mixed. Pour over the pasta mixture, tossing until well combined. Refrigerate for several hours, and serve.

Nutritional information per serving
Calories 205, Protein (g) 6, Carbohydrate (g) 37, Fat (g) 4, Calories from Fat (%) 19, Saturated Fat (g) 0, Dietary Fiber (g) 3, Cholesterol (mg) 0, Sodium (mg) 248, Diabetic Exchanges: 2 starch, 1 vegetable, 0.5 fat

Tortellini Shrimp Salad

Shrimp and tortellini tossed with a Dijon vinaigrette team up to make this a popular choice.

MAKES 8 SERVINGS

2 (8-ounce) packages tri-colored tortellini stuffed with Parmesan cheese
1 pound cooked medium shrimp, peeled
⅓ cup grated Romano cheese
4 green onions (scallions), finely chopped
⅓ cup chopped red bell pepper
2 tablespoons dried basil leaves, divided
¼ cup balsamic vinegar
2 tablespoons canola oil
1 teaspoon Dijon mustard

Cook the tortellini according to the package directions, omitting any oil and salt. Drain well and cool slightly.

In a large bowl, combine the tortellini, shrimp, cheese, green onions, red pepper, and 1 tablespoon basil.

In a small bowl, combine the vinegar, oil, remaining basil, and mustard. Toss with the pasta mixture, and refrigerate until serving.

Nutritional information per serving
Calories 270, Protein (g) 21, Carbohydrate (g) 28, Fat (g) 8, Calories from Fat (%) 27, Saturated Fat (g) 2, Dietary Fiber (g) 2, Cholesterol (mg) 145, Sodium (mg) 289, Diabetic Exchanges: 2 lean meat, 2 starch

Southwestern Tortellini Salad

These ingredients tossed with this incredibly flavored vinaigrette turn an ordinary salad into an outstanding dish.

MAKES 10 TO 12 SERVINGS

1 pound cheese-filled tri-colored tortellini or spiral pasta
1 pint grape tomatoes, cut in half
1 (15-ounce) can black beans, drained and rinsed
1 cup frozen corn, thawed
¼ cup balsamic vinegar
2 tablespoons lime juice
½ cup chopped red onion
½ teaspoon minced garlic
1 teaspoon honey
¼ cup chopped fresh cilantro
¼ cup olive oil
Salt and freshly ground pepper to taste

Prepare the tortellini according to the package directions, omitting any oil and salt. Rinse in cold water, and set aside to cool.

In a large bowl, combine the tortellini, tomatoes, black beans, and corn; toss gently.

In a food processor, combine the balsamic vinegar, lime juice, red onion, garlic, honey, and cilantro. Pulse to combine. Add the olive oil gradually through the feed tube with the motor running. Season with the salt and pepper. Pour the dressing over the salad. Toss, cover, and chill for 30 minutes before serving.

Nutritional information per serving

Calories 202, Protein (g) 8, Carbohydrate (g) 28, Fat (g) 7, Calories from Fat (%) 30, Saturated Fat (g) 2, Dietary Fiber (g) 4, Cholesterol (mg) 20, Sodium (mg) 177, Diabetic Exchanges: 1.5 starch, 1 vegetable, 1 fat

Greek Seafood Pasta Salad

Marinated shrimp and scallops tossed with pasta and Feta create this Greek wonder. To cook the scallops and shrimp, sauté them in a non-stick skillet.

MAKES 6 TO 8 SERVINGS

1 pound small shrimp, cooked and peeled
1 pound bay scallops, cooked
Dill Dressing (recipe follows)
1 (12-ounce) package tri-colored rotini (spiral) pasta
2 cups cherry tomato halves
¼ cup thinly sliced black olives
3 ounces Feta cheese, crumbled

Toss the shrimp and scallops with ¼ cup Dill Dressing (see recipe). Refrigerate the seafood and the remaining dressing until ready to toss together with the other ingredients.

Cook the pasta according to the package directions, omitting any oil and salt. Drain well.

In a large bowl, toss the pasta with the marinated seafood, tomato, olives, Feta, and reserved dressing. Refrigerate until serving.

DILL DRESSING

½ teaspoon dried dill weed leaves
½ teaspoon minced garlic
½ cup chopped red onion
¼ cup fresh lemon juice
3 tablespoons olive oil
Salt and pepper to taste

In a food processor, mix the dill weed, garlic, onion, lemon juice, olive oil, salt, and pepper until well combined.

Nutritional information per serving

Calories 374, Protein (g) 32, Carbohydrate (g) 38, Fat (g) 10, Calories from Fat (%) 24, Saturated Fat (g) 3, Dietary Fiber (g) 2, Cholesterol (mg) 144, Sodium (mg) 410, Diabetic Exchanges: 4 lean meat, 2 starch, 1 vegetable

Greek Chicken
Salad Bowl

SALADS

Throw in some Feta cheese to make a Greek chef salad. The mint gives the salad an adventurous personality.

MAKES 4 TO 6 SERVINGS

½ cup lemon juice, divided
1 teaspoon dried mint, divided
¾ teaspoon minced garlic, divided
2 tablespoons red wine vinegar
1½ pounds skinless, boneless chicken breasts,
    cut into strips
½ cup dry white wine
1 pound fresh spinach, washed, stemmed,
    and torn into pieces
1½ cups chopped tomatoes
⅓ cup chopped green onions (scallions)
1½ cups chopped peeled cucumber
Salt and pepper to taste
1 tablespoon olive oil
Feta cheese, optional

In a large bowl, mix together ¼ cup lemon juice, ½ teaspoon mint, ¼ teaspoon garlic, and the vinegar. Add the chicken; toss, cover with plastic wrap, and marinate in the refrigerator for at least 1 hour.

In a large non-stick skillet, cook the chicken over medium-high heat until brown, turning frequently, about 5 minutes. Add the wine, reduce the heat, and simmer for 8 to 10 minutes, or until the chicken is done. Remove the chicken from the pan, and refrigerate until ready to use.

In a large bowl, combine the spinach, tomatoes, green onion, cucumber, and chicken. In a small bowl, mix together the remaining lemon juice, mint, and garlic, with the salt, pepper, and oil. Pour the dressing over the salad, add Feta cheese, if desired, and toss to mix well. Serve immediately.

Nutritional information per serving
Calories 198, Protein (g) 29, Carbohydrate (g) 9, Fat (g) 4, Calories from Fat (%) 19, Saturated Fat (g) 1, Dietary Fiber (g) 3, Cholesterol (mg) 66, Sodium (mg) 141, Diabetic Exchanges: 3 very lean meat, 2 vegetable

Greek Chicken Salad Bowl

SALADS

Mandarin Chicken Salad

SALADS

This blast of color with a burst of flavor and a simple, light lemon dressing is hard to beat. It's a great way to use leftover grilled chicken.

MAKES 4 TO 6 SERVINGS

1½ pounds skinless, boneless chicken breasts, cut into chunks or strips
1 tablespoon canola oil
3 tablespoons low-sodium soy sauce, divided
½ teaspoon minced garlic
¼ teaspoon ground ginger
1 cup green grapes, cut in half
1 cup chopped celery
½ cup thinly chopped green onions (scallions)
1 (11-ounce) can mandarin orange segments, drained
¼ cup chopped pecans, toasted
1 (6-ounce) container nonfat lemon yogurt
6 cups fresh spinach, washed, stemmed, and torn into pieces
Chinese noodles, for garnish, optional

In a large bowl, combine the chicken, oil, 2 tablespoons soy sauce, garlic, and ginger, coating the chicken well. In a non-stick skillet, cook the chicken mixture over medium heat for about 5 to 7 minutes, or until the chicken is done. Set aside to cool.

In a large bowl, combine the cooled chicken, grapes, celery, green onion, orange segments, and pecans.

In a small bowl, mix together the yogurt and the remaining soy sauce, and pour over the chicken mixture. Cover and refrigerate until the mixture is well chilled, about 2 hours.

Serve on the fresh spinach leaves, and sprinkle with Chinese noodles, if desired.

Nutritional information per serving

Calories 262, Protein (g) 30, Carbohydrate (g) 18, Fat (g) 8, Calories from Fat (%) 26, Saturated Fat (g) 1, Dietary Fiber (g) 3, Cholesterol (mg) 66, Sodium (mg) 334, Diabetic Exchanges: 3.5 lean meat, 1 fruit, 1 vegetable

Chicken Fiesta Salad

Well-seasoned chicken paired with beans, cilantro, tomato, and onion will thrill your taste buds. Serve over mixed greens.

MAKES 6 SERVINGS

1 teaspoon ground cumin

1 teaspoon chili powder

¼ cup all-purpose flour

1½ pounds skinless, boneless chicken breasts, cut into strips

2 cups frozen corn, thawed

1 (15-ounce) can pinto beans, drained and rinsed

1 cup chopped tomato

½ cup chopped red onion

¼ cup chopped fresh cilantro, optional

1 tablespoon olive oil

½ teaspoon minced garlic

½ cup lime juice

¼ cup red wine vinegar

In a small bowl, combine the cumin, chili powder, and flour. Coat the chicken with the flour mixture, and in a large non-stick skillet, sauté the chicken over medium-high heat, about 5 to 7 minutes or until well done. Set aside.

In a large bowl, combine the corn, pinto beans, tomato, red onion, and cilantro.

In a small bowl, combine the oil, garlic, lime juice, and vinegar. Pour over the corn mixture. Add the chicken strips, tossing to mix. Serve immediately or refrigerate.

Nutritional information per serving

Calories 297, Protein (g) 32, Carbohydrate (g) 33, Fat (g) 5, Calories from Fat (%) 14, Saturated Fat (g) 1, Dietary Fiber (g) 5, Cholesterol (mg) 66, Sodium (mg) 230, Diabetic Exchanges: 3.5 very lean meat, 2 starch, 1 vegetable

QUICK TIP:

For the best flavor, cilantro should only be used when it is fresh. If you are not a cilantro fan, leave it out.

Curried Chicken Salad

The hint of curry (add more if you like) in the light, snappy dressing makes this a marvelous chicken salad for luncheon guests or for just the family.

MAKES 4 SERVINGS

4 cooked skinless, boneless chicken breasts, diced
¾ cup chopped celery
½ cup chopped onion
¼ cup light mayonnaise
¼ cup nonfat plain yogurt
1 teaspoon lemon juice
1 tablespoon low-sodium soy sauce
¼ teaspoon curry powder
¼ cup chopped almonds, toasted
½ cup frozen green peas, thawed

In a large bowl, combine the chicken, celery, and onion.

In a small bowl, mix the mayonnaise, yogurt, lemon juice, soy sauce, and curry powder. Pour the sauce over the chicken mixture, and mix thoroughly. Before serving, fold in the almonds and peas.

Nutritional information per serving
Calories 259, Protein (g) 30, Carbohydrate (g) 10, Fat (g) 11, Calories from Fat (%) 37, Saturated Fat (g) 1, Dietary Fiber (g) 3, Cholesterol (mg) 71, Sodium (mg) 343, Diabetic Exchanges: 4 lean meat, 0.5 starch

Marinated Italian Tuna Salad

Tuna, mozzarella, and tomatoes highlight this Italian marinade. I like to use fresh mozzarella whenever it's available.

MAKES 4 TO 6 SERVINGS

2 ounces part-skim Mozzarella cheese, cut into small cubes
2 (6-ounce) cans solid white tuna, packed in water, drained
1 cup cherry tomatoes, halved
1 small red onion, cut into thin rings, halved
⅔ cup chopped celery
2 tablespoons olive oil
3 tablespoons red wine vinegar or balsamic vinegar
1½ teaspoons dried basil leaves
¼ teaspoon crushed red pepper flakes
⅛ teaspoon pepper

In a large bowl, combine the cheese, tuna, tomatoes, onion, and celery.

In a small bowl, mix together the oil, vinegar, basil, red pepper flakes, and pepper. Pour the dressing over the tuna mixture, and toss gently to coat. Cover, and refrigerate for at least 1 hour.

Nutritional information per serving
Calories 159, Protein (g) 17, Carbohydrate (g) 5, Fat (g) 8, Calories from Fat (%) 45, Saturated Fat (g) 2, Dietary Fiber (g) 1, Cholesterol (mg) 30, Sodium (mg) 277, Diabetic Exchanges: 2 very lean meat, 1 vegetable, 1 fat

Deluxe Tuna Salad

Who knew that with a can of tuna and a can opener you could create such a sensational salad?

MAKES 8 SERVINGS

2 (6-ounce) cans solid white tuna, packed in water, drained
1 (11-ounce) can mandarin orange segments, drained
¼ pound fresh mushrooms, sliced
1 (14-ounce) can artichoke hearts, drained and halved
1 cup sliced water chestnuts, drained
¼ cup light mayonnaise
¼ cup nonfat plain yogurt
1 tablespoon lemon juice
2 teaspoons sugar
1 bunch green onions (scallions), chopped

In a large bowl, carefully combine the tuna, oranges, mushrooms, artichoke hearts, and water chestnuts.

In a small bowl, mix the mayonnaise, yogurt, lemon juice, sugar, and green onions, and fold into the tuna mixture. Serve immediately or refrigerate.

Nutritional information per serving
Calories 129, Protein (g) 12, Carbohydrate (g) 11, Fat (g) 4, Calories from Fat (%) 27, Saturated Fat (g) 1, Dietary Fiber (g) 2, Cholesterol (mg) 21, Sodium (mg) 322, Diabetic Exchanges: 1.5 lean meat, 2 vegetable

Tuna and White Bean Salad

This stylishly simple salad is packed with fiber and lots of flavor. Try this recipe with grilled fresh tuna.

MAKES 4 TO 6 SERVINGS

1 (12-ounce) can solid white tuna, packed in water, drained
1 cup chopped green onions (scallions)
1 (15-ounce) can white beans, rinsed and drained
2 tablespoons chopped parsley
½ cup diced celery
⅓ cup lemon juice
1½ tablespoons olive oil
¼ teaspoon dried rosemary leaves
¼ teaspoon pepper

In a large bowl, combine the tuna, green onion, white beans, parsley, and celery, tossing well.

In a small bowl, blend the lemon juice, olive oil, rosemary, and pepper. Pour over the tuna mixture, and stir gently to combine. Refrigerate for 2 hours, or let stand at room temperature for at least 30 minutes before serving.

Nutritional information per serving
Calories 161, Protein (g) 18, Carbohydrate (g) 14, Fat (g) 5, Calories from Fat (%) 28, Saturated Fat (g) 1, Dietary Fiber (g) 4, Cholesterol (mg) 24, Sodium (mg) 462, Diabetic Exchanges: 2 lean meat, 1 starch

FOOD FACT:

White tuna is albacore tuna. It has a milder flavor and whiter flesh than the tuna labeled "light."

Salad Niçoise

Prepare this French marinated-tuna-and-veggies presentation ahead of time. To wow your taste buds, try using grilled fresh tuna instead of canned.

MAKES 6 TO 8 SERVINGS

3 or 4 red potatoes
1 tablespoon chopped green onions (scallions)
Salt and pepper to taste
½ pound fresh green beans
Vinaigrette Dressing (recipe follows)
2 (9-ounce) cans tuna packed in water, well drained
1 cucumber, peeled and thinly sliced
2 tomatoes, quartered
2 hard-boiled eggs, sliced, optional

Place the potatoes in a medium saucepan; cover with salted water. Cook, uncovered, until tender when pierced with a fork, about 20 to 25 minutes. Drain, peel, and slice. Combine with the chopped green onion, salt, and pepper; set aside.

Snip the ends off the green beans. In a microwave-safe dish, cook the green beans in a small amount of salted water, covered, in the microwave or on the stovetop until crisp-tender. Drain.

Arrange the green beans on a large platter. Place the tuna over the green beans. Sprinkle with salt and pepper. Drizzle with ¼ cup Vinaigrette Dressing (see recipe at right). Around the edges of the platter, arrange the potato slices, cucumber slices, tomato wedges, and egg slices. Pour the remaining Vinaigrette Dressing over all. Cover with plastic wrap, and refrigerate for at least 1 hour.

VINAIGRETTE DRESSING

½ teaspoon minced garlic
1 tablespoon chopped parsley
¼ cup chopped red onion
⅓ cup red wine vinegar
2 tablespoons lemon juice
1 teaspoon Dijon mustard
3 tablespoons olive oil

In a small bowl, combine the garlic, parsley, onion, vinegar, lemon juice, mustard, and olive oil, mixing well.

Nutritional information per serving

Calories 193, Protein (g) 18, Carbohydrate (g) 16, Fat (g) 7, Calories from Fat (%) 32, Saturated Fat (g) 1, Dietary Fiber (g) 3, Cholesterol (mg) 27, Sodium (mg) 263, Diabetic Exchanges: 2 lean meat, 0.5 starch, 1 vegetable

Salad Niçoise

Grilled Tuna Salad with Wasabi-Ginger Vinaigrette

Wasabi-ginger vinaigrette turns an ordinary tuna salad into something special.

MAKES 4 SERVINGS

3 tablespoons low-sodium soy sauce
¼ cup lime juice
2 teaspoons sugar
1 teaspoon wasabi paste
½ teaspoon ground ginger
2 green onions (scallions), finely chopped
4 grilled tuna steaks, 2 inches thick
    (about 4 ounces each)
1 medium red onion, thinly sliced
4 cups mixed greens

Combine the soy sauce, lime juice, sugar, wasabi, ginger, and green onions in a large bowl, and whisk. Taste for seasoning. Set aside.

Cut the grilled tuna into large chunks, and toss with the vinaigrette. Set aside.

Combine the red onion and greens in a large bowl, and toss well. Place the mixture on four plates. Spoon the tuna on top and serve.

Nutritional information per serving

Calories 165, Protein (g) 27, Carbohydrate (g) 10, Fat (g) 1, Calories from Fat (%) 7, Saturated Fat (g) 0, Dietary Fiber (g) 2, Cholesterol (mg) 53, Sodium (mg) 351, Diabetic Exchanges: 3 very lean meat, 2 vegetable

Salmon Pasta Salad

Fresh salmon is worth the extra effort, but to save time, you can substitute a can of red salmon.

MAKES 4 TO 6 SERVINGS

1 pound fresh salmon fillet
1 (8-ounce) package rotini (spiral) pasta
⅓ cup light mayonnaise
½ cup nonfat plain yogurt
½ teaspoon sugar
2 teaspoons dried dill weed leaves
½ teaspoon white pepper
1 cup diced celery
1 (14-ounce) can artichoke hearts, drained and quartered

Preheat the oven to 325°F. Place the salmon in a shallow non-stick baking dish coated with non-stick cooking spray, and bake for 15 minutes, or pan-fry, until the salmon is thoroughly cooked and flakes easily. Set aside to cool. Cook the pasta according to the package directions, omitting any oil and salt. Drain, rinse, and set aside. In a small bowl, mix the mayonnaise, yogurt, sugar, dill weed, and pepper. Set aside. In a large bowl, mix the celery, artichoke hearts, pasta, and dressing. Remove the skin from the salmon, flake into chunks, and add to the pasta mixture, tossing gently. Chill until ready to serve.

Nutritional information per serving

Calories 305, Protein (g) 22, Carbohydrate (g) 35, Fat (g) 8, Calories from Fat (%) 23, Saturated Fat (g) 1, Dietary Fiber (g) 2, Cholesterol (mg) 44, Sodium (mg) 311, Diabetic Exchanges: 2 lean meat, 2 starch, 1 vegetable

Wild Rice
and Pork Salad

Spruce up this salad with teriyaki or peppered pork tenderloins. If you have pork tenderloin leftovers, this combination makes another hearty yet light meal.

MAKES 6 TO 8 SERVINGS

2 (6-ounce) packages long-grain and wild rice

1 (6-ounce) package frozen snow pea pods

1 (8-ounce) can sliced water chestnuts, drained

1 (11-ounce) can mandarin orange segments, drained

2 cups chopped cooked pork tenderloin
   (about 1¼ pounds)

¼ cup low-sodium soy sauce

¼ cup seasoned rice vinegar

2 tablespoons olive oil

1 teaspoon ground ginger

Prepare the rice according to the package directions, omitting any oil and salt; set aside. Prepare the pea pods according to the package directions; set aside. In a large bowl, combine the cooked rice, pea pods, water chestnut, orange, and pork, tossing well. In a small bowl, whisk together the soy sauce, vinegar, oil, and ginger. Pour over the rice salad, and gently toss. Cover and refrigerate for at least 2 hours before serving.

Nutritional information per serving

Calories 343, Protein (g) 25, Carbohydrate (g) 43, Fat (g) 7, Calories from Fat (%) 19, Saturated Fat (g) 2, Dietary Fiber (g) 3, Cholesterol (mg) 56, Sodium (mg) 1,019, Diabetic Exchanges: 3 lean meat, 1.5 starch, 0.5 fruit

Taco Rice Salad

Taco Rice Salad

This is one of my favorite Southwestern salads. Light but satisfying, it will win you over. Serve with extra salsa and chips. This recipe is also a great way to introduce the younger ones to lettuce, since the meat and rice are the stars of the salad.

MAKES 6 SERVINGS

1 pound ground sirloin
½ cup finely chopped onion
½ teaspoon minced garlic
½ teaspoon ground cumin
Salt and pepper to taste
3 cups cooked rice
½ head lettuce, shredded, or 4 cups mixed greens
2 tomatoes, chopped
½ cup shredded reduced-fat Cheddar cheese
½ cup chopped red onion
¼ cup fat-free sour cream
¼ cup salsa
Low-fat tortilla chips (optional)

In a large non-stick skillet, cook the meat, onion, and garlic over medium heat, stirring to crumble, 5 to 7 minutes or until the meat is done. Drain any excess fat. Add the cumin, salt, pepper, and rice. Remove from the heat, and let cool.

In a large bowl, combine the lettuce, tomatoes, cheese, red onion, and the rice mixture.

In a separate bowl, mix together the sour cream and salsa, and toss lightly with the lettuce-rice mixture. Serve immediately, with extra salsa and chips, if desired.

Nutritional information per serving

Calories 256, Protein (g) 21, Carbohydrate (g) 30, Fat (g) 6, Calories from Fat (%) 20, Saturated Fat (g) 3, Dietary Fiber (g) 2, Cholesterol (mg) 45, Sodium (mg) 168, Diabetic Exchanges: 2.5 lean meat, 1.5 starch, 1 vegetable

Southwestern Rice Salad

Another make-ahead lifesaver, this full-flavored rice salad is hearty enough to eat on its own and also makes an outstanding side dish for grilled chicken and other meats.

MAKES 10 TO 12 SERVINGS

1 (15-ounce) can black beans, rinsed and drained

2 cups cooked rice

1 medium tomato, chopped

1 red bell pepper, seeded and chopped

1 bunch green onions (scallions), chopped

½ cup chopped fresh cilantro leaves

1 small jalapeño pepper, seeded

3 tablespoons olive oil

½ cup lime juice

½ teaspoon ground cumin

1 cup shredded reduced-fat mild Cheddar cheese

In a large bowl, combine the beans, rice, tomato, red pepper, green onions, and cilantro. In a food processor, mince the jalapeño pepper. Add the oil, lime juice, and cumin, and process until well blended. Toss the dressing with the bean mixture. Cover and chill at least 2 hours, or overnight. Just before serving, toss the cheese with the salad.

Nutritional information per serving

Calories 130, Protein (g) 6, Carbohydrate (g) 14, Fat (g) 6, Calories from Fat (%) 38, Saturated Fat (g) 2, Dietary Fiber (g) 3, Cholesterol (mg) 5, Sodium (mg) 173, Diabetic Exchanges: 0.5 lean meat, 1 starch, .05 fat

Paella Salad

Paella is a Spanish dish of saffron-flavored rice combined with a variety of meats, shellfish, garlic, onions, peas, artichoke hearts, and tomatoes. This festive presentation of colors and textures will quickly convince even the heartiest eaters that a salad can be a satisfying, fulfilling meal, which makes this another favorite of mine. My sister loves this recipe with grilled chicken instead of shrimp.

MAKES 6 SERVINGS

2 (5-ounce) packages saffron yellow rice
¼ cup balsamic vinegar
¼ cup lemon juice
1 tablespoon olive oil
1 teaspoon dried basil leaves
⅛ teaspoon pepper
Dash cayenne pepper
1 pound medium cooked and peeled shrimp
1 (14-ounce) can quartered artichoke hearts, drained
¾ cup chopped green bell pepper
1 cup frozen green peas, thawed
1 cup chopped tomato
1 (2-ounce) jar diced pimiento, drained
½ cup chopped red onion
2 ounces chopped prosciutto

Prepare the rice according to the package directions, omitting any oil and salt. Set aside.

In a small bowl, mix together the vinegar, lemon juice, oil, basil, pepper, and cayenne; set aside.

In a large bowl, combine the cooked rice with the shrimp, artichoke hearts, green pepper, peas, tomato, pimiento, red onion, and prosciutto, mixing well. Pour the dressing over the rice mixture, tossing to coat. Cover, and refrigerate at least 2 hours before serving.

Nutritional information per serving

Calories 342, Protein (g) 25, Carbohydrate (g) 50, Fat (g) 5, Calories from Fat (%) 12, Saturated Fat (g) 1, Dietary Fiber (g) 3, Cholesterol (mg) 156, Sodium (mg) 1,106, Diabetic Exchanges: 2.5 very lean meat, 3 starch, 1 vegetable

Paella Salad

SALADS

Pretzel Strawberry Gelatin

Pretzel Strawberry Gelatin

This popular recipe may also be served for dessert. No one can ever figure out the ingredients in the pretzel crust—they think there are pecans.

MAKES 16 SERVINGS

4 tablespoons margarine, melted
2 tablespoons light brown sugar
2 cups crushed pretzels
1 (6-ounce) package strawberry gelatin
2 cups boiling water
3 cups sliced fresh strawberries
4 ounces reduced-fat cream cheese
½ cup sugar
1 envelope dry whipped topping mix
½ cup skim milk

Preheat the oven to 350°F.

Combine the margarine, brown sugar, and pretzels, and press into a 13 x 9 x 2-inch non-stick baking pan. Bake for 10 minutes; cool. Meanwhile, dissolve the strawberry gelatin in 2 cups boiling water, stirring until dissolved. Add the strawberry slices. Cool in the refrigerator until the gelatin begins to set. In a small bowl, beat the cream cheese with the sugar. Prepare the whipped topping according to the package directions, substituting skim milk. Fold into the cream cheese mixture. Spread over the cooled crust. Pour the semi-firm gelatin mixture over the cream cheese layer. Refrigerate at least 1 hour, or until set.

Nutritional information per serving

Calories 179, Protein (g) 3, Carbohydrate (g) 30, Fat (g) 5, Calories from Fat (%) 26, Saturated Fat (g) 2, Dietary Fiber (g) 1, Cholesterol (mg) 5, Sodium (mg) 275, Diabetic Exchanges: 0.5 starch, 1.5 other carbohydrate, 1 fat

Mango Salad with Citrus Sauce

A tangy citrus sauce complements this mango salad. Use fresh mangoes when in season.

MAKES 12 SERVINGS

3 (3-ounce) packages lemon gelatin
3 cups boiling water
1 (32-ounce) jar mangoes with juice
1 (8-ounce) package reduced-fat cream cheese
Citrus Sauce (recipe follows)

In a large bowl, dissolve the gelatin in the boiling water. Place the mangoes with juice in a food processor. Gradually add the cream cheese, and blend well. Stir in the gelatin mixture. Pour into a 2-quart mold coated with nonstick cooking spray. Refrigerate until set. Serve with Citrus Sauce.

CITRUS SAUCE

1 egg, slightly beaten
⅔ cup sugar
Juice of 1 lemon
Juice of 1 orange

In a small saucepan, combine the egg, sugar, lemon juice, and orange juice. Bring to a boil, lower the heat, and cook 5 minutes. Remove from the heat, and cool. Store the sauce in the refrigerator; take out 20 minutes before serving, to soften.

Nutritional information per serving
Calories 211, Protein (g) 5, Carbohydrate (g) 40, Fat (g) 5, Calories from Fat (%) 19, Saturated Fat (g) 3, Dietary Fiber (g) 0, Cholesterol (mg) 31, Sodium (mg) 166, Diabetic Exchanges: 0.5 fruit, 2 other carbohydrate, 1 fat

Cranberry Mold

Throw all these festive ingredients into a food processor—yes, even the the orange peel! This is a great cranberry choice for any holiday table.

MAKES 10 SERVINGS

1 (16-ounce) package fresh cranberries
1 whole orange, seeded
½ cup chopped pecans
1 cup crushed pineapple, in its own juices, drained
1 (3-ounce) package raspberry gelatin
1 cup boiling water

Combine the cranberries, orange, and pecans in a food processor, and mix until chopped finely. Add the crushed pineapple.

Dissolve the gelatin in the boiling water, stirring until dissolved. Combine with the cranberry mixture, mixing well. Pour into a 5-cup mold. Refrigerate until firm.

Nutritional information per serving
Calories 114, Protein (g) 2, Carbohydrate (g) 19, Fat (g) 4, Calories from Fat (%) 33, Saturated Fat (g) 0, Dietary Fiber (g) 3, Cholesterol (mg) 0, Sodium (mg) 22, Diabetic Exchanges: 1 fruit, 0.5 other carbohydrate, 1 fat

QUICK TIP:

Purchase cranberries when they're in season and freeze in airtight plastic bags for up to a year.

Vegetables
and Side Dishes

Almond Asparagus

* See photo on page 162
Asparagus is great and low in calories. The crunch of almonds adds a finishing touch.

MAKES 6 SERVINGS

1½ pounds asparagus spears
1 tablespoon margarine
2 tablespoons lemon juice
¼ cup slivered almonds, toasted
Salt and pepper to taste

Trim off the tough ends of the asparagus.

In a large non-stick skillet, melt the margarine. Add the asparagus and sauté at medium heat for 3 to 5 minutes. Add the lemon juice, cover, and simmer until crisp-tender. Add the almond slivers, and season with the salt and pepper, tossing gently. Serve.

Nutritional information per serving

Calories 83, Protein (g) 4, Carbohydrate (g) 6, Fat (g) 5, Calories from Fat (%) 51, Saturated Fat (g) 1, Dietary Fiber (g) 3, Cholesterol (mg) 0, Sodium (mg) 23, Diabetic Exchanges: 1 vegetable, 1 fat

QUICK TIP:

When selecting asparagus, pick out stalks that are firm from their closed tips to their green bottoms, avoiding spears with ridges, a sign they are drying out. Peeling asparagus is unnecessary and a lot of work—don't bother.

Baked Beans

Using canned beans makes this a great, easy-to-make version of everyone's favorite savory, sweet beans.

MAKES 12 SERVINGS

2 ounces Canadian bacon, chopped into ¼-inch pieces
½ pound ground sirloin
1 onion, chopped
½ cup light brown sugar
½ cup tomato sauce
1 tablespoon molasses
1 tablespoon cider vinegar
1 tablespoon Worcestershire sauce
1 teaspoon onion powder
1 (15-ounce) can butter beans, rinsed and drained
1 (15-ounce) can red kidney beans, rinsed and drained
2 (19-ounce) cans small white beans, rinsed and drained
Salt and pepper to taste

Preheat the oven to 350°F. In a large skillet, sauté the bacon until slightly brown. Add the sirloin and onion, and cook over medium-high heat until the sirloin is done. Drain any excess fat. Combine the meat mixture with the brown sugar, tomato sauce, molasses, vinegar, Worcestershire sauce, onion powder, butter beans, kidney beans, white beans, salt, and pepper; pour into a 2- or 3-quart baking dish. Bake for 40 to 50 minutes, or until bubbly. Serve.

Nutritional information per serving

Calories 187, Protein (g) 14, Carbohydrate (g) 37, Fat (g) 2, Calories from Fat (%) 6, Saturated Fat (g) 0, Dietary Fiber (g) 8, Cholesterol (mg) 12, Sodium (mg) 656, Diabetic Exchanges: 1.5 very lean meat, 2 starch, 1 vegetable

VEGETABLES & SIDE DISHES

White Beans ❄

White beans make a nutritious, filling side dish. They are great served over rice.

1 pound navy or pea beans
½ green bell pepper, seeded and chopped
3 stalks celery, chopped
1 onion, chopped
4 cloves garlic, minced
1 tablespoon olive oil
½ cup diced lean ham
3 bay leaves
1 tablespoon garlic powder
1 tablespoon Worcestershire sauce
2 tablespoons light brown sugar, optional
Salt and pepper to taste

Soak the beans overnight in water. Rinse and drain. Add olive oil to a large non-stick pot and sauté the green pepper, celery, onion, and garlic until tender. Add the beans and water to cover. Add the ham, bay leaves, garlic powder, Worcestershire sauce, brown sugar, salt, and pepper. Bring to a boil, lower heat, and simmer, covered, for 2 hours, or until the beans are tender. Remove the bay leaves before serving.

Nutritional information per serving
Calories 313, Protein (g) 20, Carbohydrate (g) 52, Fat (g) 4, Calories from Fat (%) 11, Saturated Fat (g) 1, Dietary Fiber (g) 20, Cholesterol (mg) 5, Sodium (mg) 218, Diabetic Exchanges: 2 very lean meat, 3 starch, 1.5 vegetable

Broccoli with Mustard Vinaigrette 🥕

Dress up broccoli with a light, mustardy dressing.

1 bunch fresh broccoli, trimmed and cut into florets
¼ cup finely chopped green onions (scallions)
2 cloves garlic, minced
½ teaspoon dried tarragon leaves
½ teaspoon dry mustard
1 tablespoon olive oil
2 tablespoons red wine vinegar
1 teaspoon Dijon mustard
⅛ teaspoon salt
¼ teaspoon freshly ground pepper

Place the broccoli in a microwave-safe dish with ¼ cup water. Cover, and cook 8 minutes, or until the broccoli is tender; drain.

Combine the green onion, garlic, tarragon, and dry mustard in a bowl. Whisk the oil into the green onion mixture. Add the vinegar, Dijon mustard, salt, and pepper. Pour the vinaigrette over the broccoli, tossing to coat. Serve hot or at room temperature.

Nutritional information per serving
Calories 39, Protein (g) 2, Carbohydrate (g) 4, Fat (g) 2, Calories from Fat (%) 41, Saturated Fat (g) 0, Dietary Fiber (g) 2, Cholesterol (mg) 0, Sodium (mg) 69, Diabetic Exchanges: 1 vegetable, 0.5 fat

Sicilian Broccoli

Sicilian Broccoli

Need a quick veggie with some spunk? Your family will adore this broccoli recipe that is prepared in the microwave.

MAKES 4 SERVINGS

1 (16-ounce) package broccoli florets
Salt and pepper to taste
⅓ cup chopped onion
¼ cup sliced kalamata olives
½ cup balsamic vinegar
1 tablespoon olive oil
½ cup shredded part-skim Mozzarella cheese

Lay the broccoli in a 10-inch microwave-safe dish. Add the salt and pepper to taste. Sprinkle with the onion, olives, vinegar, and oil, and microwave for 8 minutes, or until the broccoli is tender. Immediately sprinkle the broccoli with the cheese, and serve when the cheese is melted.

Nutritional information per serving
Calories 154, Protein (g) 7, Carbohydrate (g) 15, Fat (g) 8, Calories from Fat (%) 46, Saturated Fat (g) 2, Dietary Fiber (g) 4, Cholesterol (mg) 8, Sodium (mg) 243, Diabetic Exchanges: 3 vegetable, 1.5 fat

Broccoli with Lemon Ginger Sauce ✐

When you're bored with broccoli, this light, perky sauce will give it extra personality.

MAKES 6 SERVINGS

1 bunch broccoli (about 1½ pounds)
2 tablespoons dry sherry, optional
½ teaspoon ground ginger
½ cup fat-free canned chicken (or vegetable) broth
2 tablespoons lemon juice
1 teaspoon low-sodium soy sauce
1 teaspoon cornstarch mixed with 1½ teaspoons cold water

Cut the broccoli into medium-size florets, discarding the stems. Cook the broccoli in ¼ cup water in the microwave, in a microwave-safe covered dish, for 6 to 7 minutes, or until tender, or cook on the stove. Drain and set aside.

In the microwave or in a small pot on the stove, bring the sherry, ginger, broth, and lemon juice to a boil. Boil for 1 minute, reduce the heat, and add the soy sauce. Gradually add the cornstarch mixture, and cook over medium heat, stirring, until the mixture thickens, about 1 minute. Pour over broccoli and serve.

Nutritional information per serving
Calories 29, Protein (g) 3, Carbohydrate (g) 6, Fat (g) 0, Calories from Fat (%) 0, Saturated Fat (g) 0, Dietary Fiber (g) 3, Cholesterol (mg) 0, Sodium (mg) 96, Diabetic Exchanges: 1 vegetable

Broccoli Casserole ✐ ❄

Throw all the ingredients into one dish for a velvety, cheesy broccoli casserole.

MAKES 6 TO 8 SERVINGS

2 (10-ounce) packages frozen chopped broccoli, thawed and drained
1 egg
2 egg whites, slightly beaten
3 tablespoons all-purpose flour
1 (12-ounce) container reduced-fat cottage cheese
6 ounces reduced-fat pasteurized processed cheese spread, cut into pieces

Preheat the oven to 350°F.

Mix all ingredients in a large bowl. Pour into a 2-quart baking dish coated with non-stick cooking spray. Bake, uncovered, for 1 hour, or until bubbly. Serve.

Nutritional information per serving
Calories 121, Protein (g) 13, Carbohydrate (g) 9, Fat (g) 4, Calories from Fat (%) 26, Saturated Fat (g) 2, Dietary Fiber (g) 2, Cholesterol (mg) 37, Sodium (mg) 49, Diabetic Exchanges: 1.5 lean meat, 0.5 starch

QUICK TIP:

When buying broccoli, look for heads that are dark to almost purple in color. The purple color means that they are loaded with beta-carotene, a nutrient proven to reduce the risk of heart disease and cancer. Broccoli that is yellow in color has lost its vital nutrients.

Carrot Soufflé

I'm so excited to offer everyone this excellent, pudding-like carrot dish. From my daughter to my mother-in-law, this recipe gets high ratings.

MAKES 6 TO 8 SERVINGS

2 pounds carrots, peeled and sliced
½ cup sugar
2 egg whites
3 eggs
2 tablespoons all-purpose flour
1½ teaspoons baking powder
3 tablespoons margarine
1 teaspoon vanilla extract

Preheat the oven to 350°F.

Cook the carrot slices in a small amount of water over medium-high heat or in the microwave until very soft; drain.

In a mixing bowl, beat the carrots and add the sugar, egg whites, and eggs. Mix together the flour and baking powder, and add to the carrot mixture, mixing well. Add the margarine and vanilla, mixing well. Transfer to an oblong 2-quart non-stick baking dish coated with non-stick cooking spray, and bake for 35 to 45 minutes or until the center is set. Serve.

Nutritional information per serving

Calories 176, Protein (g) 5, Carbohydrate (g) 26, Fat (g) 6, Calories from Fat (%) 32, Saturated Fat (g) 1, Dietary Fiber (g) 3, Cholesterol (mg) 80, Sodium (mg) 219, Diabetic Exchanges: 2 vegetable, 1 other carbohydrate, 1 fat

Dijon Glazed Carrots

Spicy sweet and a delight to eat—don't miss this recipe.

MAKES 4 SERVINGS

1 pound carrots, peeled and sliced
1 tablespoon margarine
1 tablespoon Dijon mustard
2 tablespoons honey
¼ teaspoon white pepper
¼ teaspoon ground ginger

Steam the carrot slices in water until crisp-tender, about 10 minutes, or cook in the microwave. Drain the cooking liquid.

In a small saucepan, combine the margarine, mustard, honey, pepper, and ginger over low heat, stirring just until combined and the margarine is melted. Pour the sauce over the carrots, toss gently to coat, and serve.

Nutritional information per serving

Calories 111, Protein (g) 1, Carbohydrate (g) 20, Fat (g) 3, Calories from Fat (%) 24, Saturated Fat (g) 0, Dietary Fiber (g) 3, Cholesterol (mg) 0, Sodium (mg) 163, Diabetic Exchanges: 2 vegetable, 0.5 other carbohydrate, 0.5 fat

FOOD FACT:

Carrots are high in vitamin C, beta-carotene, and potassium.

VEGETABLES & SIDE DISHES

Orange Glazed Carrots

The citrus-sweet flavor of this glaze complements the carrots and adds color and nutrition.

MAKES 8 TO 10 SERVINGS

1 tablespoon margarine
¼ cup fat-free canned vegetable (or chicken) broth
2 pounds baby carrots or carrots cut into 2-inch pieces
1 cup orange marmalade
Salt and pepper to taste
2 tablespoons chopped parsley

In a large saucepan, bring the margarine and broth to a boil. Add the carrots, and cook, covered, over medium heat for 10 to 20 minutes, or until crisp-tender. Uncover, and stir in the marmalade. Cook, stirring, over low heat until the liquid has reduced to a glaze, 3 to 5 minutes. Season with the salt and pepper. Sprinkle with the parsley before serving.

Nutritional information per serving

Calories 125, Protein (g) 1, Carbohydrate (g) 30, Fat (g) 2, Calories from Fat (%) 11, Saturated Fat (g) 0, Dietary Fiber (g) 2, Cholesterol (mg) 0, Sodium (mg) 77, Diabetic Exchanges: 1.5 vegetable, 1.5 other carbohydrate

Orange Glazed Carrots

Cauliflower Supreme

A light cheese sauce coats the cauliflower in this tasty dish.

MAKES 4 SERVINGS

1 head cauliflower, cut into florets
½ cup plain nonfat yogurt
½ cup shredded reduced-fat sharp Cheddar cheese
½ teaspoon dry mustard
½ teaspoon cayenne pepper
Salt and pepper to taste

Preheat the oven to 400°F.

Place the cauliflower in a microwave-safe dish with ⅓ cup water; cook covered in the microwave for 8 minutes, or until crisp-tender. Drain and transfer to a non-stick baking dish coated with non-stick cooking spray.

In a small bowl, combine the yogurt, cheese, mustard, cayenne pepper, salt, and pepper, and spread over the cauliflower. Bake, uncovered, for 8 to 10 minutes, or until lightly browned. Serve.

Nutritional information per serving
Calories 97, Protein (g) 9, Carbohydrate (g) 10, Fat (g) 3, Calories from Fat (%) 25, Saturated Fat (g) 2, Dietary Fiber (g) 3, Cholesterol (mg) 8, Sodium (mg) 158, Diabetic Exchanges: 1 lean meat, 2 vegetable

Creamy Corn Casserole

Everyday pantry ingredients turn this into an extraordinary corn dish.

MAKES 8 TO 10 SERVINGS

2 (16-ounce) bags frozen corn
1 (7-ounce) can chopped green chilies, drained
½ cup skim milk
1 (8-ounce) package fat-free cream cheese, cut into pieces
Salt and pepper to taste
½ teaspoon paprika

Preheat the oven to 350°F.

In a 2-quart baking dish, combine the corn and green chilies.

In a small microwave- and oven-safe dish, heat the milk and cream cheese in the microwave until the cream cheese is melted, about 30 seconds. Mix with a fork to blend. Stir into the corn, and season with the salt and pepper. Sprinkle with the paprika. Bake for 30 minutes, or until bubbly. Serve.

Nutritional information per serving
Calories 108, Protein (g) 6, Carbohydrate (g) 22, Fat (g) 1, Calories from Fat (%) 6, Saturated Fat (g) 0, Dietary Fiber (g) 3, Cholesterol (mg) 2, Sodium (mg) 191, Diabetic Exchanges: 1.5 starch

VEGETABLES & SIDE DISHES

Tamale and Corn Casserole

I love tamales, and this easy casserole is a great way to enjoy them. Serve with extra salsa.

MAKES 6 TO 8 SERVINGS

2 (15-ounce) cans chicken, vegetarian, or reduced-fat
   meat tamales
1 (15-ounce) can cream-style corn
1 (4-ounce) can chopped green chilies
½ cup chopped green onions (scallions)
¼ cup evaporated skimmed milk
1 (7-ounce) can salsa verde
1½ teaspoons chili powder
1 teaspoon ground cumin
1 cup shredded reduced-fat Monterey Jack cheese

Preheat the oven to 375°F.

Cut the tamales into 1-inch pieces. Place in a single layer in a glass, 2-quart casserole dish coated with non-stick cooking spray. Cover with the corn, chilies, and green onion.

In a medium bowl, whisk the evaporated milk, salsa verde chili powder, and cumin to blend. Pour over the casserole. Sprinkle the cheese over the top. Bake until heated through and bubbling, about 30 to 35 minutes.

Nutritional information per serving

Calories 207, Protein (g) 11, Carbohydrate (g) 28, Fat (g) 6, Calories from Fat (%) 27, Saturated Fat (g) 4, Dietary Fiber (g) 4, Cholesterol (mg) 25, Sodium (mg) 913, Diabetic Exchanges: 1 lean meat, 2 starch

VEGETABLES & SIDE DISHES

Eggplant Parmesan

The ultimate version of a favorite of mine, this recipe was featured in Cooking Light *magazine in the "Make It Light" section.*

MAKES 8 SERVINGS

2 eggplants, peeled and cut into ½-inch slices
1 (28-ounce) can chopped tomatoes, with juice
2 (15-ounce) cans tomato sauce
1 (6-ounce) can tomato paste
½ cup white wine
1 teaspoon minced garlic
1 tablespoon dried basil leaves
1 tablespoon dried oregano leaves
3 egg whites
¼ cup water
1½ cups seasoned bread crumbs
2½ cups shredded reduced-fat Mozzarella cheese

Preheat the broiler.

Soak the eggplant slices in water to cover for 30 minutes. Pat dry.

In a large saucepan, combine the tomatoes with juice, tomato sauce, tomato paste, white wine, garlic, basil, and oregano. Bring to a boil, lower the heat, and cook 20 minutes.

In a medium bowl, mix the egg whites and water with a fork. Dip the eggplant slices in the egg white mixture, and coat in the bread crumbs. Place the eggplant on a non-stick baking sheet coated with non-stick cooking spray, and broil 5 minutes on each side, until lightly browned. Watch closely. Remove and set aside.

Lower the oven temperature to 350°F.

In a 2-quart oblong baking dish, layer half the sauce, half the eggplant, and half the Mozzarella cheese. Repeat the layers. Bake for 20 minutes, or until bubbly and the cheese is melted. Serve.

Nutritional information per serving
Calories 296, Protein (g) 18, Carbohydrate (g) 41, Fat (g) 6, Calories from Fat (%) 19, Saturated Fat (g) 4, Dietary Fiber (g) 8, Cholesterol (mg) 21, Sodium (mg) 1520, Diabetic Exchanges: 1.5 lean meat, 1 starch, 5 vegetable

Eggplant Parmesan

Eggplant Manicotti with Cheesy Spinach Filling

This meatless, high-fiber manicotti creatively uses eggplant instead of pasta—a fabulous way to enjoy veggies disguised in this tasty roll with a rich, wonderful tomato sauce.

MAKES 8 SERVINGS

1 (15-ounce) container reduced-fat Ricotta cheese
¼ cup grated Asiago or Parmesan cheese
1¼ cups chopped fresh baby spinach
¼ teaspoon ground nutmeg
1 egg white
Salt and pepper to taste
2 medium eggplants, peeled, cut lengthwise
    into 8⅓-inch slices
3 tablespoons olive oil
Tomato Sauce (recipe follows)
1 cup shredded part-skim Mozzarella cheese

Preheat the oven to 350°F.

In a medium bowl, mix the Ricotta and Asiago cheeses, spinach, nutmeg, egg white, salt, and pepper. Arrange the eggplants on foil-lined pans or non-stick baking pans coated with non-stick cooking spray. Drizzle with the olive oil. Sprinkle with salt and pepper. Bake until the eggplant slices are tender, about 12 to 15 minutes; cool.

Place one eggplant slice on the work surface. Place about 2 tablespoons of the Ricotta mixture near the narrower end of the eggplant slice. Roll up, enclosing the filling. Repeat with the remaining eggplant slices and filling.

Spread half the Tomato Sauce (see recipe) over the bottom of a 13 x 9 x 2-inch glass baking dish coated with non-stick cooking spray. Arrange the eggplant in a single layer atop the Tomato Sauce. Spoon the remaining sauce over the eggplant rolls. Sprinkle with the Mozzarella cheese. Bake until heated through, about 15 to 20 minutes. Serve immediately.

TOMATO SAUCE

1 onion, chopped
⅔ cup chopped carrot
1 teaspoon chopped garlic
½ cup dry red wine
1 (28-ounce) can crushed tomatoes with purée
1 cup fat-free canned chicken broth
1 teaspoon dried basil leaves
Salt and pepper to taste

In a large, heavy non-stick saucepan, sauté the onion, carrot, and garlic over medium-high heat until tender, 5 to 7 minutes. Add the wine, crushed tomatoes, broth, and basil, and bring to a boil. Reduce the heat; cover, and simmer for 15 to 20 minutes to blend the flavors. Season with salt and pepper.

Nutritional information per serving
Calories 236, Protein (g) 13, Carbohydrate (g) 20, Fat (g) 11, Calories from Fat (%) 40, Saturated Fat (g) 4, Dietary Fiber (g) 5, Cholesterol (mg) 24, Sodium (mg) 462, Diabetic Exchanges: 1 very lean meat, 4 vegetable, 1.5 fat

Green Bean and Artichoke Casserole

Close your eyes and take a bite of this fantastic casserole. You will think you are eating a stuffed artichoke.

MAKES 14 TO 16 SERVINGS

2 (16-ounce) packages frozen French-cut green
   beans, thawed
1 (14-ounce) can artichoke hearts, quartered and drained
2 cups Italian bread crumbs
½ cup olive oil
1 tablespoon minced garlic
⅓ cup grated Parmesan cheese

Preheat the oven to 350°F.

In a large mixing bowl, combine the green beans, artichoke hearts, bread crumbs, olive oil, garlic, and cheese. Place in a 3-quart oblong casserole coated with non-stick cooking spray, and bake for 30 minutes, or until lightly browned. Serve.

Nutritional information per serving

Calories 149, Protein (g) 4, Carbohydrate (g) 16, Fat (g) 8, Calories from Fat (%) 48, Saturated Fat (g) 1, Dietary Fiber (g) 2, Cholesterol (mg) 2, Sodium (mg) 300, Diabetic Exchanges: 0.5 starch, 1 vegetable, 1.5 fat

QUICK TIP:

Olive oil is a monounsaturated oil which has been shown to be particularly effective against high cholesterol. The majority of the fat in this recipe is from the olive oil, so enjoy!

Green Bean Casserole

When you're looking for a simple, tasty, green bean casserole with kid appeal, try this great recipe.

MAKES 8 SERVINGS

1 (16-ounce) package frozen French-cut green beans
1 onion, chopped
1 tablespoon margarine
2 tablespoons all-purpose flour
Salt and pepper to taste
½ cup skim milk
½ cup nonfat plain yogurt or fat-free sour cream
1 cup shredded reduced-fat sharp Cheddar cheese

Cook the green beans according to the package directions; drain well.

Preheat the boiler. In a small pot, sauté the onion in the margarine until tender. Blend in the flour, salt, and pepper. Gradually add the milk, stirring and cooking over medium heat until thickened and bubbly. Stir in the yogurt and green beans; heat thoroughly, about two minutes. Transfer to 1½-quart casserole. Sprinkle with the cheese, and broil in the oven until the cheese melts. Serve.

Nutritional information per serving

Calories 100, Protein (g) 7, Carbohydrate (g) 10, Fat (g) 4, Calories from Fat (%) 36, Saturated Fat (g) 2, Dietary Fiber (g) 2, Cholesterol (mg) 8, Sodium (mg) 129, Diabetic Exchanges: 0.5 very lean meat, 2 vegetable, 1 fat

VEGETABLES & SIDE DISHES

One-Step Macaroni and Cheese 🥕

This macaroni and cheese recipe from scratch is easier than the box. Teenagers rate it an A+. Use small shells or a small pasta for a variation.

MAKES 10 TO 12 SERVINGS

1 (16-ounce) package elbow macaroni
1 (8-ounce) package reduced-fat Cheddar cheese, shredded
1 (12-ounce) can evaporated skimmed milk
2½ cups skim milk
1 egg, beaten
¼ cup sugar, optional
Salt and pepper to taste

Preheat the oven to 350°F.

In a 2-quart casserole dish, mix together the macaroni and the cheese.

In a large bowl, mix together the evaporated milk, milk, egg, sugar, salt, and pepper, and pour over the macaroni. Bake, covered, for 1 hour, or until the liquid is almost absorbed. Uncover, and continue baking for 10 minutes. Serve.

Nutritional information per serving

Calories 240, Protein (g) 15, Carbohydrate (g) 34, Fat (g) 5, Calories from Fat (%) 17, Saturated Fat (g) 3, Dietary Fiber (g) 1, Cholesterol (mg) 30, Sodium (mg) 188, Diabetic Exchanges: 1 lean meat, 2 starch, 0.5 skim milk

Pineapple Noodle Kugel 🥕 ❄️

A kugel is a baked pudding usually made with noodles or potatoes and generally served as a side dish. This noodle pudding with pineapple makes a light side dish with a slightly sweet flavor.

MAKES 12 TO 16 SERVINGS

1 (16-ounce) package wide noodles
4 tablespoons margarine, melted
1 (16-ounce) container reduced-fat cottage cheese
2 cups nonfat plain yogurt
⅔ cup sugar
1 (20-ounce) can crushed pineapple, drained
2 teaspoons vanilla extract
4 egg whites

Preheat the oven to 350°F.

Cook the noodles according to the package directions, omitting any oil; drain. Combine with the margarine, cottage cheese, yogurt, sugar, pineapple, and vanilla.

In a medium bowl, beat the egg whites with a mixer on high speed until stiff. Fold into the noodle mixture.

Pour into a 13 x 9 x 2-inch non-stick baking pan coated with non-stick cooking spray. Bake, uncovered, for 60 to 75 minutes, or until mixture is set. Serve.

Nutritional information per serving

Calories 229, Protein (g) 10, Carbohydrate (g) 37, Fat (g) 4, Calories from Fat (%) 17, Saturated Fat (g) 1, Dietary Fiber (g) 1, Cholesterol (mg) 29, Sodium (mg) 194, Diabetic Exchanges: 1 lean meat, 1.5 starch, 0.5 fruit, 0.5 other carbohydrate

Noodle Pudding

This traditional noodle pudding, sometimes called kugel, is rich in flavor yet low in fat. It can be made ahead, refrigerated, and baked when ready to serve.

MAKES 12 TO 16 SERVINGS

1 (8-ounce) package wide noodles
3 tablespoons margarine, melted
½ cup sugar
1 cup reduced-fat cottage cheese
4 ounces reduced-fat cream cheese
1 cup nonfat plain yogurt
1 egg
2 egg whites
½ teaspoon vanilla extract

Preheat the oven to 350°F.

Boil the noodles according to the package directions, omitting any oil. Rinse, drain, and combine with the margarine, tossing evenly.

Place the noodles in a glass 13 x 9 x 2-inch baking pan coated with non-stick cooking spray.

In a food processor or mixer, mix the sugar, cottage cheese, cream cheese, yogurt, egg, egg whites, and vanilla, beating until smooth. Combine with the noodles, mixing well. Bake for 45 minutes to 1 hour, or until the mixture is set. Serve.

Nutritional information per serving

Calories 141, Protein (g) 6, Carbohydrate (g) 18, Fat (g) 5, Calories from Fat (%) 30, Saturated Fat (g) 2, Dietary Fiber (g) 0, Cholesterol (mg) 33, Sodium (mg) 138, Diabetic Exchanges: 0.5 very lean meat, 1 starch, 1 fat

Okra and Corn

Okra and Corn

Okra and tomatoes are popular Southern ingredients. The corn adds a splash of color and flavor to the okra in this simple recipe.

MAKES 6 SERVINGS

1 tablespoon margarine
1 onion, chopped
1 (16-ounce) bag frozen cut okra
1 (16-ounce) bag frozen corn
2 (10-ounce) cans diced tomatoes and green chilies

In a non-stick large pan, melt the margarine over medium heat, then sauté the onion until tender. Add the okra, and cook for 5 minutes, stirring. Add the corn and tomatoes and chilies, cooking and stirring until the okra is tender, about 20 minutes. Serve.

Nutritional information per serving

Calories 130, Protein (g) 5, Carbohydrate (g) 27, Fat (g) 3, Calories from Fat (%) 17, Saturated Fat (g) 0, Dietary Fiber (g) 5, Cholesterol (mg) 0, Sodium (mg) 406, Diabetic Exchanges: 1 starch, 2 vegetable, 0.5 fat

Garlic
Smashed Potatoes

*See photo on page 256
*I love this time-efficient, family favorite: you don't
even have to peel the potatoes! Many times, I've
added shredded Cheddar cheese and cooked bacon
for a deluxe version.*

MAKES 8 SERVINGS

3 pounds red potatoes, peeled and quartered
10 garlic cloves, peeled
2 tablespoons margarine
1 cup skim milk
⅓ cup plain nonfat yogurt
½ cup chopped green onions (scallions)
Salt and pepper to taste

Preheat the oven to 350°F.

On a non-stick baking sheet coated with non-stick cooking spray, spread the potatoes and garlic. Bake for 45 minutes, or until the potatoes are tender.

Mash potatoes in a large mixing bowl, then mix in the margarine, milk, and yogurt until creamy. Fold in the green onion, and add salt and pepper to taste.

Nutritional information per serving

Calories 173, Protein (g) 5, Carbohydrate (g) 32, Fat (g) 3, Calories from Fat (%) 16, Saturated Fat (g) 1, Dietary Fiber (g) 3, Cholesterol (mg) 1, Sodium (mg) 68, Diabetic Exchanges: 2 starch

Horseradish
Mashed Potatoes

*If you're a horseradish fan, this variation on classic
mashed potatoes will be a delightful experience. It's
especially good with beef and pork dishes.*

MAKES 8 SERVINGS

3 pounds Yukon Gold potatoes
3 tablespoons margarine
½ cup fat-free sour cream
2 tablespoons prepared horseradish
1 teaspoon minced garlic
Salt and pepper to taste

Place the potatoes in a large pot with water to cover. Bring to a boil, and boil about 30 minutes, or until the potatoes are tender. Peel the potatoes, and place in a large mixing bowl. Add the margarine, sour cream, horseradish, and garlic, beating until creamy. Season with the salt and pepper and serve.

Nutritional information per serving

Calories 181, Protein (g) 4, Carbohydrate (g) 32, Fat (g) 4, Calories from Fat (%) 22, Saturated Fat (g) 1, Dietary Fiber (g) 3, Cholesterol (mg) 0, Sodium (mg) 84, Diabetic Exchanges: 2 starch, 0.5 fat

QUICK TIP:

Beat potatoes until they are light; overbeating will only make them sticky and starchy.

Wasabi Mashed Potatoes

Adding new flavors to familiar ingredients is a great way to introduce new tastes to home cooking. Wasabi and soy sauce add an Asian flair to this incredibly tasty recipe.

MAKES 6 TO 8 SERVINGS

2½ pounds baking potatoes
2 tablespoons margarine
1 tablespoon low-sodium soy sauce
1 teaspoon minced garlic
1 to 2 teaspoons wasabi
½ cup nonfat plain yogurt

Combine the potatoes and enough water to cover in a large saucepan; bring to a boil. Lower the heat, cover, and cook until tender, about 30 to 40 minutes. Drain.

Peel the potatoes, and place them in a mixing bowl with the margarine, blending until smooth. Slowly add the soy sauce, garlic, wasabi, and yogurt, beating until creamy. Serve immediately.

Nutritional information per serving

Calories 139, Protein (g) 4, Carbohydrate (g) 25, Fat (g) 3, Calories from Fat (%) 19, Saturated Fat (g) 1, Dietary Fiber (g) 2, Cholesterol (mg) 0, Sodium (mg) 102, Diabetic Exchanges: 1.5 starch

FOOD FACT:

Wasabi is a Japanese version of horseradish that comes from the root of an Asian plant. This green condiment has a sharp, pungent, fiery flavor.

VEGETABLES & SIDE DISHES

Easy Potato Casserole

When you are overwhelmed with preparing dinner, here's a super potato recipe. One night without warning, my husband said, "Company's coming," so I threw this recipe together and everyone asked for a copy of the recipe. Make this ahead, and refrigerate it until you're ready to cook it.

MAKES 8 SERVINGS

1 (32-ounce) bag frozen hash brown potatoes
2 cups fat-free sour cream
1 onion, chopped
4 tablespoons margarine, melted
1 (10¾-ounce) can 98% fat-free cream
  of mushroom soup
6 slices reduced-fat American cheese, cut into pieces
Salt and pepper to taste
Paprika, for garnish

Preheat the oven to 350°F.

In a 3-quart casserole dish coated with non-stick cooking spray, combine the potatoes, sour cream, onion, margarine, mushroom soup, cheese, salt, and pepper, mixing well. Sprinkle with the paprika. Bake for 1¼ to 1½ hours, or until the casserole is bubbly. Serve.

Nutritional information per serving
Calories 290, Protein (g) 10, Carbohydrate (g) 37, Fat (g) 10, Calories from Fat (%) 33, Saturated Fat (g) 4, Dietary Fiber (g) 2, Cholesterol (mg) 13, Sodium (mg) 663, Diabetic Exchanges: 0.5 lean meat, 2.5 starch, 1 fat

Southwestern Stuffed Potatoes

Potatoes stuffed with easily available Mexican ingredients make this a cinch. Serve with salsa.

MAKES 6 SERVINGS

3 medium baking potatoes
2 tablespoons margarine
2 tablespoons skim milk
½ cup fat-free or light sour cream
1 (4-ounce) can diced green chilies, optional
1 (15¼-ounce) can corn, drained
4 green onions (scallions), chopped
1 cup shredded reduced-fat Cheddar cheese
Paprika, for garnish

Preheat the oven to 400°F.

Wash the potatoes well, and dry thoroughly. Place the potatoes directly on the oven rack, and bake for approximately 1 hour, or until soft when squeezed. Reduce the heat to 350°F.

Cut each potato in half lengthwise. Scoop out the inside, leaving a thin shell. In a mixer, mash the potato flesh with the margarine, skim milk, and sour cream, mixing well. Stir in the green chilies, corn, green onions, and cheese, combining well. Spoon the mixture into the shells. Top with the paprika. Bake for about 15 minutes, or until the cheese is melted and the potatoes are heated. Serve.

Nutritional information per serving
Calories 216, Protein (g) 11, Carbohydrate (g) 29, Fat (g) 8, Calories from Fat (%) 30, Saturated Fat (g) 3, Dietary Fiber (g) 4, Cholesterol (mg) 10, Sodium (mg) 381, Diabetic Exchanges: 1 lean meat, 2 starch, 0.5 fat

Sweet Potato Oven Fries

Sweet Potato Oven Fries

This recipe is requested every time I prepare it on television or for guests. It's low in saturated fat and high in fiber. For a sweet variation, sprinkle with 1 teaspoon each cinnamon and nutmeg.

MAKES 4 TO 6 SERVINGS

4 medium to large sweet potatoes (yams)
¼ cup olive oil
Salt to taste
Parsley, for garnish

FOOD FACT:

Sweet potatoes should not be refrigerated unless they have been cooked. Store them in a cool, dry location.

Preheat the oven to 400°F.

Cut the sweet potatoes lengthwise into ½-inch-thick strips, and toss with olive oil. Arrange the potatoes on a non-stick baking sheet coated with non-stick cooking spray. Bake the potatoes for 15 to 20 minutes, or until golden brown on the bottom. Turn the potatoes over, and bake for 15 to 20 more minutes, or until golden brown all over. Sprinkle with salt, add parsley for color, and serve.

Nutritional information per serving

Calories 166, Protein (g) 1, Carbohydrate (g) 22, Fat (g) 9, Calories from Fat (%) 46, Saturated Fat (g) 1, Dietary Fiber (g) 3, Cholesterol (mg) 0, Sodium (mg) 30, Diabetic Exchanges: 1.5 starch, 1.5 fat

Roasted Sweet and White Potatoes

I repeat this easy (no peeling needed) recipe whenever I want a zippy side dish.

MAKES 8 SERVINGS

3 tablespoons olive oil
1 pound sweet potatoes (yams) unpeeled,
   cut into 2-inch chunks
1 pound baking potatoes, unpeeled,
   cut into 2-inch chunks
4 cloves garlic, unpeeled
¼ cup chopped parsley
1 teaspoon dried thyme leaves
½ teaspoon pepper
Salt to taste

Preheat the oven to 450°F.

In a large roasting pan, toss the potatoes with the oil and garlic. Bake, shaking the pan every 15 minutes, until the potatoes are browned and crisp and the garlic is soft, about 45 minutes to 1 hour.

Remove the garlic, press the softened cloves, and slip from the skins, discarding the skins. Toss the potatoes with the garlic, parsley, thyme, pepper, and salt. Serve immediately.

Nutritional information per serving

Calories 143, Protein (g) 3, Carbohydrate (g) 25, Fat (g) 5, Calories from Fat (%) 29, Saturated Fat (g) 1, Dietary Fiber (g) 3, Cholesterol (mg) 0, Sodium (mg) 21, Diabetic Exchanges: 1.5 starch, 1 fat

QUICK TIP:

The sweet potato is not really a potato—not even a distant cousin. Potatoes are tubers; sweet potatoes are roots.

Praline Stuffed Yams 🥕 ❄️

Individually stuffed, nutritious, mouth-watering treats with this crumbly topping are hard to beat. Make extra and freeze until ready to serve.

MAKES 4 TO 6 SERVINGS

VEGETABLES
& SIDE DISHES

3 pounds small to medium sweet potatoes (yams), unpeeled
¼ cup sugar
½ teaspoon ground cinnamon, divided
¼ cup skim milk
2 teaspoons vanilla extract, divided
3 tablespoons margarine, melted
⅓ cup all-purpose flour
¼ cup light brown sugar
¼ cup chopped pecans

Preheat the oven to 400°F.

Place the yams on a non-stick baking sheet and cook for 1 hour, or until tender.

Cut a thin slice off the top of each potato. Carefully scoop the yam out of its skin into a large bowl, leaving ¼-inch thick shells.

In a mixing bowl, mash the yams; add the sugar, ¼ teaspoon cinnamon, milk, and 1 teaspoon vanilla, mixing until smooth. Spoon the mixture evenly into the shells. Place on a non-stick baking sheet.

In a small bowl, mix the margarine, flour, brown sugar, pecans, remaining 1 teaspoon vanilla, and remaining ¼ teaspoon cinnamon together until crumbly. Sprinkle evenly over the yams.

Reduce the oven to 350°F, and continue baking 15 minutes, or until the topping is brown. Serve.

Nutritional information per serving

Calories 412, Protein (g) 5, Carbohydrate (g) 82, Fat (g) 9, Calories from Fat (%) 19, Saturated Fat (g) 1, Dietary Fiber (g) 8, Cholesterol (mg) 0, Sodium (mg) 154, Diabetic Exchanges: 4 starch, 1.5 other carbohydrate, 1 fat

QUICK TIP:

Pricking the sweet potato keeps them from bursting during baking. Lining the pan with foil makes an easy clean up.

Praline Stuffed Yams

Sweet Potato Casserole with Praline Topping 🥕 ❄️

Use freshly baked or canned yams to create this indulgence that is just too good to save for the holidays.

MAKES 8 TO 10 SERVINGS

3 cups cooked mashed sweet potatoes (yams)
½ cup sugar
1 egg
1 egg white
1 (5-ounce) can evaporated skimmed milk
1½ teaspoons vanilla extract
Praline Topping (recipe follows)

Preheat the oven to 350°F.

In a mixing bowl, blend the potatoes, sugar, egg, egg white, evaporated skimmed milk, and vanilla. Place in a 2-quart casserole dish coated with non-stick cooking spray, and cover with Praline Topping (see recipe at right). Bake for 45 minutes until topping is browned and casserole is thoroughly heated. Serve.

PRALINE TOPPING

1 cup light brown sugar
½ cup all-purpose flour
½ teaspoon ground cinnamon
6 tablespoons margarine, melted
1 teaspoon vanilla extract
½ cup chopped pecans, optional

In a medium bowl, mix together the brown sugar, flour, and cinnamon. Add the margarine, vanilla, and pecans, stirring until crumbly.

Nutritional information per serving

Calories 333, Protein (g) 5, Carbohydrate (g) 62, Fat (g) 8, Calories from Fat (%) 20, Saturated Fat (g) 1, Dietary Fiber (g) 2, Cholesterol (mg) 22, Sodium (mg) 132, Diabetic Exchanges: 2 starch, 2 other carbohydrate, 1 fat

Parmesan Potato Sticks

Prepare plenty of these crispy, seasoned, oven-baked fries, as they disappear quickly. If your potato sticks are large, you may need more coating.

MAKES 4 TO 6 SERVINGS

½ cup Italian bread crumbs
2 tablespoons grated Parmesan cheese
2 tablespoons chopped parsley
Salt and pepper to taste
¼ teaspoon garlic powder
3 medium baking potatoes, peeled and
    cut into large sticks
¼ cup skim milk
1 tablespoon margarine, melted

Preheat the oven to 375°F.

Line a baking sheet with foil. In a shallow dish, combine the bread crumbs, cheese, parsley, salt, pepper, and garlic powder. Dip the potatoes in the milk and then in the crumb mixture. Lay the sticks on the prepared baking sheet. Drizzle with the margarine. Bake for 45 minutes to 1 hour, or until crisp. Serve.

Nutritional information per serving

Calories 117, Protein (g) 5, Carbohydrate (g) 21, Fat (g) 3, Calories from Fat (%) 20, Saturated Fat (g) 1, Dietary Fiber (g) 2, Cholesterol (mg) 2, Sodium (mg) 332, Diabetic Exchanges: 1.5 starch

Southwestern Rice

Mildly flavored with peppers and topped with cheese, this creamy baked rice dish makes you look forward to every bite. It's a great side dish with barbecue.

MAKES 10 SERVINGS

1 onion, chopped
5 cups cooked rice
2 cups nonfat plain yogurt
1 cup reduced-fat cottage cheese
2 (4-ounce) cans diced green chilies, drained
Salt and pepper to taste
¾ cup shredded reduced-fat sharp Cheddar cheese

Preheat the oven to 350°F.

In a non-stick skillet, sauté the onion until tender. Combine with the rice, yogurt, cottage cheese, green chilies, salt, pepper, and cheese. Place in a 2-quart casserole dish coated with non-stick cooking spray. Bake for 20 minutes or until thoroughly heated. Serve.

Nutritional Information per serving

Calories 205, Protein (g) 13, Carbohydrate (g) 29, Fat (g) 4, Calories from Fat (%) 16, Saturated Fat (g) 2, Dietary Fiber (g) 1, Cholesterol (mg) 11, Sodium (mg) 323, Diabetic Exchanges: 1 very lean meat, 1.5 starch, 0.5 skim milk

VEGETABLES
& SIDE DISHES

Summer Rice

Pick ingredients fresh from the garden for this exciting summer side with a Mediterranean personality.

MAKES 6 SERVINGS

1 cup chopped onion
1 teaspoon minced garlic
1 cup rice
1 (14½-ounce) can vegetable broth
2 cups chopped tomatoes
1 cup diced cucumber
½ teaspoon dried basil leaves
¼ cup thinly chopped green onions (scallions)
½ cup crumbled Feta cheese

In a medium non-stick saucepan, sauté the onion and garlic over medium heat for 5 minutes. Add the rice; cook 1 minute, stirring constantly. Add the broth, and bring to a boil. Reduce the heat; cover, and simmer 20 minutes, or until the rice is done. Stir in the tomato, cucumber, and basil, mixing well. Gradually stir in the green onion and Feta cheese. Serve.

Nutritional information per serving

Calories 180, Protein (g) 6, Carbohydrate (g) 32, Fat (g) 3, Calories from Fat (%) 17, Saturated Fat (g) 2, Dietary Fiber (g) 2, Cholesterol (mg) 11, Sodium (mg) 451, Diabetic Exchanges: 1.5 starch, 1.5 vegetable

Wild Rice and Peppers

Wild rice, peppers, and mushrooms create this enticing side dish. Here's the perfect side that keeps the plate attractive while rating very high in flavor.

MAKES 6 TO 8 SERVINGS

1 (6-ounce) box long-grain and wild rice mix
2 tablespoons olive oil
1 bunch green onions (scallions), chopped
1 red bell pepper, seeded, sliced in long, thin slices
1 green bell pepper, seeded, sliced in long, thin slices
½ pound mushrooms, sliced
½ cup cooked white rice

Cook the wild rice according to the package directions.

In a large non-stick skillet, heat the olive oil and sauté the green onions, red and green peppers, and mushrooms until tender, 5 to 7 minutes. Stir in cooked wild rice and white rice, and serve.

Nutritional information per serving

Calories 163, Protein (g) 4, Carbohydrate (g) 23, Fat (g) 7, Calories from Fat (%) 35, Saturated Fat (g) 1, Dietary Fiber (g) 2, Cholesterol (mg) 0, Sodium (mg) 352, Diabetic Exchanges: 1.5 starch, 1 fat

Rice and Noodles

When you can't decide which to serve, enjoy both rice and noodles with a toasty flavor. Kids especially like this dish.

MAKES 6 SERVINGS

1 cup uncooked rice
1 tablespoon margarine
1 cup medium noodles
2¾ cups fat-free canned vegetable (or chicken) broth
Salt and pepper to taste

In a heavy non-stick saucepan, brown the rice in the margarine, stirring. Add the noodles, broth, salt, and pepper. Bring the mixture to a boil, lower the heat, and simmer, covered, for 20 to 30 minutes, or until the rice and noodles are done. Serve.

Nutritional information per serving

Calories 160, Protein (g) 4, Carbohydrate (g) 30, Fat (g) 2, Calories from Fat (%) 13, Saturated Fat (g) 0, Dietary Fiber (g) 1, Cholesterol (mg) 6, Sodium (mg) 309, Diabetic Exchanges: 2 starch

Rice and Noodles

Wild Rice and Barley Pilaf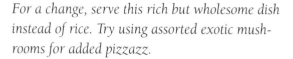

Here's a great way to try barley—hearty and simple with a fancy flair.

MAKES 6 TO 8 SERVINGS

1 (6-ounce) package long-grain and wild rice mix (with seasoning packet)
½ cup pearl barley
3 cups fat-free canned vegetable (or chicken) broth
1 tablespoon margarine
⅓ cup sliced almonds, toasted

Preheat the oven to 325°F.

In a large saucepan, combine the rice, seasoning packet, barley, broth, and margarine. Bring to a boil. Reduce the heat, cover, and simmer for 10 minutes.

Spoon into a 1½-quart casserole dish coated with non-stick cooking spray. Bake covered for 1 hour, or until the rice and barley are tender and the liquid is absorbed. Fluff with a fork; stir in the almonds.

Nutritional information per serving

Calories 164, Protein (g) 5, Carbohydrate (g) 28, Fat (g) 4, Calories from Fat (%) 21, Saturated Fat (g) 0, Dietary Fiber (g) 3, Cholesterol (mg) 0, Sodium (mg) 567, Diabetic Exchanges: 2 starch, 0.5 fat

Barley Casserole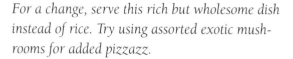

For a change, serve this rich but wholesome dish instead of rice. Try using assorted exotic mushrooms for added pizzazz.

MAKES 6 TO 8 SERVINGS

1 cup medium barley
1 (1-ounce) envelope onion soup mix
4 cups water
1 tablespoon margarine
½ pound fresh mushrooms, sliced

Preheat the oven to 350°F.

In a 3-quart casserole dish, combine the barley, onion soup mix, and water.

In a small non-stick skillet, melt the margarine over medium-low heat and sauté the mushrooms until tender, about 5 minutes. Add to the barley mixture. Cover with a lid or tightly with foil, and bake for 1 to 1¼ hours, or until the barley is done and the liquid is absorbed. Serve.

Nutritional information per serving

Calories 122, Protein (g) 4, Carbohydrate (g) 23, Fat (g) 2, Calories from Fat (%) 15, Saturated Fat (g) 0, Dietary Fiber (g) 5, Cholesterol (mg) 0, Sodium (mg), 457 Diabetic Exchanges: 1.5 starch

FOOD FACT:

Barley is a whole grain, high in fiber, which is a good way to include fiber in your diet.

Dirty Rice ❄

Seasoned meat and rice combine to create a traditional Louisiana-style side dish or meal.

MAKES 4 TO 6 SERVINGS

1 pound ground sirloin
2 cloves garlic, minced
2 stalks celery, chopped
1 onion, chopped
1 tablespoon chopped parsley
1 green bell pepper, seeded and chopped
1 tablespoon Worcestershire sauce
¼ teaspoon cayenne pepper
¼ teaspoon pepper
1 cup uncooked rice
1 (14½-ounce) can beef broth
¾ cup water

In a large non-stick skillet, cook the beef, garlic, celery, onion, parsley, and green pepper over medium-high heat until the meat is done and the vegetables are tender. Add the Worcestershire sauce, cayenne pepper, and pepper, stirring well. Add the rice, broth, and water, mixing well. Bring to a boil; reduce heat, cover, and cook for 25 to 30 minutes, or until the rice is done.

Nutritional information per serving

Calories 227, Protein (g) 19, Carbohydrate (g) 30, Fat (g) 4, Calories from Fat (%) 14, Saturated Fat (g) 1, Dietary Fiber (g) 2, Cholesterol (mg) 40, Sodium (mg) 388, Diabetic Exchanges: 2 very lean meat, 1.5 starch, 1 vegetable

QUICK TIP:

This hearty dish can be used as an entree if desired and served with a salad.

Spinach and Black Bean Enchiladas

Spinach and Black Bean Enchiladas

These simple ingredients give you a tasty and meatless enchilada that will be a quick favorite. Try different varieties of tortillas.

MAKES 8 ENCHILADAS

1 (10-ounce) package frozen chopped spinach, thawed
1 (15-ounce) can black beans, rinsed and drained
1 (1¼-ounce) package taco seasoning mix
1 cup water
1 cup fat-free sour cream, divided
8 (6- to 8-inch) flour tortillas
1 (10-ounce) can enchilada sauce
1½ cups shredded reduced-fat Cheddar cheese
2 tablespoons sliced green onions (scallions)

Preheat the oven to 375°F.

In a non-stick skillet, heat the spinach, black beans, taco seasoning mix, and water. Bring to a boil, reduce heat, and cook for 8 to 10 minutes, or until the mixture is thickened. Remove from the heat, and stir in ½ cup sour cream.

On each tortilla, spread 1 tablespoon enchilada sauce, about ⅓ cup spinach mixture, and 1 heaping tablespoon cheese. Roll up each tortilla placing the seam-side down in an oblong baking dish coated with nonstick cooking spray. Spread the remaining enchilada sauce over the filled enchiladas, cover, and bake for 15 to 18 minutes.

Uncover and garnish with the remaining cheese. Continue baking for 5 minutes longer, or until the cheese is melted. Serve with the remaining sour cream, and sprinkle with the green onion.

Nutritional information per serving

Calories 266, Protein (g) 14, Carbohydrate (g) 39, Fat (g) 5, Calories from Fat (%) 18, Saturated Fat (g) 3, Dietary Fiber (g) 5, Cholesterol (mg) 11, Sodium (mg) 1195, Diabetic Exchanges: 1.5 very lean meat, 2.5 starch

VEGETABLES & SIDE DISHES

Crêpes Florentine

Buy already made crêpes in the grocery to make this recipe very simple. The cheesy spinach filling baked in crispy crêpes was enthusiastically received at my house.

MAKES 10 TO 12 CRÊPES

2 (10-ounce) packages frozen chopped spinach
½ pound fresh mushrooms
½ cup chopped onion
⅓ cup all-purpose flour
1¼ cups skim milk
⅛ teaspoon pepper
⅛ teaspoon ground nutmeg
1 cup shredded reduced-fat Swiss cheese
Salt and pepper to taste
12 commercially prepared crêpes
1 tablespoon margarine, melted
2 tablespoons grated Parmesan cheese

Preheat the oven to 350°F.

Cook the spinach as directed on the package, and drain well; set aside. In a small non-stick skillet, sauté the mushrooms and onion until tender, about 5 minutes.

In a 2-quart saucepan, mix the flour and milk, and cook over medium heat, stirring about 5 minutes until smooth and thickened. Add the pepper, nutmeg, Swiss cheese, spinach, mushrooms, and onions. Season to taste. Blend well. Remove from the heat when the cheese is melted.

Place 1 heaping tablespoon of the spinach mixture on a crêpe, with the brown side of the crêpe facing down. Roll the crêpe and place seam down in a 2-quart baking dish coated with nonstick cooking spray. Repeat with the remaining crêpes. Drizzle the crêpes with the melted margarine, and sprinkle with the Parmesan cheese. Bake for 15 to 20 minutes, or until heated.

Nutritional information per serving

Calories 191, Protein (g) 11, Carbohydrate (g) 18, Fat (g) 9, Calories from Fat (%) 41, Saturated Fat (g) 3, Dietary Fiber (g) 2, Cholesterol (mg) 85, Sodium (mg) 177, Diabetic Exchanges: 0.5 lean meat, 1 starch, 1 vegetable, 1.5 fat

VEGETABLES & SIDE DISHES

Cheesy Spicy Spinach

This special and wonderful cheesy spinach gets requested extremely often. The Mexican cheese gives the recipe extra spice.

MAKES 10 SERVINGS

3 (10-ounce) packages frozen chopped spinach
½ cup spinach liquid, reserved from cooking spinach
1 onion, chopped
3 tablespoons all-purpose flour
1 cup skim milk
6 ounces mild Mexican processed cheese spread
1 tablespoon Worcestershire sauce
½ teaspoon garlic powder

Cook the spinach according to the package directions. Drain well, reserving ½ cup spinach liquid; set aside.

In a non-stick pan, sauté the onion until tender, about 5 minutes. Add the flour and stir. Gradually add the milk and spinach liquid to make a sauce. Cook over medium heat until the mixture thickens. Add the cheese, Worcestershire sauce, and garlic powder, cooking until the cheese is melted. Add the spinach, mixing well. Serve.

Nutritional information per serving
Calories 107, Protein (g) 8, Carbohydrate (g) 10, Fat (g) 5, Calories from Fat (%) 38, Saturated Fat (g) 3, Dietary Fiber (g) 3, Cholesterol (mg) 15, Sodium (mg) 339, Nutritional Exchanges: 0.5 very lean meat, 2 vegetable, 1 fat

Spinach Mushroom Casserole

This light spinach dish, topped with sautéed mushrooms, is great for a large party, as it is easily doubled.

MAKES 6 SERVINGS

2 (10-ounce) packages frozen chopped spinach
½ pound fresh mushrooms, sliced
3 slices reduced-fat American cheese, diced
1 (5-ounce) can evaporated skimmed milk
¼ teaspoon garlic powder
Salt and pepper, optional

Preheat the oven to 350°F.

Cook the spinach according to the package directions; drain well.

In a small non-stick skillet sauté the mushrooms until tender; set aside.

In a heavy saucepan, melt the cheese in the milk over low heat. Turn the spinach into a shallow baking dish coated with nonstick cooking spray. Sprinkle with the garlic powder. Add the cheese mixture, and stir until thoroughly mixed. Season with salt and pepper. Top with the sautéed mushrooms and drippings. Bake, uncovered, for 20 minutes, or until well heated. Serve.

Nutritional information per serving
Calories 89, Protein (g) 8, Carbohydrate (g) 9, Fat (g) 3, Calories from Fat (%) 29, Saturated Fat (g) 2, Dietary Fiber (g) 3, Cholesterol (mg) 9, Sodium (mg) 279, Diabetic Exchanges: 0.5 lean meat, 2 vegetable

VEGETABLES & SIDE DISHES

Italian Spinach Pie

Here's the perfect solution when you have vegetarians and meat eaters at one table. It makes a special spinach side for any main course and a delicious main dish in its own right.

MAKES 6 SERVINGS

½ cup chopped onion

2 (10-ounce) packages frozen chopped spinach

1 (14-ounce) can artichoke hearts, quartered, drained

1 cup fat-free or low-fat Ricotta cheese

¼ cup skim milk

2 egg whites, beaten

½ teaspoon garlic powder

1 (8-ounce) can tomato sauce

½ teaspoon dried oregano leaves

½ teaspoon dried basil leaves

1 cup shredded part-skim Mozzarella cheese

Preheat the oven to 350°F.

In a non-stick skillet, sauté the onion over medium heat until tender, about 5 minutes. Meanwhile, cook the spinach according to the package directions; drain very well.

In a large bowl, combine the onion, spinach, artichoke hearts, Ricotta cheese, milk, egg whites, and garlic powder, mixing well. Spoon the mixture into a 9-inch pie plate coated with non-stick cooking spray. Mix the tomato sauce with the oregano and basil, and spread evenly over the spinach. Bake for 15 minutes. Sprinkle with the Mozzarella cheese, and continue baking for 5 to 10 minutes longer, until the cheese is melted. Serve.

Nutritional information per serving

Calories 143, Protein (g) 16, Carbohydrate (g) 13, Fat (g) 3, Calories from Fat (%) 21, Saturated Fat (g) 2, Dietary Fiber (g) 4, Cholesterol (mg) 14, Sodium (mg) 590, Diabetic Exchanges: 1.5 very lean meat, 3 vegetable

QUICK TIP:

Some varieties of cheese may be frozen—the lower the moisture content of the cheese, the better it is for freezing. However, once the cheese has been frozen, only use it as a cooking ingredient, not as table cheese. Good freezing cheeses include Cheddar, Mozzarella, Edam, Gouda, Provolone, and Parmesan.

VEGETABLES & SIDE DISHES

Spinach Oriental

Stir-fry mushrooms and spinach with Oriental seasonings for an instant Asian dish. Prepackaged spinach and pre-sliced mushrooms are time savers.

MAKES 4 SERVINGS

½ pound fresh mushrooms, sliced
½ cup red onion, thinly sliced and separated into rings
¼ teaspoon ground ginger
1 teaspoon sesame seeds
½ teaspoon minced garlic
¼ cup water
1 teaspoon cornstarch
½ teaspoon sugar
Dash cayenne pepper
1 tablespoon low-sodium soy sauce
½ teaspoon dark sesame oil, optional
1 (10-ounce) bag fresh spinach, washed and stemmed

Heat a large non-stick skillet over medium-high heat until hot. Add the mushrooms, onion, ginger, sesame seeds, and garlic; sauté 5 minutes.

Combine the water with the cornstarch, and add to the mushroom mixture along with the sugar, cayenne, soy sauce, and sesame oil; stir well. Add the spinach, and cook about 2 minutes, while stirring constantly, until the spinach begins to wilt.

Nutritional information per serving

Calories 48, Protein (g) 4, Carbohydrate (g) 8, Fat (g) 1, Calories from Fat (%) 14, Saturated Fat (g) 0, Dietary Fiber (g) 3, Cholesterol (mg) 0, Sodium (mg) 157, Diabetic Exchanges: 1.5 vegetable

QUICK TIP:

Swiss Chard can be substituted in recipes that call for spinach. Red stemmed chard has a faint beet flavor. The best method for preparing Swiss chard is to remove the stems, cut them into pieces, and sauté them with the leaves or simmer them in a skillet with olive oil or garlic.

VEGETABLES & SIDE DISHES

Squash Rockefeller

Make ahead, refrigerate, and bake before serving. Visually attractive and full of flavor, this squash stuffed with spinach is a stand-out recipe.

MAKES 12 STUFFED SQUASH

6 medium yellow squash
2 (10-ounce) packages frozen chopped spinach
1 bunch green onions (scallions), chopped
½ cup finely chopped parsley
3 stalks celery, chopped
2 cloves garlic, minced
¼ cup margarine
½ cup Italian bread crumbs
Hot pepper sauce to taste
Salt and pepper to taste

Preheat the oven to 350°F. Cut each squash in half lengthwise. Steam in ½ inch water, covered, on the stove or in the microwave, until almost tender. Cool slightly, and scoop out the flesh, being careful not to break the shell; discard the flesh. Cook the spinach according to the package directions; drain well. In a non-stick skillet, melt the margarine and sauté the green onions, parsley, celery, and garlic until tender. Combine with the spinach, bread crumbs, hot pepper sauce, salt, and pepper, mixing well. Stuff the squash shells with the mixture. Bake for 20 minutes, or until well-heated. Serve.

Nutritional information per serving

Calories 89, Protein (g) 3, Carbohydrate (g) 11, Fat (g) 4, Calories from Fat (%) 40, Saturated Fat (g) 1, Dietary Fiber (g) 4, Cholesterol (mg) 0, Sodium (mg) 162, Diabetic Exchanges: 2 vegetable, 1 fat

Squash Rockefeller

Squash Casserole

Squash Casserole

This recipe has been in my family for years. Even if you're not a squash fan, this creamy-corn, squash casserole will win you over. You can make it ahead and freeze uncooked. Be sure to defrost to room temperature before baking.

MAKES 6 TO 8 SERVINGS

2 pounds fresh squash, thinly sliced

2 green bell peppers, seeded and chopped

1 large onion, chopped

2 tablespoons canola oil

1 (15-ounce) can cream-style corn

1 tablespoon sugar

¼ cup cornmeal

Salt and pepper to taste

Preheat the oven to 350°F. On the stove or in the microwave, steam the fresh squash in ¼ cup water for about 10 minutes or until tender. Drain and mash or purée the squash in a food processor. In a large non-stick skillet, sauté the green pepper and onion in the oil until tender. Combine the squash, onion mixture, corn, sugar, and cornmeal. Add salt and pepper. Place the mixture in a 2-quart casserole dish coated with nonstick cooking spray. Bake for 30 minutes, or until bubbly and thoroughly heated. Serve.

Nutritional information per serving

Calories 136, Protein (g) 3, Carbohydrate (g) 25, Fat (g) 4, Calories from Fat (%) 24, Saturated Fat (g) 0, Dietary Fiber (g) 4, Cholesterol (mg) 0, Sodium (mg) 173, Diabetic Exchanges: 1 starch, 1.5 vegetable, 0.5 fat

Corn Bread Dressing

Use corn bread mix as a short cut for this traditional favorite.

MAKES 8 SERVINGS

2 (8½-ounce) boxes corn muffin mix
1 egg
⅓ cup skim milk
4 ounces bulk light sausage, optional
2 onions, chopped
1 green bell pepper, seeded and chopped
1 teaspoon minced garlic
1 cup chopped celery
1 (10¾-ounce) can 98% fat-free cream
 of mushroom soup
1 (16-ounce) can fat-free vegetable (or chicken) broth
1 teaspoon poultry seasoning
Salt and pepper to taste
¼ cup chopped parsley
¼ cup chopped green onions (scallions)

Preheat the oven to 350°F.

Prepare the corn muffin mix with the egg and milk, and bake in a 13 x 9 x 2-inch non-stick pan according to the package directions. Let cool, crumble and set aside.

In a large non-stick skillet, sauté the sausage, onion, green pepper, garlic, and celery until tender. Add the cream of mushroom soup, broth, poultry seasoning, salt, pepper, and crumbled corn bread. Stir in the parsley and green onion.

Transfer to a 2-quart casserole, and bake for 30 minutes, or until lightly browned and heated. Serve.

Nutritional information per serving
Calories 292, Protein (g) 6, Carbohydrate (g) 54, Fat (g) 7, Calories from Fat (%) 20, Saturated Fat (g) 2, Dietary Fiber (g) 2, Cholesterol (mg) 28, Sodium (mg) 836, Diabetic Exchanges: 3 starch, 2 vegetable, 1 fat

VEGETABLES & SIDE DISHES

Yam Corn Bread Stuffing

Naturally sweet yams and cornbread team up for a mouthwatering savory stuffing. For a time-efficient approach, prepare the cornbread and toast the pecans a day ahead.

MAKES 10 SERVINGS

2 cups chopped, peeled, sweet potatoes (yams)

1 cup chopped onion

1 cup sliced celery

2 tablespoons margarine

¼ cup chopped parsley

1 teaspoon ground ginger

5 cups crumbled cooked corn bread

¼ cup chopped pecans, toasted

Vegetable (or chicken) broth, as needed

Preheat the oven to 375°F.

In a large non-stick skillet, cook the sweet potatoes, onion, and celery in the margarine over medium-high heat for 7 to 10 minutes, or until just tender. Spoon the mixture into a large mixing bowl.

Stir in the parsley and ginger. Add the corn bread and pecans, and toss gently to coat. Add enough broth to moisten. Place the stuffing in a 2-quart oblong casserole. Bake, uncovered, for 45 minutes, or until heated through. Serve.

Nutritional information per serving

Calories 211, Protein (g) 5, Carbohydrate (g) 29, Fat (g) 9, Calories from Fat (%) 37, Saturated Fat (g) 2, Dietary Fiber (g) 3, Cholesterol (mg) 19, Sodium (mg) 355, Diabetic Exchanges: 2 starch, 1.5 fat

VEGETABLES & SIDE DISHES

Wild Rice and Oyster Dressing

Make ahead, refrigerate, and bake before serving. The hint of sherry with wild rice and oysters is the perfect blend for a really wonderful dish.

MAKES 6 TO 8 SERVINGS

2 (6-ounce) packages long-grain and wild rice mix
2 (10-ounce) jars oysters
1 teaspoon minced garlic
½ pound fresh mushrooms, sliced
½ cup chopped onion
3 tablespoons all-purpose flour
1 (5-ounce) can evaporated skimmed milk
2 tablespoons dry sherry
¼ cup chopped green onions (scallions)
¼ cup chopped parsley

Preheat the oven to 350°F.

Prepare the wild rice according to the package directions; set aside.

Drain the oysters, reserving ½ cup oyster liquid; set the liquid aside.

In a large non-stick skillet, sauté the garlic, mushrooms, and onion until tender. Add the oysters, and cook for several minutes. Add the flour, and gradually stir in the milk and the reserved oyster liquid, mixing well. Cook over medium heat until the mixture thickens, stirring constantly. Add the sherry, wild rice, green onion, and parsley. Transfer the mixture to a 2-quart baking dish. Bake, uncovered, for 30 minutes, or until heated through. Serve.

Nutritional information per serving

Calories 270, Protein (g) 12, Carbohydrate (g) 43, Fat (g) 5, Calories from Fat (%) 17, Saturated Fat (g) 1, Dietary Fiber (g) 2, Cholesterol (mg) 40, Sodium (mg) 771, Diabetic Exchanges: 1 lean meat, 3 starch

Sautéed Cherry Tomatoes with Basil

Some choice seasonings turn ordinary tomatoes into a sensational side dish.

MAKES 6 SERVINGS

1 pound cherry or grape tomatoes
1 garlic clove, minced
1 tablespoon dried basil leaves
2 tablespoons chopped parsley
½ teaspoon dried thyme leaves
1 teaspoon sugar
Salt and freshly ground pepper to taste

Wash the tomatoes, and dry them well. In a small bowl, combine the garlic, basil, parsley, and thyme. Heat a non-stick skillet over medium heat, and add the tomatoes. Sprinkle with the sugar, salt, and pepper, and toss briefly until well heated. Stir in the garlic mixture, and sauté for 1 minute, or until the sugar melts and the mixture is heated thoroughly. Serve immediately.

Nutritional information per serving
Calories 22, Protein (g) 1, Carbohydrate (g) 5, Fat (g) 0, Calories from Fat (%) 0, Saturated Fat (g) 0, Dietary Fiber (g) 1, Cholesterol (mg) 0, Sodium (mg) 8, Diabetic Exchanges: 1 vegetable

VEGETABLES
& SIDE DISHES

Sauteed Cherry Tomatoes with Basil

Basic Eggplant Stuffing

Use as a dressing or even an eggplant casserole. Add cooked shrimp for a seafood version.

MAKES 10 TO 12 SERVINGS

16 cups peeled and cubed eggplant (about 3 large)
2 cups chopped onion
1 tablespoon minced garlic
1 cup chopped celery
1 green bell pepper, seeded and chopped
1 bunch green onions (scallions), chopped
1 (8-ounce) bag herb stuffing mix
⅓ cup grated Parmesan cheese
¾ cup fat-free canned vegetable (or chicken) broth

Preheat the oven to 350°F.

In a large pot, boil the eggplant, in water to cover, for about 20 to 25 minutes, or until tender. Drain and set aside.

In a large non-stick skillet, sauté the onion, garlic, celery, and green pepper until tender, about 8 minutes. Add the green onions, stuffing mix, cheese, and eggplant, mixing well. Gradually stir in the broth until moistened. If needed, adjust the amount of broth.

Pour the mixture into a 3-quart casserole dish coated with non-stick cooking spray. Bake for 20 to 30 minutes, or until heated through. Serve.

Nutritional information per serving

Calories 130, Protein (g) 6, Carbohydrate (g) 25, Fat (g) 2, Calories from Fat (%) 11, Saturated Fat (g) 1, Dietary Fiber (g) 5, Cholesterol (mg) 2, Sodium (mg) 454, Diabetic Exchanges: 1 starch, 2 vegetable

VEGETABLES & SIDE DISHES

Yam Veggie Wraps

This quick and wonderful flavor combo makes a wrap to remember. Shred sweet potatoes with a grater or in a food processor. This is a high-fiber recipe.

MAKES 6 WRAPS

1 sweet potato (yam), peeled and shredded (about 1 cup)
½ cup chopped red onion
1 cup canned black beans, rinsed and drained
2 green onions (scallions), chopped
¼ cup chopped roasted peanuts
2 tablespoons light Italian or Caesar dressing
1 teaspoon honey
6 (6- to 8-inch) flour tortillas, warmed to soften

In a non-stick skillet, sauté the shredded yam over medium-high heat for about 5 minutes, or until crisp-tender. Transfer to a bowl.

In the same skillet, sauté the red onion until tender. Add the onion, black beans, green onions, and peanuts to the shredded yams, mixing well.

In a small bowl, mix together the dressing and honey, and toss with the yam mixture to coat. Fill the tortillas, and wrap. Serve.

Nutritional information per serving

Calories 226, Protein (g) 8, Carbohydrate (g) 39, Fat (g) 4, Calories from Fat (%) 16, Saturated Fat (g) 0, Dietary Fiber (g) 6, Cholesterol (mg) 0, Sodium (mg) 554, Diabetic Exchanges: 0.5 very lean, 2.5 starch

FOOD FACT:

Sweet potatoes contain virtually no fat or sodium, and one medium potato is only about 150 calories. Sweet potatoes are high in vitamins A and C, beta carotene, iron, potassium, and fiber.

Chicken and Dumplings

Poultry

Oven-Fried Parmesan Chicken

This recipe continually gets rave reviews—best of all, you won't miss fried chicken.

MAKES 8 SERVINGS

¾ cup nonfat plain yogurt
¼ cup lemon juice
1½ tablespoons Dijon mustard
1 teaspoon minced garlic
½ teaspoon dried oregano leaves
8 skinless, boneless chicken breasts
2 cups Italian bread crumbs
¼ cup grated Parmesan cheese
2 tablespoons margarine, melted

Preheat the oven to 350°F.

Combine the yogurt, lemon juice, mustard, garlic, and oregano. Pour over the chicken, coating it. Marinate, covered, for 2 hours or overnight in the refrigerator.

Drain the chicken.

Mix the bread crumbs and cheese, and coat the chicken. Place on a non-stick baking sheet, and chill for 1 hour (time permitting).

Drizzle the chicken with the margarine. Bake for 45 minutes to 1 hour, or until tender and golden brown. Serve immediately.

Nutritional information per serving

Calories 293, Protein (g) 33, Carbohydrate (g) 23, Fat (g) 7, Calories from Fat (%) 21, Saturated Fat (g) 1, Dietary Fiber (g) 1, Cholesterol (mg) 69, Sodium (mg) 680, Diabetic Exchanges: 3 lean meat, 1.5 starch

QUICK TIP:

Try this recipe with chicken tenders or strips to make pick-ups. Serve with Jezebel Sauce on page 40 for a zesty dipping sauce.

POULTRY

Simple Baked
Crusty Chicken

A no-fuss favorite in my house, this is a real kid-pleaser. The gravy is also great on rice.

MAKES 8 SERVINGS

2 pounds skinless, boneless chicken breasts
⅔ cup biscuit baking mix
2 tablespoons olive oil
1 teaspoon minced garlic
1 tablespoon all-purpose flour
1 (16-ounce) can fat-free chicken broth

Preheat the oven to 375°F.

Coat the chicken in the baking mix. Place in a 3-quart oblong casserole dish coated with non-stick cooking spray. Bake for 40 minutes to 1 hour.

Meanwhile, in a saucepan, mix the olive oil and garlic, and add the flour. Whisk in the chicken broth, cooking over medium-high heat until thickened. Pour over the chicken, baking covered, for an additional 20 minutes, or until chicken is done. Serve.

Nutritional information per serving

Calories 203, Protein (g) 28, Carbohydrate (g) 7, Fat (g) 6, Calories from Fat (%) 29, Saturated Fat (g) 1, Dietary Fiber (g) 0, Cholesterol (mg) 66, Sodium (mg) 355, Diabetic Exchanges: 3 lean meat, 0.5 starch

Dijon
Rosemary Chicken

This quick-to-fix chicken pops right in the oven for those busy evenings. This dish is incredibly tasty and appealing to all.

MAKES 6 SERVINGS

1½ to 2 pounds skinless, boneless chicken breasts
2 tablespoons Dijon mustard
¼ teaspoon garlic powder
1 teaspoon dried rosemary leaves
Pepper to taste
¼ cup grated Parmesan cheese

Preheat the oven to 350°F.

Line a baking sheet with foil. Lay the chicken on the foil.

In a small bowl, mix the mustard and garlic powder, and spread on top of each chicken breast. Sprinkle with the rosemary and pepper. Top with the cheese. Bake for 45 to 50 minutes, or until the chicken is done. Serve.

Nutritional information per serving

Calories 150, Protein (g) 28, Carbohydrate (g) 0, Fat (g) 3, Calories from Fat (%) 18, Saturated Fat (g) 1, Dietary Fiber (g) 0, Cholesterol (mg) 69, Sodium (mg) 271, Diabetic Exchanges: 3 very lean meat

Honey Pecan Chicken

Honey Pecan Chicken

The honey and pecan combo create and unforget-table taste. For a glowing presentation, slice the chicken and arrange on a plate to show how moist it is inside. If you're in a pinch and don't have Wheat Chex, use bread crumbs or another wheat cereal.

MAKES 6 SERVINGS

1 cup Wheat Chex cereal crumbs
⅓ cup finely chopped pecans
2 tablespoons honey
2 tablespoons low-sodium soy sauce
6 skinless, boneless chicken breasts
Salt and pepper to taste

Preheat the oven to 425°F.

Cover a baking sheet with foil, and spray with nonstick cooking spray. On a plate or on waxed paper, combine the cereal crumbs and pecans. In a bowl, mix together the honey and soy sauce.

Season the chicken with salt and pepper. Dip both sides of the chicken breast into the honey mixture; then roll in the pecan mixture to coat. Arrange the chicken on the pan. Bake for 12 to 15 minutes on each side, or until the chicken is done. Serve.

Nutritional information per serving

Calories 262, Protein (g) 29, Carbohydrate (g) 23, Fat (g) 7, Calories from Fat (%) 22, Saturated Fat (g) 1, Dietary Fiber (g) 3, Cholesterol (mg) 66, Sodium (mg) 376, Diabetic Exchanges: 3 lean meat, 1 starch, 0.5 other carbohydrate

Company Chicken ❄

Everyday ingredients dress up chicken for a special treat, bursting with flavor.

MAKES 8 SERVINGS

8 skinless, boneless chicken breasts or thighs
Salt and pepper to taste
2 tablespoons olive oil
1 bunch green onions (scallions), chopped
½ teaspoon minced garlic
½ pound fresh mushrooms, sliced
½ cup white wine
1 (28-ounce) can diced tomatoes in juice
½ cup fat-free canned chicken broth

Season the chicken breasts with the salt and pepper.

In a large non-stick skillet, heat the olive oil and brown the chicken. Remove from the pan and set aside. Add the green onions, garlic, and mushrooms to the pan, and sauté until tender.

Add the wine, tomatoes, and broth. Bring to a boil, adjust the seasonings, and reduce to a simmer. Add the chicken, cover, and continue to cook for about 30 to 40 minutes, or until the chicken is tender. Serve.

Nutritional information per serving
Calories 197, Protein (g) 28, Carbohydrate (g) 7, Fat (g) 5, Calories from Fat (%) 23, Saturated Fat (g) 1, Dietary Fiber (g) 2, Cholesterol (mg) 66, Sodium (mg) 242, Diabetic Exchanges: 3 lean meat, 1.5 vegetable

Chicken Breasts Diane

This light and flavorful recipe is a quick dinner solution. Try serving it with wild rice, which complements the chicken.

MAKES 6 SERVINGS

6 skinless, boneless chicken breasts
Salt and pepper to taste
1 tablespoon olive oil
1 bunch green onions (scallions), chopped
Juice of 1 lemon
2 tablespoons chopped parsley
1 tablespoon Dijon mustard
⅓ cup fat-free canned chicken broth

Place the chicken breasts between sheets of waxed paper, and pound slightly with a mallet to flatten, if desired. Sprinkle with salt and pepper.

In a large non-stick skillet, heat the olive oil. Cook the chicken on each side until done, about 15 minutes total. Remove from the skillet, and set aside.

Add the green onions, lemon juice, parsley, and mustard to the skillet. Cook, stirring constantly, for 1 minute. Whisk in the broth, and stir until smooth. Return the chicken to the pan, and serve with the sauce.

Nutritional information per serving
Calories 155, Protein (g) 27, Carbohydrate (g) 2, Fat (g) 4, Calories from Fat (%) 23, Saturated Fat (g) 1, Dietary Fiber (g) 0, Cholesterol (mg) 66, Sodium (mg) 171, Diabetic Exchanges: 3 very lean meat

Chicken Divan

POULTRY

Use this recipe to make a follow-up meal out of leftover chicken. Frozen chopped broccoli can be substituted for fresh.

MAKES 6 SERVINGS

2 bunches fresh broccoli

3 cups chopped, cooked chicken breasts (about 1 pound skinless, boneless chicken breasts)

1 cup skim milk

1 (10¾-ounce) can 98% fat-free cream of chicken soup

1 teaspoon lemon juice

⅛ teaspoon pepper

3 tablespoons all-purpose flour

3 tablespoons water

½ cup finely crushed whole wheat bread crumbs or plain bread crumbs

1 tablespoon margarine, melted

1 cup shredded reduced-fat sharp Cheddar cheese

Preheat the oven to 350°F.

Cut off the stems of the broccoli, leaving florets. Place in a 2-quart casserole with ⅓ cup water. Cover and cook on high in a microwave for 8 minutes, or until tender; drain. Arrange the broccoli in an oblong dish. Spoon the chicken on top of the broccoli.

In a heavy saucepan, combine the milk, soup, lemon juice, and pepper, stirring well. In a small bowl, combine the flour and water. Add to the soup mixture. Bring to a boil over medium heat, stirring constantly with a wire whisk, about 5 minutes. The mixture will get thick and bubbly. Pour evenly over the chicken.

In a small bowl, combine the bread crumbs and margarine. Sprinkle over the soup mixture. Top with the shredded cheese. Bake for 20 minutes, or until thoroughly heated. Serve.

Nutritional information per serving
Calories 296, Protein (g) 33, Carbohydrate (g) 18, Fat (g) 10, Calories from Fat (%) 30, Saturated Fat (g) 4, Dietary Fiber (g) 2, Cholesterol (mg) 74, Sodium (mg) 678, Diabetic Exchanges: 4 lean meat, 1 starch

Easy Marinated Chicken ❄

With its intense flavors, this marinade works well with other meats.

MAKES 6 SERVINGS

2 tablespoons olive oil
⅓ cup sherry
1 tablespoon lemon juice
⅓ cup finely chopped onion
½ teaspoon minced garlic
1 teaspoon dried rosemary leaves
Pepper to taste
6 skinless, boneless chicken breasts

In a small bowl, whisk together the olive oil, sherry, lemon juice, onion, garlic, rosemary, and pepper. Place the chicken in a shallow glass dish, and pour the marinade over it. Cover, and refrigerate for 2 hours to overnight.

Broil or grill the chicken until done, 5 to 7 minutes on each side, basting with the marinade. Serve.

Nutritional information per serving

Calories 145, Protein (g) 26, Carbohydrate (g) 0, Fat (g) 4, Calories from Fat (%) 24, Saturated Fat (g) 1, Dietary Fiber (g) 0, Cholesterol (mg) 66, Sodium (mg) 74, Diabetic Exchanges: 3 very lean meat

Chicken Cherry Jubilee ❄

Try this sweet and spicy dish for a rich-tasting, festive entrée. Serve with wild rice.

MAKES 10 TO 12 SERVINGS

3 pounds skinless, boneless chicken breasts and thighs
Salt and pepper to taste
2 onions, thinly sliced
1 cup water
1 (12-ounce) bottle chili sauce
½ cup light brown sugar
1 cup sherry
1 (16-ounce) can pitted dark cherries, drained

Preheat the broiler.

Season the chicken with the salt and pepper. Place in a 3-quart oblong pan, and cover with the sliced onion. Broil until the chicken is brown, 5 to 7 minutes.

Meanwhile, in a medium saucepan, combine the water, chili sauce, brown sugar, sherry, and cherries over low heat, until melted together.

When the chicken is brown, remove and discard the onion and transfer the chicken to a baking dish. Lower the oven temperature to 325°F. Pour the sauce over the chicken. Bake, covered, for 1½ hours, or until chicken is very tender. Serve.

Nutritional information per serving

Calories 236, Protein (g) 25, Carbohydrate (g) 25, Fat (g) 3, Calories from Fat (%) 11, Saturated Fat (g) 1, Dietary Fiber (g) 1, Cholesterol (mg) 80, Sodium (mg) 849, Diabetic Exchanges: 3 very lean meat, 0.5 fruit, 1 other carbohydrate

Skillet Pizza Chicken

When there's no time to cook, prepare this family-pleasing dish. For best results, use thin chicken breasts, or pound them with a mallet.

MAKES 6 SERVINGS

1 egg white
¼ cup buttermilk
¼ cup grated Parmesan cheese
½ teaspoon dried oregano leaves
½ teaspoon dried basil leaves
½ cup all-purpose flour
½ cup bread crumbs
2 pounds skinless, boneless chicken breasts, pounded thin
2 cups tomato pasta sauce
1 cup shredded part-skim Mozzarella cheese

In a shallow bowl, combine the egg white and buttermilk, beating lightly.

On a plate, combine the Parmesan cheese, oregano, basil, flour, and bread crumbs. Dip each piece of chicken in the egg and then in the flour mixture, making sure to completely coat each piece. Set the chicken aside.

Heat a large non-stick skillet coated with non-stick cooking spray over medium heat. Add the chicken, and cook until lightly browned. Turn the chicken, and cook several more minutes, or until almost done. Lower the heat, and cover the chicken with the pasta sauce. Top with the Mozzarella, cover the pan, and cook several more minutes, or until the cheese is melted. Serve.

Nutritional information per serving

Calories 361, Protein (g) 46, Carbohydrate (g) 24, Fat (g) 8, Calories from Fat (%) 20, Saturated Fat (g) 4, Dietary Fiber (g) 2, Cholesterol (mg) 102, Sodium (mg) 736, Diabetic Exchanges: 5.5 very lean meat, 1.5 starch

Chicken Breasts Florentine ❄

This version of Chicken Florentine is full of flavor and perfect for company. Prepare early in the day, refrigerate, and bake it when you're ready.

MAKES 8 SERVINGS

8 skinless, boneless chicken breasts
⅓ cup all-purpose flour
2 tablespoons olive oil
Salt and pepper to taste
1 (10-ounce) package frozen chopped spinach
8 thin, square slices part-skim Mozzarella cheese
    (about 6 ounces)
½ cup fat-free canned chicken broth
¼ cup white wine
¼ cup lemon juice

Preheat the oven to 325°F. Dust the chicken breasts with the flour.

In a large non-stick skillet, heat the olive oil and sauté the breasts about 5 minutes on each side, until lightly browned, and season to taste. Remove to a 3-quart oblong dish coated with non-stick cooking spray.

Cook the spinach according to the package directions; squeeze and drain well. Top each chicken breast with spinach and a slice of Mozzarella.

Add the chicken broth to the same pan used to sauté the breasts. Add the wine and lemon juice, scraping the pan to remove the drippings, and stirring until heated. Pour the sauce over the chicken. If preparing the chicken ahead of time, refrigerate it at this point. Bake for 20 minutes, or until the chicken is done. The cheese should be melted and the chicken heated thoroughly. Serve.

Nutritional information per serving
Calories 241, Protein (g) 33, Carbohydrate (g) 7, Fat (g) 8, Calories from Fat (%) 32, Saturated Fat (g) 3, Dietary Fiber (g) 1, Cholesterol (mg) 78, Sodium (mg) 238, Diabetic Exchanges: 4 lean meat, 0.5 starch

QUICK TIP:

Spinach is a source of beta-carotene, vitamin C, and folate.

POULTRY

Italian Chicken

Chicken, rice, and seasonings all in one dish—it seems too easy for such a good Italian experience.

MAKES 4 SERVINGS

1½ cups water
1 cup uncooked rice
1 (10-ounce) can diced tomatoes and
    green chilies, drained
½ cup chopped onion
½ cup shredded part-skim Mozzarella cheese
2 teaspoons dried basil leaves, divided
2 teaspoons dried oregano leaves, divided
1 teaspoon minced garlic
1½ pounds skinless, boneless chicken breasts,
    cut into strips
¼ cup grated Parmesan cheese

Preheat the oven to 375°F. In a 2- to 3-quart oblong baking dish coated with non-stick cooking spray, combine the water, rice, tomatoes and chilies, onion, Mozzarella, 1 teaspoon of the basil, 1 teaspoon of the oregano, and the garlic, stirring well. Top the rice mixture with the chicken strips, and sprinkle with the remaining basil, oregano, and the Parmesan. Bake, covered, for 45 minutes. Uncover and continue baking 15 minutes longer, or until the chicken is tender and the rice is cooked. Serve.

Nutritional information per serving

Calories 444, Protein (g) 50, Carbohydrate (g) 43, Fat (g) 7, Calories from Fat (%) 14, Saturated Fat (g) 3, Dietary Fiber (g) 2, Cholesterol (mg) 112, Sodium (mg) 580, Diabetic Exchanges: 6 very lean meat, 2.5 starch, 1 vegetable

Paprika Chicken

This chicken is fast to prepare, and will disappear even faster from your plate. The paprika gives this dish a nice color.

MAKES 8 SERVINGS

8 skinless, boneless chicken breasts
Salt and pepper to taste
4 tablespoons lemon juice, divided
1 tablespoon paprika
1 teaspoon minced garlic
1 tablespoon low-sodium soy sauce
¾ cup dry sherry
1 bunch green onions (scallions), chopped

Pound the chicken breasts to a ½-inch thickness. Season with the salt, pepper, 3 tablespoons of lemon juice, and paprika.

Heat a large non-stick skillet over medium heat. Cook the chicken breasts on each side until browned, 5 to 7 minutes. Add the garlic, the remaining 1 tablespoon lemon juice, the soy sauce, and the sherry to the pan. Cook for 5 minutes. Sprinkle the green onions into the pan, and cook 3 to 5 minutes more, or until the chicken is done. Serve.

Nutritional information per serving

Calories 146, Protein (g) 27, Carbohydrate (g) 3, Fat (g) 2, Calories from Fat (%) 10, Saturated Fat (g) 0, Dietary Fiber (g) 1, Cholesterol (mg) 66, Sodium (mg) 126, Diabetic Exchanges: 3 very lean meat

POULTRY

Indoor Barbecued Chicken ❄

When you crave barbecue but don't feel like grilling or it's too chilly outside, try this indoor method. This homemade barbecue sauce works especially well with ribs or meat.

MAKES 8 SERVINGS

⅔ cup ketchup
2 tablespoons lemon juice
2 tablespoons Worcestershire sauce
2 tablespoons honey
1 teaspoon minced garlic
8 skinless, boneless chicken breast halves

Preheat the broiler.

In a small saucepan, combine the ketchup, lemon juice, Worcestershire sauce, honey, and garlic. Bring to a boil, stirring frequently, then reduce the heat and simmer 2 minutes. Remove from the heat.

Place the chicken on a foil-lined pan, and coat both sides with the sauce. Broil 10 to 15 minutes; then turn and baste, and continue cooking 10 to 15 minutes longer, or until the chicken is done. Serve.

Nutritional information per serving

Calories 166, Protein (g) 27, Carbohydrate (g) 11, Fat (g) 1, Calories from Fat (%) 8, Saturated Fat (g) 0, Dietary Fiber (g) 0, Cholesterol (mg) 66, Sodium (mg) 358, Diabetic Exchanges: 3 very lean meat, 0.5 other carbohydrate

Peanut Chicken

This dish is fast, full of flavor, and a favorite. Crunchy peanuts and soy sauce glaze accent the chicken nicely.

MAKES 8 SERVINGS

1 tablespoon peanut oil
2 pounds skinless, boneless chicken breasts, cut into strips
½ cup thinly chopped green onions (scallions)
½ teaspoon minced garlic
1 tablespoon cornstarch
¼ teaspoon ground ginger
Dash cayenne pepper
1¼ cups fat-free canned chicken broth
2 tablespoons honey
¼ cup low-sodium soy sauce
½ pound sliced mushrooms, optional
⅓ cup roasted peanuts

Heat the oil in a wok or a large skillet. Add the chicken, and brown over medium-high heat, about 7 to 10 minutes. Add the green onion, garlic, cornstarch, ginger, cayenne, chicken broth, honey, soy sauce, and mushrooms. Cook, stirring constantly, until thickened. Cover and cook over low heat, 15 to 20 minutes. Sprinkle with the peanuts, and serve.

Nutritional information per serving

Calories 204, Protein (g) 29, Carbohydrate (g) 8, Fat (g) 6, Calories from Fat (%) 27, Saturated Fat (g) 1, Dietary Fiber (g) 1, Cholesterol (mg) 66, Sodium (mg) 368, Diabetic Exchanges: 4 lean meat, 0.5 other carbohydrate

Chicken Breasts with Artichokes and Mushrooms ❄

This is my mother's standby recipe when we're all coming to town. She always makes it ahead of time, freezes it, and pulls it out to bake for an eagerly awaiting group.

MAKES 8 SERVINGS

2 pounds skinless, boneless chicken breasts
Onion powder to taste
Paprika to taste
Salt and pepper to taste
1 (14-ounce) can artichoke hearts, drained and quartered
½ pound mushrooms, sliced
1 bunch green onions (scallions), chopped
½ teaspoon minced garlic
2 tablespoons margarine
2 tablespoons all-purpose flour
⅔ cup fat-free canned chicken broth
3 tablespoons sherry

Preheat the oven to 350°F.

Season the chicken heavily with the onion powder, paprika, salt, and pepper. Place the chicken in a 3-quart casserole dish coated with non-stick cooking spray. Place the artichoke hearts around the chicken.

In a medium non-stick skillet, sauté the mushrooms, green onions, and garlic until tender. Place the mushroom mixture on top of the chicken. In the same skillet, melt the margarine, and add the flour, stirring. Gradually add the chicken broth and sherry, cooking until smooth and the sauce comes to a boil. Pour the sauce over all in the casserole. Bake, covered, for 1 hour. Remove the cover, and continue baking for 15 minutes to brown the chicken. Serve.

Nutritional information per serving

Calories 184, Protein (g) 28, Carbohydrate (g) 6, Fat (g) 4, Calories from Fat (%) 22, Saturated Fat (g) 1, Dietary Fiber (g) 1, Cholesterol (mg) 66, Sodium (mg) 250, Diabetic Exchanges: 3 very lean meat, 1 vegetable

QUICK TIP:

To omit sherry, wine, or any other alcoholic beverage from a recipe, substitute another liquid such as chicken broth or water.

Chicken Breasts with Artichokes and Mushrooms

Lemon Feta Chicken

Lemon Feta Chicken

*For a last-minute dinner, remember this
Mediterranean-inspired dish.*

MAKES 8 SERVINGS

8 skinless, boneless chicken breasts
¼ cup lemon juice, divided
1 tablespoon dried oregano leaves, divided
¼ teaspoon pepper
3 ounces crumbled Feta cheese
3 tablespoons chopped green onions (scallions)

Preheat the oven to 350ºF.

Place the chicken in a 13 x 9 x 2-inch non-stick baking dish and drizzle with half the lemon juice. Sprinkle with half the oregano and all of the pepper. Top with the cheese and green onion. Drizzle with the remaining lemon juice and oregano. Bake, covered, for 45 minutes to 1 hour, or until done. Serve.

Nutritional information per serving
Calories 158, Protein (g) 28, Carbohydrate (g) 2, Fat (g) 4, Calories from Fat (%) 22, Saturated Fat (g) 2, Dietary Fiber (g) 0, Cholesterol (mg) 75, Sodium (mg) 193, Diabetic Exchanges: 4 very lean meat

Ginger Chicken
and Black Beans

Intrigue your taste buds with peaches, ginger, and black beans, which mesh together for this sweet and savory dish.

MAKES 6 SERVINGS

2½ pounds skinless, boneless chicken breasts
Salt and pepper to taste
½ teaspoon garlic powder
1 teaspoon paprika
1 (15-ounce) can light sliced peaches,
    drained and cut into chunks
1 teaspoon ground ginger
2 tablespoons lime juice
1 teaspoon minced garlic
½ cup chopped green onions (scallions)
2 (15-ounce) cans black beans, undrained

Preheat the oven to 350°F.

Place the chicken in a 2-quart oblong baking dish. Season with the salt and pepper, garlic powder, and paprika.

In a bowl, combine the peaches, ginger, lime juice, garlic, green onions, and black beans. Spoon this mixture over the chicken, cover, and bake for 50 to 60 minutes, or until the chicken is tender. Serve.

Nutritional information per serving

Calories 361, Protein (g) 52, Carbohydrate (g) 27, Fat (g) 4, Calories from Fat (%) 9, Saturated Fat (g) 1, Dietary Fiber (g) 9, Cholesterol (mg) 110, Sodium (mg) 563, Diabetic Exchanges: 6 very lean meat, 1.5 starch, 0.5 fruit

POULTRY

QUICK TIP:

If you are watching your sodium intake, rinse the beans before using them.

Chinese Chicken and Broccoli Stir-Fry

Chicken and broccoli are stir-fried for a tasty Chinese-style meal. My kids thought the flavor was better than at our favorite Chinese restaurant. Serve over rice.

MAKES 4 TO 6 SERVINGS

2 pounds skinless, boneless chicken breasts, cut into
  strips
1 tablespoon cornstarch
½ teaspoon ground ginger
1 teaspoon crushed red pepper flakes
Salt and pepper to taste
3 tablespoons olive oil
1 bunch broccoli, florets only
1 tablespoon minced garlic
3 tablespoons low-sodium soy sauce
¼ cup sherry
1 teaspoon sugar
1 bunch green onions (scallions), cut into 2-inch slices
1 red bell pepper, seeded and cut into strips

In a large bowl, toss the chicken strips with the cornstarch, ginger, red pepper flakes, salt, and pepper.

In a large non-stick skillet, heat the olive oil. Add the chicken, broccoli, garlic, soy sauce, sherry, and sugar, stirring and cooking over high heat, about 7 minutes. Add the green onions and red pepper, and continue cooking and stirring for another 10 minutes, or until the chicken is done. Serve.

Nutritional information per serving

Calories 266, Protein (g) 37, Carbohydrate (g) 7, Fat (g) 9, Calories from Fat (%) 30, Saturated Fat (g) 1, Dietary Fiber (g) 2, Cholesterol (mg) 88, Sodium (mg) 308, Diabetic Exchanges: 4.5 lean meat, 1.5 vegetable

Chicken Full-of-Flavor ❄

Green onions, mushrooms, and white wine make this time-saving, one-pan recipe a hit. It is ideal for busy nights.

MAKES 8 SERVINGS

¼ cup all-purpose flour
Salt and pepper to taste
8 skinless, boneless chicken breasts
1 tablespoon olive oil
1 bunch green onions (scallions), chopped
½ pound fresh mushrooms, sliced
1 cup fat-free canned chicken broth
½ cup dry white wine
1 tablespoon lemon juice
1 tablespoon chopped parsley

In a small bowl, combine the flour, salt, and pepper. Dredge the chicken breasts in the flour mixture.

In a non-stick skillet, heat the olive oil; cook the chicken 7 to 10 minutes or until golden brown and no longer pink inside. Remove to a platter.

Add the green onions and mushroom slices to the skillet and cook, stirring until tender. Pour in the chicken broth, wine, and lemon juice; bring to a boil, stirring. Cook for 5 minutes, or until slightly thickened. Reduce the heat to low, and stir in the parsley.

Return the chicken to the pan; cook over low heat for 10 to 12 minutes until the chicken is tender. Serve.

Nutritional information per serving

Calories 172, Protein (g) 28, Carbohydrate (g) 5, Fat (g) 3, Calories from Fat (%) 17, Saturated Fat (g) 1, Dietary Fiber (g) 1, Cholesterol (mg) 66, Sodium (mg) 155, Diabetic Exchanges: 3 very lean meat, 0.5 starch

Cranberry Chicken with Wild Rice

Get in the holiday mood with this cranberry-orange chicken dish that's both satisfying and pretty on the plate. Include toasted pecans and dried cranberries in the rice for a dish full of texture and a flavor that's equally impressive.

MAKES 4 TO 6 SERVINGS

1 (16-ounce) can whole-berry cranberry sauce
2 tablespoons orange liqueur or orange juice
2 tablespoons lemon juice
½ teaspoon dry mustard
1½ pounds skinless, boneless chicken breasts
1 (6-ounce) package long grain and wild rice mix
2 tablespoons grated orange rind
¼ cup chopped green onions (scallions)

Preheat the oven to 350°F.

In a medium saucepan over medium heat or in a microwave-safe pan, combine the cranberry sauce, orange liqueur, lemon juice, and mustard, cooking until hot.

Place the chicken in a baking dish, and pour the cranberry sauce over the chicken. Bake, uncovered, for 45 minutes, or until the chicken is done.

Meanwhile, cook the wild rice according to the package directions, omitting any oil and salt. When the rice is done, stir in the orange rind and green onion. To serve, place the rice on a plate, and top with the chicken and cranberry sauce.

Nutritional information per serving

Calories 357, Protein (g) 29, Carbohydrate (g) 53, Fat (g) 2, Calories from Fat (%) 4, Saturated Fat (g) 0, Dietary Fiber (g) 2, Cholesterol (mg) 66, Sodium (mg) 511, Diabetic Exchanges: 3 very lean meat, 1.5 starch, 2 other carbohydrate

POULTRY

Chicken Roll-Ups

A different twist for chicken with a fancy flair—use broccoli or canned asparagus if you wish.

MAKES 4 SERVINGS

4 skinless, boneless chicken breasts
1 tablespoon Dijon mustard
⅓ pound fresh asparagus, trimmed
2 tablespoons all-purpose flour
½ teaspoon dried thyme leaves, divided
¼ teaspoon garlic powder
¼ teaspoon paprika
⅛ teaspoon white pepper
1 tomato, sliced
1 red onion, thinly sliced
½ cup fat-free canned chicken broth
½ cup dry white wine

Preheat the oven to 350°F.

Pound the chicken breasts to ½ inch thick. Spread each with the mustard. Place 2 asparagus spears on each chicken breast, and roll up, securing with a toothpick.

Combine the flour with ¼ teaspoon thyme, the garlic powder, paprika, and pepper. Roll the chicken breasts in the flour mixture.

Place the tomato and onion slices in a 1½-quart oblong baking dish coated with non-stick cooking spray. Arrange the chicken rolls on top.

In a small bowl, combine the chicken broth, wine, and remaining ¼ teaspoon thyme. Pour over the chicken. Cover loosely with foil. Bake for 30 minutes, basting occasionally. Uncover and bake 10 to 15 minutes longer, or until the chicken is done. Serve.

Nutritional information per serving

Calories 185, Protein (g) 29, Carbohydrate (g) 10, Fat (g) 2, Calories from Fat (%) 8, Saturated Fat (g) 0, Dietary Fiber (g) 2, Cholesterol (mg) 66, Sodium (mg) 246, Diabetic Exchanges: 3 very lean meat, 2 vegetable

QUICK TIP:

When buying asparagus, examine the tips for signs of freshness, as they are the part most likely to break or spoil. Try snapping off the bottom of each stalk instead of cutting. The stalk will usually separate right where the woody part ends.

Chicken and Dumplings ❄

This Southern comfort dish is great in the winter months and popular in my home. If you prefer a thicker soup, mix a little soup and flour together then return the mixture to the pot. If you like lots of dumplings, (like we do) double the dumpling recipe.

MAKES 6 TO 8 SERVINGS

2 pounds skinless, boneless chicken breasts,
    cut into small serving pieces
3 quarts water
Salt and pepper to taste
2 (10¾-ounce) cans 98% fat-free cream
    of mushroom soup
6 chicken bouillon cubes
½ cup all-purpose flour
1 celery stalk, cut into pieces
1 onion, quartered
4 carrots, peeled and sliced
2 cups self-rising flour
2 tablespoons canola oil
¾ cup skim milk

Place the chicken in a large pot with the water, salt, pepper, mushroom soup, bouillon cubes, flour mixed with a little water to make a smooth paste, celery, onion, and carrot slices. Bring to a boil. Reduce the heat to medium, and cook 30 minutes, or until the chicken is tender.

Meanwhile, make the dumplings. In a small bowl, combine with a fork the self-rising flour, oil, and milk. Turn onto a floured surface, and roll the dough ⅛-inch thick. Cut into thin strips.

Remove the celery and onion, bring the broth to a boil, and drop in the dumplings. Cook on medium heat, covered, for 10 minutes or until the dumplings are done. Serve in big bowls.

Nutritional information per serving
Calories 368, Protein (g) 32, Carbohydrate (g) 40, Fat (g) 7, Calories from Fat (%) 18, Saturated Fat (g) 1, Dietary Fiber (g) 2, Cholesterol (mg) 70, Sodium (mg) 1,869, Diabetic Exchanges: 3 lean meat, 2.5 starch, 1 vegetable

QUICK TIP:

If you're watching your sodium intake, use low sodium chicken broth instead of the bouillon cubes.

Chicken and Dumplings

Salsa Chicken

Cover the chicken with all the ingredients, and pop it into the oven. Yellow rice goes well with this recipe.

MAKES 8 SERVINGS

2 pounds skinless, boneless chicken breasts
2 cups salsa
1 (15-ounce) can corn, drained
1½ cups shredded reduced-fat Monterey Jack cheese
½ cup chopped green onions (scallions), optional

Preheat the oven to 350°F.

Place the chicken in a 2-quart casserole coated with non-stick cooking spray. Cover with the salsa and corn. Cover, and bake for 1 hour.

Uncover, sprinkle with the cheese, and continue cooking for 5 minutes, or until done. Sprinkle with the green onion, if desired. Serve.

Nutritional information per serving
Calories 240, Protein (g) 33, Carbohydrate (g) 10, Fat (g) 6, Calories from Fat (%) 23, Saturated Fat (g) 3, Dietary Fiber (g) 1, Cholesterol (mg) 77, Sodium (mg) 578, Diabetic Exchanges: 4 lean meat, 0.5 starch

QUICK TIP:

To make grating cheese easier, place soft cheese such as Monterey Jack in the freezer for 10 to 15 minutes before grating.

Tequila Chicken

Homemade salsa baked with the tequila-infused chicken makes this quick dish a simple sensation. If you don't want to flame this dish, just bring the mixture to a boil for several minutes. Be careful when flaming any dish—make sure the area is clear.

MAKES 6 SERVINGS

1¾ pounds skinless, boneless chicken breasts
2 teaspoons ground cumin
2 tablespoons triple sec
2 tablespoons tequila
2 tomatoes, chopped
2 tablespoons chopped fresh cilantro
1 tablespoon lime juice
1 teaspoon chopped jalapeño pepper
⅓ cup chopped onion
⅔ cup shredded reduced-fat Monterey Jack cheese

Preheat the oven to 350°F.

Coat the chicken breasts on both sides with the cumin.

In a large non-stick skillet, sauté the breasts over medium heat until brown on both sides, 5 minutes in all.

In a medium bowl, mix together the tomatoes, cilantro, lime juice, jalapeño, and onion. Set aside.

In a small bowl, combine the triple sec and tequila. Remove the pan from the heat, add the liqueur, and ignite very carefully with a match—a high flame will arise. Add the salsa to the chicken when the flame goes out. Transfer to a baking dish, and bake for 15 minutes. Sprinkle with the shredded cheese, and continue baking until the cheese is melted, about 5 more minutes. Serve immediately.

Nutritional information per serving

Calories 226, Protein (g) 35, Carbohydrate (g) 6, Fat (g) 4, Calories from Fat (%) 17, Saturated Fat (g) 2, Dietary Fiber (g) 1, Cholesterol (mg) 84, Sodium (mg) 170, Diabetic Exchanges: 4.5 very lean meat, 1 vegetable

POULTRY

Southwestern Chicken with Bean Sauce ❄

The beans dissolve to create a great tasting secret sauce for the chicken. Top with cheese and chopped green onions, and serve with yellow rice.

MAKES 6 TO 8 SERVINGS

2 pounds skinless, boneless chicken breasts
1 (16-ounce) can fat-free refried beans
½ cup chopped red onion
1 (16-ounce) jar salsa
1 cup shredded reduced-fat sharp Cheddar cheese, optional
¼ cup chopped green onions (scallions), optional

Preheat the oven to 350°F.

Place the chicken breasts in a 2-quart oblong baking dish coated with non-stick cooking spray. Spread the beans to cover the top of the chicken. Sprinkle with the onions. Pour the salsa evenly over the top. Cover with foil, and bake 80 minutes, or until the chicken is done. Sprinkle with the cheese and green onion, if desired, and serve.

Nutritional information per serving

Calories 193, Protein (g) 29, Carbohydrate (g) 11, Fat (g) 1, Calories from Fat (%) 7, Saturated Fat (g) 0, Dietary Fiber (g) 3, Cholesterol (mg) 66, Sodium (mg) 558, Diabetic Exchanges: 3.5 very lean meat, 1 starch

QUICK TIP:

Try different flavored salsas for a twist to this recipe. Make sure you purchase fat-free refried beans!

Mexican Chicken Casserole ❄

This recipe is so good that it once won the heart of a man and inspired a proposal. I just think it's a great-tasting casserole—I have my man.

MAKES 6 TO 8 SERVINGS

1½ cups fat-free canned chicken broth

1 cup skim milk

½ cup all-purpose flour

½ cup nonfat plain yogurt

1 (10-ounce) can diced tomatoes and green chilies, drained

1 (4-ounce) can diced green chilies, drained

1 tablespoon chili powder

1 teaspoon dried oregano leaves

Salt and pepper to taste

1 onion, chopped

1 red or green bell pepper, seeded and chopped

½ teaspoon minced garlic

10 (6- to 8-inch) flour tortillas, cut into quarters

1 pound cooked skinless, boneless, chicken breasts cut into chunks

1 cup shredded reduced-fat sharp Cheddar cheese

Preheat the oven to 350°F.

In a large saucepan, bring the chicken broth to a simmer.

In a small bowl, whisk the milk into the flour to make a smooth paste. Add to the chicken broth, bring to a boil, reduce heat, and cook until thickened and smooth, stirring constantly. Remove from the heat, and stir in the yogurt, tomatoes and green chilies, diced green chilies, chili powder, and oregano. Season with the salt and pepper; set aside.

In a medium skillet coated with nonstick cooking spray, sauté the onion, bell pepper, and garlic until tender. Line the bottom of a shallow 3-quart baking dish with half the tortillas. Sprinkle half the chicken and half the onion mixture over the tortillas. Spoon half the sauce evenly on the top. Repeat the layers, ending with the cheese. Bake for 25 to 30 minutes, or until bubbly. Serve.

Nutritional Information per serving
Calories 278, Protein (g) 22, Carbohydrate (g) 37, Fat (g) 4, Calories from Fat (%) 14, Saturated Fat (g) 2, Dietary Fiber (g) 3, Cholesterol (mg) 38, Sodium (mg) 791, Diabetic Exchanges: 2.5 very lean meat, 2 starch, 1 vegetable

POULTRY

Chicken Fajita Pizza ❄

Try this pizza with a Mexican flair. This quick dish is simple enough to please the kids while still satisfying the adults.

MAKES 8 SERVINGS

1 pound skinless, boneless chicken breasts,
   cut into strips
1 teaspoon chili powder
Salt and pepper to taste
½ teaspoon garlic powder
1 small onion, thinly sliced
1 green bell pepper, seeded and thinly sliced into strips
1 (10-ounce) can prepared pizza crust or Boboli crust
½ cup picante sauce
1 cup shredded reduced-fat Monterey Jack cheese

Preheat the oven to 425°F.

In a large non-stick skillet, sauté the chicken over medium heat until done, 7 to 10 minutes. Stir in the chili powder, salt, pepper, and garlic powder. Add the onion and green pepper, cooking until the vegetables are tender, another 3 minutes.

On a non-stick pizza pan coated with non-stick cooking spray, unroll the dough. Starting at the center, press out the dough with your hands. Bake for 6 to 8 minutes, or until light golden brown.

Remove from the oven, and spoon the picante sauce over the partially baked crust. Top with the chicken, and sprinkle with the cheese. Return to the oven, and bake for 10 to 12 minutes, or until the crust is crisp.

Nutritional information per serving
Calories 214, Protein (g) 21, Carbohydrate (g) 21, Fat (g) 5, Calories from Fat (%) 20, Saturated Fat (g) 2, Dietary Fiber (g) 2, Cholesterol (mg) 41, Sodium (mg) 471, Diabetic Exchanges: 2.5 lean meat, 1 starch, 1 vegetable

Chicken Fajita Pizza

POULTRY

Chicken and Black Bean Enchiladas

Chicken and Black Bean Enchiladas ❄

Try flavored salsas to kick up the flavor in this super recipe that is full of flavor and color.

MAKES 6 SERVINGS

1¼ pounds skinless, boneless chicken breasts
3 slices center-cut bacon
½ teaspoon minced garlic
1½ cups salsa, divided
1 (15-ounce) can black beans, undrained
1 red or green bell pepper, seeded and chopped, optional
1 teaspoon ground cumin
Salt and pepper to taste
1 bunch green onions (scallions), chopped
12 (6- to 8-inch) flour tortillas
6 ounces reduced-fat Monterey Jack cheese, shredded

Preheat the oven to 350°F. Cut the chicken into chunks; set aside.

In a non-stick skillet, cook the bacon until crisp. Remove the bacon to a paper towel to soak any excess grease; discard any grease in the skillet.

In the same skillet, sauté the chicken and garlic until the chicken is almost done, 5 to 7 minutes. Stir in ½ cup salsa, the beans, bell pepper, cumin, salt, and pepper. Simmer until thickened, about 5 minutes, stirring occasionally, or until the chicken is done. Stir in the green onions and reserved bacon.

Divide the chicken-bean mixture among 12 tortillas, placing the mixture down the center of each tortilla. Top with 1 tablespoon shredded cheese. Roll up and place seam-side down in a 13 x 9 x 2-inch non-stick baking dish coated with non-stick cooking spray. Spoon the remaining 1 cup salsa evenly over the enchiladas. Top with the remaining cheese. Bake for 15 minutes, or until thoroughly heated and the cheese is melted.

Nutritional information per serving
Calories 455, Protein (g) 40, Carbohydrate (g) 50, Fat (g) 8, Calories from Fat (%) 17, Saturated Fat (g) 4, Dietary Fiber (g) 6, Cholesterol (mg) 73, Sodium (mg) 1326, Diabetic Exchanges: 4 lean meat, 3 starch, 1 vegetable

POULTRY

Cornish Hens with Wild Rice Stuffing ❄

These glazed hens with fruits and a superb stuffing make a special-occasion dish. The stuffing may be used with any main dish. Make sure you remove the skin before eating.

MAKES 16 SERVINGS

8 Cornish game hens (about 1½ pounds each)
1 tablespoon paprika
1 tablespoon garlic powder
Salt and pepper to taste
2 onions, chopped
2 green bell peppers, seeded and chopped
4 celery stalks, chopped
1 tablespoon minced garlic
1 bunch green onions (scallions), chopped
3 (6-ounce) packages long-grain and wild rice mix
1 cup peach preserves
3 tablespoons honey
2 tablespoons light brown sugar
½ cup golden raisins
4 baking apples, cored and sliced

Preheat the oven to 350°F.

Clean and rinse the hens. Lay them in a large casserole dish, and pat dry. Season with the paprika, garlic powder, salt, and pepper; set aside.

In a large non-stick pot, sauté the onion, green pepper, celery, garlic, and green onions until tender, about 7 minutes. Add all of the long grain and wild-rice mix and water according to the package directions, omitting any oil and salt. Cook until the rice is done and the liquid is absorbed, about 35 to 40 minutes. Stuff each hen with equal amounts of the wild rice mixture.

In another saucepan, heat the peach preserves, honey, and brown sugar over medium-low heat until the mixture is bubbly, about 4 minutes. Pour over the hens. Sprinkle with the raisins and apples. Bake for 1½ to 2 hours, or until the hens are done. You might have to cover them with foil during the last 30 minutes if the hens get too brown. To serve, cut each hen in half, and serve with the dressing.

Nutritional information per serving
Calories 404, Protein (g) 34, Carbohydrate (g) 58, Fat (g) 5, Calories from Fat (%) 11, Saturated Fat (g) 1, Dietary Fiber (g) 3, Cholesterol (mg) 132, Sodium (mg) 574, Diabetic Exchanges: 4 medium-fat meat, 1.5 starch, 1 fruit, 1.5 other carbohydrate

Cornish Hens with Wild Rice Stuffing

Turkey Steaks with Prosciutto

Turkey cutlets are a nice change of fare. Topped with prosciutto, they will leave quite an impression on you.

MAKES 4 SERVINGS

4 turkey breast cutlets or steaks (about 1 pound)
Salt and pepper to taste
¼ cup all-purpose flour
2 tablespoons olive oil
½ cup fat-free canned chicken broth
½ teaspoon minced garlic
4 thin slices prosciutto (about 2 ounces)
¼ cup Marsala wine
2 tablespoons chopped parsley

Place the turkey steaks between sheets of waxed paper, and pound them to about ¼ inch thick. Sprinkle with salt and pepper. Coat lightly in the flour, and shake off the excess.

Heat the oil, and cook the turkey steaks until golden brown, 5 to 7 minutes; turn, and cook until done on other side. Add the chicken broth and garlic to the pan, and heat. Top each steak with prosciutto. Pour in the Marsala wine, and cook for a few minutes, reducing the sauce. Sprinkle with the parsley; serve.

Nutritional information per serving

Calories 263, Protein (g) 32, Carbohydrate (g) 8, Fat (g) 10, Calories from Fat (%) 35, Saturated Fat (g) 2, Dietary Fiber (g) 0, Cholesterol (mg) 89, Sodium (mg) 383, Diabetic Exchanges: 4 lean meat, 0.5 starch

Honey-Glazed Turkey Breast

A sweet, spicy glaze infuses the turkey with flavor for a great everyday meal. Enjoy the leftovers for sandwiches the next day.

MAKES 10 TO 12 SERVINGS

1 (5-pound) turkey breast
Salt and pepper to taste
⅓ cup honey
3 tablespoons Dijon mustard
1½ teaspoons dried rosemary leaves

Preheat the oven to 325°F.

Remove the skin from the turkey breast and discard; place the breast in a roaster pan. Season with the salt and pepper.

In a small bowl, mix together the honey, mustard, and rosemary. Pour half the glaze over the turkey breast, and bake, uncovered, for about 2 hours, or until the meat thermometer registers 170° to 175°F in the thickest part of the breast. You may need to add a little water to the bottom of pan.

During the final 15 minutes of baking, brush the remaining glaze over the turkey breast. Serve.

Nutritional information per serving

Calories 188, Protein (g) 33, Carbohydrate (g) 8, Fat (g) 1, Calories from Fat (%) 7, Saturated Fat (g) 0, Dietary Fiber (g) 0, Cholesterol (mg) 95, Sodium (mg) 152, Diabetic Exchanges: 4.5 very lean meat, 0.5 carbohydrate

POULTRY

Turkey Jambalaya

Turkey Jambalaya ❄

The word Jambalaya *refers to a Spanish Cajun seasoned rice dish with a mixture of several combinations of meat, poultry, sausage, and vegetables. This is an easy, yet sophisticated, version. Turn leftover turkey into another meal with this superb combination of ingredients, or buy a roasted chicken to use instead of turkey.*

MAKES 8 TO 10 SERVINGS

1 pound reduced-fat sausage
1 large onion, chopped
1 pound fresh mushrooms, sliced
2 (6-ounce) packages long-grain and wild rice mix
4 cups cooked, diced turkey breasts or thighs
1 (2¼-ounce) can sliced black olives, drained
1 (14-ounce) can artichoke hearts, drained and quartered
½ cup chopped green onions (scallions)

Cut the sausage into slices, and brown about 5 minutes in a large non-stick pot. Add the onion and mushrooms, cooking until tender. Drain off any excess grease. Add the wild rice, seasoning packet, and water to the sausage mixture, and cook according to the package directions. Add the turkey, olives, and artichoke hearts, tossing gently. Top with the chopped green onion, and serve.

Nutritional information per serving
Calories 294, Protein (g) 28, Carbohydrate (g) 38, Fat (g) 3, Calories from Fat (%) 9, Saturated Fat (g) 1, Dietary Fiber (g) 2, Cholesterol (mg) 64, Sodium (mg) 1,055, Diabetic Exchanges: 3 very lean meat, 2 starch, 1.5 vegetable

Glazed Pork Tenderloin

Meat

Italian-Style Pot Roast ❄

Everyone always enjoys a pot roast, and this hearty Italian-seasoned version with a wonderful gravy will win you over. Serve rice or potatoes with the gravy.

MAKES 8 TO 10 SERVINGS

1 (4- to 5-pound) round roast
2 cups canned beef broth
½ cup Burgundy wine
3 tablespoons tomato paste
1 (28-ounce) can chopped tomatoes, with juice
1 teaspoon minced garlic
1 tablespoon dried basil leaves
1 tablespoon dried oregano leaves
2 bay leaves
1 pound carrots, peeled and cut into 1-inch pieces
3 onions, quartered
1 pound fresh mushrooms, halved
3 tablespoons all-purpose flour

Preheat the oven to 350°F.

Place the roast in a large pot or Dutch oven. Pour in the beef broth and wine. Add the tomato paste, and stir. Add the tomatoes with juice. Blend in the garlic, basil, oregano, and bay leaves. Cover, and cook in the oven for 1½ hours. Turn the meat over, and add the carrots, onions, and mushrooms. Cover, and continue cooking for 1 to 1½ hours, or until the meat is tender. Transfer the meat to a carving board.

Remove a small amount of the sauce, and mix with the flour to form a paste. Place the Dutch oven over medium-high heat, and bring the remaining sauce to a boil. Whisk in the paste to thicken the sauce. Slice the meat against the grain. Remove the bay leaves from the sauce, and discard. Serve the sliced meat with the vegetables and the sauce.

Nutritional information per serving
Calories 332, Protein (g) 41, Carbohydrate (g) 18, Fat (g) 10, Calories from Fat (%) 27, Saturated Fat (g) 3, Dietary Fiber (g) 5, Cholesterol (mg) 111, Sodium (mg) 384, Diabetic Exchanges: 5 lean meat, 3 vegetable

FOOD FACT:

Round roasts include top round, bottom round, rump, and eye of round, which are leaner than other cuts of meat.

MEAT

Italian-Style Pot Roast

MEAT

Barbecued Brisket ❄

Who needs to mess with a grill when you have this wonderful recipe that cooks itself? Put it in the oven, forget about it, and return to a tender, tasty brisket.

MAKES 12 TO 14 SERVINGS

1 (5-pound) trimmed beef brisket
Salt and pepper to taste
1 tablespoon garlic powder
½ cup light brown sugar
½ cup Worcestershire sauce
2 cups chipotle salsa

Trim any excess fat from the brisket.

Season the brisket with the salt, pepper, and garlic powder.

In a small bowl, mix together the brown sugar, Worcestershire sauce, and salsa, and spread over the brisket. Cover, and refrigerate overnight.

Preheat the oven to 300°F.

Place the brisket and marinade in the oven in a heavy pot. Bake, covered, for 5 to 6 hours, or until the brisket is tender. To serve, slice the meat against the grain.

Nutritional information per serving

Calories 289, Protein (g) 35, Carbohydrate (g) 11, Fat (g) 10, Calories from Fat (%) 33, Saturated Fat (g) 3, Dietary Fiber (g) 0, Cholesterol (mg) 96, Sodium (mg) 378, Diabetic Exchanges: 5 lean meat, 0.5 other carbohydrate

Tenderloin Mexicana ❄

Tender fillets seasoned with Southwestern seasonings create a magnificent meal. Splurge with a reasonable portion of this treat. This tastes even better when it's grilled.

MAKES 4 SERVINGS

4 (5-ounce) beef tenderloin steaks
¼ cup lime juice
2 tablespoons chili powder
1 tablespoon minced garlic
½ teaspoon ground cumin
¼ teaspoon crushed red pepper flakes
Salt and pepper

Place the steaks in a wide, shallow dish.

In a small bowl, combine the lime juice, chili powder, garlic, cumin, and red pepper flakes. Pour over the steaks, and rub to coat. Marinate if time permits.

Heat a large, heavy non-stick skillet over medium-high heat. Add the steaks, and cook 4 minutes on each side for medium-rare. Season with salt and pepper to taste. Serve.

Nutritional information per serving

Calories 237, Protein (g) 30, Carbohydrate (g) 3, Fat (g) 11, Calories from Fat (%) 43, Saturated Fat (g) 4, Dietary Fiber (g) 1, Cholesterol (mg) 88, Sodium (mg) 105, Diabetic Exchanges: 4 lean meat

MEAT

Grilled Flank Steak

My family requests this simple savory sensation often. The marinade packs the steak with flavor. Broil inside if desired.

MAKES 6 SERVINGS

2 pounds flank steak
2 tablespoons dry red wine
1 tablespoon red wine vinegar
1 tablespoon prepared horseradish
1 tablespoon ketchup
½ teaspoon pepper
1 teaspoon dried thyme leaves
1 teaspoon minced garlic

Trim any visible fat from the meat.

Combine the wine, vinegar, horseradish, ketchup, pepper, thyme, and garlic, and pour over meat. Cover, and marinate in the refrigerator for 8 hours or overnight, turning occasionally.

Grill, covered, over a hot fire about 7 minutes on each side. Serve rare, and cut diagonally across the grain into thin slices.

Nutritional information per serving
Calories 241, Protein (g) 32, Carbohydrate (g) 0, Fat (g) 12, Calories from Fat (%) 46, Saturated Fat (g) 5, Dietary Fiber (g) 0, Cholesterol (mg) 78, Sodium (mg) 135, Diabetic Exchanges: 4.5 meat

MEAT

Stuffed Flank Steak

Stuffed Flank Steak ❄

Roasted peppers are available in the grocery stores in jars for a time saver. The stuffing infuses the meat with intense flavors—quite a presentation, with a taste to match. If you like, the butcher can butterfly your meat.

MAKES 6 TO 8 SERVINGS

1 red bell pepper, roasted (recipe follows)
  or jarred peppers, drained
1 (10-ounce) bag fresh baby spinach
1 teaspoon minced garlic
½ cup Italian bread crumbs
½ cup grated Parmesan cheese
3 pounds lean flank steak, butterflied
Salt and pepper to taste

Preheat the oven to 350°F.

Combine the roasted pepper (see recipe at right), spinach, garlic, bread crumbs, and Parmesan cheese in a food processor, and process until chopped into small pieces and well mixed.

Place the mixture on the flank steak. Starting with the long side, roll the steak up jelly roll style. Season with the salt and pepper. Secure with a toothpick.

Place in a baking pan, and bake for 45 minutes. Slice into pinwheels, and serve.

ROASTED PEPPERS

Preheat the oven to 400°F.

Place the peppers on a pan, and bake for 30 minutes, or until browned.

Place in a paper bag for 20 minutes. Take out of the bag, remove the skins, and use the rest of the peppers in the recipe.

Nutritional information per serving
Calories 343, Protein (g) 40, Carbohydrate (g) 9, Fat (g) 16, Calories from Fat (%) 42, Saturated Fat (g) 7, Dietary Fiber (g) 2, Cholesterol (mg) 93, Sodium (mg) 361, Diabetic Exchanges: 5 lean meat, 0.5 starch

MEAT

Sirloin Steak Strips ❄

You'll find yourself preparing this recipe for its excellent, quick, rich sauce.

MAKES 6 TO 8 SERVINGS

2 pounds sirloin steak, trimmed of fat
Salt and pepper to taste
1 teaspoon minced garlic
½ cup dry red wine
½ cup canned beef broth
2 tablespoons Dijon mustard
3 tablespoons minced parsley

Cut the steak into strips about ¾ inch thick. Heat a large non-stick skillet over medium-high heat, and sauté the steak on both sides until done, about 5 to 7 minutes. Season with the salt and pepper. Remove the meat, and add the garlic and wine to the pan. Boil until reduced by half, stirring well. Add the beef broth and mustard, stirring until blended. Boil until slightly thickened, and add the parsley. Return the meat to the pan, heat with the sauce, and serve.

Nutritional information per serving

Calories 159, Protein (g) 24, Carbohydrate (g) 0, Fat (g) 5, Calories from Fat (%) 30, Saturated Fat (g) 2, Dietary Fiber (g) 0, Cholesterol (mg) 69, Sodium (mg) 219, Diabetic Exchanges: 3 lean meat

Smothered Round Steak ❄

My family likes this terrific gravy with rice. Toss in some baby carrots if desired.

MAKES 4 TO 6 SERVINGS

2 pounds round steak, trimmed of fat
Salt and pepper to taste
¼ cup all-purpose flour
1 medium onion, chopped
1 teaspoon minced garlic
1 (10-ounce) can diced tomatoes and green chilies
2 cups canned beef broth

Season the meat with the salt and pepper, and dust both sides with the flour.

In a large non-stick skillet, brown the steak over medium-high heat on both sides, about 6 minutes in all. Add the onion, garlic, tomato and green chilies, and broth, and bring to a boil. Reduce the heat, cover, and simmer for 1½ hours, or until the meat is tender. Serve.

Nutritional information per serving

Calories 245, Protein (g) 38, Carbohydrate (g) 8, Fat (g) 6, Calories from Fat (%) 22, Saturated Fat (g) 2, Dietary Fiber (g) 1, Cholesterol (mg) 94, Sodium (mg) 592, Diabetic Exchanges: 4.5 lean meat, 1.5 vegetable

QUICK TIP:

Even though round steak is a less tender cut of meat, this recipe cooks the meat for a long time, and the meat is extremely soft.

MEAT

Beef Stir-Fry ❄

Early in the morning, marinate and refrigerate the meat. The honey and ginger infuse the meat, so you'll get a sweet and spicy flavor in every bite. For your quick evening meal, toss the ingredients together and serve over rice.

MAKES 6 TO 8 SERVINGS

⅓ cup low-sodium soy sauce

¼ cup honey

1 teaspoon ground ginger

2 teaspoons minced garlic

2 pounds flank steak, trimmed of fat and cut into strips

1 onion, coarsely chopped

4 cups broccoli florets

1 green or red bell pepper, seeded and cut into strips

½ cup quartered fresh mushrooms

1 large tomato, chopped

1 (8-ounce) can sliced water chestnuts, drained

Combine the soy sauce, honey, ginger, and garlic in a baking dish; coat both sides of the meat with the mixture, and marinate in the refrigerator, covered, for at least 1 hour.

In a wok or large shallow non-stick skillet, stir-fry the steak, onion, broccoli, and pepper over medium-high heat for 5 to 7 minutes. Add the mushrooms, tomato, and water chestnuts, and cook for 3 more minutes, or until the vegetables are tender and the meat is done. The meat is best served rare.

Nutritional information per serving

Calories 258, Protein (g) 26, Carbohydrate (g) 18, Fat (g) 9, Calories from Fat (%) 32, Saturated Fat (g) 4, Dietary Fiber (g) 3, Cholesterol (mg) 59, Sodium (mg) 348, Diabetic Exchanges: 3 lean meat, 0.5 starch, 1.5 vegetable

MEAT

FOOD FACT:

The best cuts of beef for stir-frying are flank and sirloin, which are more tender and full-flavored. To make slicing beef into strips easier, freeze for 15 to 30 minutes.

Traditional Meat-and-Macaroni Casserole ❄

Turn America's favorite side into a main dish meal. Who can resist macaroni with meat?

MAKES 8 SERVINGS

1 onion, chopped
1 green bell pepper, seeded and chopped
½ pound fresh mushrooms, sliced
1 pound ground sirloin
1 cup shell macaroni
1 (15-ounce) can tomato sauce
3 tablespoons tomato paste
1 (15 ¼-ounce) can corn, drained
1 tablespoon chili powder
Salt and pepper to taste
1 cup shredded reduced-fat Cheddar cheese

Preheat the oven to 350°F.

In a large non-stick pot, sauté the onion, green pepper, mushrooms, and meat until the vegetables are tender and the meat is done. Cook the macaroni according to the package directions, omitting any oil and salt. Drain; add to the meat mixture. Add the tomato sauce, tomato paste, corn, and chili powder. Season with the salt and pepper. Transfer to a 2-quart casserole, and top with the shredded cheese. Bake for 20 minutes, or until well heated. Serve.

Nutritional information per serving

Calories 227, Protein (g) 20, Carbohydrate (g) 26, Fat (g) 6, Calories from Fat (%) 22, Saturated Fat (g) 3, Dietary Fiber (g) 3, Cholesterol (mg) 38, Sodium (mg) 527, Diabetic Exchanges: 2 lean meat, 1 starch, 2 vegetable

Southwestern Grilled Beef Fajitas ❄

This marinade is packed with flavor and makes the best fajitas. Serve with tortillas, cheese, tomatoes, and salsa or the condiments of your choice.

MAKES 6 TO 8 SERVINGS

1 (10-ounce) can light beer
¼ cup chopped cilantro
½ teaspoon minced garlic
¼ cup lime juice
2 tablespoons red wine vinegar
1 tablespoon Worcestershire sauce
1 tablespoon grated lime peel
1 teaspoon ground cumin
1 tablespoon chili powder
Salt and pepper
2 pounds flank steak

In a zipper-lock bag, combine the beer, cilantro, garlic, lime juice, vinegar, Worcestershire sauce, lime peel, cumin, chili powder, salt, and pepper. Add the meat, seal the bag, and refrigerate overnight.

Drain well, and grill or broil the meat until done—flank steak should be served rare. Slice and serve.

Nutritional information per serving

Calories 185, Protein (g) 24, Carbohydrate (g) 1, Fat (g) 9, Calories from Fat (%) 45, Saturated Fat (g) 4, Dietary Fiber (g) 0, Cholesterol (mg) 59, Sodium (mg) 103, Diabetic Exchanges: 3 lean meat

MEAT

Beef and Chicken Shish Kabobs

This recipe has one of the best marinades. I prepared this quick recipe on the Today show for a grilled, one-dish meal. It's also great for parties.

MAKES 8 TO 10 SKEWERS

2 pounds skinless, boneless chicken breasts,
    cut into 1½-inch cubes
2 pounds sirloin tip, cut into 1½-inch cubes
1 pint cherry tomatoes
1 pound fresh mushrooms
2 green bell peppers, seeded and cut into chunks
1 onion, cut into chunks
Orange and Wine Marinade (recipe follows)

Place the chicken, meat, tomatoes, mushrooms, peppers, and onion in a large bowl, and pour the Orange and Wine Marinade (see recipe at right) over them. Refrigerate overnight.

Assemble the chicken, meat, and vegetables on metal skewers, without crowding the pieces together, and grill on a hot grill 5 to 10 minutes or until done, turning frequently. Baste with the remaining marinade while grilling. Serve.

ORANGE AND WINE MARINADE

1 cup dry red wine
¼ cup low-sodium soy sauce
1 cup orange juice
1 tablespoon dried thyme leaves
1 tablespoon dried rosemary leaves
2 tablespoons Worcestershire sauce
1 teaspoon pepper
1 tablespoon minced garlic

In a medium bowl, mix together the wine, soy sauce, orange juice, thyme, rosemary, Worcestershire sauce, pepper, and garlic.

Nutritional information per serving

Calories 252, Protein (g) 43, Carbohydrate (g) 8, Fat (g) 5, Calories from Fat (%) 18, Saturated Fat (g) 2, Dietary Fiber (g) 2, Cholesterol (mg) 107, Sodium (mg) 311, Diabetic Exchanges: 6 very lean meat, 1.5 vegetable

MEAT

QUICK TIP:

When making kabobs, don't crowd the ingredients on the skewers—leave a little space between each piece.

Crispy Southwestern Lasagna ❄

This popular and exciting twist to lasagna is simple to prepare, with no noodles to cook. I prefer blending the cottage cheese in a food processor until it's smooth. Ricotta cheese may be substituted for the cottage cheese. After preparing this recipe on the Today *show, the first edition of this book shot to #4 on Amazon.com!*

MAKES 8 TO 10 SERVINGS

1 pound ground sirloin
1 (14½-ounce) can diced tomatoes, with juice
1 (4-ounce) can diced green chilies, drained
2 teaspoons chili powder
1½ teaspoons ground cumin
1 teaspoon minced garlic
Salt and pepper to taste
2 egg whites
2 cups reduced-fat or fat-free cottage cheese
14 (6-inch) corn or flour tortillas, cut into quarters
1 (15¼-ounce) can corn, drained
8 ounces reduced-fat Monterey Jack cheese, shredded

Preheat the oven to 350°F.

In a large non-stick skillet, cook the meat over medium heat until done, and drain any excess liquid. Add the tomatoes and juice, green chilies, chili powder, cumin, garlic, salt, and pepper; set aside.

In a small bowl, blend the egg whites and cottage cheese well; set aside. In a 13 x 9 x 2-inch non-stick baking dish coated with non-stick cooking spray, place six quartered tortillas. Layer of all the corn, half the meat mixture, half the cheese, four quartered tortillas, then all of the cottage cheese mixture, the remaining half of the meat mixture, and the remaining four quartered tortillas, and top with the remaining cheese. Bake, uncovered, for 30 minutes. Serve.

Nutritional information per serving

Calories 239, Protein (g) 25, Carbohydrate (g) 20, Fat (g) 7, Calories from Fat (%) 26, Saturated Fat (g) 3, Dietary Fiber (g) 3, Cholesterol (mg) 40, Sodium (mg) 537, Diabetic Exchanges: 3 lean meat, 1 starch, 1 vegetable

QUICK TIP:

Purchase ground meat in bulk for savings. Mold into patties, wrap well, and freeze to pull out later for hamburgers on the spot.

MEAT

Crispy Southwestern Lasagna

Mexican Lasagna

No boiling noodles for this lasagna. Use tortillas and Mexican salsas to satisfy that south-of-the-border craving.

MAKES 8 SERVINGS

1 pound ground sirloin
½ cup chopped celery
½ cup chopped onion
½ teaspoon minced garlic
¼ cup chopped green bell pepper
1 (16-ounce) jar salsa
1 (14-ounce) can enchilada sauce, divided
Salt and pepper to taste
4 slices reduced-fat American cheese
1 cup fat-free cottage cheese
1 egg white, beaten
6 (6- to 8-inch) flour tortillas, cut into thirds

Preheat the oven to 350°F.

In a large non-stick skillet, cook the meat, celery, onion, garlic, and green pepper over medium heat until the meat is done, about 8 to 10 minutes. Drain any excess liquid. Add the salsa, two-thirds of the enchilada sauce, and the salt and pepper. Bring to a boil; reduce the heat, and simmer 10 minutes.

Meanwhile, combine the American and cottage cheeses and the egg white in a food processor, mixing until blended and the American cheese is in pieces; set aside.

In a non-stick skillet, heat the remaining enchilada sauce a little at a time, and fry the flour tortillas until soft. Remove, continuing to add sauce and fry tortillas until all have been cooked. Spoon one-third of the meat mixture into a 2-quart oblong baking dish coated with non-stick cooking spray. Spoon half the cheese mixture over the meat. Top with half the tortillas. Repeat the layers, ending with the meat. Bake for 25 minutes. Let stand for 5 minutes before serving.

Nutritional information per serving
Calories 230, Protein (g) 20, Carbohydrate (g) 22, Fat (g) 5, Calories from Fat (%) 22, Saturated Fat (g) 3, Dietary Fiber (g) 2, Cholesterol (mg) 40, Sodium (mg) 998, Diabetic Exchanges: 2.5 lean meat, 1.5 starch

MEAT

Tamale Pie

In the mood for tamales? This easy-to-make layered tortilla-and-meat dish is great for a crowd of all ages.

MAKES 10 TO 12 SERVINGS

2 pounds ground sirloin
1 onion, chopped
1 teaspoon minced garlic
1 (8-ounce) can tomato sauce
1 (16-ounce) jar thick and chunky salsa
1 teaspoon ground cumin
1 teaspoon chili powder
1 (15-ounce) can cream-style corn
6 (6- to 8-inch) flour tortillas, cut into 1-inch strips
¾ cup shredded reduced-fat Cheddar cheese

Preheat the oven to 350°F.

In a large non-stick skillet, cook the meat, onion, and garlic over medium heat, until the meat is done, about 7 minutes. Drain any excess grease. Add the tomato sauce, salsa, cumin, chili powder, and corn, mixing well.

In a 13 x 9 x 2-inch non-stick baking pan coated with non-stick cooking spray, layer one-third of the meat mixture. Cover the mixture with one-third of the tortilla strips, and repeat the layers, starting with a fourth of the remaining meat mixture and topping with a third of the tortilla strips. Continue layering, ending with the meat mixture. Cover and bake for 35 to 40 minutes, or until thoroughly heated. Sprinkle with the cheese, and continue cooking for another 5 minutes, or until the cheese is melted. Cool for 5 minutes, and serve.

Nutritional information per serving
Calories 200, Protein (g) 19, Carbohydrate (g) 20, Fat (g) 5, Calories from Fat (%) 22, Saturated Fat (g) 2, Dietary Fiber (g) 1, Cholesterol (mg) 44, Sodium (mg) 605, Diabetic Exchanges: 2 lean meat, 1 starch, 1 vegetable

MEAT

Italian Meat Loaf with Garlic Smashed Potatoes

Italian Meat Loaf ❄

Layers of Mozzarella and ham will make anyone a fan of this meatloaf. The tomato juice keeps it moist. Try adding spinach for a twist.

MAKES 6 SERVINGS

2 pounds ground sirloin

1 egg white

1 cup tomato juice

Salt and pepper to taste

½ teaspoon minced garlic

1 teaspoon dried oregano leaves

1 teaspoon dried basil leaves

1 onion, chopped

4 ounces sliced part-skim Mozzarella cheese

4 ounces sliced lean ham

Preheat the oven to 350°F.

In a large bowl, combine the meat, egg white, tomato juice, salt, pepper, garlic, oregano, and basil. In a small non-stick skillet, sauté the onion until tender. Add the cooked onion to the meat mixture, mixing well. Put half the meat mixture into a 9 x 5 x 3-inch non-stick loaf pan, top with the Mozzarella cheese and ham, and cover with the remaining meat mixture. Bake for 1 hour, or until meat is done. Serve.

Nutritional information per serving

Calories 266, Protein (g) 39, Carbohydrate (g) 5, Fat (g) 11, Calories from Fat (%) 35, Saturated Fat (g) 5, Dietary Fiber (g) 1, Cholesterol (mg) 98, Sodium (mg) 532, Diabetic Exchanges: 5 lean meat, 1 vegetable

Italian Eggplant, Meat, and Rice

Eggplant and zucchini are disguised in this rice dressing-style dish topped with tomato sauce and cheese. It's a wonderful, crowd-pleasing Italian casserole.

MAKES 6 TO 8 SERVINGS

2 medium eggplants, peeled and cubed

1 zucchini, thinly sliced

1 tablespoon minced garlic

4 ounces light bulk sausage

½ pound ground sirloin

Salt and pepper to taste

1 tablespoon plus 1 teaspoon dried basil leaves, divided

1 tablespoon plus 1 teaspoon dried oregano leaves, divided

3 cups cooked rice

1 (15-ounce) can tomato sauce

1½ cups shredded part-skim Mozzarella cheese

Preheat the oven to 350°F.

In a large non-stick pot, sauté the eggplants, zucchini, garlic, sausage, and meat over medium heat until the meat is done and the vegetables are very tender, about 10 minutes. Drain any excess liquid. Add the salt and pepper, 1 tablespoon basil, 1 tablespoon oregano, and the cooked rice, tossing well. Spread the mixture in a 2-quart casserole dish coated with non-stick cooking spray.

In a small bowl, combine the tomato sauce with the remaining basil and oregano, and spread over the eggplant-rice mixture. Sprinkle with the Mozzarella, and bake, uncovered, for 20 to 30 minutes, or until the mixture is hot and the cheese is melted. Serve.

Nutritional information per serving

Calories 246, Protein (g) 17, Carbohydrate (g) 30, Fat (g) 7, Calories from Fat (%) 24, Saturated Fat (g) 3, Dietary Fiber (g) 4, Cholesterol (mg) 39, Sodium (mg) 502, Diabetic Exchanges: 2 lean meat, 1 starch, 3 vegetable

MEAT

QUICK TIP:

For added fiber, use brown or wild rice in dishes that call for rice.

Stuffed Peppers

Stuffed Peppers ❄

This stuffing is so delicious, you can put this hearty mixture in a casserole dish, bake it, and make a meal of it. If you feel creative, use red, yellow, or orange bell peppers.

MAKES 6 SERVINGS

6 medium green bell peppers, seeded
1 pound ground sirloin
1 cup chopped fresh mushrooms
¾ cup chopped onion
1 cup tomato sauce
1 tablespoon minced garlic
1 teaspoon dried basil leaves
1 teaspoon dried oregano leaves
1 tablespoon Worcestershire sauce
Salt and pepper to taste
2 cups cooked rice
½ cup (2 ounces) shredded part-skim Mozzarella cheese

Preheat the oven to 350°F.

Cut the tops off the green peppers, and remove the cores. Trim the stems from the tops, and discard. Chop the remaining tops; set aside.

Arrange the pepper shells in a steamer over boiling water, cover, and steam for 5 to 10 minutes, or until tender. Drain the shells, and set aside.

In a large non-stick skillet, combine the meat, mushrooms, onion, and reserved chopped green pepper. Cook over medium heat until the meat is brown, about 7 minutes; drain off any excess grease. Add the tomato sauce, garlic, basil, oregano, Worcestershire sauce, salt, and pepper. Bring to a boil; reduce the heat and simmer 5 minutes. Mix in the rice.

Spoon the mixture into the pepper shells; then place the peppers upright in an 8-inch square baking dish. Sprinkle with the Mozzarella. Bake for 15 minutes, or until the cheese is melted and the peppers are thoroughly heated. Serve.

Nutritional information per serving
Calories 242, Protein (g) 21, Carbohydrate (g) 29, Fat (g) 5, Calories from Fat (%) 19, Saturated Fat (g) 2, Dietary Fiber (g) 3, Cholesterol (mg) 45, Sodium (mg) 346, Diabetic Exchanges: 2 lean meat, 1 starch, 3 vegetable

MEAT

Meatballs for a Crowd ❄

This recipe makes a huge pot of these meatballs, so I usually serve them and freeze the remainder.

MAKES 14 TO 16 SERVINGS

4 pounds ground sirloin
1 tablespoon onion powder
1 tablespoon dried oregano leaves
1 tablespoon dried basil leaves
½ teaspoon pepper
1 tablespoon minced garlic
2 tablespoons Worcestershire sauce
2 tablespoons low-sodium soy sauce
1 cup Italian bread crumbs
3 egg whites
Tomato Sauce (recipe follows)

Preheat the broiler.

In a large bowl, mix together the meat, onion powder, oregano, basil, pepper, garlic, Worcestershire sauce, soy sauce, bread crumbs, and egg whites until well combined. Shape the mixture into meatballs, using about ¼ cup of the mixture for each.

Place the meatballs on a non-stick baking sheet coated with non-stick cooking spray. Broil about 6 to 8 minutes on each side. Transfer the meatballs to the pot of Tomato Sauce (see recipe at right), and continue cooking for 30 minutes. Serve with pasta.

TOMATO SAUCE

1 cup finely chopped onion
2 (28-ounce) cans chopped tomatoes, with juice
2 (6-ounce) cans tomato paste
2 cups water
1 tablespoon minced garlic
1 tablespoon dried oregano leaves
1 tablespoon dried basil leaves
¼ teaspoon pepper

While the meatballs are broiling, place the onion in a large non-stick pot. Over medium-high heat, sauté the onion until tender, about 5 minutes. Add the tomatoes, tomato paste, water, garlic, oregano, basil, and pepper. Bring to a boil, lower the heat, and simmer for 30 minutes. Add the meatballs to the sauce.

Nutritional information per serving
Calories 213, Protein (g) 26, Carbohydrate (g) 17, Fat (g) 5, Calories from Fat (%) 22, Saturated Fat (g) 2, Dietary Fiber (g) 4, Cholesterol (mg) 60, Sodium (mg) 395, Diabetic Exchanges: 3 lean meat, 0.5 starch, 2 vegetable

QUICK TIP:

To keep your hands from getting sticky when shaping meatballs or other sticky foods, moisten them with cool water.

Mock Cabbage Rolls ❄

This recipe is a quick and easy alternative to individually stuffing all those cabbage leaves. Shredded cabbage is available in bags at the grocery store to make preparation a snap.

MAKES 6 TO 8 SERVINGS

1½ pounds ground sirloin
1 onion, chopped
1 teaspoon minced garlic
¼ teaspoon pepper
3 cups cooked rice
1(¾-pound) head cabbage, coarsely shredded
1 (26-ounce) jar pasta sauce
¼ cup light brown sugar
1 cup shredded part-skim Mozzarella cheese, optional

Preheat the oven to 350°F.

In a large skillet, cook the meat, onion, and garlic over medium heat until the meat is done, about 7 minutes. Drain any excess liquid. Add the pepper and cooked rice, mixing well.

Spoon the meat mixture into a 4-quart casserole dish coated with non-stick cooking spray. Top with shredded cabbage.

In a medium bowl, mix together the pasta sauce and brown sugar. Pour the sauce over the cabbage. Bake, covered, for 1¼ hours, or until the cabbage is tender. Sprinkle with Mozzarella, and continue baking for 5 minutes, or until the cheese is melted. Serve.

Nutritional information per serving
Calories 307, Protein (g) 24, Carbohydrate (g) 37, Fat (g) 7, Calories from Fat (%) 22, Saturated Fat (g) 3, Dietary Fiber (g) 3, Cholesterol (mg) 53, Sodium (mg) 541, Diabetic Exchanges: 3 lean meat, 1 starch, 1 vegetable, 1 other carbohydrate

MEAT

Stuffed Cabbage ❄

This recipe is from my grandmother. Storing the cabbage overnight in the freezer simplifies the typical preparation of boiling cabbage leaves to soften, so I usually double the recipe and freeze some.

3 pounds green cabbage (about 2 large heads)
2 pounds ground sirloin
1 onion, chopped
2 egg whites
1 cup uncooked rice
Salt and pepper to taste
1 (15-ounce) can tomato sauce
¾ cup water
½ cup light brown sugar
½ cup crushed ginger snap cookie crumbs
¼ cup lemon juice

Freeze the cabbage overnight.

Defrost the cabbage, and cut out the core. Carefully tear the leaves away from the head (they will pull off easily now); set aside.

Preheat the oven to 350°F.

In a large bowl, combine the meat, onion, egg whites, rice, salt, and pepper. Place about ¼ cup meat mixture in the hollow of each cabbage leaf. Fold the sides of the leaf over the stuffing; roll up from the thick end of the leaf. Repeat with all leaves large enough to roll up, until the stuffing is used up.

Place the stuffed leaves in a deep, oblong 3- to 4-quart casserole dish. A roaster also works well. To make the sauce, in another bowl combine the tomato sauce, water, brown sugar, cookie crumbs, and lemon juice. Pour over the stuffed cabbage. Cover, and bake for 2 to 2½ hours. When the cabbage rolls are done, the rice and meat will be cooked and the cabbage will be tender.

Nutritional information per serving

Calories 248, Protein (g) 19, Carbohydrate (g) 35, Fat (g) 4, Calories from Fat (%) 15, Saturated Fat (g) 1, Dietary Fiber (g) 3, Cholesterol (mg) 40, Sodium (mg) 306, Diabetic Exchanges: 2 lean meat, 1 starch, 1 vegetable, 1 other carbohydrate

QUICK TIP:

When you're buying cabbage, look for tight, firm, heavy heads with no broken or bruised leaves.

MEAT

Old-Fashioned Pork Chop Casserole ❄️

In this simple dish, you get gravy, meat, and rice in a no-fail combination that makes a nice dinner.

MAKES 6 TO 8 SERVINGS

⅔ cup uncooked rice
1 (6-ounce) package long-grain and wild rice mix
3 cups hot water
8 bone-in loin pork chops, trimmed of fat (½ inch thick)
Salt and pepper to taste
1 (10¾-ounce) can 98% fat-free cream of celery soup
⅔ cup skim milk
⅓ cup chopped green onions (scallions)

Preheat the oven to 350°F.

In a medium bowl, combine the rice, the wild rice with its seasoning packet, and the hot water. Place the rice mixture in a 13 x 9 x 2-inch non-stick baking dish coated with nonstick cooking spray; lay the pork chops on top, and season with salt and pepper. Cover, and bake for 1 hour.

In a small bowl, mix together the cream of celery soup, milk, and green onion. Uncover the casserole, and pour the soup mixture over the pork chops. Return the casserole, uncovered, to the oven, and bake for 15 minutes longer, or until thoroughly heated. Serve.

Nutritional information per serving

Calories 292, Protein (g) 26, Carbohydrate (g) 33, Fat (g) 5, Calories from Fat (%) 17, Saturated Fat (g) 2, Dietary Fiber (g) 1, Cholesterol (mg) 66, Sodium (mg) 640, Diabetic Exchanges: 3 lean meat, 2 starch

MEAT

Moussaka ❄

My Greek neighbor showed me how to make moussaka, a traditional Greek lasagna with a unique taste that serves a crowd. This hearty meal is worth the time spent preparing it.

MAKES 12 SERVINGS

2 large eggplants, peeled and cut into ½-inch slices
2 baking potatoes, peeled and cut into ½-inch slices
½ teaspoon sugar
Meat Sauce (recipe follows)
White Sauce (recipe follows)
1 cup shredded reduced-fat Cheddar cheese

Preheat the broiler.

Place the eggplant and the potato on a non-stick baking sheet, and spray the vegetables with non-stick cooking spray. Broil about 4 inches from the heat until the vegetables are golden in color, about 5 minutes on each side.

Preheat the oven to 350°F.

In a 13 x 9 x 2-inch non-stick baking pan coated with non-stick cooking spray, lay half the potato slices. Layer half the eggplant on top, and sprinkle with the sugar. Layer with all of the Meat Sauce (see recipe at right). Top with the remaining potato and eggplant. Pour the White Sauce (see recipe at right) over the top to cover. Bake for 35 to 40 minutes, or until the vegetables are tender. Sprinkle with the cheese, and continue baking for 5 to 10 minutes, or until the cheese is melted. Cool for 5 minutes, and serve.

MEAT SAUCE

1 onion, chopped
1 teaspoon minced garlic
1 pound ground sirloin
½ cup dry white wine
½ cup chopped parsley
1 (14½-ounce) can diced tomatoes
1 (10¾-ounce) can tomato pureé
Dash allspice
¼ teaspoon ground cinnamon
Salt and pepper to taste

In a large non-stick skillet, sauté the onion, garlic, and meat over medium heat until the meat is done and the vegetables are tender, about 5 minutes. Drain any excess grease. Add the white wine, parsley, tomato, tomato pureé, allspice, cinnamon, salt, and pepper. Bring to a boil, stirring constantly. Reduce the heat, and simmer, uncovered, for 20 minutes.

WHITE SAUCE

¼ cup all-purpose flour
2 cups skim milk
⅛ teaspoon allspice
Salt and pepper to taste

In a medium saucepan, stir together the flour and milk. Bring to a boil over medium-high heat, stirring until thickened, about 5 minutes. Remove from the heat, and add the allspice, salt, and pepper.

Moussaka

Nutritional information per serving

Calories 158, Protein (g) 14, Carbohydrate (g) 19, Fat (g) 4, Calories from Fat (%) 20, Saturated Fat (g) 2, Dietary Fiber (g) 4, Cholesterol mg) 26, Sodium (mg) 252, Diabetic Exchanges: 1.5 lean meat, 0.5 starch, 2 vegetable

FOOD FACT:

Traditional Greek moussaka is a baked, layered casserole typically made with lamb.

MEAT

Barbecued Pork Roast

Barbecued Pork Roast ❄

A pork roast is a nice change, and this tasty barbe-cued meat is a no-trouble approach for barbecue cravings. The leftovers make great sandwiches.

MAKES 6 TO 8 SERVINGS

1 (3-pound) boneless, rolled loin pork roast
3 large cloves garlic, sliced thinly
1 teaspoon pepper
1 teaspoon dried thyme leaves
1 onion, sliced
½ cup fat-free canned chicken broth
½ cup cider vinegar
1 (6-ounce) can tomato paste
¼ cup lemon juice
2 tablespoons Worcestershire sauce
2 tablespoons light brown sugar
1 tablespoon Dijon mustard
½ teaspoon paprika

Preheat the oven to 350°F.

Trim any excess fat from the pork roast. Cut deep slits in the roast, and insert the garlic slices. Combine the pepper and thyme; rub over the surface of the roast. In a non-stick saucepan, sauté the onion over medium heat. Add the chicken broth, vinegar, tomato paste, lemon juice, Worcestershire sauce, brown sugar, Dijon mustard, and paprika, stirring until the mixture comes to a boil. Remove from heat. Place the roast in a non-stick pot coated with non-stick cooking spray, and cover with the barbecue sauce. Bake for 1½ to 2 hours, or until very tender. Slice, and serve with the sauce.

Nutritional information per serving
Calories 314, Protein (g) 39, Carbohydrate (g) 13, Fat (g) 11, Calories from Fat (%) 33, Saturated Fat (g) 4, Dietary Fiber (g) 2, Cholesterol (mg) 94, Sodium (mg) 198, Diabetic Exchanges: 6 lean meat, 2 vegetable

MEAT

Pork Tenderloin Diane with Wild Rice ❄

Brown the tenderloins while the rice is cooking, for a fast-to-fix, one-dish meal with pizzazz.

MAKES 6 TO 8 SERVINGS

1 (6-ounce) package long-grain and wild rice mix
2 pounds pork tenderloin, trimmed of fat, cut crosswise
   into 16 slices, each about 1 inch thick
Salt and pepper to taste
2 tablespoons margarine
¼ cup lemon juice
2 tablespoons Worcestershire sauce
1 tablespoon Dijon mustard
1 tablespoon chopped parsley

Cook the wild rice according to the package directions, omitting any oil and salt.

Meanwhile, season the pork with salt and pepper. Heat the margarine in a heavy non-stick skillet and cook the slices 3 to 4 minutes on each side, until browned and cooked through, working in batches if necessary. Remove to a serving platter, and cover to keep warm.

Add the lemon juice, Worcestershire sauce, and mustard to the skillet. Cook over medium heat, stirring with the pork juices, until heated thoroughly, about 3 minutes. Return the pork to the sauce. Serve the pork and sauce over the rice, sprinkled with the parsley.

Nutritional information per serving
Calories 248, Protein (g) 26, Carbohydrate (g) 18, Fat (g) 7, Calories from Fat (%) 27, Saturated Fat (g) 2, Dietary Fiber (g) 0, Cholesterol (mg) 67, Sodium (mg) 483, Diabetic Exchanges: 3 lean meat, 1 starch

MEAT

Florentine Pork Wellington with Green Peppercorn Sauce ❄

Easy elegance with a terrific taste. It literally took me only minutes to wrap these tenderloins for such an impressive pork preparation. Wonderful stuffing with a very tasty Peppercorn Sauce.

MAKES 6 TO 8 SERVINGS

2 (10-ounce) packages frozen chopped spinach
½ pound fresh mushrooms, sliced
1 onion, chopped
½ teaspoon minced garlic
2 (1-pound) pork tenderloins, trimmed of fat
Salt and pepper to taste
1 package phyllo dough
Green Peppercorn Sauce (recipe follows)

Preheat the oven to 375°F.

Cook the spinach according to the package directions; drain, squeeze dry, and set aside.

In a large non-stick skillet, sauté the mushrooms, onion, and garlic until tender. Add the spinach. Transfer the mixture to a food processor, and pulse until puréed.

Season each tenderloin with the salt and pepper. Mold the spinach mixture around the sides and top of each tenderloin.

On waxed paper, lay each sheet of phyllo dough, coated with non-stick cooking spray, until 10 sheets of phyllo dough are stacked. Place a spinach-covered tenderloin on one end of the phyllo dough, and roll up, tucking the ends on each side under. Repeat the procedure with another 10 sheets of phyllo dough and the other tenderloin.

Spray each wrapped tenderloin with non-stick cooking spray, and transfer to a non-stick baking sheet. Bake for 45 minutes, or until a meat thermometer reads 160°F. Slice, and serve with Green Peppercorn Sauce (see recipe on next page).

MEAT

GREEN PEPPERCORN SAUCE

MAKES 1½ CUPS

1 cup beef broth
2 teaspoons Dijon mustard
¼ cup dried green peppercorns
1 cup evaporated skimmed milk

In a small saucepan, combine the beef broth, mustard, and peppercorns. Bring to a boil over medium heat. Lower the heat, and cook until the sauce is reduced by half and thickens. Add the milk, and heat until the sauce thickens. Do not boil.

Nutritional information per serving

Calories 385, Protein (g) 34, Carbohydrate (g) 43, Fat (g) 8, Calories from Fat (%) 19, Saturated Fat (g) 2, Dietary Fiber (g) 6, Cholesterol (mg) 75, Sodium (mg) 582, Diabetic Exchanges: 3 lean meat, 2 starch, 0.5 skim milk, 1.5 vegetable

FOOD FACT:

Phyllo is tissue-thin pastry dough found frozen in most grocery stores. Phyllo sheets become dry and brittle quickly, so don't remove the sheets from their wrapping until you're ready to use them.

MEAT

Glazed Pork Tenderloin ❄

Pork tenderloin is a lean cut of meat that can be kept in the freezer to pull out for a quick dinner. This glaze enhances the meat with a subtly sweet, spicy flavor. If time permits, let the meat marinate in the sauce before cooking.

MAKES 6 TO 8 SERVINGS

2 tablespoons Dijon mustard
½ teaspoon minced garlic
½ teaspoon dried rosemary leaves
½ teaspoon dried thyme leaves
¼ teaspoon pepper
2 tablespoons honey
2 (1-pound) pork tenderloins, trimmed of fat

Preheat the oven to 325°F.

In a small bowl, mix together the mustard, garlic, rosemary, thyme, pepper, and honey. Coat the tenderloins with the mixture.

Place the tenderloins on a non-stick baking sheet coated with non-stick cooking spray or on a rack in a shallow roasting pan. Bake for 40 to 45 minutes, or until a meat thermometer inserted into the thickest portion registers 160°F. Slice the tenderloins, and serve.

Nutritional information per serving
Calories 160, Protein (g) 24, Carbohydrate (g) 5, Fat (g) 4, Calories from Fat (%) 24, Saturated Fat (g) 1, Dietary Fiber (g) 0, Cholesterol (mg) 67, Sodium (mg) 138, Diabetic Exchanges: 3 lean meat, 1 other carbohydrate

QUICK TIP:

Tenderloins come two to a package. If one will be enough for you to serve, halve the recipe and freeze the other tenderloin.

MEAT

Glazed Pork Tenderloin

Grilled Pork Tenderloin Oriental ❄

This fabulous marinade (also great with flank steak) infuses the meat with tons of flavor.

SERVES 6 TO 8

¼ cup orange juice

¼ cup low-sodium soy sauce

3 tablespoons honey

1 tablespoon chopped garlic

1 bay leaf

½ teaspoon pepper

½ teaspoon dry mustard

½ teaspoon ground ginger

½ teaspoon onion powder

2 (1-pound) pork tenderloins, trimmed of fat

In a shallow dish, combine the orange juice, soy sauce, honey, garlic, bay leaf, pepper, mustard, ginger, and onion powder. Add the pork tenderloins. Marinate in the refrigerator at least 4 hours (time permitting) or overnight.

Grill the pork over medium-hot coals for 20 to 25 minutes, or bake at 350°F, basting with the marinade mixture, for 50 minutes, or until a meat thermometer registers 160°F. Discard unused marinade. Serve.

Nutritional information per serving

Calories 144, Protein (g) 24, Carbohydrate (g) 1, Fat (g) 4, Calories from Fat (%) 27, Saturated Fat (g) 1, Dietary Fiber (g) 0, Cholesterol (mg) 67, Sodium (mg) 243, Diabetic Exchanges: 3 lean meat

QUICK TIP:

The best way to test pork's doneness is with a meat thermometer. Cutting it to check on doneness lets too many good juices run out.

MEAT

Pork Medallions
with Brandy Sauce ❄

This succulent, moist tenderloin is served with a rich, intensely flavored sauce.

MAKES 6 TO 8 SERVINGS

1 (2 to 2½-pound) boneless pork tenderloin, trimmed of fat
Black pepper as needed
Brandy Sauce
⅔ cup canned fat-free chicken broth
2 tablespoons chopped green onions (scallions)
½ cup evaporated skimmed milk
2 tablespoons brandy
2 tablespoons margarine
1 tablespoon lemon juice
Salt to taste
⅛ teaspoon white pepper

Preheat the oven to 325°F.

Rub the tenderloin with the black pepper. Place on a rack in a shallow non-stick baking pan coated with non-stick cooking spray. Roast until a meat thermometer registers 160°F (about 30 minutes per pound).

Meanwhile, make the Brandy Sauce. In a saucepan, combine the chicken broth and green onions. Bring to a boil; reduce the heat, cover, and simmer 2 minutes. Add the evaporated milk and brandy. Simmer, uncovered, over medium heat until the sauce is reduced to ⅔ cup, about 5 minutes. Add the margarine to the sauce, 1 tablespoon at a time, stirring constantly with a wire whisk. Stir in the lemon juice, salt, and white pepper. To serve, cut the meat and top with the sauce.

Nutritional information per serving
Calories 188, Protein (g) 25, Carbohydrate (g) 2, Fat (g) 7, Calories from Fat (%) 35, Saturated Fat (g) 2, Dietary Fiber (g) 0, Cholesterol (mg) 68, Sodium (mg) 151, Diabetic Exchanges: 3 lean meat

MEAT

Pork Tenderloin with Mustard Sauce ❄

Many times I've served this on a buffet line with rolls. The mustard sauce superbly complements the tenderloin, adding a touch of sophistication.

MAKES 6 TO 8 SERVINGS

¼ cup low-sodium soy sauce
¼ cup bourbon
2 tablespoons light brown sugar
2 pounds pork tenderloin, trimmed of fat
Mustard Sauce (recipe follows)

In an 11 x 7 x 1½-inch non-stick baking dish, combine the soy sauce, bourbon, and brown sugar. Add the tenderloins. Cover and refrigerate at least 2 hours, turning occasionally.

Preheat the oven to 325°F.

Remove the meat from the marinade, discarding the marinade; place the tenderloins on a rack in a shallow roasting pan. Bake for 45 minutes, or until a meat thermometer inserted into the thickest portion registers 160°F. Serve with the Mustard Sauce (see recipe at right).

MUSTARD SAUCE

MAKES ABOUT 1½ CUPS

⅔ cup fat-free sour cream
⅔ cup light mayonnaise
2 tablespoons dry mustard
½ cup thinly chopped green onions (scallions)

In a small bowl, combine the sour cream, mayonnaise, dry mustard, and green onion. Cover, and chill in the refrigerator until ready to serve.

Nutritional information per serving
Calories 249, Protein (g) 27, Carbohydrate (g) 7, Fat (g) 11, Calories from Fat (%) 43, Saturated Fat (g) 2, Dietary Fiber (g) 0, Cholesterol (mg) 74, Sodium (mg) 420, Diabetic Exchanges: 3.5 lean meat, 0.5 other carbohydrate

QUICK TIP:

The leanest cuts of pork have "loin" names. Pork rib chops and boneless rib roasts are also good choices.

MEAT

Sweet-and-Sour Pork

Thumbs up for this version of sweet-and-sour pork. Everyone will clean their plates and say, "Forget going to Chinese restaurants, when I can enjoy this dish at home."

MAKES 6 SERVINGS

1½ pounds lean boneless pork tenderloin, trimmed of fat, sliced into thin slices
1 (8-ounce) can tomato sauce
¼ cup rice wine vinegar
2 tablespoons light brown sugar
1 tablespoon low-sodium soy sauce
¼ teaspoon minced garlic
⅛ teaspoon cayenne pepper
1 (20-ounce) can pineapple chunks with juice
1 green bell pepper, seeded and cut into 1-inch pieces
½ cup chopped green onions (scallions)
1 (11-ounce) can mandarin orange segments, drained
2 tablespoons cornstarch
3 cups cooked rice

In a non-stick skillet, cook the pork over medium-high heat for 3 to 5 minutes, or until browned, stirring frequently. Add the tomato sauce, vinegar, brown sugar, soy sauce, garlic, and cayenne pepper, and bring to a boil. Cover, reduce the heat, and simmer for 10 minutes, or until the pork is tender.

Drain the pineapple, reserving the juice. To the pork mixture, add the pineapple, green pepper, green onion, and mandarin oranges; cover and simmer 5 minutes longer, or until the vegetables are crisp-tender.

Combine the cornstarch with the reserved pineapple juice, and stir into the pork mixture. Cook, stirring constantly, until thickened and boiling. To serve, spoon the pork mixture over the rice.

Nutritional information per serving

Calories 366, Protein (g) 27, Carbohydrate (g) 52, Fat (g) 4, Calories from Fat (%) 11, Saturated Fat (g) 1, Dietary Fiber (g) 2, Cholesterol (mg) 67, Sodium (mg) 339, Diabetic Exchanges: 3 lean meat, 1.5 starch, 1.5 fruit, 1 vegetable

MEAT

Italian Pork, Squash, and Tomatoes

This summer specialty showcases seasonal squash in a one-dish skillet with an array of wonderful herbs and seasonings.

MAKES 6 TO 8 SERVINGS

2 pounds pork tenderloin, trimmed of fat, cut into 1½-inch cubes
2 cups sliced yellow squash (about 3 squash)
1 large zucchini, sliced
1 green bell pepper, seeded and coarsely chopped
1 onion, coarsely chopped
1 teaspoon minced garlic
4 large Roma (plum) tomatoes, quartered
1 teaspoon dried basil leaves
1 teaspoon dried oregano leaves
1 (28-ounce) can chopped tomatoes, with juice

Heat a large non-stick skillet over high heat, and add the pork, squash, zucchini, green pepper, onion, garlic, Roma tomatoes, basil, and oregano. Cook, stirring, until the meat begins to brown and the vegetables are crisp-tender, about 10 minutes. Add the chopped tomatoes, and continue cooking, covered, over medium heat until the meat is done and the vegetables are tender, about 20 minutes. Serve.

Nutritional information per serving
Calories 199, Protein (g) 26, Carbohydrate (g) 13, Fat (g) 4, Calories from Fat (%) 19, Saturated Fat (g) 1, Dietary Fiber (g) 5, Cholesterol (mg) 67, Sodium (mg) 177, Diabetic Exchanges: 3 lean meat, 3 vegetable

Veal Marengo

This intensely herb-flavored sauce cooked with the veal teams up with fresh tomatoes and mushrooms. Quick and tasty, it's perfect to serve with pasta.

MAKES 8 SERVINGS

½ cup white wine, divided
2 pounds lean veal scallopine
1 onion, chopped
½ pound fresh mushrooms, sliced
½ teaspoon minced garlic
1 teaspoon dried basil leaves
1 teaspoon dried oregano leaves
1 bay leaf
1 cup chopped Roma (plum) tomato
1 bunch green onions (scallions), chopped
2 tablespoons chopped parsley

In a large non-stick skillet, bring ¼ cup white wine to a simmer. Add the veal, and brown on both sides. Add the onion, mushrooms, garlic, basil, oregano, bay leaf, tomato, and the remaining white wine. Cook, stirring, until the mushrooms and onions are tender and the veal is cooked through, about 7 minutes. Add the green onions and parsley, and continue cooking for 5 more minutes. Remove and discard the bay leaf before serving.

Nutritional information per serving
Calories 157, Protein (g) 24, Carbohydrate (g) 5, Fat (g) 3, Calories from Fat (%) 20, Saturated Fat (g) 1, Dietary Fiber (g) 1, Cholesterol (mg) 94, Sodium (mg) 104, Diabetic Exchanges: 3 very lean meat, 1 vegetable

MEAT

Veal Saltimbocca

Veal Saltimbocca ❄

This impressive dish is made company-capable by preparing it early and transferring it to a 2-quart casserole dish to reheat. My friends enjoy this combination of veal and prosciutto in a light cheese sauce.

MAKES 4 TO 6 SERVINGS

10 small lean veal scallopine (thin slices)
¼ cup all-purpose flour
10 tablespoons shredded part-skim Mozzarella cheese
10 slices prosciutto (about 2 ounces)
1½ cups fat-free canned chicken broth
½ cup white wine
Chopped parsley, for garnish

Dust the veal with the flour. In a non-stick skillet coated with non-stick cooking spray, brown the veal on both sides. Remove the veal from the pan and top with the cheese. Place the prosciutto over the cheese (it will adhere to the cheese). Add the chicken broth and wine to the pan, scraping to get all pieces off the pan. Reduce the liquid by half by boiling for about 5 minutes. Carefully place the prepared veal in the pan, cooking over low heat for 10 minutes, or until heated. Garnish with the chopped parsley, and serve.

Nutritional information per serving

Calories 195, Protein (g) 26, Carbohydrate (g) 5, Fat (g) 6, Calories from Fat (%) 28, Saturated Fat (g) 3, Dietary Fiber (g) 0, Cholesterol (mg) 94, Sodium (mg) 461, Diabetic Exchanges: 3.5 lean meat, 0.5 starch

MEAT

Veal Elegante ❄

This veal, with a wonderful savory sauce, goes well with capellini.

MAKES 6 SERVINGS

1½ pounds thinly sliced veal scallopine
½ cup all-purpose flour
Salt and pepper to taste
2 tablespoons olive oil
1 cup sliced fresh mushrooms
1 green bell pepper, seeded and sliced
½ cup chopped green onions (scallions)
1 teaspoon minced garlic
1⅓ cups fat-free canned chicken broth
2 tablespoons lemon juice

Trim any fat from the veal.

Combine the flour with the salt and pepper, and dredge the veal in the flour. In a large non-stick skillet, heat the olive oil over medium-high heat. Sauté the veal cutlets about 1½ minutes on each side, or just until done. Remove from the skillet, and set aside.

In the same skillet, add the mushrooms, green pepper, green onion, and garlic, cooking over low heat for about 5 minutes, or until almost tender. Add the chicken broth and lemon juice, scraping up the browned bits from the bottom of the pan. Bring to a boil, lower the heat, and return the veal to the sauce. Cook for 3 to 5 minutes, or until the veal is heated through. Serve immediately.

Nutritional information per serving

Calories 222, Protein (g) 25, Carbohydrate (g) 11, Fat (g) 8, Calories from Fat (%) 33, Saturated Fat (g) 2, Dietary Fiber (g) 1, Cholesterol (mg) 94, Sodium (mg) 238, Diabetic Exchanges: 3 lean meat, 0.5 starch

QUICK TIP:

When a recipe calls for mushrooms, try substituting shiitake or portabella mushrooms for a more intense mushroom flavor.

MEAT

Veal with Tomatoes ❄

Veal and pasta together is a natural, and with its spices, olives, and prosciutto, this dish has a distinct, flavorful personality.

MAKES 6 SERVINGS

1 large onion, thinly sliced
1 pound veal scallopine, cut into 1-inch strips
2 tablespoons all-purpose flour
½ cup dry white wine
1 teaspoon minced garlic
Salt and pepper to taste
1 teaspoon dried oregano leaves
1 teaspoon dried thyme leaves
5 medium Roma (plum) tomatoes, cut into wedges
1 (2¼-ounce) can sliced ripe black olives, drained
2 ounces prosciutto, cut into 1-inch slices
2 tablespoons chopped parsley

In a large non-stick skillet, sauté the onion over medium heat until tender, about 5 minutes.

Sprinkle the veal with the flour, and add to the skillet, stirring constantly, cooking the veal until lightly browned. Stir in the wine, garlic, salt, pepper, oregano, and thyme. Bring to a boil; cover, reduce the heat, and simmer 8 to 10 minutes, or until the veal is almost tender. Add the tomatoes and olives; cover and simmer 5 minutes, or until thoroughly heated. Add the prosciutto; cover, and let stand 2 minutes. Sprinkle with the parsley, and serve.

Nutritional information per serving

Calories 162, Protein (g) 19, Carbohydrate (g) 9, Fat (g) 5, Calories from Fat (%) 27, Saturated Fat (g) 1, Dietary Fiber (g) 2, Cholesterol (mg) 71, Sodium (mg) 334, Diabetic Exchanges: 2.5 lean meat, 1.5 vegetable

MEAT

QUICK TIP:

Overcooking any cut of veal will toughen and ruin its delicate texture.

MEAT

Lamb Loin Chops with Mint Sauce

The light mint sauce perfectly complements the lamb. Marinate this savory sensation ahead to cook when needed.

MAKES 4 SERVINGS

1 tablespoon dried mint
1 teaspoon ground cumin
1 teaspoon garlic powder
½ teaspoon ground cinnamon
Salt and pepper to taste
1½ pounds lamb loin chops
Mint Sauce (recipe follows)

In a large zipper-lock bag, combine the mint, cumin, garlic powder, cinnamon, salt, and pepper. Add the lamb chops, and shake the bag. Refrigerate until ready to cook.

Heat a large non-stick skillet coated with non-stick cooking spray over medium-high heat. Place the lamb chops in the skillet, and cook until crusty and browned, about 5 minutes on each side. Serve with the Mint Sauce (see recipe below).

MINT SAUCE

1 tablespoon olive oil
¼ teaspoon minced garlic
1 tablespoon lemon juice
1 teaspoon dried mint
¼ cup fat-free canned chicken broth

In a microwave-safe dish or in a small pot on the stove, heat the oil, garlic, lemon juice, mint, and chicken broth until bubbly hot.

Nutritional information per serving

Calories 170, Protein (g) 20, Carbohydrate (g) 2, Fat (g) 9, Calories from Fat (%) 49, Saturated Fat (g) 2, Dietary Fiber (g) 0, Cholesterol (mg) 61, Sodium (mg) 104, Diabetic Exchanges: 3 lean meat

Honey Mustard Lamb Chops

When you're in the mood for lamb, rosemary and honey mustard pair together to make this simple preparation of a very special dish.

MAKES 4 SERVINGS

3 tablespoons honey
2 tablespoons Dijon mustard
8 (4-ounce) lean lamb loin chops (2 pounds)
1 teaspoon minced garlic
1 tablespoon dried rosemary leaves
⅛ teaspoon pepper

In a small bowl, combine the honey and mustard; set aside.

Trim any excess fat from the chops.

Rub both sides of the chops with the garlic, and press the rosemary and pepper onto both sides. Place on a broiler pan covered with foil. Broil the chops close to heat for about 5 minutes. Turn the chops, and spread with the honey mixture; broil for several minutes more, or until done. Serve.

Nutritional information per serving

Calories 235, Protein (g) 26, Carbohydrate (g) 14, Fat (g) 7, Calories from Fat (%) 30, Saturated Fat (g) 3, Dietary Fiber (g) 0, Cholesterol (mg) 81, Sodium (mg) 264, Diabetic Exchanges: 4 lean meat, 1 other carbohydrate

Asian Meat Marinade ❄️

This recipe makes enough marinade that you could increase the amount of meat if necessary. Marinade-infused flavor colors every bite of this marvelous dish. Try with different cuts of beef or pork.

MAKES 6 SERVINGS

1 cup mirin
1 teaspoon ground ginger
1 serrano chile pepper, minced
1 teaspoon minced garlic
2 green onions (scallions), sliced
1 cup light beer
1 cup low-sodium soy sauce
½ cup chopped cilantro, optional
6 (4-ounce) beef tenderloin fillets

In a shallow dish, combine the mirin, ginger, serrano chile, garlic, green onions, beer, soy sauce, and cilantro; add the fillets. Marinate the fillets for at least 2 hours, time permitting.

Grill, or pan-sear on a hot skillet about 5 to 10 minutes on each side, depending on how well-cooked you like the meat. Serve immediately.

Nutritional information per serving

Calories 177, Protein (g) 24, Carbohydrate (g) 0, Fat (g) 8, Calories from Fat (%) 44, Saturated Fat (g) 3, Dietary Fiber (g) 0, Cholesterol (mg) 70, Sodium (mg) 1,093, Diabetic Exchanges: 3 lean meat

QUICK TIP:

If mirin is not available, substitute 2 tablespoons vermouth mixed with 1 teaspoon sugar. If you don't have vermouth, use another light sweet wine.

MEAT

Glazed Salmon

Seafood

Pecan Trout with Dijon Sauce

Pecan Trout
with Dijon Sauce

This dish is elegant enough for company. The simple sauce and toasted pecans are prepared in a snap, and the fish can be sautéed in a skillet, if you prefer.

MAKES 6 SERVINGS

6 (4-ounce) trout fillets
Salt and pepper to taste
½ cup Italian bread crumbs
¼ cup nonfat plain yogurt
1 tablespoon Dijon mustard
1 tablespoon lemon juice
3 tablespoons chopped pecans, toasted
½ cup chopped green onions (scallions), optional

Preheat the broiler. Season the fillets with salt and pepper.

In a rectangular non-stick baking dish coated with non-stick cooking spray, arrange the fillets in a single layer. Top evenly with the bread crumbs. Cook under the broiler about 5 to 7 minutes, or until the fish flakes easily when tested with a fork. Combine the yogurt, mustard, and lemon juice in a small bowl. Transfer to a serving dish. Spoon 1 tablespoon sauce over the hot fish, and sprinkle the pecans evenly over each fillet. Sprinkle with green onions, if desired. Serve immediately.

Nutritional information per serving

Calories 206, Protein (g) 26, Carbohydrate (g) 8, Fat (g) 7, Calories from Fat (%) 32, Saturated Fat (g) 1, Dietary Fiber (g) 1, Cholesterol (mg) 67, Sodium (mg) 246, Diabetic Exchanges: 3 lean meat, 0.5 starch

Spicy Baked Fish

A quick, tasty, and popular choice for preparing trout, catfish, orange roughy, or any mild-flavored fish.

MAKES 4 SERVINGS

1 pound fish fillets
2 tablespoons light mayonnaise
1 teaspoon lemon juice
½ teaspoon prepared mustard
½ teaspoon sugar
¼ teaspoon Worcestershire sauce
½ teaspoon garlic powder
⅛ teaspoon cayenne pepper
Paprika, as needed

Preheat the oven to 500°F. Rinse the fish fillets, and pat dry.

In a small dish, combine the mayonnaise, lemon juice, mustard, sugar, Worcestershire sauce, garlic powder, and cayenne pepper.

Lay the fish in a non-stick oblong baking dish coated with non-stick cooking spray. Spread the mayonnaise mixture over the fillets. Let sit to marinate for 30 minutes.

Sprinkle with paprika. Bake for 10 to 15 minutes, or until the fish flakes easily with a fork. Serve immediately.

Nutritional information per serving

Calories 108, Protein (g) 17, Carbohydrate (g) 2, Fat (g) 3, Calories from Fat (%) 29, Saturated Fat (g) 0, Dietary Fiber (g) 0, Cholesterol (mg) 25, Sodium (mg) 142, Diabetic Exchanges: 3 very lean meat

QUICK TIP:

To test fish for doneness, prod it with a fork at its thickest point. Properly cooked fish is opaque, has milky white juices and just begins to flake easily. Don't overcook or it will be dry.

SEAFOOD

Mediterranean Catch

Feta, tomatoes, peppers, and oregano give this delectable fish dish a Greek flair.

MAKES 6 SERVINGS

1 large onion, sliced

1 large green bell pepper, seeded and cut into thin strips

1 cup sliced Roma (plum) tomatoes

1 tablespoon minced garlic

2 pounds firm-textured fish fillets (such as redfish, snapper, grouper)

Salt and pepper to taste

1 teaspoon dried oregano leaves

½ cup crumbled Feta cheese

1 tablespoon chopped parsley, optional

Preheat the oven to 375°F.

In a large non-stick skillet, sauté the onion and green pepper over medium heat until tender, about 5 minutes. Add the tomato and garlic, stirring for several more minutes. Arrange the fish in a single layer in a 3-quart oblong baking dish coated with non-stick cooking spray. Season with salt and pepper, and sprinkle with oregano. Spoon the vegetable mixture over the fish. Sprinkle with Feta. Bake for 20 to 25 minutes, or until the fish flakes easily with a fork. Sprinkle with parsley, and serve immediately.

Nutritional information per serving

Calories 204, Protein (g) 31, Carbohydrate (g) 7, Fat (g) 5, Calories from Fat (%) 24, Saturated Fat (g) 2, Dietary Fiber (g) 2, Cholesterol (mg) 75, Sodium (mg) 257, Diabetic Exchanges: 4 lean meat, 1.5 vegetable

Mediterranean Catch

SEAFOOD

Fish Florentine

Any fresh fish such as flounder, trout, or orange roughy would work well with this recipe. Creamy spinach and dill-seasoned fish pair together for simple gourmet dining.

2 (10-ounce) packages frozen chopped spinach
¼ cup all-purpose flour
1 cup skim milk
½ cup fat-free canned chicken broth
½ cup fat-free sour cream
2 pounds fish fillets
1 teaspoon dried dill weed leaves
Salt and pepper to taste
2 tablespoons lemon juice

Preheat the oven to 350°F.

Cook the spinach according to the package directions. Drain very well; set aside.

Place the flour in a small saucepan, and gradually whisk in the milk and chicken broth. Cook over medium heat until thickened, stirring about 5 minutes. Remove from the heat, and fold in the sour cream. Stir 1 cup of the sauce into the spinach, mixing well. Spread the creamed spinach on the bottom of a 2-quart casserole dish coated with nonstick cooking spray.

Arrange the fish fillets over the spinach. Sprinkle the fish with dill weed, salt, and pepper; drizzle with lemon juice. Pour the remaining sauce over the fish. Bake, covered with foil, for 30 minutes, or until the fish is done and flakes easily when tested with a fork. Serve immediately.

Nutritional information per serving
Calories 220, Protein (g) 35, Carbohydrate (g) 14, Fat (g) 2, Calories from Fat (%) 9, Saturated Fat (g) 1, Dietary Fiber (g) 3, Cholesterol (mg) 73, Sodium (mg) 282, Diabetic Exchanges: 4 very lean meat, 0.5 starch, 1 vegetable

SEAFOOD

Pizza Baked Fish ❄

Now you can have all the appealing flavors of pizza in a fish dish.

MAKES 6 SERVINGS

½ pound sliced fresh mushrooms, divided
⅔ cup chopped onion
½ teaspoon minced garlic
¾ cup water
½ cup tomato paste
1 teaspoon dried basil leaves
1 teaspoon dried oregano leaves
¼ teaspoon sugar
⅛ teaspoon crushed red pepper flakes
Salt and pepper
2 pounds red snapper fillets or fish of choice
1 green bell pepper, seeded and sliced into rings
1 cup shredded part-skim Mozzarella cheese

Preheat the oven to 400°F.

In a non-stick skillet, combine half the mushrooms, the onion, and the garlic, and sauté over medium heat until tender, about 5 minutes. Add the water, tomato paste, basil, oregano, sugar, red pepper flakes, salt, and pepper. Bring to a boil, reduce the heat, and simmer, uncovered, for 5 minutes, stirring occasionally. Remove from the heat.

Place the fish in a 2-quart oblong baking dish coated with nonstick cooking spray. Season with salt and pepper, and pour the sauce over the fish. Top with the remaining mushrooms and the green pepper rings. Bake the fish for 15 minutes. Sprinkle with Mozzarella, and continue baking for 5 minutes, or until the fish flakes with a fork and the cheese is melted. Serve immediately.

Nutritional information per serving

Calories 243, Protein (g) 38, Carbohydrate (g) 10, Fat (g) 5, Calories from Fat (%) 20, Saturated Fat (g) 2, Dietary Fiber (g) 3, Cholesterol (mg) 67, Sodium (mg) 204, Diabetic Exchanges: 5 very lean meat, 2 vegetable

SEAFOOD

Baked Fish
with Shrimp Stuffing

Fish sandwiched with a shrimp stuffing baked in a tomato sauce is the ultimate! Make ahead and refrigerate until time to bake. Use the fish of your choice.

1 tablespoon minced garlic
¾ cup chopped green onions (scallions), divided
1 pound small peeled shrimp
1½ cups Italian bread crumbs
Salt and pepper to taste
2 pounds fish fillets (such as trout)
1 (15-ounce) can tomato sauce
½ cup dry white wine or clam juice
1 teaspoon sugar
1 tablespoon minced parsley

Preheat the oven to 350°F. Coat a 2-quart oblong baking dish with nonstick cooking spray.

In a large non-stick skillet, sauté the garlic, ½ cup green onion, and the shrimp, stirring, until done. Add the bread crumbs, and season to taste; set aside.

Arrange half the fish fillets along the bottom of the prepared baking dish. Season with salt and pepper. Top the fish with all the shrimp mixture. Arrange the remaining fish fillets on top, and season with salt and pepper.

In a small bowl, combine the tomato sauce, wine, sugar, and parsley. Pour over the fish. Bake, uncovered, for 30 to 40 minutes, or until the fish flakes easily with a fork. Sprinkle with the remaining ¼ cup green onion, and serve immediately.

Nutritional information per serving

Calories 391, Protein (g) 48, Carbohydrate (g) 27, Fat (g) 7, Calories from Fat (%) 17, Saturated Fat (g) 1, Dietary Fiber (g) 2, Cholesterol (mg) 197, Sodium (mg) 1,000, Diabetic Exchanges: 6 very lean meat, 1.5 starch, 1 vegetable

SEAFOOD

Trout Eggplant Parmesan

This recipe gets a thumbs-up and is well worth the extra steps for the eggplant, topped with fried fish, red sauce, and cheese. Prepare early in the day, and bake just before serving.

MAKES 6 SERVINGS

1 eggplant, peeled
1 cup chopped tomatoes
1 (15-ounce) can tomato sauce
1 onion, chopped
1 green bell pepper, seeded and chopped
1 teaspoon dried oregano leaves
1 teaspoon dried basil leaves
1 tablespoon minced garlic
Salt and pepper to taste
⅛ teaspoon cayenne pepper
⅓ cup grated Parmesan cheese
½ cup Italian bread crumbs
½ cup all-purpose flour
1 tablespoon chopped parsley
½ cup skim milk
1½ pounds trout fillets
1½ cups shredded part-skim Mozzarella cheese

Preheat the broiler. Coat a 2-quart oblong casserole dish with non-stick cooking spray.

Cut the eggplant into ½-inch slices. Place the eggplant in a broiler pan, and broil for 5 minutes on each side. Remove the eggplant, and place in the bottom of the prepared casserole dish.

Preheat the oven to 350°F.

In a large saucepan, stir together the tomatoes, tomato sauce, onion, green pepper, oregano, basil, garlic, salt, pepper, and cayenne pepper. Bring the mixture to a boil, reduce the heat, and cook for about 7 minutes; set aside.

In a small shallow bowl, combine the Parmesan cheese, bread crumbs, flour, and parsley. Place the milk in another small, shallow bowl. Dip the fillets first in the milk and then in the Parmesan cheese mixture, pressing to coat.

In a large non-stick skillet, sauté the fish until crisp and cooked through, several minutes on each side. Remove the fillets from the skillet, and place them on top of the eggplant in the casserole dish. Spread the tomato mixture over the cooked fillets. Sprinkle with Mozzarella. Bake for 10 minutes, or until the cheese is melted. Serve immediately.

Nutritional information per serving

Calories 382, Protein (g) 38, Carbohydrate (g) 32, Fat (g) 11, Calories from Fat (%) 26, Saturated Fat (g) 5, Dietary Fiber (g) 4, Cholesterol (mg) 88, Sodium (mg) 826, Diabetic Exchanges: 4 lean meat, 1 starch, 3 vegetable

SEAFOOD

Fish Fry

Fish Fry

In the South, we love fish frys with fresh fish. Here's my version without the usual guilt. If you can't find the seasoned fish fry, substitute it with cornmeal and seasonings.

MAKES 6 SERVINGS

½ cup skim milk
1 teaspoon garlic powder
Dash cayenne pepper
1 teaspoon Dijon mustard
Salt and pepper to taste
2 pounds fish fillets (such as trout)
1 cup commercially prepared seasoned fish fry
1 teaspoon baking powder
2 tablespoons canola oil
¼ cup lemon juice
2 tablespoons chopped parsley

In a large bowl, combine the milk, garlic powder, cayenne pepper, mustard, salt, and pepper. Add the fish fillets, and refrigerate for at least 30 minutes and up to several hours.

On a plate, combine the fish fry and baking powder. Remove each fillet, and roll in the fish fry mix to cover; set aside.

In a large non-stick frying pan, heat the oil over medium-high heat, and sauté the fish on each side for several minutes, or until flaky. Sprinkle with the lemon juice and parsley, heat for a minute longer, and serve immediately.

Nutritional information per serving
Calories 313, Protein (g) 33, Carbohydrate (g) 19, Fat (g) 10, Calories from Fat (%) 31, Saturated Fat (g) 1, Dietary Fiber (g) 1, Cholesterol (mg) 90, Sodium (mg) 853, Diabetic Exchanges: 4 lean meat, 1.5 starch

SEAFOOD

Tuna Steaks with Horseradish Sauce

Impressive, intensely herb-flavored tuna seared in the pan is a winning selection with this distinctive sauce. Serve the Horseradish Sauce with other recipes, too.

MAKES 4 SERVINGS

1½ to 2 pounds tuna steaks, 1- to 2-inches thick
3 tablespoons finely chopped blanched almonds
¼ cup all-purpose flour
1 teaspoon minced garlic
1 tablespoon dried basil leaves
1 tablespoon dried thyme leaves
1 tablespoon dried rosemary leaves
1 teaspoon coarsely ground pepper
2 tablespoons water
2 tablespoons white wine, optional
Horseradish Sauce (recipe follows)

Rinse and trim the tuna steaks.

In a food processor or with a fork, combine the almonds, flour, garlic, basil, thyme, rosemary, pepper, and water to make a paste. Spread the paste on both sides of the tuna steaks, and refrigerate until ready to use.

Heat a non-stick skillet over medium heat until hot, and cook the tuna steaks 3 to 5 minutes on each side, depending on thickness, until done. Tuna is usually served rare. If desired, wine can be added to the pan while cooking. Serve with Horseradish Sauce (see recipe at right).

HORSERADISH SAUCE

MAKES 1 CUP SAUCE

⅔ cup light mayonnaise
1½ tablespoons prepared horseradish
1½ tablespoons grainy or other spicy mustard

In a small bowl, combine the mayonnaise, horseradish, and mustard, mixing well.

Nutritional information per serving
Calories 386, Protein (g) 40, Carbohydrate (g) 14, Fat (g) 18, Calories from Fat (%) 43, Saturated Fat (g) 3, Dietary Fiber (g) 2, Cholesterol (mg) 94, Sodium (mg) 497, Diabetic Exchanges: 5 very lean meat, 1 starch, 2.5 fat

SEAFOOD

Superb Salmon Steaks

Fast and easy, salmon topped with tomatoes and capers never fails to wow diners. Double the recipe as needed.

MAKES 2 TO 3 SERVINGS

1 tablespoon Dijon mustard
1 tablespoon honey
1 pound 1-inch-thick salmon steaks
½ teaspoon dried tarragon leaves
1 Roma (plum) tomato, sliced
1 tablespoon drained capers
¼ cup white wine

Preheat the oven to 400°F.

In a small bowl, combine the mustard and honey. Place the salmon steaks in a baking dish, and coat with the mustard mixture. Sprinkle with the tarragon, sliced tomato, and capers. Pour the wine in the dish. Bake for 18 to 25 minutes, or until done as desired. Serve immediately.

Nutritional information per serving

Calories 215, Protein (g) 31, Carbohydrate (g) 7, Fat (g) 5, Calories from Fat (%) 23, Saturated Fat (g) 1, Dietary Fiber (g) 0, Cholesterol (mg) 79, Sodium (mg) 309, Diabetic Exchanges: 4 very lean meat, 0.5 other carbohydrate

Salmon Framboise

This is fine dining with simple elegance that will thrill your taste buds.

MAKES 4 SERVINGS

1 cup dry white wine
¼ cup raspberry preserves
1 tablespoon green peppercorns
4 (6-ounce) salmon fillets

In a small bowl, mix the wine, preserves, and peppercorns. Pour over the salmon fillets, and refrigerate for 4 hours.

Preheat the oven to 375°F.

Bake the fillets for 20 minutes, or until done as desired. Serve immediately.

Nutritional information per serving

Calories 277, Protein (g) 34, Carbohydrate (g) 15, Fat (g) 6, Calories from Fat (%) 20, Saturated Fat (g) 1, Dietary Fiber (g) 1, Cholesterol (mg) 88, Sodium (mg) 128, Diabetic Exchanges: 5 very lean meat, 1 other carbohydrate

FOOD FACT:

Salmon is a fatty fish providing a good supply of health protective omega-3 fatty acids. It's also a good source of high-quality protein.

Glazed Salmon

SEAFOOD

Glazed Salmon

This may be the best salmon you've ever had. The glaze on the crispy, crusted salmon takes only minutes to prepare—and to disappear from the plate.

MAKES 4 SERVINGS

¼ cup honey
2 tablespoons low-sodium soy sauce
2 tablespoons lime juice
1 tablespoon Dijon mustard
4 (6-ounce) salmon fillets

In a small bowl, whisk together the honey, soy sauce, lime juice, and mustard. Marinate the salmon in the sauce in the refrigerator for several hours, or until ready to cook.

In a non-stick skillet coated with non-stick cooking spray, cook the salmon on each side, 3 to 5 minutes, until golden brown, crispy, and just cooked through. Transfer the salmon to a platter.

Add the remaining honey glaze to the skillet, and simmer, stirring, until the mixture comes to a boil. Return the salmon to the pan, heat thoroughly, and serve immediately.

Nutritional information per serving

Calories 273, Protein (g) 35, Carbohydrate (g) 19, Fat (g) 6, Calories from Fat (%) 20, Saturated Fat (g) 1, Dietary Fiber (g) 0, Cholesterol (mg) 88, Sodium (mg) 400, Diabetic Exchanges: 5 very lean meat, 1 other carbohydrate

SEAFOOD

Salmon Patties with Horseradish Caper Sauce

Try using fresh salmon to whip up these wonderful patties for a light evening meal or lunch or as an appetizer. The sauce adds fat to the recipe, so watch your portions. It's so good.

MAKES 6 PATTIES

1¼ pounds salmon fillets, skinned
⅓ cup finely chopped onion
3 tablespoons light mayonnaise
½ teaspoon dried dill weed leaves
½ cup Italian bread crumbs
Salt and pepper to taste
Horseradish Caper Sauce (recipe follows)

Trim the salmon, and cut into 2-inch cubes; place in a food processor, or chop finely by hand. Add the onion, mayonnaise, dill weed, and bread crumbs, mixing well. Season to taste with salt and pepper. Shape the salmon mixture into 6 patties. Heat a non-stick skillet and brown the patties over high heat for 1 minute. Lower the heat, and continue cooking for a few minutes; turn over, and continue cooking about 3 more minutes, or until the salmon is done. Do not overcook. Serve with Horseradish Caper Sauce (see recipe at right).

HORSERADISH CAPER SAUCE

¼ cup light mayonnaise
2 tablespoons prepared horseradish
1 tablespoon lemon juice
1 tablespoon finely chopped onion
1 teaspoon capers, drained

In a small bowl, combine the mayonnaise, horseradish, lemon juice, onion, and capers. Refrigerate until serving.

Nutritional information per serving

Calories 212, Protein (g) 21, Carbohydrate (g) 10, Fat (g) 10, Calories from Fat (%) 41, Saturated Fat (g) 1, Dietary Fiber (g) 1, Cholesterol (mg) 55, Sodium (mg) 377, Diabetic Exchanges: 3 lean meat, 0.5 starch

SEAFOOD

Salmon Patties with Horseradish Caper Sauce

Crabmeat au Gratin

Lump crabmeat and white sauce ensure that you won't even be able to tell this is a healthier version of one of the Louisiana greats.

MAKES 6 TO 8 SERVINGS

1 cup thinly chopped green onions (scallions)
2 tablespoons finely chopped fresh parsley
3 tablespoons margarine
3 tablespoons all-purpose flour
Salt and pepper to taste
1½ cups skim milk
1 tablespoon sherry, optional
1½ to 2 pounds lump crabmeat
1 cup shredded reduced-fat sharp Cheddar cheese

Preheat the oven to 375°F.

In a non-stick saucepan, sauté the green onion and parsley in the margarine until tender. Stir in the flour. Add the salt and pepper. Gradually add the milk, stirring over low heat until the mixture thickens and is bubbly. Remove the pan from the heat; add the sherry. Gently fold in the crabmeat. Place the mixture in a casserole dish or individual ramekins. Sprinkle with cheese. Bake for 10 to 15 minutes, or until the cheese is melted. Serve.

Nutritional information per serving

Calories 204, Protein (g) 25, Carbohydrate (g) 6, Fat (g) 8, Calories from Fat (%) 36, Saturated Fat (g) 3, Dietary Fiber (g) 1, Cholesterol (mg) 73, Sodium (mg) 488, Diabetic Exchanges: 3.5 lean meat, 0.5 starch

Crabmeat au Gratin

SEAFOOD

Crabmeat Enchiladas ❄

These simple enchiladas are filled with crab, cheese, and chilies, resulting in a creamy Southwestern sensation.

MAKES 8 SERVINGS

1 pound lump white crabmeat, picked for shells
½ cup chopped onion
¾ cup shredded reduced-fat Monterey Jack cheese
1 (4-ounce) can chopped green chilies
16 to 18 (6- to 8-inch) tortillas (flour, flavored, or whole wheat)
White Sauce (recipe follows)
¼ cup shredded reduced-fat Cheddar cheese
Sliced green onion, optional

Preheat the oven to 350°F.

In a mixing bowl, combine the crabmeat, onion, Monterey Jack cheese, and green chilies.

Warm the tortillas a few seconds in the microwave to make them easier to roll.

Place 1 heaping tablespoon of the filling on the edge of each tortilla, rolling up with the filling in the center. Place the filled tortillas in a 2-quart baking dish. Pour the White Sauce over the filled tortillas. Sprinkle with the Cheddar cheese and green onion. Bake for 30 minutes, or until thoroughly heated, and serve.

WHITE SAUCE

2 tablespoons chopped onion
2 cloves garlic, minced
1 tablespoon margarine
¼ cup all-purpose flour
1 (14½-ounce) can fat-free chicken broth
1 (4-ounce) can chopped green chilies, drained
1 cup nonfat plain yogurt or sour cream

In a medium non-stick saucepan, sauté the onion and garlic in the margarine until tender. Add the flour, and gradually add the chicken broth and green chilies. Bring to a boil, stirring, until the mixture thickens; reduce heat. Stir in the yogurt until smooth. Pour over the filled enchiladas.

Nutritional information per serving
Calories 316, Protein (g) 22, Carbohydrate (g) 45, Fat (g) 5, Calories from Fat (%) 13, Saturated Fat (g) 2, Dietary Fiber (g) 3, Cholesterol (mg) 42, Sodium (mg) 1,065, Diabetic Exchanges: 2 very lean meat, 3 starch

SEAFOOD

QUICK TIP:

When you're watching your fat intake, the sharper the cheese, the better—you can use less of it for the same amount of flavor.

Crab Cakes

Go gourmet with ease by preparing this mouth-watering recipe—an absolutely terrific crab cake. Make early in the day, refrigerate, and cook before serving.

MAKES 12 CRAB CAKES

1 pint lump white crabmeat, picked for shells
⅓ cup finely diced green bell pepper
½ cup thinly sliced green onions (scallions)
1 (11-ounce) can Mexi-corn, drained
⅓ cup light mayonnaise
¾ cup Italian bread crumbs
1 egg, beaten
½ teaspoon hot pepper sauce
½ cup cornmeal

In a large bowl, combine the crabmeat, green pepper, green onion, corn, mayonnaise, bread crumbs, egg, and hot pepper sauce. Mix well.

Place the cornmeal in a shallow dish. Shape the crabmeat mixture into 12 equal cakes. Dredge each cake in the cornmeal to coat both sides well.

In a large non-stick skillet set over medium-low heat, carefully add the crab cakes; cook until golden brown and cooked through, about 4 minutes on each side. Serve warm.

Nutritional information per serving
Calories 116, Protein (g) 7, Carbohydrate (g) 14, Fat (g) 3, Calories from Fat (%) 26, Saturated Fat (g) 1, Dietary Fiber (g) 1, Cholesterol (mg) 35, Sodium (mg) 347, Diabetic Exchanges: 0.5 lean meat, 1 starch

Broiled Marinated Shrimp

Broil large shrimp in this distinctive sauce for an easy but tasty meal. You can marinate early in the day and prepare later.

MAKES 4 TO 6 SERVINGS

2 pounds unpeeled large shrimp
Salt and pepper to taste
2 tablespoons olive oil
1 lemon, thinly sliced
¼ cup lemon juice
¼ cup Worcestershire sauce
1 teaspoon minced garlic
2 bay leaves
1 teaspoon dried oregano leaves

Spread the shrimp in a 13 x 9 x 2-inch non-stick baking pan coated with non-stick cooking spray or lined with foil. Sprinkle with salt and pepper.

In a small bowl, combine the olive oil, lemon, lemon juice, Worcestershire sauce, garlic, bay leaves, and oregano. Mix well, and pour evenly over the shrimp. Refrigerate, and marinate 30 minutes to 1 hour.

When ready to cook, preheat the broiler. Place the pan under the broiler for 10 to 15 minutes, until the shrimp are done, turning the shrimp once. Serve immediately.

Nutritional information per serving
Calories 143, Protein (g) 19, Carbohydrate (g) 3, Fat (g) 6, Calories from Fat (%) 36, Saturated Fat (g) 1, Dietary Fiber (g) 0, Cholesterol (mg) 179, Sodium (mg) 317, Diabetic Exchanges: 3 lean meat

SEAFOOD

Shrimp Fried Rice

This favorite tastes like you ordered it from a Chinese restaurant. For vegetable fried rice, just leave out the shrimp; you can even add cooked chicken to please your taste buds. A good choice!

MAKES 6 SERVINGS

2 eggs, lightly beaten
1 tablespoon peanut oil
1 pound peeled small shrimp
1 cup chopped onion
½ pound fresh mushrooms, sliced
3 tablespoons low-sodium soy sauce, plus additional
   for serving
1 tablespoon minced garlic
4 cups cooked rice
1 cup chopped green onions (scallions)
1 (5-ounce) can sliced water chestnuts, drained
1 cup frozen green peas
1 tablespoon sesame oil

In a large non-stick skillet, cook the eggs without stirring (as with an omelet) until the eggs are almost dry; set aside.

In a large skillet, heat the peanut oil over high heat. Add the shrimp, onion, and mushroom slices, sautéing until the mushroom slices are tender, 5 to 7 minutes. Stir in 3 tablespoons soy sauce, the garlic, and rice; cook about 3 minutes, stirring frequently. Add the green onion, water chestnuts, peas, and sesame oil.

Cut the egg into thin strips, add to the skillet, and stir. Stir-fry 1 minute more to heat the water chestnuts and peas. Serve with additional soy sauce, if desired.

Nutritional information per serving

Calories 320, Protein (g) 20, Carbohydrate (g) 42, Fat (g) 7, Calories from Fat (%) 21, Saturated Fat (g) 2, Dietary Fiber (g) 4, Cholesterol (mg) 178, Sodium (mg) 376, Diabetic Exchanges: 2 lean meat, 2 starch, 2 vegetables

Shrimp with Caper Clam Sauce

Clam juice, found with the canned seafood in the grocery store, adds a nice touch to the sauce in this quick, tasty recipe.

MAKES 8 SERVINGS

2 pounds peeled large shrimp
¼ cup all-purpose flour
2 tablespoons olive oil
1 to 1½ cups clam juice or fat-free canned chicken broth
1 tablespoon Dijon mustard
1 teaspoon Worcestershire sauce
½ teaspoon minced garlic
¼ cup chopped green onions (scallions)
1 tablespoon capers, drained
1 tablespoon minced parsley
¼ cup white wine, optional

Toss the shrimp with the flour.

In a large non-stick skillet, heat the olive oil, and cook the shrimp until done, 5 to 7 minutes. Remove the shrimp from the pan.

In the same skillet, combine 1 cup clam juice and the mustard, Worcestershire sauce, garlic, and green onion, scraping the pan to remove the bits, cooking 2 minutes. Add the capers, parsley, and white wine, and continue cooking 1 minute. Add the shrimp to the pan, tossing gently with the sauce. Add more clam juice or water if the sauce is too thick. Serve.

Nutritional information per serving

Calories 130, Protein (g) 18, Carbohydrate (g) 4, Fat (g) 4, Calories from Fat (%) 31, Saturated Fat (g) 1, Dietary Fiber (g) 0, Cholesterol (mg) 161, Sodium (mg) 470, Diabetic Exchanges: 2.5 lean meat, 0.5 starch

FOOD FACT:

Capers are little buds from a plant native to the Mediterranean that are picked, sun dried, and then pickled in a vinegar brine. They are high in sodium, so use in moderation or even rinse before using.

SEAFOOD

Shrimp Clemanceau

A heavenly green onion and mushroom sauce tops off this mixture of crispy potatoes, shrimp, and peas, for a great one-dish meal.

MAKES 8 SERVINGS

2 large baking potatoes, cubed (about 5 cups)
2 tablespoons margarine
2 tablespoons minced garlic
2 bunches green onions (scallions), chopped
½ pound fresh mushrooms, sliced
2½ pounds peeled medium shrimp
2 tablespoons finely chopped parsley
¼ cup white wine
1 tablespoon lemon juice
1 tablespoon Worcestershire sauce
1 (10-ounce) package frozen green peas
Salt and pepper to taste

Preheat the oven to 400°F.

Place the potatoes on a non-stick baking sheet coated with non-stick cooking spray. Bake, stirring occasionally, for 30 to 40 minutes, or until browned and crisp-tender.

In a large non-stick skillet, melt the margarine, and sauté the garlic, green onions, and mushrooms until tender, stirring frequently. Add the shrimp, parsley, wine, lemon juice, and Worcestershire sauce, and cook, stirring, until the shrimp are done, 5 to 7 minutes. Cook the peas according to the package directions; drain.

In a 2-quart oblong casserole, combine the cooked potatoes, peas, and the shrimp mixture removed from the skillet with a slotted spoon. Reduce the liquid in the skillet by half, and pour over the shrimp-potato mixture. Season to taste. Toss gently, and serve.

Nutritional information per serving

Calories 254, Protein (g) 27, Carbohydrate (g) 27, Fat (g) 4, Calories from Fat (%) 15, Saturated Fat (g) 1, Dietary Fiber (g) 4, Cholesterol (mg) 202, Sodium (mg) 337, Diabetic Exchanges: 3 very lean meat, 1.5 starch, 1 vegetable

SEAFOOD

Shrimp with Mango Salsa

The jalapeños and cilantro with the sweet mango make exotic, exciting flavors. Serve this wonderful combination over rice or as a salsa.

MAKES 4 SERVINGS

2 tablespoons sliced pickled jalapeño pepper
⅓ cup chopped red onion
½ cup chopped red bell pepper
½ cup fresh cilantro leaves
2 ripe medium-size mangoes
4 tablespoons lime juice, divided
1 tablespoon olive oil
1 pound peeled medium shrimp
1 teaspoon minced garlic
¼ cup tequila

Place the jalapeño, onion, red pepper, and cilantro in a food processor, and pulse until chopped. Peel the mangoes and chop, adding tothe jalapeño mixture. Add 2 tablespoons lime juice, and transfer to a bowl. Heat the oil in a large skillet over medium heat, and stir-fry the shrimp and garlic until the shrimp is almost done, about 5 minutes. Add the remaining 2 tablespoons lime juice and the tequila, and cook for about 5 minutes, or until the shrimp are done. Add the salt and pepper. Stir the shrimp into the salsa mixture, and serve.

Nutritional information per serving

Calories 230, Protein (g) 18, Carbohydrate (g) 22, Fat (g) 5, Calories from Fat (%) 18, Saturated Fat (g) 1, Dietary Fiber (g) 3, Cholesterol (mg) 161, Sodium (mg) 226, Diabetic Exchanges: 2.5 lean meat, 1.5 fruit

Shrimp Sauté

A few ingredients sautéed with shrimp created this family favorite. It's great over rice, fettuccine, or inside patty shells.

MAKES 6 SERVINGS

2 tablespoons margarine
1 bunch green onions (scallions), chopped
2 cloves garlic, minced
1 tablespoon Worcestershire sauce
1 teaspoon dried basil leaves
2 pounds peeled medium shrimp
2 cups nonfat plain yogurt

In a large non-stick skillet, melt the margarine, and sauté the green onions and garlic until tender. Add the Worcestershire sauce and basil. Add the shrimp, and cook until the shrimp are done (turn pink), 5 to 7 minutes. Gradually stir in the yogurt, and heat thoroughly. Do not boil. Serve.

Nutritional information per serving

Calories 197, Protein (g) 28, Carbohydrate (g) 8, Fat (g) 5, Calories from Fat (%) 24, Saturated Fat (g) 1, Dietary Fiber (g) 0, Cholesterol (mg) 217, Sodium (mg) 384, Diabetic Exchanges: 3.5 very lean meat, 0.5 skim milk

SEAFOOD

Grilled Shrimp (in kebabs)

Grilled Shrimp

The shrimp burst with flavor from this simple citrus marinade. Have fun—use the shrimp in shish kabobs.

MAKES 6 SERVINGS

⅓ cup lime juice
1 tablespoon honey
2 tablespoons low-sodium soy sauce
2 tablespoons Worcestershire sauce
1 cup orange juice
1 tablespoon minced garlic
2 pounds peeled large shrimp

In a small glass or stainless steel bowl, mix the lime juice, honey, soy sauce, Worcestershire sauce, orange juice, and garlic. Add the shrimp, and marinate 15 minutes.

Grill the shrimp on hot coals, or broil in the oven for several minutes on each side, or until done. Serve.

Nutritional information per serving

Calories 116, Protein (g) 23, Carbohydrate (g) 1, Fat (g) 1, Calories from Fat (%) 10, Saturated Fat (g) 0, Dietary Fiber (g) 0, Cholesterol (mg) 215, Sodium (mg) 433, Diabetic Exchanges: 3.5 very lean meat

Shrimp Tacos
with Tropical Salsa

*Seasoned shrimp and veggie tacos make
an unbeatable meal.*

MAKES 8 SHRIMP TACOS

1 yellow or red bell pepper, seeded and sliced
1 red onion, sliced
½ teaspoon minced garlic
1½ pounds peeled medium shrimp
½ teaspoon ground cumin
½ teaspoon chili powder
1 cup chopped tomatoes
1 (11-ounce) can Mexi-corn, drained (optional)
8 (6- to 8-inch) flour tortillas
1 cup shredded reduced-fat Monterey Jack cheese
Tropical Salsa (recipe follows)

In a large non-stick skillet, sauté the bell pepper, onion, and garlic over medium-high heat for 2 minutes. Add the shrimp, cumin, chili powder, and tomatoes, cooking until the shrimp are done, 5 to 7 minutes. Stir in Mexi-corn.

On each tortilla, evenly divide the shrimp mixture and the cheese. Fold the tortilla in half. If desired, heat in the microwave or heat the tortillas before filling. Serve with Tropical Salsa (see recipe at right).

TROPICAL SALSA

1 (8-ounce) can pineapple chunks in own juice, drained
1 (11-ounce) can mandarin orange segments, drained
1 tablespoon lemon juice
2 green onions (scallions), chopped
1 tablespoon diced green chilies
1 tablespoon chopped fresh cilantro

Coarsely chop the pineapple and oranges.

In a medium bowl, combine the pineapple, oranges, lemon juice, green onions, green chilies, and cilantro. Refrigerate until ready to use.

Nutritional information per serving
Calories 238, Protein (g) 20, Carbohydrate (g) 31, Fat (g) 3, Calories from Fat (%) 13, Saturated Fat (g) 2, Dietary Fiber (g) 2, Cholesterol (mg) 129, Sodium (mg) 506, Diabetic Exchanges: 2.5 very lean meat, 1 starch, 0.5 fruit, 1 vegetable

QUICK TIP:

To heat tortillas, wrap them loosely in plastic wrap and heat them in a microwave on high for about 1 minute. If you prefer, wrap in foil and warm in a 250°F oven for 10 minutes.

SEAFOOD

Shrimp Tacos with Tropical Salsa

Scampi Italian Style

When you arrive home from work exhausted and starving, turn to this dish with pasta for an irresistible dinner.

MAKES 4 SERVINGS

2 tablespoons olive oil
1 pound peeled large shrimp
1 teaspoon minced garlic
2 green onions (scallions), chopped
3 tablespoons dry sherry
1 tomato, diced
1 teaspoon Worcestershire sauce
½ teaspoon hot pepper sauce
¼ teaspoon white pepper
⅛ teaspoon dried oregano leaves
⅛ teaspoon dried thyme leaves
2 tablespoons chopped parsley

Heat the olive oil in a large non-stick skillet and sauté the shrimp until they begin to turn pink. Add the garlic and green onions, sautéing for 1 minute longer. Add the remaining ingredients, cook about 5 minutes, or until the shrimp are fully cooked and the sauce has thickened slightly. Serve.

Nutritional information per serving
Calories 161, Protein (g) 18, Carbohydrate (g) 3, Fat (g) 8, Calories from Fat (%) 44, Saturated Fat (g) 1, Dietary Fiber (g) 1, Cholesterol (mg) 161, Sodium (mg) 209, Diabetic Exchanges: 2.5 very lean meat, 1 fat

Cheesy Shrimp Rice Casserole ❄

Shrimp and rice team up with cheese and salsa for a quick dinner. Use leftover rice or rice of your choice.

MAKES 6 SERVINGS

1 onion, chopped
1 teaspoon minced garlic
1½ pounds peeled medium shrimp
1 (8-ounce) can mushroom stems and pieces
⅓ cup chunky salsa
1½ cups shredded reduced-fat Cheddar cheese
1 tablespoon Worcestershire sauce
½ cup evaporated skimmed milk
1 bunch green onions (scallions), chopped
3 cups cooked rice

In a large non-stick skillet, sauté the onion, garlic, shrimp, and mushrooms over medium-high heat for 5 to 7 minutes. Add the salsa, cheese, Worcestershire sauce, milk, and green onions. Stir in the rice, and cook until the cheese is melted and well combined, about 10 minutes. Serve.

Nutritional information per serving
Calories 313, Protein (g) 31, Carbohydrate (g) 30, Fat (g) 6, Calories from Fat (%) 19, Saturated Fat (g) 4, Dietary Fiber (g) 2, Cholesterol (mg) 177, Sodium (mg) 623, Diabetic Exchanges: 3.5 very lean meat, 1.5 starch, 1 vegetable

SEAFOOD

Italian Shrimp (Barbecue Shrimp)

This is probably one of the best recipes in this book. I've made it all over the country to the same overwhelmingly positive response. Make sure to have a loaf of hot French bread to dip in the unbelievable sauce.

MAKES 4 TO 6 SERVINGS

¼ cup olive oil

½ cup fat-free Italian dressing

6 cloves garlic, minced

1 teaspoon hot pepper sauce

¼ cup Worcestershire sauce

8 bay leaves

2 teaspoons paprika

1 teaspoon dried oregano leaves

1 teaspoon dried rosemary leaves

1 teaspoon dried thyme leaves

1 teaspoon pepper

1 teaspoon salt, optional

2 pounds unpeeled headless large shrimp

2 ounces dry white wine

In a large, heavy non-stick skillet, combine the oil, Italian dressing, garlic, hot pepper sauce, Worcester-shire sauce, bay leaves, paprika, oregano, rosemary, thyme, pepper, and salt. Cook over medium heat until the sauce begins to boil. Add the shrimp. Cook approximately 10 minutes. Add the wine, and cook another 5 to 7 minutes, or until the shrimp are done. Serve the shrimp with the sauce.

Nutritional information per serving

Calories 206, Protein (g) 20, Carbohydrate (g) 6, Fat (g) 10, Calories from Fat (%) 46, Saturated Fat (g) 2, Dietary Fiber (g) 1, Cholesterol (mg) 180, Sodium (mg) 610, Diabetic Exchanges: 3 lean meat, 0.5 other carbohydrate

SEAFOOD

Italian Shrimp

Shrimp-and-Spinach White Pizza

Shrimp in a white sauce topped with spinach adds intrigue to the traditional pizza. For a different twist, use Brie instead of Mozzarella in this recipe.

MAKES 8 SERVINGS

1 (12-inch) Italian Boboli crust
1¼ cups evaporated skimmed milk
2 tablespoons cornstarch
½ teaspoon minced garlic
Salt and pepper to taste
1 pound peeled small shrimp
½ pound sliced fresh mushrooms
3 cups fresh spinach, washed and stemmed
½ teaspoon dried oregano leaves
½ teaspoon dried basil leaves
1 cup shredded part-skim Mozzarella cheese

Preheat the oven to 425°F.

Place the pizza crust on a round 12-inch non-stick pizza pan coated with non-stick cooking spray. In a small pot, whisk the milk and cornstarch until blended. Cook over medium-high heat, stirring until thickened. Stir in the garlic, and season with salt and pepper. Spread sauce over the crust, and set aside.

In a non-stick skillet, cook the shrimp until pink, about 5 minutes; drain. Add the mushroom slices, and continue cooking for several minutes. Add the spinach, stirring until. Drain and spoon the shrimp mixture over the white sauce. Sprinkle with oregano and basil. Top with the Mozzarella cheese. Bake for 8 to 10 minutes, or until the crust is golden brown and the cheese is melted. Slice and serve.

Nutritional information per serving
Calories 275, Protein (g) 23, Carbohydrate (g) 33, Fat (g) 6, Calories from Fat (%) 19, Saturated Fat (g) 3, Dietary Fiber (g) 1, Cholesterol (mg) 93, Sodium (mg) 503, Diabetic Exchanges: 2 very lean meat, 1.5 starch, 0.5 skim milk

SEAFOOD

Shrimp-and-Spinach Skillet Surprise

Mandarin oranges and pine nuts give this dish a burst of flavor. This incredible recipe takes minutes to prepare and is great served over wild rice.

MAKES 6 TO 8 SERVINGS

2 tablespoons olive oil

1 red bell pepper, seeded and chopped

1 cup sliced red onion

1 teaspoon minced garlic

2 pounds peeled medium shrimp

3 sprigs fresh basil leaves, chopped, or ½ teaspoon dried basil leaves

½ cup cherry or grape tomatoes, halved

2 cups fresh baby spinach, washed and stemmed

2 tablespoons pine nuts

1 (11-ounce) can mandarin orange segments, drained

In a large non-stick skillet, heat the olive oil, and sauté the red pepper, onion, and garlic for 5 to 7 minutes. Add the shrimp, cooking over medium-high heat until the shrimp are done, 5 to 7 minutes. Add the basil, tomatoes, and spinach, cooking until the spinach begins to wilt. Add the pine nuts and oranges, cooking until well heated. Serve.

Nutritional information per serving

Calories 156, Protein (g) 18, Carbohydrate (g) 8, Fat (g) 5, Calories from Fat (%) 31, Saturated Fat (g) 1, Dietary Fiber (g) 1, Cholesterol (mg) 161, Sodium (mg) 196, Diabetic Exchanges: 2.5 lean meat, 0.5 fruit

Speedy Shrimp Jambalaya

Talk about easy, talk about good. A jar of salsa, smoked sausage, and shrimp help you make this classic easily. Serve over rice, pasta, patty shells, corn bread, or biscuits.

MAKES 4 TO 6 SERVINGS

1 (16-ounce) jar roasted-pepper-and-garlic chunky salsa or other flavored salsa

8 ounces reduced-fat smoked sausage, diced

½ pound peeled small shrimp

1 teaspoon dried thyme leaves

1 bunch green onions (scallions), chopped, divided

¼ teaspoon cayenne pepper

¾ cup fat-free sour cream

In a large non-stick skillet, mix the salsa, sausage, shrimp, thyme, and ⅓ cup green onions. Heat to a boil. Reduce the heat to low, and cook 10 minutes. Meanwhile, in a small bowl, mix the cayenne pepper and sour cream. Serve the jambalaya with a dollop of sour cream mixture, and sprinkle with the remaining green onions.

Nutritional information per serving

Calories 140, Protein (g) 13, Carbohydrate (g) 14, Fat (g) 1, Calories from Fat (%) 10, Saturated Fat (g) 0, Dietary Fiber (g) 1, Cholesterol (mg) 67, Sodium (mg) 766, Diabetic Exchanges: 1.5 very lean meat, 1 starch

QUICK TIP:

One-half cup salsa is equal to one serving of vegetables. Add salsa to your favorite recipe to sneak in those veggies.

Crawfish Elegante ❄

This healthier version of a classic favorite will satisfy even gourmets. Crabmeat may be substituted for crawfish. For dinner, serve over rice, patty shells, or pasta, and for an amazing appetizer, serve with melba rounds.

MAKES 6 TO 8 SERVINGS

3 tablespoons margarine
1 bunch green onions (scallions), chopped
½ cup chopped parsley
3 tablespoons all-purpose flour
1 (12-ounce) can evaporated skimmed milk
3 tablespoons sherry
1 pound crawfish tails, rinsed and drained
Salt and pepper to taste
Dash cayenne pepper

In a small non-stick skillet, melt the margarine, and sauté the green onions and parsley. Blend in the flour. Gradually add the milk, stirring constantly until the sauce thickens and bubbles. Add the sherry and crawfish tails, stirring gently. Season with the salt, pepper, and cayenne pepper; serve.

Nutritional information per serving

Calories 141, Protein (g) 14, Carbohydrate (g) 9, Fat (g) 5, Calories from Fat (%) 33, Saturated Fat (g) 1, Dietary Fiber (g) 0, Cholesterol (mg) 77, Sodium (mg) 163, Diabetic Exchanges: 1.5 lean meat, 0.5 skim milk

Crawfish Étouffée

Étouffée is a very popular Louisiana recipe, and this quick and "better for you" version is the best one of them all. Purchase crawfish tails in sealed bags in the freezer section of the grocery store.

MAKES 4 SERVINGS

1 cup finely chopped onions
⅓ cup finely chopped green bell pepper
½ teaspoon minced garlic
2 tablespoons margarine
2 tablespoons all-purpose flour
1 pound peeled crawfish tails, rinsed and drained
1 cup water
Dash cayenne pepper
Dash Worcestershire sauce
Salt and pepper to taste
Juice of 1 lemon
1 bunch green onions (scallions), tops only, finely sliced

In a large non-stick skillet, sauté the onions, green pepper, and garlic in the margarine until tender. Stir in the flour, and cook 1 minute. Add the crawfish tails and water. Cover, and simmer over low heat for 10 minutes. Add the cayenne pepper, Worcester-shire sauce, salt, pepper, and lemon juice. Add the green onions, and cook for 5 minutes longer. If the mixture is too thick, add more water. Serve over cooked rice.

Nutritional information per serving

Calories 195, Protein (g) 21, Carbohydrate (g) 12, Fat (g) 7, Calories from Fat (%) 33, Saturated Fat (g) 1, Dietary Fiber (g) 2, Cholesterol (mg) 151, Sodium (mg) 179, Diabetic Exchanges: 2.5 lean meat, 2 vegetable

SEAFOOD

Crawfish and Rice Casserole

Crawfish and Rice Casserole ❄

Cooked shrimp may be substituted in this crowd-pleasing dish. Use wild rice if desired.

MAKES 12 TO 14 SERVINGS

2 tablespoons olive oil

2 large onions, chopped

2 large green bell peppers, seeded and chopped

2 pounds crawfish tails, rinsed and drained

1 (8-ounce) package fat-free cream cheese, cubed

1 (10¾-ounce) can 98% fat-free cream of mushroom soup

4 ounces light pasteurized processed cheese spread, cubed

6 cups cooked rice

2 bunches green onions (scallions), chopped

1 teaspoon minced garlic

¼ teaspoon cayenne pepper

Dash white pepper

Preheat the oven to 350°F. Coat a 2- or 3-quart casserole dish with non-stick cooking spray.

In a large non-stick skillet, heat the oil over medium heat, and sauté the onion and pepper until tender, about 5 minutes. Add the crawfish tails and cream cheese, cooking until the cream cheese is creamy. Add the cream of mushroom soup and cheese spread, cooked rice, green onions, garlic, cayenne, and white pepper. Transfer the mixture to the prepared dish coated with non-stick cooking spray. Bake, uncovered, for 30 minutes, or until well heated. Serve.

Nutritional information per serving

Calories 225, Protein (g) 18, Carbohydrate (g) 28, Fat (g) 4, Calories from Fat (%) 18, Saturated Fat (g) 1, Dietary Fiber (g) 2, Cholesterol (mg) 92, Sodium (mg) 414, Diabetic Exchanges: 2 very lean meat, 1.5 starch, 1 vegetable

Scallop Stir-Fry with Crispy Noodle Pancakes

This scallop specialty is equally good served over rice—if you feel adventurous, try the noodle pancakes, as they are a tasty complement to the dish.

MAKES 4 SERVINGS

2 cups fat-free canned chicken broth
¼ cup oyster sauce
1 tablespoon cornstarch
½ teaspoon sesame oil
2 tablespoons canola oil, divided
½ pound fresh mushrooms, sliced
1 (6-ounce) package frozen snow peas, thawed
4 green onions (scallions), chopped
½ pound sea scallops, halved crosswise
½ teaspoon ground ginger
Crispy Noodle Pancakes (recipe follows)

In a small bowl, combine the chicken broth, oyster sauce, cornstarch, and sesame oil. Heat 1 tablespoon canola oil in a wok or large, heavy skillet over high heat. Stir-fry the mushrooms; add the snow peas, and stir-fry until crisp-tender, about 3 minutes. Transfer to a bowl. In the same skillet, heat the remaining 1 tablespoon canola oil over high heat; add the green onions and scallops, stir-frying several minutes, or until the scallops turn opaque. Stir the broth mixture and ginger into the skillet, stirring until the sauce thickens. Return the vegetables to the skillet, stirring until thoroughly heated. Spoon over Noodle Pancakes (see recipe at right), and serve.

CRISPY NOODLE PANCAKES

8 ounces plain Chinese noodles
½ cup chopped green onions (scallions)
1 teaspoon plus 1 tablespoon canola oil, divided
1 tablespoon sesame oil

Cook the noodles according to the package directions, stirring occasionally. Drain. Rinse with cold water, and drain well.

In a medium bowl, toss noodles with the green onion and 1 teaspoon canola oil. Heat 1 tablespoon canola oil and the sesame oil in a heavy 9-inch skillet over medium heat. Drop the mixture onto the skillet, and flatten slightly. Cook without stirring, until light brown, about 6 minutes. Flip, and cook the second side until light brown, about 6 minutes. Drain on paper towels.

Nutritional information per serving

Calories 449, Protein (g) 22, Carbohydrate (g) 57, Fat (g) 17, Calories from Fat (%) 33, Saturated Fat (g) 1, Dietary Fiber (g) 10, Cholesterol (mg) 19, Sodium (mg) 1,082, Diabetic Exchanges: 1.5 very lean meat, 3.5 starch, 1 vegetable, 3 fat

FOOD FACT:

To best cook scallops, dry with paper towels to remove excess moisture before sautéing them. Cook in a single layer in the skillet, making sure they don't touch one another; otherwise, they will steam instead of brown.

SEAFOOD

Seafood and Wild Rice Casserole

This dish is easy and excellent for your family or friends. Shrimp, crabmeat, and wild rice make this quick casserole a must-try

MAKES 6 TO 8 SERVINGS

1 (6-ounce) package long-grain and wild rice mix
1 pound peeled cooked shrimp
1 pound white or lump crabmeat picked for shells
1 (10-ounce) package frozen green peas
1 cup chopped celery
1 green bell pepper, seeded and chopped
1 onion, chopped
½ cup light mayonnaise
1 teaspoon Worcestershire sauce
Salt and pepper to taste

Preheat the oven to 350°F.

Cook the rice mix according to the package directions, omitting any oil. Add the shrimp, crabmeat, peas, celery, green pepper, onion, mayonnaise, Worcester-shire sauce, salt, and pepper, tossing carefully. Pour into a 2-quart casserole coated with nonstick cooking spray. Bake for 20 to 30 minutes, or until heated through; serve.

Nutritional information per serving

Calories 287, Protein (g) 29, Carbohydrate (g) 27, Fat (g) 7, Calories from Fat (%) 21, Saturated Fat (g) 1, Dietary Fiber (g) 3, Cholesterol (mg) 159, Sodium (mg) 837, Diabetic Exchanges: 4 very lean meat, 1.5 starch, 1 vegetable

Seafood and Wild Rice Casserole

Broiled Scallops

Honey mustard with a touch of curry glazes these simple scallops for tons of flavor.

MAKES 8 SERVINGS

¼ cup Dijon mustard
¼ cup honey
½ teaspoon ground curry
1 teaspoon lemon juice
2 pounds sea scallops

In a large bowl, combine the mustard, honey, curry, and lemon juice, mixing well. Add the scallops, and marinate 15 minutes.

Transfer to a baking pan, and broil in the oven about 4 inches from the heat until golden brown on the outside and opaque in the middle, 4 to 5 minutes. (Do not turn.) Serve.

Nutritional information per serving
Calories 140, Protein (g) 19, Carbohydrate (g) 12, Fat (g) 1, Calories from Fat (%) 6, Saturated Fat (g) 0, Dietary Fiber (g) 0, Cholesterol (mg) 37, Sodium (mg) 363, Diabetic Exchanges: 3 very lean meat, 1 other carbohydrate

Seafood Casserole

This mouthwatering dish can also be served as an appetizer or in a chafing dish with patty shells or melba toasts.

MAKES 6 SERVINGS

½ cup chopped onion
2 cloves garlic, minced
1 pound peeled shrimp
¼ cup all-purpose flour
¾ cup fat-free canned chicken broth
1 (5-ounce) can evaporated skimmed milk
1 teaspoon dried dill weed leaves
1 (14-ounce) can quartered artichoke hearts, drained
1 pound lump crabmeat, picked for shells
1 cup shredded reduced-fat sharp Cheddar cheese

In a non-stick skillet, sauté the onion, garlic, and shrimp until pink, about 5 minutes. Stir in the flour and gradually add the chicken broth, stirring until smooth and it comes to a boil. As the sauce thickens, add the milk, stirring until mixed. Add the dill weed. Gently fold in the artichoke hearts, crabmeat, and cheese, heating until the cheese is melted and thoroughly heated. Serve in individual dishes or a in casserole dish.

Nutritional information per serving
Calories 254, Protein (g) 38, Carbohydrate (g) 12, Fat (g) 5, Calories from Fat (%) 18, Saturated Fat (g) 3, Dietary Fiber (g) 1, Cholesterol (mg) 176, Sodium (mg) 756, Diabetic Exchanges: 5 very lean meat, 0.5 starch, 1 vegetable

SEAFOOD

Baked Italian Oysters

Baked Italian Oysters ❄

Here's a lighter version of a New Orleans restaurant favorite. This one has all the taste but not all the fat.

MAKES 10 SERVINGS

⅓ cup olive oil
1 tablespoon minced garlic
1 bunch green onions (scallions), chopped
½ cup chopped parsley
2 cups bread crumbs
2 cups Italian bread crumbs
⅓ cup grated Parmesan cheese
2 tablespoons lemon juice
2 teaspoons dried oregano leaves
¼ teaspoon cayenne pepper
1 teaspoon dried tarragon leaves
Salt and pepper to taste
2 pints oysters, with liquid

Preheat the oven to 450°F.

In a large non-stick skillet, heat the olive oil, and sauté the garlic, green onions, and parsley for several minutes. Add the bread crumbs, Parmesan cheese, lemon juice, oregano, cayenne pepper, tarragon, salt, and pepper. Stir in the oysters and enough oyster liquid to make the mixture moist.

Transfer the mixture to a shallow 2-quart casserole dish. Bake for 20 to 30 minutes, or until the oysters are cooked and the mixture browned. Serve.

Nutritional information per serving

Calories 327, Protein (g) 15, Carbohydrate (g) 37, Fat (g) 13, Calories from Fat (%) 36, Saturated Fat (g) 3, Dietary Fiber (g) 2, Cholesterol (mg) 55, Sodium (mg) 805, Diabetic Exchanges: 1 very lean meat, 2.5 starch, 2 fat

SEAFOOD

Chicken Primavera

Pasta

Perfect Pasta

I find myself making this recipe time and time again when I need a pasta side dish with a little something extra.

MAKES 6 TO 8 SERVINGS

12 ounces capellini (angel hair) pasta
3 tablespoons olive oil
½ teaspoon minced garlic
1 tablespoon finely chopped parsley

Cook the pasta according to the package directions, omitting any oil and salt. Drain and set aside.

In a small skillet, heat the olive oil and sauté the garlic and parsley for a few minutes. Toss with the pasta, and serve.

Nutritional information per serving
Calories 204, Protein (g) 6, Carbohydrate (g) 32, Fat (g) 6, Calories from Fat (%) 26, Saturated Fat (g) 1, Dietary Fiber (g) 1, Cholesterol (mg) 0, Sodium (mg) 3, Diabetic Exchanges: 2 starch, 1 fat

QUICK TIP:

Always cook pasta uncovered at a fast, continuous boil so that the pasta can move freely and will cook more evenly. The rapid boil also helps to prevent sticking.

Penne with Spinach, Sun-Dried Tomatoes, and Goat Cheese

This easy recipe has the fabulous characteristics of a trendy restaurant dish.

MAKES 4 TO 6 SERVINGS

½ cup sun-dried tomatoes (not oil-packed)
⅔ cup boiling water
12 ounces penne or other tubular pasta
2 tablespoons olive oil
1 tablespoon minced garlic
6 cups stemmed fresh spinach, washed
1 tablespoon dried basil leaves
2 tablespoons balsamic vinegar
Salt and pepper to taste
½ cup crumbled goat cheese

In a small bowl, combine the tomatoes and boiling water; set aside to soften, about 10 minutes.

Coarsely chop the tomatoes, and reserve the soaking liquid. Meanwhile, prepare the pasta according to the package directions, omitting any oil and salt. Drain, and set aside.

In a large non-stick skillet, heat the oil and add the garlic, tomatoes with soaking liquid, spinach, basil, vinegar, salt, and pepper, cooking until the spinach is just wilted, about 5 minutes. Stir in the goat cheese and pasta, heating until the cheese begins to melt. Serve immediately.

Nutritional information per serving
Calories 322, Protein (g) 12, Carbohydrate (g) 48, Fat (g) 9, Calories from Fat (%) 25, Saturated Fat (g) 3, Dietary Fiber (g) 3, Cholesterol (mg) 10, Sodium (mg) 63, Diabetic Exchanges: 3 starch, 1 vegetable, 1.5 fat

PASTA

Vermicelli with Fresh Tomatoes

Here's an incredible and satisfying recipe, best for when tomatoes are in season.

MAKES 8 SERVINGS

2 pounds tomatoes, chopped

1 onion, chopped

½ teaspoon minced garlic

1 tablespoon dried basil leaves

⅓ cup olive oil

Salt and pepper to taste

1 (16-ounce) package vermicelli pasta

1 cup shredded reduced-fat Cheddar cheese, optional

In a large bowl, mix the tomatoes, onion, garlic, basil, olive oil, salt, and pepper. Let stand at room temperature for 1 hour.

Cook the vermicelli according to the package directions, omitting any oil and salt. Drain, and toss with the tomato mixture. Sprinkle with the cheese, and serve.

Nutritional information per serving

Calories 324, Protein (g) 9, Carbohydrate (g) 50, Fat (g) 10, Calories from Fat (%) 28, Saturated Fat (g) 1, Dietary Fiber (g) 3, Cholesterol (mg) 0, Sodium (mg) 15, Diabetic Exchanges: 3 starch, 1.5 vegetable, 1.5 fat

Vermicelli with Fresh Tomatoes

PASTA

Thai Pasta Dish

Here's a quick trip to Bangkok, in a mainstreamed version you can enjoy in your own home. The Thai stir-fry sauce gives this dish a surprising, sweet, and fiery flavor.

MAKES 4 TO 6 SERVINGS

1 (8-ounce) package vermicelli pasta
1 cup fresh bean sprouts
½ cup chopped green onions (scallions)
½ cup whole baby corn, drained
1 (4-ounce) can mushrooms, drained
3 egg whites
½ teaspoon garlic powder
1 cup bottled pad thai or sweet-and-sour stir-fry sauce
2 tablespoons chopped peanuts

Cook the pasta according to the package directions, omitting any oil and salt. Drain; set aside.

In a small bowl, toss together the bean sprouts, green onion and corn; set aside.

In a large non-stick skillet, sauté the mushrooms over medium heat until hot, about 1 minute.

In a small bowl, beat the egg whites slightly with the garlic powder. Pour over the mushrooms, cooking and stirring for 1 minute. Stir in the sauce, pasta, and vegetable mixture. Continue cooking, tossing gently, until the pasta is heated through and the egg whites are cooked, about 5 to 8 minutes. Toss in the peanuts, and serve immediately.

Nutritional information per serving

Calories 236, Protein (g) 10, Carbohydrate (g) 45, Fat (g) 2, Calories from Fat (%) 8, Saturated Fat (g) 0, Dietary Fiber (g) 4, Cholesterol (mg) 0, Sodium (mg) 453, Diabetic Exchanges: 2 starch, 1 other carbohydrate

QUICK TIP:

If you can't find fresh bean sprouts, substitute 1 (14-ounce) can of bean sprouts, drained. If you can't find or don't like baby corn, substitute one (14-ounce) can of white corn, drained. The dish is very tasty either way.

PASTA

Vodka Pasta

Don't let the vodka scare you; it cooks into a very light creamy tomato sauce that you will adore.

MAKES 6 TO 8 SERVINGS

2 tablespoons olive oil
¾ cup finely chopped onion
1 (28-ounce) can diced tomatoes, drained
½ cup vodka
1 (12-ounce) can evaporated skimmed milk
¼ teaspoon crushed red pepper flakes
Salt and pepper to taste
1 (16-ounce) package penne or other tubular pasta
¼ cup grated Parmesan cheese
¼ cup sliced green onions (scallions) stems, optional

In a large non-stick skillet over medium heat, heat the olive oil and sauté the onion until tender, about 5 minutes. Add the tomatoes. Stir in the vodka, and cook over medium-high heat until it comes to a boil, about 5 minutes. Reduce the heat and add the milk, stirring constantly. Add the crushed red pepper, salt, and pepper Continue cooking for 3 to 5 minutes, or until thoroughly heated.

Meanwhile, prepare the pasta according to the package directions, omitting any oil and salt. Drain well. Add to the sauce, mixing well. Toss with the cheese, and sprinkle with green onion to serve.

Nutritional information per serving

Calories 349, Protein (g) 13, Carbohydrate (g) 54, Fat (g) 5, Calories from Fat (%) 14, Saturated Fat (g) 1, Dietary Fiber (g) 3, Cholesterol (mg) 4, Sodium (mg) 244, Diabetic Exchanges: 3 starch, 0.5 skim milk, 1 vegetable

Rigatoni with Roasted Tomato Sauce

The roasted tomatoes give this sauce a smoky flavor.

MAKES 6 SERVINGS

1 (16-ounce) package rigatoni or other tubular pasta
8 to 10 Roma (plum) tomatoes
1 tablespoon minced garlic
½ cup sliced fresh mushrooms
¼ cup green peas
Salt and pepper to taste
1 tablespoon dried basil leaves
¼ cup grated Parmesan cheese

Cook the rigatoni according to the package directions, omitting any oil and salt. Drain, and set aside.

Broil or grill the tomatoes until black on the outside, turning occasionally, about 15 minutes. Do not peel! Purée in a food processor. Set aside.

In a large non-stick skillet, sauté the garlic over medium heat until light brown, about 1 minute. Add the mushrooms; cook until the mushrooms are tender, about 4 minutes. Add the tomato purée and peas, and cook 3 minutes or until well heated. Add salt and pepper, basil, and Parmesan cheese, mixing well. Toss with the rigatoni, and serve.

Nutritional information per serving

Calories 327, Protein (g) 13, Carbohydrate (g) 63, Fat (g) 3, Calories from Fat (%) 8, Saturated Fat (g) 1, Dietary Fiber (g) 3, Cholesterol (mg) 3, Sodium (mg) 91, Diabetic Exchanges: 4 starch

PASTA

Spicy Southwestern Pasta

This sensational Southwestern meatless pasta will be devoured in minutes. Use a food processor to purée the tomatoes until they are mushy.

MAKES 6 TO 8 SERVINGS

1 (28-ounce) can whole tomatoes, puréed, with their juice
1 onion, chopped
1½ teaspoons chili powder
½ teaspoon ground cumin
1 teaspoon dried oregano leaves
½ teaspoon minced garlic
½ teaspoon sugar
¼ teaspoon ground cinnamon
¼ teaspoon crushed red pepper flakes
Salt and pepper to taste
1 (16-ounce) package rotini pasta
1 (16-ounce) can black beans, drained and rinsed
1 (10-ounce) package frozen corn kernels
1 (4-ounce) can chopped green chilies, drained
1 cup shredded reduced-fat Cheddar cheese, optional

In a large non-stick pot, add the tomato purée with juice, onion, chili powder, cumin, oregano, garlic, sugar, cinnamon, red pepper flakes, salt, and pepper. Bring to a boil, reduce the heat, and simmer, covered, to blend the flavors, about 15 minutes.

Cook the pasta according to the package directions, omitting any oil and salt. Drain well. Stir the black beans, corn, and green chilies into the sauce. Cook until the corn is crisp-tender, about 5 minutes. Remove from the heat. To serve, toss the black bean mixture with the pasta. If desired, serve with shredded cheese.

Nutritional information per serving
Calories 323, Protein (g) 13, Carbohydrate (g) 65, Fat (g) 2, Calories from Fat (%) 5, Saturated Fat (g) 0, Dietary Fiber (g) 8, Cholesterol (mg) 0, Sodium (mg) 349, Diabetic Exchanges: 4 starch, 1 vegetable

Spicy Southwestern Pasta

Sensational Meatless Spaghetti Sauce

You can put this classic red sauce on the stove late in the afternoon and let it cook while you get other things done. It reheats and freezes well, so make a big batch.

MAKES 6 TO 8 SERVINGS

1 onion, chopped
1 teaspoon minced garlic
¼ cup chopped parsley
1 green bell pepper, seeded and chopped
1 pound fresh mushrooms, chopped
2 (6-ounce) cans tomato paste
1 (28-ounce) can whole Italian tomatoes, chopped, with their juice
1 (15-ounce) can tomato sauce
1 cup water
1 tablespoon Worcestershire sauce
1 tablespoon sugar
½ cup dry red wine
1 tablespoon dried basil leaves
2 bay leaves
1 (16-ounce) package spaghetti
Grated Parmesan cheese, optional

In a large, heavy non-stick pot, sauté the onion and garlic over medium heat until tender, about 5 minutes. Add the parsley, green pepper, mushrooms, tomato paste, tomatoes with their juice, tomato sauce, water, Worcestershire sauce, sugar, wine, basil, and bay leaves. Simmer over low heat for at least 1 hour.

Cook the spaghetti according to the package directions, omitting any oil and salt. Drain, and serve with the sauce, discarding the bay leaves. Sprinkle with Parmesan cheese, if desired. Serve immediately.

Nutritional information per serving

Calories 333, Protein (g) 12, Carbohydrate (g) 67, Fat (g) 1, Calories from Fat (%) 3, Saturated Fat (g) 0, Dietary Fiber (g) 7, Cholesterol (mg) 0, Sodium (mg) 485, Diabetic Exchanges: 3 starch, 4 vegetable

Excellent Eggplant Pasta

A one-pan, high-fiber dinner that eggplant lovers will praise.

MAKES 4 TO 6 SERVINGS

1 (12-ounce) package vermicelli pasta

1½ tablespoons olive oil

1 small (1-pound) eggplant, peeled and sliced ¼-inch thick

1 teaspoon minced garlic

1 green bell pepper, seeded and cut into thin strips

½ pound fresh mushrooms, sliced

1 tablespoon dried basil leaves

½ teaspoon crushed red pepper flakes

1 large tomato, chopped

2 tablespoons grated Parmesan cheese

Cook the vermicelli according to the package directions, omitting any oil and salt. Drain, set aside, and keep warm. While the pasta is cooking, heat the olive oil in a large skillet. Add the eggplant and garlic, cover, and cook about 5 minutes, or until the eggplant is just tender, stirring occasionally. Stir in the pepper strips, mushrooms, basil, and red pepper flakes; cook until tender, about 6 minutes. Stir in the chopped tomatoes, and cook until the mixture is heated through, 5 to 7 minutes. Toss with the cooked pasta and Parmesan cheese. Serve immediately.

Nutritional information per serving

Calories 293, Protein (g) 11, Carbohydrate (g) 52, Fat (g) 5, Calories from Fat (%) 16, Saturated Fat (g) 1, Dietary Fiber (g) 5, Cholesterol (mg) 2, Sodium (mg) 50, Diabetic Exchanges: 3 starch, 2 vegetable, 0.5 fat

PASTA

Mediterranean Capellini

Mediterranean Capellini

A deluxe red sauce enhanced with capers and seasonings makes this a light dinner or pasta side dish. Feta cheese may be substituted for Parmesan.

MAKES 4 TO 6 SERVINGS

1 (12-ounce) package capellini (angel hair) pasta

2 tablespoons olive oil

1 tablespoon minced garlic

1 red onion, chopped

1 red bell pepper, seeded and finely chopped

1 (14½-ounce) can chopped tomatoes with their juice

1 (10-ounce) can diced tomatoes and green chilies

1 teaspoon drained capers

2 teaspoons dried basil leaves

1 teaspoon dried oregano leaves

½ teaspoon crushed red pepper flakes

¼ cup grated Parmesan cheese

Cook the capellini according to the package directions, omitting any oil and salt. Drain, set aside.

Heat the oil in a large non-stick pan and sauté the garlic, onion, and red pepper over medium heat until tender, about 5 minutes. Add the tomatoes with their juice, tomatoes and green chilies, capers, basil, oregano, and red pepper flakes. Simmer for 20 minutes. Toss with the pasta and Parmesan cheese. Serve immediately.

Nutritional information per serving

Calories 309, Protein (g) 11, Carbohydrate (g) 52, Fat (g) 7, Calories from Fat (%) 20, Saturated Fat (g) 2, Dietary Fiber (g) 4, Cholesterol (mg) 3, Sodium (mg) 389, Diabetic Exchanges: 3 starch, 1.5 vegetable, 1 fat

PASTA

Eggplant, Spinach, and Pasta

Eggplant, tomatoes, and basil together make a true Sicilian dish. This light red sauce highlights these wonderful veggies, which are standouts. A good dish during tomato season. For a different version, I made this dish without the eggplant, and it was wonderful.

MAKES 6 TO 8 SERVINGS

2 tablespoons olive oil
1 cup chopped onion
1 teaspoon minced garlic
5 cups peeled and cubed eggplant
4 cups fresh stemmed spinach, chopped
2 cups chopped tomatoes
2 tablespoons chopped fresh basil leaves
Salt and pepper to taste
1 (8-ounce) can tomato sauce
1 (16-ounce) package tubular pasta
⅓ cup grated fresh Parmesan cheese

In a large non-stick skillet, heat the olive oil over medium-high heat, and sauté the onion and garlic until tender, about 5 minutes. Add the eggplant; sauté about 5 minutes, or until lightly browned. Add the spinach, tomatoes, basil, salt, pepper, and tomato sauce; reduce the heat, and simmer 15 minutes.

Meanwhile, cook the pasta according to the package directions, omitting any oil and salt. Add the pasta to the eggplant mixture, and toss. Sprinkle with Parmesan cheese, and serve.

Nutritional information per serving
Calories 303, Protein (g) 11, Carbohydrate (g) 52, Fat (g) 6, Calories from Fat (%) 17, Saturated Fat (g) 1, Dietary Fiber (g) 4, Cholesterol (mg) 3, Sodium (mg) 258, Diabetic Exchanges: 3 starch, 2 vegetable, 0.5 fat

QUICK TIP:

When you're buying eggplant, look for smooth, taut skin with a fresh-looking green cap at the stem. Store eggplant in your refrigerator, and use it as soon as possible because the inside will become soft and bitter within a few days.

PASTA

Tortellini and Eggplant Casserole 🥕

This great and easy combination creates a delicious vegetarian meal that is a variation on Eggplant Parmesan.

MAKES 4 SERVINGS

1 (9-ounce) package cheese tortellini
1 medium eggplant, peeled and cut into 1-inch cubes
1 medium green bell pepper, seeded and chopped
1 cup chopped onion
1 teaspoon minced garlic
1 (15-ounce) can tomato sauce
1 teaspoon balsamic or red wine vinegar
1 teaspoon dried basil leaves
Salt and pepper to taste
½ cup shredded part-skim Mozzarella cheese

Preheat the oven to 350°F.

Cook the tortellini according to the package directions, omitting any oil and salt. Drain, and set aside.

In a large non-stick skillet, sauté the eggplant, green pepper, onion, and garlic. Cook, stirring often, 10 to 12 minutes, or until the vegetables are tender. Add the tomato sauce, vinegar, basil, salt, and pepper. Bring to a boil, reduce heat, and simmer for 5 minutes.

Spoon half the eggplant mixture into a baking dish coated with non-stick cooking spray. Top with half the tortellini. Repeat the layers with the remaining eggplant and tortellini. Sprinkle Mozzarella over the top. Cook for 10 to 15 minutes, or until the cheese melts and the casserole is heated through. Serve immediately.

Nutritional information per serving

Calories 300, Protein (g) 15, Carbohydrate (g) 48, Fat (g) 6, Calories from Fat (%) 17, Saturated Fat (g) 3, Dietary Fiber (g) 7, Cholesterol (mg) 42, Sodium (mg) 769, Diabetic Exchanges: 0.5 lean meat, 2 starch, 4 vegetable, 0.5 fat

QUICK TIP:

Store eggplants in a cool, dry place and use within one to two days of purchase. For longer storage (up to 5 days) place the eggplant in a plastic bag and store it in a refrigerator or vegetable drawer.

Double Squash Pasta Toss

Great for a light evening dinner or lunch, this is one of my favorite simple summer recipes to take advantage of farmers' markets or homegrown squash and tomatoes.

MAKES 6 TO 8 SERVINGS

2 tablespoons olive oil
1 tablespoon minced garlic
2 cups thinly sliced zucchini
2 cups thinly sliced yellow squash
2 cups coarsely chopped red onion
1 teaspoon dried basil leaves
1 teaspoon dried oregano leaves
2 cups coarsely chopped tomatoes
3 tablespoons balsamic vinegar
Salt and pepper to taste
1 (16-ounce) package ziti or other tubular pasta
¼ cup grated Parmesan cheese

In a large non-stick skillet, heat the olive oil over medium-high heat, and cook the garlic, zucchini, yellow squash, and onion until very tender, about 5 to 8 minutes. Add the basil, oregano, tomatoes, vinegar, salt, and pepper; lower the heat and cook 2 minutes longer, or until well heated.

Prepare the pasta according to the package directions, omitting any oil and salt. Drain, and add to the squash mixture. Add the Parmesan cheese, toss, and serve.

Nutritional information per serving

Calories 298, Protein (g) 10, Carbohydrate (g) 52, Fat (g) 6, Calories from Fat (%) 17, Saturated Fat (g) 1, Dietary Fiber (g) 4, Cholesterol (mg) 3, Sodium (mg) 70, Diabetic Exchanges: 3.5 starch, 3 vegetable, 1 fat

FOOD FACT:

Crookneck (yellow) squash and zucchini are referred to as summer squash. Summer squash have thin, edible skins and soft seeds. In general, the smaller the squash, the more tender it will be.

PASTA

Chicken Primavera

This is one of my standby favorites when I want a satisfying dish packed with flavor that looks as good as it is to eat.

MAKES 6 TO 8 SERVINGS

1 (12-ounce) package linguine
1½ pounds skinless, boneless chicken breasts,
   cut into chunks or strips
¼ cup olive oil
1 teaspoon minced garlic
½ pound mushrooms, sliced
1 onion, chopped
1 red bell pepper, seeded and chopped
½ teaspoon dried oregano leaves
½ teaspoon dried basil leaves
½ teaspoon thyme leaves
Salt and pepper to taste
1 cup frozen peas
¼ cup grated Parmesan cheese

Cook the linguine according to the package directions, omitting any oil and salt; drain.

In a large non-stick skillet, cook the chicken pieces in the olive oil and garlic over medium high heat until lightly brown and done, about 7 minutes. Watch carefully, tossing to keep from sticking. Add the mushrooms, onion, red pepper, oregano, basil, thyme, salt, and pepper, sautéing until tender. Add the peas, tossing until heated. Add the pasta to the vegetable mixture, combining well. Add the Parmesan cheese and serve.

Nutritional information per serving

Calories 359, Protein (g) 29, Carbohydrate (g) 38, Fat (g) 10, Calories from Fat (%) 24, Saturated Fat (g) 2, Dietary Fiber (g) 3, Cholesterol (mg) 52, Sodium (mg) 139, Diabetic Exchanges: 3 very lean meat, 2 starch, 1.5 vegetable, 1 fat

PASTA

Chicken Primavera

Chicken and Linguine

The roasted chicken and onion add an abundance of flavor to this simple preparation. If you're in the mood for a really quick and great tasting chicken dish, serve the chicken as an entrée and make your choice of sides.

MAKES 4 SERVINGS

3 tablespoons olive oil

1 medium onion, thinly sliced in rings

2 cloves garlic, minced

1 teaspoon dried basil leaves

¼ teaspoon crushed red pepper flakes

1½ pounds skinless, boneless chicken breasts, cut into pieces

8 ounces linguine pasta

¼ cup grated Parmesan cheese

Salt and pepper, optional

Preheat the oven to 400°F.

In a 2-quart oblong pan, combine the olive oil, onion rings, garlic, basil, and red pepper. Roll the chicken pieces in the oil mixture, and leave in the pan. Bake the chicken, uncovered, about 45 minutes.

Approximately 10 minutes before the chicken is done, cook the linguine according to the package directions, omitting any oil and salt. Drain. When the chicken is done, add the pasta, cheese, salt, and pepper to the dish, mixing well. Serve immediately.

Nutritional information per serving

Calories 534, Protein (g) 50, Carbohydrate (g) 47, Fat (g) 15, Calories from Fat (%) 26, Saturated Fat (g) 3, Dietary Fiber (g) 2, Cholesterol (mg) 104, Sodium (mg) 233, Diabetic Exchanges: 4.5 very lean meat, 3 starch, 2 fat

PASTA

Greek Lemon
Chicken over Pasta

With its touch of Greek flair, this wonderfully marinated, lemony chicken in a light sauce with Feta and pasta is a delightful eating experience.

MAKES 8 SERVINGS

½ cup white wine
3 tablespoons olive oil, divided
¼ cup plus 1 tablespoon lemon juice
Salt and pepper to taste
4 cloves garlic, minced
8 skinless, boneless chicken breasts
½ cup skim milk
2 tablespoons all-purpose flour
1 tablespoon prepared mustard
1 teaspoon dried dill weed leaves
¼ cup finely chopped parsley
1 cup nonfat plain yogurt
1 (16-ounce) capellini (angel hair) pasta
½ cup crumbled Feta cheese
½ cup shredded Muenster or reduced-fat Swiss cheese

In a small bowl, combine the wine, 1 tablespoon olive oil, ¼ cup lemon juice, the salt, pepper, and garlic. Mix well.

Pound the chicken breasts slightly, and place in a shallow casserole. Pour the marinade over the chicken to cover, and refrigerate up to 12 hours. Discard the marinade.

In a non-stick skillet, heat the remaining oil. Sauté the chicken until tender, 7 to 10 minutes. Slice and set aside.

In a small saucepan, stir the milk into the flour, and add the mustard. Cook over medium heat, stirring constantly until thickened. Remove from the heat, and add the remaining lemon juice, the dill weed, and the parsley. Stir in the yogurt, mixing well.

Cook the pasta according to the package directions, omitting any oil and salt. Gently toss the pasta with the sauce and the Feta cheese. Place in a 13 x 9 x 2-inch non-stick baking dish, and top with the chicken breasts and Muenster cheese. Broil until the cheese is golden. Serve immediately.

Nutritional information per serving
Calories 478, Protein (g) 39, Carbohydrate (g) 49, Fat (g) 12, Calories from Fat (%) 22, Saturated Fat (g) 4, Dietary Fiber (g) 2, Cholesterol (mg) 82, Sodium (mg) 428, Diabetic Exchanges: 4 lean meat, 3.5 starch

PASTA

Chicken
Mediterranean Pasta

Use leftover chicken in this dish or leave it out completely for a vegetarian dish. My mother-in-law came over and enjoyed this dish for dinner, then again the next day as a cold pasta salad.

MAKES 6 SERVINGS

1 cup chopped onion
1 tablespoon minced garlic
1 tablespoon dried basil leaves
1 teaspoon dried thyme leaves
1 (10-ounce) can diced green chilies and tomatoes
1 (8-ounce) can tomato sauce
4 skinless, boneless chicken breasts, cut into strips
Salt and pepper to taste
2 tablespoons capers, drained
1 (2¼-ounce) can chopped black olives, drained
1 (16-ounce) package linguine pasta
¼ cup grated Parmesan cheese
½ cup finely minced parsley

In a large non-stick skillet, sauté the onion and garlic over medium heat until tender, about 5 minutes. Add the basil, thyme, chilies and tomatoes, tomato sauce, and chicken. Season with salt and pepper. Simmer slowly for 15 to 20 minutes, stirring occasionally until the chicken is cooked through. Add the capers and olives.

Meanwhile, cook the pasta according to the package directions, omitting any oil and salt. Drain, and toss with Parmesan cheese. Pour the sauce over the pasta; toss, sprinkle with parsley, and serve immediately.

Nutritional information per serving

Calories 428, Protein (g) 31, Carbohydrate (g) 65, Fat (g) 4, Calories from Fat (%) 9, Saturated Fat (g) 1, Dietary Fiber (g) 4, Cholesterol (mg) 47, Sodium (mg) 717, Diabetic Exchanges: 2.5 very lean meat, 4 starch, 1 vegetable

PASTA

Chicken and Spinach Cannelloni ❄

With a simple white sauce, spinach, and shells, turn leftover chicken into a scrumptious meal.

MAKES 8 SERVINGS

3 cups skim milk, divided
1 onion, quartered
3 bay leaves
2 whole cloves
2 tablespoons cornstarch
¼ cup grated Parmesan cheese
¼ teaspoon white pepper
1 cup finely chopped mushrooms
½ cup finely chopped onion
½ teaspoon minced garlic
1 (10-ounce) bag fresh spinach, coarsely chopped
1 pound cooked skinless, boneless chicken breasts, cut into small chunks
⅛ teaspoon white pepper
1 (8-ounce) package cannelloni shells

Preheat the oven to 350ºF.

In a large saucepan, combine 2 cups milk and the onion, bay leaves, and cloves; heat until hot.

In a small bowl, combine remaining milk and the cornstarch; stir well. Gradually add the cornstarch mixture to the hot milk mixture, stirring constantly and cooking until thickened and bubbly, 5 to 7 minutes. Remove the onion, bay leaves, and cloves. Add the Parmesan cheese and ¼ teaspoon white pepper to the milk mixture; set the sauce aside.

In a non-stick skillet, sauté the mushrooms, onion, and garlic until tender, 5 to 7 minutes. Add the spinach, cooking and stirring occasionally until the spinach wilts and the liquid has evaporated, 3 to 5 minutes. Remove from the heat, and add the chicken and ⅛ teaspoon white pepper; mix well and set aside.

Meanwhile, cook the shells according to the package directions, omitting any oil and salt. Spoon ½ cup sauce over the bottom of a 13 x 9 x 2-inch non-stick baking dish. Fill the shells with the chicken mixture, and arrange in the dish. Pour the remaining sauce over the shells. Cover, and bake for 30 minutes, or until bubbly and heated. Serve.

Nutritional information per serving

Calories 237, Protein (g) 23, Carbohydrate (g) 30, Fat (g) 2, Calories from Fat (%) 9, Saturated Fat (g) 1, Dietary Fiber (g) 2, Cholesterol (mg) 37, Sodium (mg) 173, Diabetic Exchanges: 2 very lean meat, 1.5 starch, 0.5 skim milk

PASTA

Chicken Vermicelli ❄

This great and very tasty recipe is perfect to take to a friend or freeze for another time, since it makes enough to fill two casseroles. If you plan to freeze the chicken vermicelli, don't bake it beforehand. For a quick and equally good version, use leftover or rotisserie chicken and canned broth.

MAKES 14 TO 16 SERVINGS

6 pounds skinless chicken breasts
Salt and pepper to taste
2 celery stalks, cut in half
2 onions, 1 halved and 1 chopped
1 (16-ounce) package vermicelli pasta
1 tablespoon margarine
1 green bell pepper, seeded and chopped
2 cups chopped celery
½ teaspoon minced garlic
1 (8-ounce) can mushrooms, drained
1 cup all-purpose flour
4 cups reserved chicken broth
1 (10-ounce) can diced tomatoes and green chilies
¼ teaspoon cayenne pepper
1 tablespoon Worcestershire sauce
½ cup grated Parmesan cheese
¼ cup chopped parsley
1 cup chopped green onions (scallions)

Preheat the oven to 300°F.

Place the chicken in a large pot, and add water to cover. Add salt and pepper, celery stalks, and halved onion; bring to a boil. Reduce heat and cook for 30 minutes, or until the chicken is done. Reserve the broth, discarding the celery and onion. Cool slightly; then debone the chicken and cut into bite-size pieces.

Cook the vermicelli according to the package directions, omitting any oil and salt. Drain and set aside.

In a large non-stick pot, melt the margarine over medium heat, and sauté the chopped onion, green pepper, celery, and garlic until tender. Add the mushrooms. Gradually stir in the flour, mixing for 30 seconds. Gradually add the chicken broth, stirring. Add the tomatoes and green chilies, cayenne pepper, and Worcestershire sauce. Add the chicken and vermicelli, mixing well.

Divide the mixture into two 2-quart shallow casseroles coated with nonstick cooking spray. Top each casserole with half the Parmesan cheese, parsley, and green onion, and bake for 20 to 30 minutes, or until thoroughly heated. Serve immediately.

Nutritional information per serving
Calories 329, Protein (g) 30, Carbohydrate (g) 30, Fat (g) 9, Calories from Fat (%) 24, Saturated Fat (g) 3, Dietary Fiber (g) 2, Cholesterol (mg) 74, Sodium (mg) 291, Diabetic Exchanges: 3 lean meat, 2 starch

PASTA

Angel Hair with Crabmeat

There is no compromise on flavor when crabmeat and Italian seasonings create a light, lovely sauce.

MAKES 4 TO 6 SERVINGS

1 (8-ounce) package capellini (angel hair) pasta
2 tablespoons olive oil
½ cup chopped onion
1 teaspoon minced garlic
½ pound fresh mushrooms, sliced
2 tablespoons chopped parsley
1 teaspoon dried basil leaves
1 teaspoon dried oregano leaves
1 teaspoon lemon juice
1 pound lump white crabmeat
Salt and pepper to taste

Cook the pasta according to the package directions, omitting any oil. Drain and set aside.

In a large non-stick skillet, heat the oil. Sauté the onion, garlic, and mushrooms over medium-high heat until tender, 5 to 7 minutes. Add the parsley, basil, oregano, and lemon juice, cooking a few more minutes. Gently stir in the crabmeat. Add the pasta, carefully tossing to mix well. Season to taste, and serve.

Nutritional information per serving

Calories 282, Protein (g) 23, Carbohydrate (g) 33, Fat (g) 6, Calories from Fat (%) 20, Saturated Fat (g) 1, Dietary Fiber (g) 2, Cholesterol (mg) 57, Sodium (mg) 291, Diabetic Exchanges: 2.5 very lean meat, 2 starch, 1 vegetable

Shrimp Fettuccine

A stylishly simple, family-favorite, one-dish evening meal.

MAKES 6 TO 8 SERVINGS

1 pound peeled large shrimp
¼ cup white wine
1 bunch green onions (scallions), chopped
2 cloves garlic, minced
½ pound fresh mushrooms, sliced
1 (6-ounce) package frozen snow peas
2 tablespoons olive oil
1 (8-ounce) package fettuccine pasta
¼ cup chopped parsley
½ cup grated Romano cheese

Marinate the shrimp in the white wine for 30 minutes, if time permits.

In a large non-stick skillet, stir-fry the green onions, garlic, mushrooms, and snow peas in the olive oil over medium-high heat for about 5 minutes. When the vegetables are crisp-tender, add the shrimp and wine, and sauté until the shrimp are pink.

Prepare the fettuccine according to the package directions, omitting any oil. Drain. Add the fettuccine to the shrimp mixture along with the parsley and Romano cheese, tossing gently. Serve immediately.

Nutritional information per serving

Calories 220, Protein (g) 15, Carbohydrate (g) 25, Fat (g) 6, Calories from Fat (%) 25, Saturated Fat (g) 2, Dietary Fiber (g) 2, Cholesterol (mg) 74, Sodium (mg) 160, Diabetic Exchanges: 1.5 very lean meat, 1.5 starch, 0.5 fat

PASTA

Shrimp with Feta and Pasta

This is an easy recipe, since most of the work is done ahead of time with the ingredients marinating. During tomato season, this is a super stand-by recipe. Try different varieties of Feta to intensify the flavor of this dish.

MAKES 6 TO 8 SERVINGS

2 pounds peeled, cooked shrimp
½ cup crumbled Feta cheese
1 bunch green onions (scallions), sliced
2 teaspoons dried oregano leaves
2½ cups chopped tomatoes
2 tablespoons sliced black olives
Salt and pepper to taste
1 (16-ounce) package fettuccine pasta

In a large bowl, combine the shrimp, Feta, green onions, oregano, tomatoes, olives, salt, and pepper. Let stand at room temperature for at least 1 hour.

Cook the pasta according to the package directions omitting any oil; drain. Add the pasta to the shrimp mixture, tossing. Serve immediately.

Nutritional information per serving
Calories 366, Protein (g) 33, Carbohydrate (g) 47, Fat (g) 5, Calories from Fat (%) 11, Saturated Fat (g) 2, Dietary Fiber (g) 3, Cholesterol (mg) 230, Sodium (mg) 388, Diabetic Exchanges: 3.5 very lean meat, 3 starch

Shrimp with Oranges and Pasta

A burst of citrus flavor, shrimp, pasta, and Brie cheese make this an easy gourmet delight.

MAKES 6 TO 8 SERVINGS

1 (16-ounce) package ziti or other tubular pasta
1 red onion, sliced
1 teaspoon chopped jalapeño chile pepper
2 pounds peeled, medium shrimp
1 teaspoon minced garlic
½ cup orange juice
2 oranges, seeded and separated into segments
1 teaspoon dried basil leaves
6 ounces Brie cheese, rind removed, sliced

Cook the pasta according to the package directions, omitting any oil and salt. Drain; set aside.

In a large non-stick skillet, sauté the onion, jalapeño, shrimp, and garlic over medium-high heat until the shrimp are done, 5 to 8 minutes. Add the orange juice, orange segments, and basil, stirring well, and cook just until heated through. Toss the pasta with the shrimp sauce, and add the Brie, stirring gently until the cheese is melted.

Nutritional information per serving
Calories 382, Protein (g) 27, Carbohydrate (g) 50, Fat (g) 8, Calories from Fat (%) 18, Saturated Fat (g) 4, Dietary Fiber (g) 3, Cholesterol (mg) 156, Sodium (mg) 294, Diabetic Exchanges: 3 lean meat, 3 starch, 0.5 fruit

PASTA

Shrimp Ziti Primavera

For a vegetarian meal, leave out the shrimp, and don't worry about losing any of the flavor—this intense sauce is a winner on its own. Be creative with your choice of veggies.

MAKES 8 SERVINGS

1 (16-ounce) package ziti or other tubular pasta

2 pounds peeled, medium shrimp

2 tablespoons minced garlic

1 bunch green onions (scallions), chopped

1 pound fresh asparagus spears, cut into 2-inch pieces

½ pound fresh mushrooms, sliced

2 cups chopped tomatoes

Salt and pepper to taste

⅛ teaspoon crushed red pepper flakes

½ cup dry white wine

1 tablespoon dried basil leaves

1 tablespoon dried oregano leaves

1 tablespoon dried thyme leaves

¼ cup grated Parmesan cheese

1 tablespoon chopped parsley

Cook the pasta according to the package directions, omitting any oil and salt. Drain; set aside.

Heat a large non-stick skillet, and cook the shrimp, garlic, and green onions, stirring constantly, until the shrimp just turn pink. Add the asparagus, mushrooms, tomatoes, salt, pepper, red pepper flakes, wine, basil, oregano, and thyme to the skillet, and continue cooking until the shrimp are done and the vegetables are tender, 5 to 7 minutes. Add the pasta, Parmesan, and parsley, tossing well. Serve immediately.

Nutritional information per serving

Calories 346, Protein (g) 26, Carbohydrate (g) 51, Fat (g) 3, Calories from Fat (%) 8, Saturated Fat (g) 1, Dietary Fiber (g) 4, Cholesterol (mg) 137, Sodium (mg) 225, Diabetic Exchanges: 2 very lean meat, 3 starch, 1.5 vegetable

Shrimp and Angel Hair

I prepared this snappy and spicy recipe on The Phil Donahue *Show years ago, and it stole the show.*

MAKES 8 TO 10 SERVINGS

5 ounces Canadian bacon, diced
1 green bell pepper, seeded and chopped
1 onion, chopped
3 stalks celery, chopped
5 cloves garlic, minced
2 teaspoons dried basil leaves
2 teaspoons dried oregano leaves
1 bay leaf
¼ cup all-purpose flour
1 (10-ounce) can chopped tomatoes and green chilies
2 pounds peeled medium shrimp
1 (16-ounce) package capellini (angel hair) pasta
1 large bunch green onions (scallions), thinly chopped

In a large non-stick skillet, cook the Canadian bacon over medium heat until it begins to brown, about 3 minutes. Add the green pepper, onion, celery, garlic, basil, oregano, and bay leaf, sautéing until tender, 5 to 7 minutes. Gradually add the flour and the tomatoes and green chilies, stirring. Add the shrimp, cooking 7 to 10 minutes or until pink and done, still stirring.

Cook the angel hair according to the package directions, omitting any oil; drain. Toss with the shrimp mixture, and add the green onions. Serve immediately.

Nutritional information per serving
Calories 279, Protein (g) 22, Carbohydrate (g) 42, Fat (g) 2, Calories from Fat (%) 8, Saturated Fat (g) 1, Dietary Fiber (g) 3, Cholesterol (mg) 115, Sodium (mg) 453, Diabetic Exchanges: 2 very lean meat, 2.5 starch, 1 vegetable

QUICK TIP:

Drain but don't rinse pasta unless you are using it for a cold salad. Always reserve a small amount of the pasta cooking liquid. Toss pasta with the sauce, and if the sauce is too thick, add some of the reserved cooking liquid a little at a time.

PASTA

Shrimp and Angel Hair

Basil Shrimp with Fettuccine

I usually don't insist on fresh herbs, but it's a must here as fresh basil is the star ingredient.

MAKES 4 SERVINGS

2 tablespoons olive oil

1 pound peeled, medium shrimp

4 cups chopped tomatoes

⅓ cup chopped fresh basil leaves

¼ cup sliced black olives

1 teaspoon minced garlic

1 bunch green onions (scallions), chopped

Salt and pepper to taste

¼ teaspoon cayenne pepper

1 (8-ounce) package fettuccine pasta

Grated Romano cheese, optional

In a large non-stick skillet, heat the oil over medium-high heat, and cook the shrimp, tomatoes, basil, olives, garlic, and green onions. Season with salt, pepper, and cayenne pepper. Cook, stirring frequently, until the shrimp are pink, about 7 minutes.

Meanwhile, cook the fettuccine according to the package directions, omitting any oil and salt. Drain, and place in a serving dish. Pour the shrimp and sauce over the pasta, and toss together. Sprinkle with the cheese. Serve immediately.

Nutritional information per serving

Calories 397, Protein (g) 24, Carbohydrate (g) 54, Fat (g) 10, Calories from Fat (%) 22, Saturated Fat (g) 1, Dietary Fiber (g) 4, Cholesterol (mg) 135, Sodium (mg) 252, Diabetic Exchanges: 2 very lean meat, 3 starch, 2 vegetable, 1 fat

QUICK TIP:

Drain but do not rinse pasta when it is used in a hot dish. Toss the pasta immediately with the sauce, and if the sauce is too thick, try adding some reserved cooking liquid a little at a time until the desired consistency is reached.

PASTA

Shrimp, Salsa, and Pasta Casserole

The combination of a custardy layer, salsa, shrimp, and cheese makes this the perfect light evening meal.

MAKES 6 SERVINGS

1 (8-ounce) package capellini (angel hair) pasta
1 egg white
1 egg
1 (5-ounce) can evaporated skimmed milk
1 cup nonfat plain yogurt
⅓ cup chopped green onions (scallions)
1 teaspoon dried basil leaves
1 teaspoon dried oregano leaves
1 teaspoon minced garlic
1 (16-ounce) jar mild chunky salsa
1 pound peeled, medium shrimp
1½ cups shredded reduced-fat Cheddar cheese

Preheat the oven to 350°F.

Cook the pasta according to the package directions, omitting any oil and salt. Drain and set aside.

In a medium bowl, blend the egg white, egg, evaporated milk, yogurt, green onions, basil, oregano, and garlic; set aside.

Spread half the pasta over the bottom of a 13 x 9 x 2-inch non-stick baking dish coated with non-stick cooking spray. Cover with the salsa. Layer the shrimp over the salsa. Spread the remaining pasta over the shrimp. Pour the egg mixture evenly over the pasta.

Bake, uncovered, 30 minutes, or until the shrimp are pink and the liquid is absorbed. Sprinkle with the cheese and continue baking for 5 to 10 minutes, or until the cheese is melted. Remove from the oven, and let stand 10 minutes before serving.

Nutritional information per serving

Calories 334, Protein (g) 24, Carbohydrate (g) 40, Fat (g) 6, Calories from Fat (%) 18, Saturated Fat (g) 3, Dietary Fiber (g) 1, Cholesterol (mg) 99, Sodium (mg) 640, Diabetic Exchanges: 2 very lean meat, 2 starch, 0.5 skim milk

Crawfish Fettuccine

Crawfish Fettuccine ❄

If you're a crawfish fan, this dish will soon be high on your list. It is great for crowds, and it freezes well. Cooked shrimp may be used instead of crawfish.

MAKES 8 TO 10 SERVINGS

1 (16-ounce) package fettuccine pasta
2 pounds crawfish tails
¼ cup margarine
1 large onion, chopped
2 green bell peppers, seeded and chopped
1 red bell pepper, seeded and chopped
1 teaspoon minced garlic
¼ cup all-purpose flour
1½ cups skim milk
½ pound light pasteurized cheese spread
2 tablespoons chopped parsley
1 tablespoon Worcestershire sauce
¼ teaspoon cayenne pepper

Cook the fettuccine according to the package directions, omitting any oil and salt. Drain; set aside.

Rinse the crawfish tails; drain well, and set aside.

In a large non-stick pot, melt the margarine and sauté the onion, green pepper, red pepper, and garlic over medium heat until tender, 5 to 7 minutes. Add the flour, stirring until mixed. Gradually add the milk, stirring until smooth. Add the cheese, stirring until melted. Add the crawfish, parsley, Worcestershire sauce, and cayenne pepper. Toss with the pasta, heat thoroughly, and serve.

Nutritional information per serving
Calories 378, Protein (g) 28, Carbohydrate (g) 45, Fat (g) 9, Calories from Fat (%) 22, Saturated Fat (g) 3, Dietary Fiber (g) 2, Cholesterol (mg) 131, Sodium (mg) 539, Diabetic Exchanges: 3 lean meat, 3 starch

Scallop, Pepper, and Pasta Toss

With an abundance of color and flavor, this fabulous dish is a great way to serve scallops. Use either bay or sea scallops, and increase the amount, if desired.

MAKES 4 TO 6 SERVINGS

1 (8-ounce) package fettuccine pasta

1 tablespoon olive oil

1 cup chopped red onion

1 red bell pepper, seeded and cut in strips

1 green bell pepper, seeded and cut in strips

8 ounces bay scallops

1 teaspoon minced garlic

1 cup frozen corn

2 tablespoons lemon juice

1 teaspoon dried basil leaves

½ cup chopped green onions (scallions)

Cook the fettuccine according to the package directions, omitting any oil and salt. Drain, set aside.

In a large non-stick skillet, heat the olive oil. Sauté the onion, red pepper, and green pepper over medium-high heat for 5 to 7 minutes until tender; set aside.

Over medium-high heat, stir-fry the scallops, garlic, and corn until the scallops are opaque. Stir in the lemon juice, basil, green onion, and pepper. Toss the scallop and pepper mixture with the pasta, and serve.

Nutritional information per serving

Calories 244, Protein (g) 13, Carbohydrate (g) 41, Fat (g) 3, Calories from Fat (%) 13, Saturated Fat (g) 0, Dietary Fiber (g) 3, Cholesterol (mg) 12, Sodium (mg) 68, Diabetic Exchanges: 1 very lean meat, 2.5 starch, 1 vegetable

PASTA

Smoked Salmon, Snap Peas, and Pasta

Add the salmon before serving—it loses its translucency and delicate texture when heated.

MAKES 8 SERVINGS

1 (16-ounce) package fusilli (corkscrew) pasta
1 cup chopped onion
½ pound fresh sugar snap peas
2 tablespoons olive oil
1 (12-ounce) can evaporated skimmed milk
2 tablespoons capers, drained
1 tablespoon chopped fresh dill weed
Salt and pepper to taste
4 ounces smoked salmon

Cook the fusilli in boiling water according to the package directions, omitting any oil and salt; drain well.

In a large non-stick skillet coated with non-stick cooking spray, sauté the onion and snap peas in the olive oil over medium-high heat until tender, 3 to 5 minutes. Add the evaporated skimmed milk, capers, dill weed, salt, and pepper, cooking until well heated, about 5 minutes. Remove from the heat, dice the smoked salmon, and toss with the pasta. Serve immediately.

Nutritional information per serving

Calories 315, Protein (g) 14, Carbohydrate (g) 52, Fat (g) 5, Calories from Fat (%) 15, Saturated Fat (g) 1, Dietary Fiber (g) 3, Cholesterol (mg) 5, Sodium (mg) 407, Diabetic Exchanges: 0.5 very lean meat, 3 starch, 0.5 skim milk

Smoked Salmon, Snap Peas, and Pasta

PASTA

Old-Fashioned Lasagna

Here is a lighter version of our traditional family-favorite lasagna, without any compromise on taste.

MAKES 8 SERVINGS

½ pound lasagna noodles

1 teaspoon minced garlic

1 onion, chopped

1½ pounds ground sirloin

Salt and pepper to taste

2 teaspoons dried basil leaves

1 tablespoon chopped parsley

1 teaspoon dried oregano leaves

½ cup finely chopped carrots

2 (6-ounce) cans tomato paste

1½ cups hot water

1 large egg white

1 (15-ounce) container reduced fat or light ricotta cheese

1 cup shredded part-skim Mozzarella cheese

QUICK TIP:

When layering lasagna, always spread a little sauce on the bottom of your lasagna dish so the pasta doesn't stick. End with sauce on top, to keep the exposed noodles from turning dry and hard.

Preheat the oven to 350°F.

Cook the noodles according to the package directions, omitting any oil and salt. Drain and set aside.

In a large non-stick skillet, sauté the garlic and onion over medium-high heat until tender. Add the ground meat, salt, pepper, basil, parsley, oregano, and carrots, cooking until the meat is done, about 7 minutes; drain excess liquid. Add the tomato paste and hot water; simmer for 5 minutes, and then set aside.

In a small bowl, blend the egg white and Ricotta cheese.

In a 13 x 9 x 2-inch non-stick baking dish coated with non-stick cooking spray, put a thin layer of the meat sauce, half the noodles, all of the ricotta cheese mixture, and half the Mozzarella cheese. Repeat with half the remaining meat sauce, all of the remaining noodles, then the remainder of the meat sauce, and top with the remainder of the Mozzarella. Bake for 30 minutes, or until bubbly and well-heated. Let sit for 10 minutes before serving.

Nutritional information per serving

Calories 380, Protein (g) 33, Carbohydrate (g) 37, Fat (g) 11, Calories from Fat (%) 26, Saturated Fat (g) 6, Dietary Fiber (g) 4, Cholesterol (mg) 74, Sodium (mg) 273, Diabetic Exchanges: 4 lean meat, 1.5 starch, 2 vegetable

PASTA

Quick Chicken Lasagna

PASTA

Quick Chicken Lasagna ❄

Take the easy but delicious way out with this recipe from a good friend who doesn't have time to cook. It's made with jarred pasta sauce, rotisserie chicken, and no-boil noodles to create one of my very favorite lasagnas. This recipe is also high in fiber and full of flavor. My daughter in college prepares this recipe all the time.

MAKES 8 SERVINGS

1 rotisserie chicken, skin removed and chicken cut into pieces (about 3 cups)

2 (26-ounce) jars red pasta sauce

1 (8-ounce) package no-boil lasagna noodles

2 cups shredded part-skim Mozzarella cheese

2 (10-ounce) packages chopped spinach, thawed and drained

1 (4-ounce) package crumbled goat cheese

Preheat the oven to 350ºF.

Combine chicken with of the pasta sauce. In an oblong baking dish, spread a thin layer of this chicken sauce. Top with a layer of noodles, one-third of the chicken sauce, Mozzarella cheese, half the spinach, and one-third of the goat cheese. Repeat layering with noodles, chicken sauce, Mozzarella, the remaining spinach, and one-third of the goat cheese. Continue with the remaining noodles, chicken sauce, Mozzarella, and goat cheese.

Bake, covered, for 50 minutes. Uncover and bake 5 minutes longer, or until bubbly. Serve immediately.

Nutritional information per serving

Calories 462, Protein (g) 36, Carbohydrate (g) 42, Fat (g) 16, Calories from Fat (%) 32, Saturated Fat (g) 8, Dietary Fiber (g) 7, Cholesterol (mg) 78, Sodium (mg) 1,107, Diabetic Exchanges: 4 lean meat, 1.5 starch, 1 vegetable, 1 other carbohydrate

QUICK TIP:

Try different flavored pasta sauces, such as roasted garlic, for bonus flavor.

PASTA

Vegetable Lasagna

This lasagna is packed with everyday veggies and is so good that a local restaurant once used the recipe.

MAKES 8 SERVINGS

1 onion, chopped
1 teaspoon minced garlic
1 green bell pepper, seeded and chopped
1 (6-ounce) can tomato paste
1 (10-ounce) can diced tomatoes and green chilies
1 (10-ounce) can chopped tomatoes
1 (11.5-ounce) can tomato juice
1 teaspoon dried basil leaves
1 teaspoon dried oregano leaves
1 teaspoon dried thyme leaves
1½ tablespoons red wine vinegar
1 bay leaf
½ pound fresh mushrooms, sliced
½ cup peeled and shredded carrots
1 bunch broccoli, cut into florets
½ pound lasagna noodles
Cheese Mixture (recipe follows)
1½ cups shredded part-skim Mozzarella cheese

Preheat the oven to 350°F.

In a large non-stick skillet, sauté the onion, garlic, and green pepper over medium-high heat for 5 to 7 minutes, or until tender. Add the tomato paste, diced tomatoes and green chilies, chopped tomatoes, and tomato juice, bringing to a boil. Add the basil, oregano, thyme, vinegar, bay leaf, mushrooms, carrots, and broccoli, lower the heat, and simmer 20 to 30 minutes, or until the vegetables are tender and the sauce has slightly thickened. Discard the bay leaf.

Cook the lasagna noodles according to the package directions, omitting any oil and salt; drain.

In a 13 x 9 x 2-inch non-stick baking dish, spoon a layer of vegetable sauce along the bottom. Layer one-third each of the lasagna noodles, Cheese Mixture (see recipe below), vegetable sauce, and Mozzarella cheese. Repeat the layers. Bake, covered, for 30 minutes. Let stand 10 minutes before cutting.

CHEESE MIXTURE

2 cups fat-free cottage cheese
1 egg white
2 tablespoons chopped parsley
¼ cup grated Parmesan cheese

In a food processor, combine the cottage cheese, egg white, parsley, and cheese, blending well.

Nutritional information per serving

Calories 290, Protein (g) 22, Carbohydrate (g) 40, Fat (g) 5, Calories from Fat (%) 16, Saturated Fat (g) 3, Dietary Fiber (g) 5, Cholesterol (mg) 20 , Sodium (mg) 721, Diabetic Exchanges: 2 lean meat, 1.5 starch, 3 vegetable

PASTA

Seafood Lasagna ❄

This lasagna is a divine creation. Sometimes, I layer the Swiss cheese instead of putting it in the sauce, which is a delicious alternative method.

MAKES 8 SERVINGS

2 (14½-ounce) cans diced tomatoes, undrained
1 cup sliced fresh mushrooms
1 teaspoon dried oregano leaves
1 clove garlic, minced
Salt and pepper to taste
1 pound cooked, peeled small shrimp
1 tablespoon margarine
3 tablespoons all-purpose flour
1¾ cups skim milk
1 cup shredded reduced-fat Swiss cheese
1 pound white crabmeat, picked for shells
¼ cup dry white wine (optional)
8 lasagna noodles

Preheat the oven to 350°F.

In a large saucepan, combine the tomatoes, mushrooms, oregano, garlic, salt, and pepper. Bring to a boil. Reduce the heat, and simmer, uncovered, about 15 minutes, or until thickened. Stir in the shrimp. Set aside.

In another saucepan, melt the margarine and stir in the flour. Add the milk, and cook, stirring constantly, over medium heat until thickened and bubbly, 5 to 7 minutes. Stir in the Swiss cheese until melted. Add the crabmeat and wine, stirring carefully.

Cook the lasagna noodles according to the package directions, omitting any oil or salt; drain.

In a 13 x 9 x 2-inch non-stick pan coated with non-stick cooking spray, layer half the shrimp sauce, half the noodles, and half the cheese sauce. Repeat the layering. Bake for 25 minutes, or until heated. Let stand 10 minutes. Serve.

Nutritional information per serving

Calories 265, Protein (g) 33, Carbohydrate (g) 19, Fat (g) 6, Calories from Fat (%) 21, Saturated Fat (g) 2, Dietary Fiber (g) 2, Cholesterol (mg) 162, Sodium (mg) 608, Diabetic Exchanges: 4 lean meat, 1 starch, 1 vegetable

Mediterranean Lasagna

This Mediterranean-inspired, vegetarian version of the classic recipe is chock-full of fabulous ingredients and packed with intense flavor. I absolutely love this recipe and don't even miss the meat. I also prefer roasted red peppers and no-boil lasagna.

MAKES 8 SERVINGS

1 large onion
1 teaspoon minced garlic
1 teaspoon dried mint flakes
2 (14-ounce) cans artichoke hearts, drained and coarsely chopped
½ cup chopped roasted red pepper, optional
1 (14-ounce) can Great Northern or navy beans, drained and rinsed
1 (10-ounce) package fresh spinach, torn in pieces
5 tablespoons all-purpose flour
3 cups skim milk
½ pound lasagna noodles, either cooked or no-boil
¾ cup crumbled Feta cheese
¾ cup part-skim shredded Mozzarella cheese

Preheat the oven to 375ºF.

In a non-stick skillet, sauté the onion, garlic, mint, artichoke hearts, red pepper, beans, and spinach over medium-high heat until tender; set aside.

In a large saucepan, whisk the flour and milk to make a white sauce, and cook over medium heat until thickened, 5 to 7 minutes.

In a 13 x 9 x 2-inch non-stick pan coated with non-stick cooking spray, spread a thin layer of the white sauce, half the noodles, half the spinach mixture, half the remaining white sauce, half the Feta, and half the Mozzarella. Repeat the layers. Cover, and bake 30 to 40 minutes, until bubbly and the noodles are done (if using no-boil noodles).

Nutritional information per serving

Calories 402, Protein (g) 24, Carbohydrate (g) 47, Fat (g) 14, Calories from Fat (%) 30, Saturated Fat (g) 9, Dietary Fiber (g) 6, Cholesterol (mg) 52, Sodium (mg) 948, Diabetic Exchanges: 2 lean meat, 2 starch, 0.5 skim milk, 1.5 vegetable, 1 fat

PASTA

Magnificent Meat Sauce with Spaghetti ❄

Here's a fabulous classic meat sauce to satisfy all spaghetti-and-meat-sauce fans. Substitute one large jar spaghetti sauce for the tomatoes and seasonings, and add to the cooked ground meat for an even faster meat sauce.

MAKES 6 TO 8 SERVINGS

1 celery stalk with leaves, finely chopped
1 carrot, peeled and finely chopped
1 onion, finely chopped
½ teaspoon minced garlic
2 pounds ground sirloin
1 tablespoon dried oregano leaves
½ cup dry red wine
1 (28-ounce) can chopped tomatoes, in juice
2 tablespoons tomato paste
1 cup canned beef broth
1 teaspoon sugar
Salt and pepper to taste
1 (16-ounce) package pasta of your choice

In a heavy non-stick pot, sauté the celery, carrot, onion, and garlic over medium heat until tender, about 5 minutes. Add the meat and oregano. Cook, stirring, until the meat begins to brown, about 4 minutes. Add the wine, and simmer another 5 minutes or until meat is done. Then add the tomatoes, tomato paste, beef broth, and sugar. Simmer over medium heat for 20 minutes (it can simmer longer). Add the salt and pepper.

Meanwhile, cook the pasta according to the package directions, omitting any oil and salt. Drain, and serve with the meat sauce.

Nutritional information per serving
Calories 394, Protein (g) 31, Carbohydrate (g) 52, Fat (g) 6, Calories from Fat (%) 14, Saturated Fat (g) 2, Dietary Fiber (g) 4, Cholesterol (mg) 60, Sodium (mg) 332, Diabetic Exchanges: 3 very lean meat, 3 starch, 1.5 vegetable

QUICK TIP:

Store leftover tomato paste in a zipper lock bag in the freezer. To reuse the paste, break off chunks or defrost it in the microwave.

PASTA

Jumbo Stuffed Shells ❄

This dish, definitely a family favorite, is often requested before I go out of town, since I make it ahead of time and freeze it for my family.

MAKES 6 TO 8 SERVINGS

1 (12-ounce) package jumbo shells
1½ pounds ground sirloin
2 egg whites
¼ cup grated Parmesan cheese
¼ cup Italian bread crumbs
1 tablespoon chopped parsley
1 teaspoon dried basil leaves
½ teaspoon dried oregano leaves
Salt and pepper to taste
Tomato Sauce (recipe follows)
1 cup shredded part-skim Mozzarella cheese

Preheat the oven to 350°F.

Cook the pasta shells according to the package directions, omitting any oil and salt; drain and set aside.

In a non-stick skillet, cook the meat until done, 5 to 7 minutes over medium-high heat. Drain any excess fat. Add the egg whites, Parmesan cheese, bread crumbs, parsley, basil, oregano, salt, and pepper. Stuff the shells with the filling.

Pour half of the Tomato Sauce (see recipe at right) in a 2-quart baking dish. Arrange the stuffed shells on top, and cover with the remaining sauce. Bake for 20 minutes, or until well-heated. Sprinkle with the Mozzarella cheese, and continue baking for 10 minutes longer, or until cheese is melted. Serve immediately.

TOMATO SAUCE

1 medium onion, chopped
½ teaspoon minced garlic
3 cups tomato juice
1 (6-ounce) can tomato paste
½ teaspoon sugar
Salt and pepper to taste

In a large non-stick pot, sauté the onion over medium heat until tender, about 5 minutes. Add the garlic, tomato juice, tomato paste, sugar, salt, and pepper; simmer at least 10 minutes to allow the flavors to blend.

Nutritional information per serving
Calories 406, Protein (g) 33, Carbohydrate (g) 45, Fat (g) 10, Calories from Fat (%) 23, Saturated Fat (g) 5, Dietary Fiber (g) 3, Cholesterol (mg) 64, Sodium (mg) 776, Diabetic Exchanges: 3.5 lean meat, 2.5 starch, 1.5 vegetable

QUICK TIP:

When you're in a hurry, purchase a jar of commercial red pasta sauce to use in this recipe instead of making the Tomato Sauce.

Jumbo Stuffed Shells

PASTA

Meaty Spinach Manicotti with Tomato Sauce ❄

Sneak spinach into your meal with this creamy, meaty filling with a light tomato sauce. For a smooth sauce, substitute tomato sauce for tomatoes.

MAKES 8 SERVINGS

1 (8-ounce) package manicotti shells
1 pound ground sirloin
½ cup chopped onion
1 teaspoon minced garlic
1 cup reduced-fat Ricotta cheese
4 ounces reduced-fat cream cheese
1 (10-ounce) package frozen chopped spinach, thawed and squeezed dry
1 (28-ounce) can chopped tomatoes, with their juice
1 teaspoon dried oregano leaves
1 teaspoon dried basil leaves
Salt and pepper to taste

Preheat the oven to 350ºF.

Cook the manicotti shells according to the package directions, omitting any oil and salt. Rinse, drain, and set aside.

In a large non-stick skillet, cook the meat, onion, and garlic over medium-high heat until the meat is done, about 7 minutes. Drain any excess grease. Mix in the Ricotta, cream cheese, and spinach.

Stuff the shells with the meat mixture, and arrange in a 2-to 3-quart oblong baking dish coated with nonstick cooking spray.

In a large bowl, combine the tomatoes, oregano, basil, salt, and pepper. Pour the sauce over the shells. Cover, and bake for 15 minutes. Uncover, and bake for 10 minutes longer, or until bubbly and well-heated.

Nutritional information per serving

Calories 270, Protein (g) 21, Carbohydrate (g) 30, Fat (g) 7, Calories from Fat (%) 29, Saturated Fat (g) 4, Dietary Fiber (g) 4, Cholesterol (mg) 48, Sodium (mg) 276, Diabetic Exchanges: 2 lean meat, 1.5 starch, 1.5 vegetable

QUICK TIP:

To prevent tomato based sauces (such as spaghetti sauce) from staining plastic storage containers, spray the containers liberally with nonstick cooking spray before adding the sauce.

PASTA

Meaty Spinach Manicotti with Tomato Sauce

PASTA

Chinese Pork Vermicelli

Chinese flavors and pasta pair up, so there's no need for Chinese takeout. Marinate the pork early in the day to prepare when you're ready to eat.

MAKES 6 SERVINGS

⅓ cup reduced-sodium soy sauce

1 teaspoon ground ginger

¼ teaspoon crushed red pepper flakes

1 teaspoon minced garlic

1½ pounds pork tenderloin, trimmed of fat and cut into 1-inch cubes

1 (6-ounce) package frozen snow pea pods

1 cup (1½-inch) red bell pepper slices

1 (8-ounce) package vermicelli pasta

⅓ cup fat-free canned chicken broth

Combine the soy sauce, ginger, red pepper, and garlic in a large zipper-lock, heavy-duty plastic bag. Add the pork; seal the bag, shake it, and marinate in the refrigerator for at least 20 minutes to overnight.

Heat a large non-stick skillet over medium-high heat; add the pork mixture to the skillet, and stir-fry 3 minutes, or until the pork is browned. Add the snow peas and red bell pepper, sautéing until the vegetables are crisp-tender, 3 to 5 minutes.

Cook the pasta according to the package directions, omitting any oil and salt. Drain.

Add the chicken broth and pasta to the skillet. Cook 1 minute longer, or until heated through. Serve immediately.

Nutritional information per serving

Calories 307, Protein (g) 31, Carbohydrate (g) 33, Fat (g) 5, Calories from Fat (%) 14, Saturated Fat (g) 1, Dietary Fiber (g) 2, Cholesterol (mg) 74, Sodium (mg) 634, Diabetic Exchanges: 3 very lean meat, 2 starch, 1 vegetable

QUICK TIP:

Stir-frying is a healthier method of cooking because the technique requires the ingredients to move constantly in the skillet, so very little oil is needed to prevent sticking.

PASTA

Veal with Angel Hair in a Mushroom, Broccoli and Tomato Sauce

This divine one-dish meal is hearty enough to satisfy big appetites but light enough to serve to guests.

MAKES 6 SERVINGS

2 cups broccoli florets

1½ pounds thinly sliced veal (scaloppini)

1 tablespoon dried rosemary leaves

Salt and pepper to taste

¼ cup all-purpose flour

2 tablespoons olive oil

½ pound mushrooms, sliced

½ cup chopped green onions (scallions)

1½ cups canned fat-free chicken broth

2 teaspoons cornstarch

1 tablespoon water

1 tablespoon balsamic vinegar

1 teaspoon Dijon mustard

2 cups chopped Roma (plum) tomatoes

1 (12-ounce) package angel hair pasta

2 tablespoons chopped parsley

In a microwave-proof dish, cook the broccoli in ½ cup water until crisp-tender, about 5 to 7 minutes. Drain water and set aside.

Sprinkle the veal with rosemary, salt and pepper, and then dust with flour.

In a large non-stick skillet, heat the olive oil over a medium-high heat. Add the veal and cook about 1 minute per side. Add the mushrooms and cook for 3 to 5 minutes or until the mushrooms are tender. Add the green onions and chicken broth.

In a small cup, blend the cornstarch and water and add to the pan, cooking and stirring until the sauce is thickened. Stir in the vinegar and mustard and cook for 30 seconds. Add the tomatoes and broccoli, cooking until heated through.

Meanwhile, prepare the pasta according to the package directions, omitting any salt and oil. Drain and toss with the parsley. Serve the veal and sauce over the angel hair.

Nutritional information per serving

Calories 450, Protein (g) 41, Carbohydrate (g) 43, Fat (g) 13, Calories from Fat (%) 25, Saturated Fat (g) 3, Cholesterol (mg) 124, Sodium (g) 375, Dietary exchanges: 2.5 starch, 5 very lean meat, 1 vegetable, 1.5 fat.

PASTA

Strawberry Custard Cake

Cookies and Cakes

Oatmeal Cookies ▧ ❄

I tested many recipes before coming up with this perfect oatmeal cookie: crispy, moist, and tasty. Toss in chocolate chips for a "loaded" version.

MAKES 36 TO 48 COOKIES

⅓ cup canola oil
¾ cup light brown sugar
¾ cup sugar
1 egg
1 egg white
1 teaspoon vanilla extract
1½ cups all-purpose flour
1 teaspoon ground cinnamon
1 teaspoon baking soda
1½ cups old-fashioned oatmeal
½ cup chopped pecans

Preheat the oven to 400°F.

In a large bowl, combine the oil, brown sugar, sugar, egg, egg white, and vanilla. In a small bowl, mix together the flour, cinnamon, and baking soda. Add the flour mixture to the sugar mixture. Stir in the oatmeal and pecans, mixing well. Drop by rounded teaspoonfuls onto a non-stick baking sheet coated with non-stick cooking spray. Bake for 10 to 12 minutes, or until lightly browned. Remove and let cool on wax paper.

Nutritional information per serving

Calories 73, Protein (g) 1, Carbohydrate (g) 11, Fat (g) 3, Calories from Fat (%) 33, Saturated Fat (g) 0, Dietary Fiber (g) 1, Cholesterol (mg) 4, Sodium (mg) 30, Diabetic Exchanges: 1 other carbohydrate, 0.5 fat

Chocolate Chip Cookies ▧ ❄

My daughters could make these cookies with their eyes closed—their friends all request them. This recipe doubles easily and is great to put in your freezer for a late night snack.

MAKES 48 COOKIES

½ cup margarine
⅔ cup sugar
⅔ cup light brown sugar
1 egg
2 cups all-purpose flour
1 teaspoon baking soda
1 teaspoon vanilla extract
⅔ cup semisweet chocolate chips

Preheat the oven to 375°F.

In a large mixing bowl, beat the margarine, sugar, and brown sugar until creamy. Add the egg, and beat well.

In another bowl, combine the flour and baking soda. Add to the margarine mixture, and beat just until blended. Add the vanilla. Stir in the chocolate chips. Drop spoonfuls of dough onto a non-stick baking sheet coated with non-stick cooking spray. Bake for 8 to 10 minutes or until lightly browned. Remove from the cookie sheet, and cool completely on a wire rack before serving.

Nutritional information per serving

Calories 71, Protein (g) 1, Carbohydrate (g) 11, Fat (g) 3, Calories from Fat (%) 34, Saturated Fat (g) 1, Dietary Fiber (g) 0, Cholesterol (mg) 4, Sodium (mg) 51, Diabetic Exchanges: 1 other carbohydrate, 0.5 fat

COOKIES & CAKES

Chocolate Chip, Peanut Butter, and Holiday Cookies

Peanut Butter Cookies

Nothing beats a rich, crumbly, nutty peanut butter cookie.

MAKES 36 COOKIES

¼ cup margarine
½ cup light brown sugar
½ cup confectioners' sugar
1 egg
½ cup reduced-fat peanut butter
1 teaspoon vanilla extract
1½ cups all-purpose flour
½ teaspoon baking soda
⅓ cup chopped peanuts

Preheat the oven to 375°F.

In a large mixing bowl, blend the margarine, brown sugar, and confectioners' sugar until fluffy. Add the egg, peanut butter, and vanilla. Mix until smooth.

In a medium bowl, combine the flour and baking soda. Add to the peanut butter mixture. Stir in the peanuts until just blended.

Drop the dough by rounded spoonfuls onto a non-stick baking sheet coated with non-stick cooking spray. Flatten each round with the back side of a fork two times (making a cross pattern). Bake for 10 to 12 minutes, or until lightly browned. Remove to a rack, and cool.

Nutritional information per serving

Calories 76, Protein (g) 2, Carbohydrate (g) 10, Fat (g) 3, Calories from Fat (%) 38, Saturated Fat (g) 1, Dietary Fiber (g) 0, Cholesterol (mg) 6, Sodium (mg) 55, Diabetic Exchanges: 0.5 other carbohydrate, 0.5 fat

Holiday Cookies

Tart cranberries team up with white chocolate for this cookie that is fabulous year-round.

MAKES 48 COOKIES

½ cup margarine
1 cup sugar
1 egg
1 teaspoon vanilla extract
2 cups all-purpose flour
½ teaspoon baking powder
¼ cup cocoa
1 (7-ounce) jar marshmallow creme
½ cup chopped white chocolate chips
½ cup dried cranberries
½ cup chopped pecans

Preheat the oven to 350°F.

In a large mixing bowl, cream the margarine and sugar. Add the egg and vanilla, mixing well.

In a medium bowl, combine the flour, baking powder, and cocoa; add to the margarine mixture. Add the marshmallow creme, stirring until combined. Stir in the white chocolate chips, cranberries, and pecans just until blended. The batter will be thick.

Drop by spoonfuls onto a non-stick baking sheet coated with non-stick cooking spray. Bake for 10 to 12 minutes, or until lightly browned. Remove to wire rack, and cool.

Nutritional information per serving

Calories 91, Protein (g) 1, Carbohydrate (g)14, Fat (g) 4, Calories from Fat (%) 35, Saturated Fat (g) 1, Dietary Fiber (g) 0, Cholesterol (mg) 5, Sodium (mg) 32, Diabetic Exchanges: 1 other carbohydrate, 1 fat

COOKIES & CAKES

No-Bake Cookies

Keep these pantry ingredients available to make this popular and quick recipe at any time. It's so simple the kids will make these treats for you. Creamy or crunchy peanut butter will work equally well here.

MAKES 48 COOKIES

½ cup graham cracker crumbs
3 cups old-fashioned oatmeal
1½ cups sugar
½ cup cocoa
½ cup skim milk
½ cup margarine
½ cup reduced-fat peanut butter
1 teaspoon vanilla extract

In a medium bowl, combine the graham cracker crumbs and oatmeal; set aside.

In a large saucepan, stir the sugar, cocoa, milk, and margarine over medium heat until dissolved. Bring the mixture to a boil, and boil for 2 minutes—this is important. Remove from heat. Stir in the peanut butter and vanilla until well combined. Quickly blend in the oatmeal mixture. Beat by hand until thickened (a few minutes), if necessary.

Drop by teaspoonfuls onto waxed paper. Refrigerate until firm, and store in the refrigerator or another cool place.

Nutritional information per serving

Calories 82, Protein (g) 2, Carbohydrate (g) 12, Fat (g) 3, Calories from Fat (%) 35, Saturated Fat (g) 1, Dietary Fiber (g) 1, Cholesterol (mg) 0, Sodium (mg) 46, Diabetic Exchanges: 1 other carbohydrate, 0.5 fat

COOKIES & CAKES

Ultimate Chocolate Cookies

These chewy, rich, double-chocolate cookies are outstanding. The espresso powder enhances the chocolate flavor, and I particularly love the toasted pecans.

MAKES 36 COOKIES

½ cup margarine, softened
½ cup sugar
½ cup light brown sugar
1 egg
1 teaspoon vanilla extract
1 teaspoon instant espresso powder
1 teaspoon hot water
1¼ cups all-purpose flour
½ teaspoon baking soda
2 tablespoons cocoa
⅔ cup semisweet chocolate chips
⅓ cup chopped pecans, toasted, optional

Preheat the oven to 350°F.

In a large mixing bowl, mix by hand the margarine, sugar, and brown sugar. Add the egg and vanilla, mixing until creamy. Dissolve the espresso powder in the hot water, and add to the sugar mixture.

In a medium bowl, combine the flour, baking soda, and cocoa; add to the sugar mixture, mixing well. Stir in the chocolate chips and pecans.

Drop by rounded spoonfuls onto a non-stick baking sheet coated with non-stick cooking spray. Bake for 8 to 10 minutes or until lightly browned. Don't overcook, as they harden as they cool. Remove from the baking sheet, and cool on wax paper or a wire rack.

Nutritional information per serving
Calories 79, Protein (g) 1, Carbohydrate (g) 11, Fat (g) 4, Calories from Fat (%) 40, Saturated Fat (g) 1, Dietary Fiber (g) 0, Cholesterol (mg) 6, Sodium (mg) 50, Diabetic Exchanges: 1 other carbohydrate, 1 fat

Lemon Sours

These luscious lemon bars are great for any occasion.

MAKES 25 SQUARES

1 cup all-purpose flour
2 tablespoons sugar
4 tablespoons margarine
2 eggs
1 cup light brown sugar
4 tablespoons lemon juice, divided
2 teaspoons grated lemon rind, divided
⅔ cup confectioners' sugar

Preheat the oven to 350°F.

In a medium bowl, combine the flour and sugar.

Cut in the margarine with a pastry blender or fork until the mixture resembles coarse meal. Press into an ungreased 9-inch square pan. Bake 13 to 15 minutes, or until light brown.

In a mixing bowl, beat together the eggs, brown sugar, 2 tablespoons lemon juice, and 1 teaspoon lemon rind until well mixed and light. Spread over the baked crust. Return to the oven, and bake for 20 minutes longer, or until the top is browned and puffed.

In a small bowl, mix together the remaining lemon juice and lemon rind, and the confectioners' sugar. Spread on the baked sours while warm. Cool, and slice into squares.

Nutritional information per serving

Calories 90, Protein (g) 1, Carbohydrate (g) 17, Fat (g) 2, Calories from Fat (%) 22, Saturated Fat (g) 0, Dietary Fiber (g) 0, Cholesterol (mg) 17, Sodium (mg) 30, Diabetic Exchanges: 1 other carbohydrate, 0.5 fat

QUICK TIP:

Room-temperature lemons will yield more juice than those that have been refrigerated.

COOKIES & CAKES

Lemon Squares

Here's the ultimate lemon bar recipe. Beware, lemon lovers, as you might find yourself eating lots of these lemon luxuries.

MAKES 48 SQUARES

1¾ cups all-purpose flour, divided
⅓ cup plus 3 tablespoons confectioners' sugar
⅓ cup margarine
1⅓ cups sugar
1 tablespoon grated lemon rind
1 teaspoon baking powder
3 egg whites
1 egg
⅓ cup plus 1 tablespoon lemon juice
½ teaspoon butter extract

Preheat the oven to 350°F. Coat a 13 x 9 x 2-inch non-stick baking dish with non-stick cooking spray.

In a medium bowl, combine 1½ cups of the flour and ⅓ cup of the confectioners' sugar; cut in the margarine with a pastry blender or two knives until the mixture resembles coarse meal. Press the mixture firmly and evenly into the bottom of the baking pan. Bake for 20 minutes, or until lightly browned.

In a medium bowl, whisk the sugar, remaining flour, lemon rind, baking powder, egg whites, and egg. Stir in ⅓ cup lemon juice and the butter extract. Pour the mixture over the prepared crust. Bake for 20 minutes, or until set.

In a small dish, combine the remaining confectioners' sugar with the remaining lemon juice to make a glaze. Carefully spread the glaze over the hot lemon squares. Cool completely in the pan, and cut into squares.

Nutritional information per serving
Calories 58, Protein (g) 1, Carbohydrate (g) 11, Fat (g) 1, Calories from Fat (%) 22, Saturated Fat (g) 0, Dietary Fiber (g) 0, Cholesterol (mg) 4, Sodium (mg) 30, Diabetic Exchanges: 0.5 other carbohydrate

QUICK TIP:

Purchase a jar of dried lemon rind in the spice section of the grocery store for those times when you don't have fresh lemons around.

Lemon Squares and Chocolate Chess Bars

Strudel

Strudel

Here's an easy but delectable version of an involved recipe. Don't be afraid of this recipe if you are nervous with dough—this is a workable dough with a sweet, nutty filling.

MAKES 48 SLICES

2¼ cups all-purpose flour
1 tablespoon sugar
½ teaspoon salt
½ cup margarine, melted
1 cup nonfat plain yogurt
1 (15.5-ounce) jar apricot spread or apricot preserves
½ cup light brown sugar
1 tablespoon ground cinnamon
⅔ cup chopped walnuts
½ cup golden raisins
2 tablespoons confectioners' sugar

In a large bowl, combine the flour, sugar, salt, margarine, and yogurt, and stir until the mixture forms a ball. Wrap the dough in waxed paper, and refrigerate for 1 hour.

Preheat the oven to 350°F.

Remove the dough from the refrigerator, and divide into four equal parts. Roll each piece of dough out on floured waxed paper to form a rectangle. Spread ¼ of the apricot spread over each entire rectangle.

Combine the brown sugar, cinnamon, walnuts, and raisins. Sprinkle one-fourth of the mixture over each rectangle. Roll each rectangle up lengthwise to form a roll. Place each roll on a non-stick baking sheet coated with non-stick cooking spray. Bake for 40 minutes to 1 hour. Sprinkle with confectioners' sugar. Let cool, and slice into 1-inch slices.

Nutritional information per serving
Calories 84, Protein (g) 1, Carbohydrate (g) 13, Fat (g) 3, Calories from Fat (%) 32, Saturated Fat (g) 0, Dietary Fiber (g) 1, Cholesterol (mg) 0, Sodium (mg) 53, Diabetic Exchanges: 1 other carbohydrate, 0.5 fat

Apricot Oatmeal Bars

Crumbly oatmeal topping with tart apricot filling is a great combination here. Try different preserves to create new cookies.

MAKES 36 TO 48 BARS

½ cup margarine, melted
1½ cups old-fashioned oatmeal
1½ cups all-purpose flour
1 cup light brown sugar
1 teaspoon vanilla extract
1 teaspoon baking soda
¼ teaspoon ground cinnamon
⅓ cup chopped walnuts
1 (12-ounce) jar apricot preserves or spreadable fruit

Preheat the oven to 350°F.

In a large mixing bowl, mix together the margarine, oatmeal, flour, brown sugar, vanilla, baking soda, and cinnamon, mixing until it forms a crumbly dough. Stir in the walnuts.

Press half the mixture into the bottom of a 13 x 9 x 2-inch non-stick baking pan coated with non-stick cooking spray. Spread the preserves over top. Crumble the other half of the oatmeal mixture over the preserves. Bake for 30 to 35 minutes, or until lightly browned. Cool, and cut into bars.

Nutritional information per serving

Calories 76, Protein (g) 1, Carbohydrate (g) 12, Fat (g) 3, Calories from Fat (%) 31, Saturated Fat (g) 0, Dietary Fiber (g) 1, Cholesterol (mg) 0, Sodium (mg) 52, Diabetic Exchanges: 1 other carbohydrate, 0.5 fat

QUICK TIP:

Walnuts may be high in fat, but 70% of the fat is polyunsaturated, the healthier form of fat.

COOKIES & CAKES

Heavenly Hash

Simple and sensational! These addictive brownies are soooo good. Toss in some toasted pecans with the marshmallows for the height of indulgence.

MAKES 48 SERVINGS

2 cups all-purpose flour
1½ cups sugar
⅓ cup cocoa
1 cup water
⅓ cup canola oil
½ cup buttermilk
1 teaspoon baking soda
1 egg white, well beaten
1 (10-ounce) package miniature marshmallows
Chocolate Icing (recipe follows)

Preheat the oven to 400°F.

Combine the flour, sugar, and cocoa in a mixing bowl. In a small saucepan, combine the water and oil; bring to a boil. Add the hot water to the flour mixture, and stir well.

In a small bowl, combine the buttermilk and baking soda, mixing well. Add the buttermilk mixture and the egg white to the batter; mix well. Spoon the batter into a 15 x 10 x 1-inch non-stick jelly-roll pan coated with non-stick cooking spray. Bake for 12 to 15 minutes. Remove from oven, and immediately top with the marshmallows. Slowly and evenly pour hot Chocolate Icing (see recipe at right) on top of the marshmallows. Cool before cutting.

CHOCOLATE ICING

6 tablespoons margarine
⅓ cup buttermilk
¼ cup cocoa
1 (16-ounce) box confectioners' sugar
1 teaspoon vanilla extract

Combine the margarine, buttermilk, and cocoa in a medium saucepan; bring to a boil, and boil for 1 minute. Remove from the heat, and add the confectioners' sugar and vanilla. Blend until smooth.

Nutritional information per serving

Calories 131, Protein (g) 1, Carbohydrate (g) 25, Fat (g) 3, Calories from Fat (%) 21, Saturated Fat (g) 0, Dietary Fiber (g) 0, Cholesterol (mg) 0, Sodium (mg) 52, Diabetic Exchanges: 1.5 other carbohydrate, 0.5 fat

FOOD FACT:

If you don't have buttermilk, mix 1 tablespoon distilled vinegar or lemon juice with 1 cup milk.

COOKIES & CAKES

Chocolate Chess Bars

*See photo on page 371
These rich-tasting, easy-to-make brownies with a baked cream cheese topping get loads of praise every time I make them.

MAKES 48 SQUARES

1 (18.25-ounce) package devil's food cake mix
1 egg
½ cup margarine, melted
1 tablespoon water
1 (8-ounce) package reduced-fat cream cheese
1 (16-ounce) box confectioners' sugar
3 egg whites
1 teaspoon vanilla extract

Preheat the oven to 350°F.

In a large mixing bowl, combine the cake mix, egg, margarine, and water. Beat by hand until well blended. Pat the batter into the bottom of a 13 x 9 x 2-inch non-stick baking pan coated with nonstick cooking spray.

In a mixing bowl, beat the cream cheese, confectioners' sugar, and egg whites until the mixture is smooth and creamy. Add the vanilla. Pour over the batter in the pan. Bake for 45 minutes, or until the top is golden brown. Cool, and cut into squares.

Nutritional information per serving
Calories 114, Protein (g) 2, Carbohydrate (g) 17, Fat (g) 4, Calories from Fat (%) 34, Saturated Fat (g) 1, Dietary Fiber (g) 0, Cholesterol (mg) 15, Sodium (mg) 139, Diabetic Exchanges: 1 other carbohydrate, 1 fat

Chocolate Raisin Peanut Butter Bars

Sweet and salty blends with a chocolate covering on a crust to make this one of the best bar cookies.

MAKES 4 DOZEN BARS

1 (18.25-ounce) package yellow cake mix
½ cup margarine
1 egg
1 tablespoon water
⅔ cup raisins
⅔ cup peanuts
⅓ cup reduced fat creamy peanut butter
1 cup semisweet chocolate chips

Preheat oven to 350°F.

In mixing bowl, combine the cake mix, margarine, egg, and water until well mixed. Spread the batter into the bottom of a 13 x 9 x 2-inch non-stick baking pan coated with non-stick baking spray and bake for 17 to 20 minutes or until golden brown.

In a medium pot over low heat, combine raisins, peanuts, peanut butter, and chocolate chips over a low heat stirring until melted. Spread over baked crust. Refrigerate for 1 hour before cutting.

Nutrition information per serving
Calories 116, Protein (g) 2, Carbohydrate (g) 15, Fat (g) 6, Calories from Fat (%) 44, Saturated Fat (g) 2, Dietary Fiber (g) 1, Cholesterol (mg) 4, Sodium (mg) 110, Diabetic Exchanges: 1 other carbohydrate, 1 fat

COOKIES & CAKES

Coffee Toffee Brownies

The rich caramel flavor with a hint of coffee and chocolate makes this a wonderful specialty brownie.

MAKES 48 BROWNIES

½ cup margarine
1 (16-ounce) box dark brown sugar
2 tablespoons instant coffee
1 tablespoon hot water
2 eggs
1 tablespoon vanilla extract
2 cups all-purpose flour
2 teaspoons baking soda
⅛ teaspoon salt
½ cup semisweet chocolate chips

Preheat the oven to 350°F. Coat a 13 x 9 x 2-inch non-stick baking pan with non-stick cooking spray.

In a small saucepan, melt the margarine and brown sugar over low heat or place in a microwave oven for 1 minute in a suitable container. Combine the instant coffee with the hot water to dissolve, and combine with the brown sugar mixture in a mixing bowl. Stir and cool.

In a small bowl, whisk the eggs and vanilla; mix into the brown sugar mixture. Combine the flour, baking soda, and salt, and stir into the brown sugar mixture. Stir in the chocolate chips.

Pour the batter into the prepared pan, and bake for 30 to 35 minutes, or until a toothpick inserted in the middle comes out clean. Do not overcook. Cool in the pan, and cut into squares.

Nutritional information per serving

Calories 84, Protein (g) 1, Carbohydrate (g) 14, Fat (g) 3, Calories from Fat (%) 28, Saturated Fat (g) 1, Dietary Fiber (g) 0, Cholesterol (mg) 9, Sodium (mg) 87, Diabetic Exchanges: 1 other carbohydrate, 0.5 fat

FOOD FACT:

Brown sugar comes in light and dark granulated forms. The lighter the brown sugar, the more delicate the flavor. The very dark brown sugar has a pronounced molasses flavor.

COOKIES & CAKES

Chewy Chocolate Caramel Brownies

This sensational chocolate brownie with chewy caramel filling is a simple success! One time we even used a yellow cake mix for a not-so-chocolatey version.

MAKES 48 BROWNIES

8 ounces chewy caramels
⅔ cup evaporated skimmed milk, divided
1 (18.25-ounce) package German chocolate cake mix
½ cup margarine, softened
½ cup semisweet chocolate chips

Preheat the oven to 350°F.

In a microwave-safe dish, combine the caramels and ⅓ cup milk and microwave until melted, about 2 minutes, stirring after 1 minute.

In a large mixing bowl, combine the cake mix, the remaining milk, and the margarine. Spread half the mixture in the bottom of a 13 x 9 x 2-inch non-stick pan coated with non-stick cooking spray. Bake for 6 minutes. Remove from the oven, and sprinkle with chocolate chips. Pour the caramel evenly over the chocolate chips, and drop the remaining cake mixture over the partially baked layer. Continue baking for 15 minutes, or until the sides pull away from the pan. Do not overbake; the brownie hardens as it cools. Cool before cutting.

Nutritional information per serving

Calories 94, Protein (g) 1, Carbohydrate (g) 13, Fat (g) 4, Calories from Fat (%) 39, Saturated Fat (g) 1, Dietary Fiber (g) 0, Cholesterol (mg) 3, Sodium (mg) 116, Diabetic Exchanges: 1 other carbohydrate, 1 fat

Gooey Chocolate Peanut Butter Brownies

Rich and gooey yet simple to make, these incredible brownies taste like a candy bar. I love the peanuts.

MAKES 36 BROWNIES

1 (18.25-ounce) package devil's food cake mix
1 (12-ounce) can fat-free sweetened condensed milk, divided
¼ cup margarine, melted
1 egg white
1 (7-ounce) jar marshmallow creme
½ cup peanut butter morsels
½ cup chopped peanuts, optional

Preheat the oven to 350°F. Coat a 13 x 9 x 2-inch non-stick baking pan with non-stick cooking spray.

In a mixing bowl, mix together the cake mix, ½ cup sweetened condensed milk, margarine, and egg white.

Pat two-thirds of the batter into the bottom of the prepared pan (the batter will be stiff and sticky). Bake for 10 minutes.

In a mixing bowl, mix the remaining sweetened condensed milk and the marshmallow creme. Stir in the peanut butter morsels and peanuts. Carefully spread the mixture evenly over the partially baked brownie layer. Drop the remaining batter by spoonfuls over the marshmallow mixture. Bake for 25 to 30 minutes or until set.

Nutritional information per serving

Calories 138, Protein (g) 3, Carbohydrate (g) 23, Fat (g) 4, Calories from Fat (%) 25, Saturated Fat (g) 1, Dietary Fiber (g) 1, Cholesterol (mg) 10, Sodium (mg) 161, Diabetic Exchanges: 1.5 other carbohydrate, 1 fat

COOKIES & CAKES

Almost-Better-than-Sex Cake

Almost-Better-than-Sex Cake

Don't let the name scare you, as the recipe has been around for years. This is my lightened version of a highly requested recipe, but no one will ever be able to tell the difference.

MAKES 20 SERVINGS

1 (18.25-ounce) package yellow cake mix
½ cup skim milk
¼ cup water
⅓ cup canola oil
2 eggs
2 egg whites
1 cup nonfat plain yogurt
1 (4-serving) box instant vanilla pudding
1 (4-ounce) bar German chocolate, grated
⅓ cup semisweet chocolate chips
½ cup chopped pecans

Preheat the oven to 350°F. Coat a 10-inch non-stick Bundt pan with non-stick cooking spray.

In a large mixing bowl, combine the cake mix, milk, water, oil, eggs, egg whites, yogurt, and vanilla pudding. Beat slightly, only until the mixture is combined. Stir in the grated chocolate, chocolate chips, and pecans.

Pour the batter into the prepared pan. Bake for 45 to 55 minutes, or until an inserted toothpick comes out clean. Do not overbake. Cool 10 minutes, and invert onto a serving plate.

Nutritional information per serving

Calories 240, Protein (g) 4, Carbohydrate (g) 32, Fat (g) 12, Calories from Fat (%) 43, Saturated Fat (g) 2, Dietary Fiber (g) 1, Cholesterol (mg) 22, Sodium (mg) 263, Diabetic Exchanges: 2 other carbohydrate, 2.5 fat

COOKIES & CAKES

Apple Cake with Broiled Topping

This moist, chunky apple cake has the perfect amount of spice complemented by the toasty broiled topping. A winner!

MAKES 20 SERVINGS

6 tablespoons margarine

2 cups sugar

2 eggs

1 teaspoon vanilla extract

2 cups all-purpose flour

2 teaspoons ground cinnamon

1 teaspoon baking soda

½ cup buttermilk

4 cups peeled and diced tart cooking apples

Broiled Brown Sugar Topping (recipe follows)

Preheat the oven to 350°F. Coat a 13 x 9 x 2-inch non-stick baking pan with non-stick cooking spray.

In a large mixing bowl, beat the margarine and sugar until creamy. Add the eggs and vanilla, mixing well.

In another bowl, combine the flour, cinnamon, and baking soda; add the flour mixture alternately with the buttermilk to the margarine mixture. Stir in the apples, and pour the batter into the prepared pan. Bake for 45 minutes, and cover with the Broiled Brown Sugar Topping (see recipe at right).

BROILED BROWN SUGAR TOPPING

2 tablespoons margarine

¼ cup evaporated skimmed milk

⅔ cup light brown sugar

1 teaspoon vanilla extract

½ cup chopped walnuts

In a saucepan, heat the margarine, milk, and brown sugar until the mixture comes to a boil. Boil 2 minutes, and add the vanilla and walnuts. Spread on top of the cake, and broil in the oven for 2 minutes. Watch carefully.

Nutritional information per serving

Calories 237, Protein (g) 3, Carbohydrate (g) 41, Fat (g) 7, Calories from Fat (%) 27, Saturated Fat (g) 1, Dietary Fiber (g) 1, Cholesterol (mg) 22, Sodium (mg) 136, Diabetic Exchanges: 3 other carbohydrate, 1.5 fat

FOOD FACT:

Granny Smith apples are available year-round, and their tartness makes them a good cooking apple. Rome apples are primarily used for cooking, a their flavor grows richer when baked.

COOKIES & CAKES

Apricot Cake 🥕 ❄

Begin with a cake mix and add a few pantry ingredients to whip up an outstanding three-layer cake with a burst of flavor.

MAKES 16 SLICES

⅓ cup canola oil
1 (16-ounce) can light apricot halves, drained and chopped
½ cup apricot nectar
1 (18.25-ounce) package white cake mix
1 (3-ounce) box apricot gelatin
3 eggs
1 teaspoon vanilla extract
1 teaspoon butter extract
Apricot Frosting (recipe follows)

Preheat the oven to 350°F. Coat three non-stick 9-inch round cake pans with non-stick cooking spray.

In a mixing bowl, combine the oil, apricot, and apricot nectar. In another bowl, combine the cake mix and gelatin; add to the liquid mixture, and beat well.

Add the eggs and extracts, beating well.

Pour the batter into the prepared cake pans, and bake for 20 to 25 minutes, or until the center springs back when touched. Cool for 10 minutes in the pans; then remove to wire racks. Frost the cooled layers with Apricot Frosting (see recipe at right).

APRICOT FROSTING

6 tablespoons margarine
1 (16-ounce) box confectioners' sugar
¼ cup apricot nectar
1 teaspoon vanilla extract
½ teaspoon butter extract

In a medium mixing bowl, blend the margarine, confectioners' sugar, nectar, and extracts until smooth.

Nutritional information per serving

Calories 374, Protein (g) 4, Carbohydrate (g) 62, Fat (g) 13, Calories from Fat (%) 31, Saturated Fat (g) 2, Dietary Fiber (g) 1, Cholesterol (mg) 42, Sodium (mg) 85, Diabetic Exchanges: 4 other carbohydrate, 2.5 fat

Banana Cake with Cream Cheese Frosting

Nothing beats a good banana cake. For the ultimate version, add toasted walnuts and/or mini chocolate chips.

MAKES 16 SLICES

2½ cups all-purpose flour
1 teaspoon baking powder
1½ teaspoons baking soda
1 teaspoon ground cinnamon
¼ cup canola oil
1 cup dark brown sugar
1 egg
2 egg whites
2 cups mashed banana
2 teaspoons vanilla extract
1 cup buttermilk
Cream Cheese Frosting (recipe follows)

Preheat the oven to 350°F. Coat three non-stick 9-inch round cake pans with non-stick cooking spray.

In a medium bowl, combine the flour, baking powder, baking soda, and cinnamon; set aside.

In a large mixing bowl, beat the oil and brown sugar until light, add the egg and egg whites. Add the banana and vanilla, beating well. Add the mixed dry ingredients alternately with the buttermilk.

Pour the batter into the prepared pans, and bake for 15 to 20 minutes or until the center springs back when touched. Frost with the Cream Cheese Frosting (see recipe at right).

CREAM CHEESE FROSTING

1 (8-ounce) package reduced-fat cream cheese
3 tablespoons margarine, softened
1 (16-ounce) box confectioners' sugar
1 teaspoon vanilla extract

In a medium mixing bowl, beat the cream cheese and margarine until smooth. Add the confectioners' sugar, and beat until light. Blend in the vanilla.

Nutritional information per serving

Calories 359, Protein (g) 5, Carbohydrate (g) 65, Fat (g) 9, Calories from Fat (%) 23, Saturated Fat (g) 3, Dietary Fiber (g) 1, Cholesterol (mg) 24, Sodium (mg) 267, Diabetic Exchanges: 4.5 other carbohydrate, 2 fat

QUICK TIP:

When you have old bananas, peel and place them in zipper-lock bags in the freezer to pull out for banana cake and bread. Ripe bananas are the best for baking.

Blueberry Pound Cake

This quick cake will impress anyone who takes a bite. If blueberries aren't in season, substitute frozen for fresh.

MAKES 20 SERVINGS

1 (18.25-ounce) package yellow cake mix
1 (8-ounce) package reduced-fat cream cheese
2 eggs
1⅓ cups water
1½ teaspoons vanilla extract
2 cups blueberries
½ cup chopped pecans
Confectioners' sugar, optional

Preheat the oven to 350°F. Coat a non-stick 10-inch Bundt pan with non-stick cooking spray.

In a large mixing bowl, mix the cake mix, cream cheese, eggs, water, and vanilla. Fold in the blueberries and pecans.

Pour the batter into the prepared pan. Bake for 40 minutes, or until inserted toothpick comes out clean. Do not overcook. Cool in the pan for 20 minutes, invert onto a serving plate, and sprinkle with confectioners' sugar, if desired.

Nutritional information per serving

Calories 172, Protein (g) 4, Carbohydrate (g) 23, Fat (g) 8, Calories from Fat (%) 40, Saturated Fat (g) 3, Dietary Fiber (g) 1, Cholesterol (mg) 31, Sodium (mg) 223, Diabetic Exchanges: 1.5 other carbohydrate, 1.5 fat

Cream Cheese Coffee Cake

Lovers of coffee cake and cheesecake will enjoy this rich, creamy cake.

MAKES 12 SERVINGS

2½ cups all-purpose flour
¾ cup sugar, divided
½ cup margarine
½ teaspoon baking powder
½ teaspoon baking soda
1 cup nonfat plain yogurt
1 teaspoon almond extract
4 egg whites, divided
1 (8-ounce) package reduced-fat cream cheese
¼ cup sliced almonds

Preheat the oven to 350°F. Coat a 9-inch non-stick springform pan with non-stick cooking spray.

In a large bowl, combine the flour and ½ cup sugar. Cut in the margarine until the mixture resembles coarse crumbs. Reserve 1 cup of the crumb mixture.

To the remaining crumb mixture, add the baking powder, baking soda, yogurt, almond extract, and 2 egg whites. Spread the batter over the bottom and up the sides of the prepared pan.

In a small bowl, mix together the cream cheese, remaining sugar and egg whites until creamy. Pour into the batter-lined pan. Sprinkle with the sliced almonds and the reserved crumb mixture. Bake for 45 minutes, or until the mixture is set and the crust is golden brown. Serve warm or cold. Refrigerate leftovers.

Nutritional information per serving

Calories 271, Protein (g) 7, Carbohydrate (g) 31, Fat (g) 13, Calories from Fat (%) 43, Saturated Fat (g) 4, Dietary Fiber (g) 1, Cholesterol (mg) 14, Sodium (mg) 278, Diabetic Exchanges: 2 other carbohydrate, 2.5 fat

COOKIES & CAKES

Coffee Cake with Streusel Filling

Sometimes a plain, rich coffee cake with a cinnamon crumble filling hits the spot.

MAKES 24 SERVINGS

½ cup margarine
1¼ cups sugar
2 cups nonfat plain yogurt
3 egg whites
1 teaspoon vanilla extract
1 teaspoon butter extract
3 cups all-purpose flour
1½ teaspoons baking powder
1 teaspoon baking soda
½ cup light brown sugar
1½ teaspoons ground cinnamon
½ cup chopped pecans

Preheat the oven to 350°F. Coat a 10-inch non-stick Bundt pan with non-stick cooking spray.

In a large mixing bowl, beat the margarine and sugar until fluffy. Add the yogurt, egg whites, and extracts, mixing well. In a medium bowl, combine the flour, baking powder, and baking soda. Gradually add to the yogurt mixture, mixing well.

Pour one-third of the batter into the prepared pan. Combine the brown sugar, cinnamon, and pecans, and sprinkle half the mixture over the batter. Repeat the layers, ending with the batter. Bake for 55 minutes, or until a toothpick inserted in the center of the cake comes out clean. Cool in the pan 15 minutes, and invert onto a serving plate.

Nutritional information per serving
Calories 180, Protein (g) 4, Carbohydrate (g) 29, Fat (g) 6, Calories from Fat (%) 28, Saturated Fat (g) 1, Dietary Fiber (g) 1, Cholesterol (mg) 0, Sodium (mg) 152, Diabetic Exchanges: 2 other carbohydrate, 1 fat

QUICK TIP:

When measuring flour, don't use the measuring cup to scoop the flour out of the canister. Lightly spoon the flour into a dry measuring cup and level it with a knife for a more accurate measurement.

Orange Cranberry Cake

Orange Cranberry Cake

I always prepare this festive citrus cake during the holiday season, but I use dried cranberries year-round. The dates and cranberries give it a fruitcake personality.

MAKES 16 SERVINGS

½ cup margarine

1 cup sugar

1 egg

1 tablespoon grated orange rind

2¼ cups all-purpose flour

1 teaspoon baking soda

½ cup orange juice

½ cup skim milk

1½ cups chopped fresh or dried cranberries

⅔ cup chopped dates

½ cup confectioners' sugar

1½ tablespoons orange juice

Preheat the oven to 350°F. Coat a 10-inch non-stick Bundt pan with non-stick cooking spray.

In a large mixing bowl, cream the margarine and sugar until light and fluffy. Add the egg and orange rind, beating well. In a medium bowl, combine the flour and baking soda, and add to the creamed mixture alternately with the orange juice and milk. Stir in the cranberries and dates. Pour into the prepared pan, and bake for 40 minutes or until a toothpick inserted comes out clean. Cool 10 minutes. Invert the cake onto a serving platter.

Meanwhile, in a small saucepan, combine the confectioners' sugar and orange juice over low heat or in the microwave oven until smooth. Pour the orange glaze over the hot cake. Cool before serving.

Nutritional information per serving

Calories 215, Protein (g) 3, Carbohydrate (g) 38, Fat (g) 6, Calories from Fat (%) 26, Saturated Fat (g) 1, Dietary Fiber (g) 2, Cholesterol (mg) 13, Sodium (mg) 154, Diabetic Exchanges: 2.5 other carbohydrate, 1 fat

COOKIES & CAKES

Cranberry Cake

This heavenly white cake with a cranberry-and-almond topping can be enjoyed year-round using canned cranberry sauce.

MAKES 16 SERVINGS

½ cup margarine
1 cup sugar
1 egg
2 egg whites
½ teaspoon almond extract
2 cups all-purpose flour
1 tablespoon baking powder
1 cup nonfat plain yogurt
1 cup whole-berry cranberry sauce
½ cup sliced almonds
1 cup confectioners' sugar
2 tablespoons skim milk
½ teaspoon vanilla extract

Preheat the oven to 350°F. Coat a 13 x 9 x 2-inch non-stick baking pan with non-stick cooking spray.

In a large mixing bowl, cream the margarine and sugar until light and fluffy. Add the egg and egg whites, beating after each addition. Add the almond extract. In a small bowl, combine the flour and baking powder. Add to the sugar mixture alternately with the yogurt, beginning and ending with the flour mixture.

Pour the batter into the prepared pan. Spoon the cranberry sauce evenly over the batter; spread slightly, but do not try to cover the batter. Sprinkle with the almonds. Bake for 35 minutes, or until the cake slightly pulls away from the sides of pan.

In a small bowl, combine the confectioners' sugar, milk, and vanilla, stirring until smooth. Drizzle the glaze over the hot cake. Cool before serving.

Nutritional information per serving

Calories 247, Protein (g) 4, Carbohydrate (g) 41, Fat (g) 8, Calories from Fat (%) 28, Saturated Fat (g) 1, Dietary Fiber (g) 1, Cholesterol (mg) 14, Sodium (mg) 187, Diabetic Exchanges: 2.5 other carbohydrate, 1.5 fat

QUICK TIP:

Fresh cranberries can be stored in an airtight plastic bag for at least a month. They can be frozen for up to year, so stock up during cranberry season. There's no need to defrost cranberries before using them in a recipe.

COOKIES & CAKES

Citus
Sensational Cake

If you enjoy a plain yellow cake, you'll love this citrus infused cake which has a simple flavor and is easy to make.

MAKES 16 SERVINGS

1 (18.25-ounce) box yellow cake mix
3 eggs
2 tablespoons canola oil
1 (6-ounce) can orange juice concentrate, thawed,
    plus water to equal 1 cup
⅓ cup peach nectar
1 teaspoon grated orange rind
Citrus Frosting (recipe follows)

Preheat the oven to 350°F. Coat two non-stick 9-inch round cake pans with non-stick cooking spray.

In a mixing bowl, beat the cake mix, eggs, oil, and orange juice, mixing well. Add the peach nectar and orange rind. Pour the batter into the pans, and bake for 20 to 25 minutes, or until the center springs back when touched. Cool for 10 minutes; then remove to wire racks. Ice with Citrus Frosting (see recipe at right).

CITRUS FROSTING

6 tablespoons margarine
1 (16-ounce) box confectioners' sugar
4 tablespoons orange juice
4 tablespoons orange rind

In a medium mixing bowl, cream the margarine, confectioners' sugar, and orange juice.

Add in the orange rind.

Nutritional information per serving
Calories 224, Protein (g) 3, Carbohydrate (g) 51, Fat (g) 10, Calories from Fat (%) 40, Saturated Fat (g) 2, Dietary Fiber (g) 1, Cholesterol (mg) 40, Sodium (mg) 266, Diabetic Exchanges: 4 other carbohydrate, 2 fat

COOKIES & CAKES

Lemon
Poppy Seed Cake

Poppy seed cakes are popular bakery items, but this simple recipe made with a cake mix allows you to have your cake without ever leaving home.

MAKES 16 TO 20 SLICES

1 (18.25-ounce) package yellow cake mix
¼ cup canola oil
¼ cup water
1⅓ cups nonfat plain yogurt
1 egg
3 egg whites
1 teaspoon almond extract
⅓ cup plus 3 tablespoons lemon juice
1 tablespoon poppy seeds
1 cup confectioners' sugar

Preheat the oven to 350°F. Coat a 10-inch non-stick Bundt pan with non-stick cooking spray.

In a large mixing bowl, combine the cake mix, oil, water, yogurt, egg, egg whites, almond extract, and ⅓ cup lemon juice. Beat until creamy. Stir in the poppy seeds. Pour the batter into the Bundt pan, and bake for 40 minutes, or until a wooden toothpick inserted in the center of the cake comes out clean. Cool in the pan on a wire rack for 10 minutes.

Meanwhile, combine the confectioners' sugar and remaining lemon juice, stirring until smooth. Remove the cake from the pan onto a serving plate, and drizzle with the lemon glaze. Cool.

Nutritional information per serving

Calories 176, Protein (g) 3, Carbohydrate (g) 28, Fat (g) 6, Calories from Fat (%) 28, Saturated Fat (g) 1, Dietary Fiber (g) 1, Cholesterol (mg) 11, Sodium (mg) 187, Diabetic Exchanges: 2 other carbohydrate, 1 fat

COOKIES
& CAKES

Boston Cream Pie

Cake, custard, and chocolate are three great tastes guaranteeing instant success.

MAKES 10 TO 12 SERVINGS

2 egg yolks
½ cup sugar, divided
4 large egg whites
½ teaspoon cream of tartar
⅔ cup all-purpose flour
2 tablespoons margarine, melted
Custard Filling (recipe follows)
Glaze (recipe follows)

Preheat the oven to 325°F. Line a 9-inch non-stick round cake pan with waxed paper and coat with non-stick cooking spray.

In a large bowl, combine the egg yolks and ¼ cup sugar. Beat with a mixer until thick and lemon colored. In a small bowl, beat the egg whites and cream of tartar with a mixer until foamy. Gradually add the remaining sugar, 1 tablespoon at time, beating until stiff peaks form. Gently fold the egg white mixture into the yolk mixture. Carefully fold the flour and margarine alternately into the egg mixture.

Spoon into the prepared pan. Bake for 25 minutes or until a toothpick comes out clean. Cool in the pan 10 minutes; remove to a wire rack, and peel off the waxed paper. Cool.

Split the cake into 2 layers. Spread the Custard Filling (see recipe at right) between the layers. Spread the Glaze (see recipe at right) over the top. Refrigerate.

CUSTARD FILLING

3 tablespoons sugar
1 tablespoon cornstarch
1 cup skim milk
1 egg yolk, beaten
1 teaspoon vanilla extract

In a saucepan, combine the sugar and cornstarch. Gradually stir in the milk and egg yolk. Cook over medium heat, stirring constantly, until the mixture comes to a boil. Boil 1 minute, or until thickened. Remove from the heat; stir in the vanilla. Transfer to a medium bowl, cover with plastic wrap, and refrigerate until chilled, about 30 minutes.

GLAZE

½ cup confectioners' sugar
3 tablespoons cocoa
2 tablespoons boiling water
1 tablespoon margarine
½ teaspoon vanilla extract

Combine the confectioners' sugar and cocoa; stir until well blended. Add the boiling water, margarine, and vanilla, stirring until smooth.

Nutritional information per serving

Calories 151, Protein (g) 4, Carbohydrate (g) 24, Fat (g) 4, Calories from Fat (%) 26, Saturated Fat (g)1, Dietary Fiber (g) 1, Cholesterol (mg) 54, Sodium (mg) 64, Diabetic Exchanges: 1.5 other carbohydrate, 1 fat

Sweet Potato Bundt Cake

Moist and spicy with a surprise streusel filling and almond glaze—this cake is a must to try!

MAKES 16 SERVINGS

⅓ cup canola oil
1½ cups sugar
1 cup light brown sugar
2 cups mashed sweet potatoes (yams) (canned or fresh)
½ cup skim milk
1 teaspoon vanilla extract
1 egg
3 egg whites
2 cups all-purpose flour
1 teaspoon baking powder
1 teaspoon baking soda
3 teaspoons cinnamon, divided
½ cup light brown sugar
½ teaspoon ground nutmeg
½ cup chopped pecans
2 tablespoons skim milk
1 cup confectioners' sugar
½ teaspoon almond extract

Preheat the oven to 350°F. Coat a 10-inch non-stick Bundt pan with non-stick cooking spray.

In a large mixing bowl, mix together the oil, sugar, brown sugar, sweet potato, milk, and vanilla. Add the egg and egg whites, one at a time, beating well with each addition.

In another bowl, mix together the flour, baking powder, baking soda, and 2 teaspoons cinnamon. Gradually add to the sugar mixture.

In a small bowl, combine the brown sugar, the remaining cinnamon, the nutmeg, and the pecans.

Sprinkle the bottom of the prepared pan with half the pecan mixture. Carefully cover with half of the batter, then the remaining pecan mixture and remaining batter. Bake 40 to 45 minutes, or until a wooden toothpick inserted in the center comes out clean. Cool in the pan for 10 minutes; then invert on a serving plate.

In a small bowl, mix the milk, confectioners' sugar, and almond extract to make a glaze. Spoon over the cake. Cool and serve.

Nutritional information per serving
Calories 299, Protein (g) 34, Carbohydrate (g) 54, Fat (g) 8, Calories from Fat (%) 23, Saturated Fat (g) 1, Dietary Fiber (g) 2, Cholesterol (mg) 14, Sodium (mg) 158, Diabetic Exchanges: 3.5 other carbohydrate, 1.5 fat

Quick
Pineapple Cake

These few ingredients (that's right, there are no eggs!) make a melt-in-your-mouth cake.

MAKES 24 SERVINGS

1 (20-ounce) can crushed pineapple in its own juice (undrained)
2 cups all-purpose flour
1 cup sugar
1 teaspoon baking soda
Cream Cheese Frosting (recipe follows)

Preheat the oven to 350°F. Coat a 13 x 9 x 2-inch non-stick baking pan with non-stick cooking spray.

In a large bowl, mix the pineapple, flour, sugar, and baking soda. Pour into the prepared pan. Bake for 30 to 40 minutes or until an inserted toothpick comes out clean.

Frost with the Cream Cheese Frosting (see recipe at right) while the cake is warm. Cool and serve.

CREAM CHEESE FROSTING

4 ounces reduced-fat cream cheese
1 tablespoon margarine
1 teaspoon vanilla extract
1⅔ cups confectioners' sugar

In a medium mixing bowl, combine the cream cheese and margarine until creamy. Add the vanilla and confectioners' sugar, mixing until well combined.

Nutritional information per serving

Calories 133, Protein (g) 2, Carbohydrate (g) 28, Fat (g) 2, Calories from Fat (%) 11, Saturated Fat (g) 1, Dietary Fiber (g) 1, Cholesterol (mg) 3, Sodium (mg) 81, Diabetic Exchanges: 2 other carbohydrate

COOKIES & CAKES

Strawberry Custard Cake

For a quicker version of this marvelous creation, just use a yellow cake mix and instant vanilla pudding layered with the fresh strawberries and whipped topping.

MAKES 16 SLICES

4 eggs, separated
2 tablespoons water
1 cup sugar
1 cup all-purpose flour
1 teaspoon baking powder
1½ tablespoons cornstarch
1 teaspoon vanilla extract
Strawberry Mixture (recipe follows)
Custard Filling (recipe follows)
1 (8-ounce) container fat-free whipped topping, thawed

Preheat the oven to 325°F. Coat two 9-inch non-stick round cake pans with non-stick cooking spray.

In a large mixing bowl, beat the egg yolks (reserving the whites) with the water. Add the sugar gradually, and beat well. In a separate bowl, combine the flour, baking powder, and cornstarch, and add to the sugar mixture. Add the vanilla.

In another bowl, beat the egg whites until stiff, and fold into the batter. Pour batter into the prepared pans. Bake for 30 to 40 minutes, or until the top springs back when lightly touched. Remove from the pans, and cool on wire racks.

To assemble the cake, place the bottom layer on a serving plate. Top with the Strawberry Mixture (see recipe at right). Spread all of the Custard Filling (see recipe below) on top. Top with the second layer. Frost the sides and top with the whipped topping.

STRAWBERRY MIXTURE

¼ cup water
¼ cup sugar
1 pint strawberries, hulled and cut in half

In a small saucepan, bring the water and sugar to a boil, boiling just until the sugar dissolves. Pour over the strawberries in a bowl, and refrigerate until chilled. Let the strawberries marinate in the syrup for 2 hours or as time permits.

CUSTARD FILLING

3 tablespoons sugar
2 tablespoons cornstarch
⅛ teaspoon salt
1½ cups skim milk
1 egg
2 teaspoons vanilla extract

Combine the sugar, cornstarch, and salt in a saucepan. Gradually add the milk, stirring until blended. Cook over medium heat, stirring constantly, until the mixture thickens and comes to a boil. Boil 1 minute, stirring. Remove from heat. In a small bowl, beat the egg at high speed until thick and lemon colored. Gradually stir one-fourth of the hot mixture into the beaten egg, then add to the remaining hot mixture. Cook,

Strawberry Custard Cake

stirring constantly, for several minutes. Remove from heat; add the vanilla. Cover and refrigerate until chilled, about 20 minutes.

Nutritional information per serving

Calories 168, Protein (g) 4, Carbohydrate (g) 33, Fat (g) 2, Calories from Fat (%) 10, Saturated Fat (g) 1, Dietary Fiber (g) 1, Cholesterol (mg) 67, Sodium (mg) 89, Diabetic Exchanges: 2 other carbohydrate

COOKIES & CAKES

Tropical Upside-Down Cake

Coconut transforms this picture-perfect cake into a tropical dream.

MAKES 24 SQUARES

½ cup margarine, divided
1 cup dark brown sugar
1 (20-ounce) can pineapple chunks, undrained
2 tablespoons flaked coconut
¾ cup sugar
1 egg white
1 egg
1 teaspoon vanilla extract
1 teaspoon coconut extract
1 teaspoon butter extract
2 cups all-purpose flour
1½ teaspoons baking soda
½ cup fat-free sour cream
½ cup pineapple juice, reserved from the can

Preheat the oven to 350°F.

Melt ¼ cup margarine, and pour into the bottom of a 13 x 9 x 2-inch non-stick baking pan. Press the brown sugar evenly over the margarine. Drain the pineapple chunks, reserving the juice, and arrange the pineapple chunks on top of the brown sugar. Sprinkle the coconut evenly over the pineapple.

In a large mixing bowl, cream the remaining margarine and the sugar. Beat in the egg white, egg, and vanilla, coconut, and butter extracts.

In a separate bowl, combine the flour and baking soda. Gradually add to the creamed mixture, alternating with the sour cream and the reserved pineapple juice. Carefully spoon the batter into the pan, so as not to disturb the fruit. Bake for 30 minutes, or until a toothpick inserted in the center comes out clean. Invert the cake onto a serving platter, and cool before serving.

Nutritional information per serving
Calories 157, Protein (g) 2, Carbohydrate (g) 28, Fat (g) 4, Calories from Fat (%) 24, Saturated Fat (g) 1, Dietary Fiber (g) 1, Cholesterol (mg) 9, Sodium (mg) 139, Diabetic Exchanges: 2 other carbohydrate, 1 fat

Piña Colada Bundt Cake

Make this cake and it'll save you a trip to Hawaii.

MAKES 16 SLICES

1 (18.25-ounce) package yellow cake mix
1 (4-serving) package instant vanilla pudding
1½ cups piña colada drink mix, divided
⅓ cup canola oil
2 eggs
2 egg whites
⅓ cup flaked coconut
1 (8-ounce) can crushed pineapple in its own juice, undrained
1 cup confectioners' sugar

Preheat the oven to 350°F. Coat a 10-inch non-stick Bundt pan with non-stick cooking spray.

In a large mixing bowl, blend together the cake mix, pudding mix, 1 cup piña colada mix, oil, eggs, and egg whites until creamy. Stir in the coconut and pineapple, mixing well.

Pour the batter into the prepared pan. Bake for 45 minutes, or until a toothpick inserted in the center comes out clean. Cool in the pan 10 minutes, and then invert on a serving platter. Poke holes with a toothpick in the top of the cake.

In a small bowl, combine the remaining piña colada mix and the confectioners' sugar, mixing well. Slowly drizzle over the cake. Cool before serving.

Nutritional information per serving
Calories 277, Protein (g) 3, Carbohydrate (g) 46, Fat (g) 9, Calories from Fat (%) 29, Saturated Fat (g) 2, Dietary Fiber (g) 1, Cholesterol (mg) 27, Sodium (mg) 309, Diabetic Exchanges: 3 other carbohydrate, 2 fat

Italian Cream Cake

Italian Cream Cake

This recipe was featured as Cooking Light *magazine's "Best Cake Ever" for their ten-year anniversary. I was thrilled when I created this lighter version of my very favorite cake.*

MAKES 16 TO 20 SLICES

½ cup margarine
¼ cup canola oil
2 cups sugar
2 eggs, separated
2 cups all-purpose flour
1 teaspoon baking soda
1 cup buttermilk
1 teaspoon vanilla extract
1 teaspoon butter extract
1 teaspoon coconut extract
½ cup chopped pecans
½ cup coconut flakes (optional)
4 egg whites
Cream Cheese Frosting (recipe follows)

Preheat the oven to 350°F. Coat three 9-inch non-stick round cake pans with non-stick cooking spray.

In a large mixing bowl, cream the margarine and oil. Gradually add the sugar, and beat until light and fluffy. Add 2 egg yolks (reserving the egg whites), one at a time, beating well after each addition.

In a small bowl, mix the flour and baking soda together. Add the flour to the sugar mixture, alternating with the buttermilk and ending with the flour. Beat after each addition. Add the vanilla, butter, and coconut extracts, pecans, and coconut.

In another mixing bowl, beat all 6 egg whites until stiff peaks form. Fold the beaten egg whites into the batter mixture. Pour the batter evenly into the prepared pans. Bake for 20 to 25 minutes, or until the tops spring back when lightly touched.

Cool the cakes in the pans for 10 minutes; then turn them out onto racks to cool thoroughly. Frost the layers and sides with the Cream Cheese Frosting (see recipe below).

CREAM CHEESE FROSTING

1 (8-ounce) package reduced-fat cream cheese
3 tablespoons margarine
1 (16-ounce) box confectioners' sugar
1 teaspoon vanilla extract

In a medium mixing bowl, beat the cream cheese and margarine until smooth. Add the confectioners' sugar, and beat until light. Blend in the vanilla.

Nutritional information per serving

Calories 358, Protein (g) 5, Carbohydrate (g) 54, Fat (g) 14, Calories from Fat (%) 35, Saturated Fat (g) 3, Dietary Fiber (g) 1, Cholesterol (mg) 30, Sodium (mg) 216, Diabetic Exchanges: 3.5 other carbohydrate, 3 fat

COOKIES & CAKES

Quick Italian Cream Cake

This easy version of my favorite three-layer cake. It hits the spot for an indulgent quick dessert.

MAKES 28 SERVINGS

1 (18.25-ounce) package white cake mix
1 cup buttermilk
2 egg whites
1 egg
¼ cup canola oil
3 tablespoons light brown sugar
¼ cup flaked coconut
2 tablespoons chopped pecans
Cream Cheese Frosting (recipe follows)

Preheat the oven to 350°F. Coat a 13 x 9 x 2-inch non-stick pan with non-stick cooking spray.

In a large mixing bowl, combine the cake mix, buttermilk, egg whites, egg, and oil, beating until well mixed.

In a small mixing bowl, combine the brown sugar, coconut, and pecans; set aside.

Spread half the batter in the bottom of the prepared pan, sprinkle with the brown sugar mixture, and carefully top with the remaining batter, spreading it out. Bake for 30 minutes, or until a toothpick inserted in the center comes out clean. Let cool, and frost with the Cream Cheese Frosting (see recipe at right).

CREAM CHEESE FROSTING

1 (8-ounce) package reduced-fat cream cheese
2 tablespoons margarine
1 (16-ounce) box confectioners' sugar
1 teaspoon vanilla extract

In a medium mixing bowl, beat the cream cheese and margarine together. Blend in the confectioners' sugar, mixing well. Add the vanilla, mixing well again.

Nutritional information per serving

Calories 206, Protein (g) 2, Carbohydrate (g) 33, Fat (g) 7, Calories from Fat (%) 31, Saturated Fat (g) 2, Dietary Fiber (g) 0, Cholesterol (mg) 14, Sodium (mg) 179, Diabetic Exchanges: 2 other carbohydrate, 1.5 fat

COOKIES & CAKES

Chocolate Pudding Cake 🥕

A surprise chocolate pudding forms on the bottom of this cake, which is perfect for chocoholics everywhere.

MAKES 12 TO 16 SERVINGS

½ cup sugar
1 cup all-purpose flour
2 teaspoons baking powder
2 tablespoons plus ¼ cup cocoa
½ cup skim milk
1 teaspoon vanilla extract
1 tablespoon margarine, melted
¾ cup light brown sugar
1½ cups boiling water

Preheat the oven to 350°F. Coat a 9 x 9 x 2-inch non-stick baking pan with non-stick cooking spray.

In a bowl, combine the sugar, flour, baking powder, and 2 tablespoons cocoa. Stir in the milk, vanilla, and margarine. Spread the batter in the prepared pan.

Mix together the brown sugar and the remaining cocoa and sprinkle over the batter. Pour the boiling water over all; bake for 25 to 30 minutes. Serve hot.

Nutritional information per serving

Calories 109, Protein (g) 2, Carbohydrate (g) 24, Fat (g) 1, Calories from Fat (%) 8, Saturated Fat (g) 0, Dietary Fiber (g) 1, Cholesterol (mg) 0, Sodium (mg) 78, Diabetic Exchanges: 1.5 other carbohydrate

Strawberry Angel Food Cake 🥕❄️

When strawberries are in season, try this easy yet impressive dessert. This recipe is so simple, it makes a great emergency dessert.

MAKES 10 TO 12 SLICES

1 (16-ounce) angel food cake
1 (8-ounce) package reduced-fat cream cheese
½ cup sugar
¼ cup evaporated skimmed milk
2 pints strawberries, hulled and sliced

With a serrated knife, slice the angel food cake horizontally into three equal layers. In a mixing bowl, beat together the cream cheese, sugar, and evaporated milk until creamy.

Top the bottom cake layer with the filling and strawberries. Repeat the layers. Frost the top with the remaining filling. Refrigerate until serving.

Nutritional information per serving

Calories 196, Protein (g) 5, Carbohydrate (g) 35, Fat (g) 5, Calories from Fat (%) 21, Saturated Fat 3, Dietary Fiber (g) 1, Cholesterol (mg) 19, Sodium (mg) 225, Diabetic Exchanges: 2.5 other carbohydrate, 1 fat

COOKIES & CAKES

Wait Cake

The hardest part of making this decadent cake is waiting to cut it per the directions and the title! (We have cheated and cut it after 24 hours, but it's best to wait for the moistest cake.)

MAKES 16 TO 20 SLICES

1 (18.25-ounce) package yellow cake mix
1 teaspoon baking powder
3 egg whites
1 egg
2 tablespoons canola oil
1⅓ cups water
2 cups light sour cream
1½ cups sugar
1 teaspoon almond extract
½ cup flaked coconut, optional
1½ cups fat-free frozen whipped topping, thawed

Preheat the oven to 350°F. Coat two 9-inch non-stick round cake pans with non-stick cooking spray.

In a large mixing bowl, beat together the cake mix, baking powder, egg whites, egg, oil, and water until well mixed. Pour the batter into the prepared pans, and bake for 25 to 30 minutes or until the top springs back when touched. Cool the layers on wire racks in the pans for 10 minutes, then turn onto wire racks to cool.

Meanwhile, in a medium bowl, combine the sour cream, sugar, and almond extract, blending well. Add coconut, if desired. Chill in the refrigerator while the cake is baking.

When the cake has cooled, split each layer in half with a serrated knife. Spread the filling between the layers, reserving 1 cup for the frosting.

Combine the reserved filling with the whipped topping, mixing until smooth. Spread the frosting on the sides and top of the cake. Seal the cake in an airtight container or cover tightly with plastic wrap; refrigerate for 36 to 48 hours before serving.

Nutritional information per serving

Calories 223, Protein (g) 3, Carbohydrate (g) 41, Fat (g) 46, Calories from Fat (%) 22, Saturated Fat (g) 2, Dietary Fiber (g) 1, Cholesterol (mg) 19, Sodium (mg) 225, Diabetic Exchanges: 2.5 other carbohydrate, 1 fat

Wait Cake

COOKIES
& CAKES

Mocha Chocolate Bundt Cake

This magnificent mocha cake begins with a mix! The only challenge about making this cake is letting it sit before serving.

MAKES 16 SLICES

1 (18.25-ounce) box devil's food cake mix
¼ cup canola oil
1 (4-serving) package instant chocolate pudding
1 egg
3 egg whites
¾ cup strong brewed coffee
⅓ cup coffee liqueur
⅓ cup créme de cacao liqueur
Mocha Glaze (recipe follows)

Preheat the oven to 350°F. Coat a 10-inch non-stick Bundt pan with non-stick cooking spray.

In a large mixing bowl, combine the cake mix, oil, pudding mix, egg, egg whites, coffee, and liqueurs, blending very well.

Transfer the batter into the prepared pan. Bake for 40 to 45 minutes. Cool 15 minutes, and invert onto a serving platter. Using a fork or toothpick, pierce the cake every few inches; then spoon the Mocha Glaze (see recipe at right) over the cake. Let the cake absorb flavors for one hour before serving.

MOCHA GLAZE

1 cup confectioners' sugar
2 tablespoons strongly brewed coffee
2 tablespoons créme de cacao liqueur

Combine all ingredients in a small bowl. Spoon over the cake according to the directions above.

Nutritional information per serving

Calories 272, Protein (g) 3, Carbohydrate (g) 44, Fat (g) 7, Calories from Fat (%) 23, Saturated Fat (g) 2, Dietary Fiber (g) 1, Cholesterol (mg) 13, Sodium (mg) 353, Diabetic Exchanges: 4 other carbohydrate, 2 fat

QUICK TIP:

For a reduced-calorie version of this dessert, substitute milk for the liqueur in the cake and glaze.

Coffee Angel Food Cake

An angel food cake with a touch of coffee and almond makes for a heavenly indulgence. For an extra treat, top with toasted almond slices.

MAKES 16 SLICES

1 (14½-ounce) package angel food cake mix
1 teaspoon vanilla extract
1 teaspoon almond extract
1 tablespoon instant coffee dissolved in
   1 tablespoon water
Coffee Icing (recipe follows)
⅓ cup sliced almonds, toasted

Mix the angel food cake according to the package directions, adding vanilla and almond extracts and coffee to the batter. Bake according to the package directions. Cool and frost with the Coffee Icing (see recipe at right). Sprinkle the almonds on the top and sides of the cake, and serve.

COFFEE ICING

6 tablespoons margarine
1 (16-ounce) box confectioners' sugar
2 tablespoons instant coffee dissolved in
   1 tablespoon water
3 to 4 tablespoons skim milk

In a mixing bowl, cream the margarine, confectioners' sugar, and dissolved coffee, adding milk as needed until the icing reaches good spreading consistency. Ice the top, sides, and center of the cake.

Nutritional information per serving

Calories 261, Protein (g) 3, Carbohydrate (g) 50, Fat (g) 5, Calories from Fat (%) 19, Saturated Fat (g) 1, Dietary Fiber (g) 0, Cholesterol (mg) 0, Sodium (mg) 276, Diabetic Exchanges: 3.5 other carbohydrate, 1 fat

COOKIES & CAKES

Tiramisu Cake

If you like tiramisu, this candy-filled cake and Chocolate Cream Cheese Frosting will excite your taste buds. For a great presentation, drizzle chocolate syrup on top. It's a great make-ahead cake—the longer it sits, the better it gets.

Makes 16 servings

1 (18.25-ounce) package white cake mix
1½ cups strongly brewed coffee, cooled, divided
4 egg whites
4 (1.4-ounce) bars toffee candy, finely chopped
1 tablespoon sugar
1 tablespoon cocoa
Chocolate Cream Cheese Frosting (recipe follows)

Preheat the oven to 350°F. Coat two 9-inch non-stick round cake pans with non-stick cooking spray.

In a large bowl, combine the cake mix, 1 cup coffee, and the egg whites. Beat until well mixed and creamy. Gently fold in the chopped candy. Spread the batter evenly into the prepared pans. Bake for 30 to 40 minutes, or until a toothpick inserted in the center comes out clean. Cool for 10 minutes; then remove from the pans and cool completely on wire rack.

In a small bowl, mix together the sugar, cocoa, and coffee. Lay the bottom cake layer on a serving plate, and spoon half the cocoa mixture evenly over the cake layer. Frost the bottom layer with the Chocolate Cream Cheese Frosting (see recipe at right); then add the top layer. Spoon the remaining cocoa mixture onto the top layer, and ice the top and sides of the cake with the remaining frosting. Refrigerate until serving.

CHOCOLATE CREAM CHEESE FROSTING

¼ cup sugar
⅓ cup chocolate syrup
1 (8-ounce) package reduced-fat cream cheese
1 (8-ounce) container fat-free frozen whipped topping, thawed
1 teaspoon vanilla extract

In a mixing bowl, beat the sugar, chocolate syrup, and cream cheese until smooth. Fold in the whipped topping and vanilla until well combined.

Nutritional information per serving

Calories 290, Protein (g) 4, Carbohydrate (g) 45, Fat (g) 10, Calories from Fat (%) 31, Saturated Fat (g) 5, Dietary Fiber (g) 1, Cholesterol (mg) 15, Sodium (mg) 319 , Diabetic Exchanges: 3 other carbohydrate, 2 fat

QUICK TIP:

For a lighter version of any cake mix, combine the cake mix with 1 teaspoon baking powder, 3 egg whites, 1 whole egg, 2 tablespoons canola oil, and 1⅓ cups water. Bake according to the directions. Ice the cake with your favorite frosting.

Tiramisu Cake

Triple Chocolate Cake

Triple Chocolate Cake

This is chocolate cake at its best and at its easiest to prepare—you will repeat this recipe very often. Easy beginnings make fabulous results here.

MAKES 16 SLICES

Cocoa as needed
1 (18.25-ounce) package devil's food cake mix
1 (4-serving) box instant chocolate pudding
1 cup fat-free sour cream
¼ cup canola oil
⅓ cup plus ¼ cup skim milk
1 egg
3 egg whites
⅓ cup almond liqueur (such as Amaretto)
2 teaspoons almond extract, divided
⅓ cup semisweet chocolate chips
1½ cups confectioners' sugar

Preheat the oven to 350°F. Coat a 10-inch non-stick Bundt pan with non-stick cooking spray and dust with cocoa.

In a large mixing bowl, combine the cake mix, pudding, sour cream, oil, ⅓ cup milk, egg, egg whites, liqueur, and 1 teaspoon almond extract. Beat with a mixer until well blended. Stir in the chocolate chips.

Pour batter into the prepared pan, and bake for 40 to 50 minutes, or until a toothpick inserted in the center comes out clean.

Meanwhile, mix the confectioners' sugar, remaining milk and almond extract together in a small bowl.

Cool the cake on a rack for 10 minutes before inverting onto a serving plate. Drizzle the glaze over the warm cake. Cool before serving.

Nutritional information per serving
Calories 296, Protein (g) 4, Carbohydrate (g) 49, Fat (g) 8, Calories from Fat (%) 24, Saturated Fat (g) 2, Dietary Fiber (g) 1, Cholesterol (mg) 14, Sodium (mg) 371, Diabetic Exchanges: 3.5 other carbohydrate, 1.5 fat

QUICK TIP:

When testing this cake for doneness, a toothpick might hit a chocolate chip, and you might think the cake isn't done. For an accurate reading, test it a few times.

COOKIES & CAKES

German Chocolate Bundt Cake

This healthier variation of a light chocolate cake with a streusel filling and a wonderful coconut-flavored glaze seems more like a piece of indulgence.

MAKES 16 SERVINGS

1 cup light brown sugar, divided
⅓ cup flaked coconut
⅓ cup chopped pecans
⅓ cup unsweetened cocoa
2 ounces German sweet baking chocolate
½ cup boiling water
1 cup sugar
⅓ cup margarine
2 teaspoons vanilla extract
1 egg
2 egg whites
2 cups all-purpose flour
2 teaspoons baking powder
½ teaspoon baking soda
1 cup buttermilk
Coconut Glaze (recipe follows)

Preheat the oven to 325°F. Coat a 10-inch non-stick Bundt pan with non-stick cooking spray.

Combine ½ cup brown sugar, the coconut, and pecans in a small bowl.

In a small bowl, combine the cocoa and chocolate; add the boiling water, stirring until the chocolate melts. Set aside.

In a large mixing bowl, beat the sugar, the remaining brown sugar, and the margarine until creamy. Add the vanilla, egg, and egg whites, one at a time, beating well after each addition.

In another bowl, combine the flour, baking powder, and baking soda. Add the flour mixture to the sugar mixture alternately with the buttermilk, beginning and ending with the flour mixture. Stir in the cocoa mixture. Spoon half the batter into the prepared pan, and top with the coconut-pecan mixture. Spoon the remaining batter over the streusel. Bake 50 to 60 minutes, or until a wooden toothpick inserted in the center comes out clean. Cool in the pan on a wire rack 10 minutes; invert onto serving platter. Cool completely. Drizzle with the Coconut Glaze (see recipe below).

COCONUT GLAZE

1 cup confectioners' sugar
1 tablespoon margarine
½ teaspoon coconut extract
½ teaspoon vanilla extract
2 tablespoons skim milk

Combine the confectioners' sugar and margarine in a small bowl. Add the coconut and vanilla extracts and the milk, stirring well.

Nutritional information per serving
Calories 290, Protein (g) 4, Carbohydrate (g) 51, Fat (g) 9, Calories from Fat (%) 26, Saturated Fat (g) 2, Dietary Fiber (g) 1, Cholesterol (mg) 14, Sodium (mg) 191, Diabetic Exchanges: 3.5 other carbohydrate, 2 fat

COOKIES & CAKES

German Chocolate Sheet Cake

There will be lots of oohs and ahs for this gooey, one-layer version of the all-time favorite. When cut into small squares, it's great for party pickups and makes tons.

MAKES 48 SQUARES

1 (18.25-ounce) package German chocolate cake mix
1 egg
2 egg whites
1¾ cups water
1 (14-ounce) can fat-free sweetened condensed milk
⅓ cup flaked coconut
⅓ cup chopped pecans
¼ cup margarine
⅓ cup cocoa
1 (16-ounce) box confectioners' sugar
1 teaspoon vanilla extract
3 to 4 tablespoons skim milk

Preheat the oven to 350°F. Coat a 15 x 11 x 1-inch non-stick baking pan with non-stick cooking spray.

In a large mixing bowl, beat the cake mix, egg, egg whites, and water until creamy. Pour the batter into the prepared pan, and bake for 15 minutes.

Meanwhile, in a small bowl, combine the condensed milk, coconut, and pecans.

Preheat the broiler.

Pour the coconut mixture over the top of the cake, spreading it evenly. Broil for about 2 minutes, or until golden. Watch carefully. Remove from the oven, and let cool.

In a mixing bowl, beat together the margarine, cocoa, confectioners' sugar, and vanilla, adding the milk gradually until the frosting reaches spreading consistency. Spread over the cake. Cool before serving.

Nutritional information per serving

Calories 127, Protein (g) 2, Carbohydrate (g) 24, Fat (g) 3, Calories from Fat (%) 21, Saturated Fat (g) 1, Dietary Fiber (g) 0, Cholesterol (mg) 5, Sodium (mg) 93, Diabetic Exchanges: 1.5 other carbohydrate, 0.5 fat

COOKIES & CAKES

Old-Fashioned German Chocolate Layered Cake

German chocolate cake is one of my absolute favorites, so I created this lighter, yet equally good, version that both satisfies my craving and is kinder to my waistline.

MAKES 16 SERVINGS

2 tablespoons cocoa
2 ounces German sweet baking chocolate
½ cup boiling water
3 tablespoons margarine
2 tablespoons canola oil
2 cups sugar
1 egg yolk
1 tablespoon vanilla extract
½ teaspoon coconut extract
2 cups all-purpose flour
1 teaspoon baking soda
1 cup buttermilk
4 egg whites
Coconut Pecan Frosting (recipe follows)

Preheat the oven to 350°F. Coat three 9-inch non-stick round cake pans with non-stick cooking spray and dust with flour.

Add the cocoa and baking chocolate to the boiling water, and stir until melted; set aside to cool slightly.

In a large mixing bowl, beat together the margarine, oil, and sugar until creamy. Add the egg yolk, mixing well. Add the vanilla and coconut extracts. Gradually add the chocolate mixture. In a small bowl, mix together the flour and baking soda. Add the flour mixture to the creamed mixture alternately with the buttermilk, beginning and ending with the flour mixture.

In another mixing bowl, beat the egg whites until stiff peaks form. Gradually fold the egg whites into the chocolate mixture.

Pour the batter into the prepared pans. Bake for 20 minutes, or until a toothpick inserted in the center comes out clean. Cool in the pans 10 minutes, and remove to wire racks. Place a layer on a serving plate; spread with one-third of the Coconut Pecan Frosting (see recipe on the next page). Repeat with remaining layers and frosting.

QUICK TIP:

To toast pecans or coconut: spread evenly on a baking sheet; bake, stirring occasionally, at 350°F for 7 to 10 minutes, or until lightly browned.

COCONUT PECAN FROSTING
(for Old-Fashioned German Chocolate Layered Cake)

1 (12-ounce) can evaporated skimmed milk
1 (5-ounce) can evaporated skimmed milk
1 cup sugar
3 tablespoons cornstarch
1 egg yolk
2 teaspoons vanilla extract
½ teaspoon coconut extract
½ cup flaked coconut
½ cup chopped pecans, toasted

In a saucepan, combine both cans of evaporated milk and the sugar, cornstarch, and egg yolk. Bring to a boil over medium-high heat, stirring constantly until the mixture thickens and bubbles about 7 to 10 minutes. Remove from heat, and stir in the vanilla and coconut extracts, coconut, and pecans. Cool slightly, and frost the cake as directed.

Nutritional information per serving

Calories 343, Protein (g) 7, Carbohydrate (g) 59, Fat (g) 9, Calories from Fat (%) 24, Saturated Fat (g) 2, Dietary Fiber (g) 1, Cholesterol (mg) 28, Sodium (mg) 176, Diabetic Exchanges: 4 other carbohydrate, 2 fat

Oatmeal Chocolate Cake 🥕 ❄

The oatmeal and chocolate in this not-too-sweet snack cake makes a great combination of flavors.

MAKES 24 TO 28 SQUARES

1½ cups boiling water
1 cup old-fashioned oatmeal
1 cup light brown sugar
½ cup sugar
½ cup margarine
1 egg
2 egg whites
1½ cups all-purpose flour
1 teaspoon baking soda
1 tablespoon cocoa
½ cup semisweet chocolate chips

Preheat the oven to 350°F. Coat a 13 x 9 x 2-inch non-stick baking pan with non-stick cooking spray.

In a large bowl, pour the boiling water over the oatmeal, and let stand for 10 minutes. Add the brown sugar, sugar, and margarine, stirring until the margarine melts. Add the egg and egg whites; mix well.

In a small bowl, combine the flour, baking soda, and cocoa. Add the dry ingredients to the sugar mixture, mixing well. Stir in the chocolate chips. Pour into the prepared pan, and bake for about 40 minutes, or until a toothpick inserted in the center comes out clean. Don't overbake.

Nutritional information per serving

Calories 127, Protein (g) 2, Carbohydrate (g) 20, Fat (g) 5, Calories from Fat (%) 32, Saturated Fat (g) 1, Dietary Fiber (g) 1, holesterol (mg) 8, Sodium (mg) 93, Diabetic Exchanges: 1.5 other carbohydrate, 1 fat

Red Velvet Cake

This classic is lightened up a bit so you can enjoy it guilt-free. While it's perfect for Christmas or Valentine's Day, we make this luscious favorite year-round.

MAKES 16 SERVINGS

6 tablespoons margarine
¼ cup canola oil
1¾ cups sugar
1 teaspoon vinegar
2 large eggs
1 cup buttermilk
1 (1-ounce) bottle red food coloring
1 teaspoon vanilla extract
2 cups all-purpose flour
2 teaspoons cocoa
1 teaspoons baking soda
Cream Cheese Icing (recipe follows)

Preheat the oven to 350°F. Coat three 9-inch non-stick round cake pans with non-stick cooking spray.

In a mixing bowl, cream the margarine, oil, sugar, and vinegar until light and fluffy. Add the eggs, mixing well. Add the buttermilk, food coloring and vanilla.

In another bowl, combine the flour, cocoa, and baking soda. Gradually add to the sugar mixture. Pour the batter into the pans and bake for 18 to 23 minutes or until a toothpick inserted in the middle comes out clean.

Cool layers on racks and frost with Cream Cheese Icing (see recipe below).

CREAM CHEESE ICING

1 (8-ounce) package reduced-fat cream cheese
3 tablespoons margarine
1 (16-ounce) box confectioners' sugar
1 teaspoon vanilla extract

In a mixing bowl, beat the cream cheese and margarine until smooth. Add the confectioners' sugar and beat until light. Blend in the vanilla.

Nutrition information per serving
Calories 388, Protein (g) 4, Carbohydrate (g) 63, Fat (g) 14, Calories from Fat (%) 32, Saturated Fat (g) 4, Dietary Fiber (g) 0, Cholesterol (mg) 37, Sodium (mg) 239, Diabetic Exchanges: 4 other carbohydrate, 3 fat

COOKIES & CAKES

Red Velvet Cake

COOKIES
& CAKES

Tiramisu

Desserts and Pies

Mock Chocolate Éclair

Layers of pudding and graham crackers topped with a chocolate sauce make this a simple but indulgent dessert. It can be the made the night before and refrigerated until ready to serve.

MAKES 15 TO 20 SERVINGS

2 wrapped packages graham crackers from 16-ounce box
2 (4-serving) packages vanilla instant pudding
3 cups skim milk
4 ounces fat-free frozen whipped topping, thawed
Chocolate Topping (recipe follows)

Layer the bottom of a 13 x 9 x 2-inch non-stick baking dish with one-third of the graham crackers.

In a mixing bowl, beat the pudding mix with the milk until it thickens; set aside for several minutes. Fold in the whipped topping.

Spread half of the pudding mixture over the graham crackers. Repeat the layers, ending with the graham crackers on top (three layers of graham crackers). Spread with the Chocolate Topping (see recipe at right).

CHOCOLATE TOPPING

¼ cup cocoa
⅔ cup sugar
¼ cup skim milk
1 tablespoon vanilla extract
1 tablespoon margarine

Combine the cocoa, sugar, and milk in a saucepan. Bring to a boil for 1 minute. Remove from heat, and add the vanilla and margarine. Cool slightly, and pour over top the graham cracker layer.

Nutritional information per serving

Calories 156, Protein (g) 3, Carbohydrate (g) 31, Fat (g) 2, Calories from Fat (%) 13, Saturated Fat (g) 0, Dietary Fiber (g) 1, Cholesterol (mg) 1, Sodium (mg) 250, Diabetic Exchanges: 2 other carbohydrate

Chocolate Layered Dessert

Because it's simple to make and everyone's favorite, I frequently make this recipe for family and friends and still get wonderful remarks. This is a great make-ahead dessert that appeals to all ages.

MAKES 16 SERVINGS

1 cup all-purpose flour
7 tablespoons margarine
½ cup chopped pecans
1 (8-ounce) package reduced-fat cream cheese
⅔ cup confectioners' sugar
2 cups fat-free frozen whipped topping, thawed, divided
Pudding Layer (recipe follows)

Preheat the oven to 350°F.

With a fork, mix together the flour and margarine until crumbly. Stir in the pecans, and press into an ungreased 13 x 9 x 2-inch nonstick pan. Bake for 20 minutes or until lightly browned. Cool completely.

In a mixer, blend the cream cheese and confectioners' sugar until creamy. Fold in the whipped topping. Spread on top of the first layer. Top with the Pudding Layer (see recipe at right). Cover with the remaining whipped topping. Refrigerate.

PUDDING LAYER

2 (4-serving) packages instant chocolate pudding
3 cups skim milk
1 teaspoon vanilla extract

Mix the pudding mix with the milk, and prepare according to package directions. Add the vanilla.

Nutritional information per serving

Calories 223, Protein (g) 4, Carbohydrate (g) 27, Fat (g) 11, Calories from Fat (%) 44, Saturated Fat (g) 3, Dietary Fiber (g) 1, Cholesterol (mg) 11, Sodium (mg) 305, Diabetic Exchanges: 2 other carbohydrate, 2 fat

QUICK TIP:

For variety, use different flavored puddings in this recipe, from white chocolate to pistachio.

Tropical Pizza

Every time I make this tropical decadence, everyone wants the recipe. Easy and picture-perfect, it's a great way to enjoy fruit, especially when the fruit is in season. Be creative and substitute your favorite fruits.

MAKES 12 SERVINGS

1 (18-ounce) roll refrigerated ready-to-slice
  sugar cookie dough
⅓ cup sugar
1 (8-ounce) package fat-free cream cheese
1 teaspoon coconut extract
1½ teaspoons grated orange rind
1 cup fat-free frozen whipped topping, thawed
1 (26-ounce) jar mango slices, drained, or 1 fresh mango,
  sliced
1 (16-ounce) can pineapple slices, drained, or 1 fresh
  pineapple, sliced
1 (11-ounce) can mandarin orange segments, drained
¼ cup apricot preserves
1 tablespoon orange liqueur or orange juice
2 tablespoons coconut, toasted, optional

Preheat the oven to 350°F.

Press the cookie dough into a 12- to 14-inch non-stick pizza pan coated with non-stick cooking spray. Bake for 12 minutes, and cool completely.

In a medium mixing bowl, blend the sugar, cream cheese, and coconut extract until well mixed. Stir in the orange rind and whipped topping, mixing until smooth. Spread the cream cheese mixture on top of the cooled crust. Arrange the mango slices around the edge of the iced pizza. Then, arrange a roll of the pineapple slices around the edge. Next, arrange the mandarin orange slices in another ring to fill the center of the pizza.

In a small saucepan or in the microwave, heat the apricot preserves and orange liqueur just until melted. Spoon the glaze over the fruit. Sprinkle with the toasted coconut, if desired. Refrigerate until serving.

Nutritional information per serving
Calories 269, Protein (g) 4, Carbohydrate (g) 48, Fat (g) 6, Calories from Fat (%) 21, Saturated Fat (g) 2, Dietary Fiber (g) 0, Cholesterol (mg) 5, Sodium (mg) 253, Diabetic Exchanges: 1 fruit, 2 other carbohydrate, 1 fat

QUICK TIP:

Go ahead and grate more orange rind than you'll need for the recipe—you can grate a whole orange or lemon and freeze the rind until needed.

Tropical Pizza

Bread Pudding

Here's a lighter version of a Southern delight.
Serve warm with the Rum Sauce.

MAKES 10 TO 12 SERVINGS

8 cups French bread, cut into small pieces
½ cup raisins
¼ cup light brown sugar
½ cup sugar
½ teaspoon ground cinnamon
1½ cups skim milk
1 (12-ounce) can evaporated skimmed milk
1 teaspoon vanilla extract
1 teaspoon butter extract
1 egg yolk
4 egg whites
Rum Sauce (recipe follows)

Preheat the oven to 350°F.

Spread the French bread in a 3-quart baking dish. Sprinkle the raisins over the bread.

In a medium bowl, combine the brown sugar, sugar, cinnamon, milk, evaporated milk, vanilla and butter extracts, and the egg yolk.

In a mixing bowl, beat the egg whites until stiff peaks form; fold into the sugar mixture. Pour over the bread and raisins in the pan. Let sit 5 minutes. Bake for 30 to 40 minutes or until set, and serve hot with Rum Sauce (see at right).

RUM SAUCE

2 tablespoons all-purpose flour
2 tablespoons margarine
½ cup sugar
1 cup skim milk
1 tablespoon dark rum or 1 teaspoon rum extract

In a small saucepan over medium heat, combine the flour, margarine, and sugar. Gradually add the milk, stirring constantly. Cook until the mixture comes to a boil and thickens, 10 to 12 minutes. Remove from heat, and stir in the rum. Serve over the hot bread pudding.

Nutritional information per serving

Calories 251, Protein (g) 8, Carbohydrate (g) 46, Fat (g) 3, Calories from Fat (%) 12, Saturated Fat (g) 1, Dietary Fiber (g) 1, Cholesterol (mg) 20, Sodium (mg) 251, Diabetic Exchanges: 0.5 skim milk, 0.5 fruit, 2 other carbohydrate

QUICK TIP:

Folding egg whites into a mixture means combining ingredients lightly while preventing loss of air by using two motions. To fold whites, first lighten the mixture by stirring a small portion of the beaten whites into it. Then gently fold in the rest of the egg whites, scooping under the mixture and smoothing over the top.

Cream Cheese Bread Pudding

Baked cream cheese topping over bread pudding takes this favorite dessert to a new level. When preparing bread pudding, use bread that is slightly hard to ensure the proper texture after it's baked.

MAKES 10 TO 12 SERVINGS

1 (16-ounce) loaf French bread
2 eggs, divided
4 egg whites, divided
1 cup sugar, divided
1 teaspoon vanilla extract
1 teaspoon butter extract
3 cups skim milk
1 teaspoon ground cinnamon
1 (8-ounce) package fat-free cream cheese

Preheat the oven to 350°F. Cut the French bread into 1-inch squares. Place the bread in a 13 x 9 x 2-inch non-stick baking dish coated with non-stick cooking spray.

In a large bowl, lightly beat together 1 egg and 3 egg whites. Add ½ cup of the sugar and the vanilla and butter extracts; mix well. Slowly add the milk to the egg mixture, mixing well. Pour over the bread squares. Sprinkle the mixture with cinnamon.

In a large mixing bowl, beat the cream cheese with the remaining sugar. Add the remaining egg and egg white, blending until smooth. Spread the mixture evenly over the soaked bread. Bake, uncovered, for 45 minutes, or until firm. Let cool slightly before serving.

Nutritional information per serving

Calories 227, Protein (g) 10, Carbohydrate (g) 41, Fat (g) 2, Calories from Fat (%) 8, Saturated Fat (g) 1, Dietary Fiber (g) 1, Cholesterol (mg) 38, Sodium (mg) 382, Diabetic Exchanges: 1 very lean meat, 2.5 other carbohydrate

DESSERTS & PIES

Pineapple Bread Pudding with Lemon Apricot Sauce

With the fabulous Lemon Apricot Sauce, this incredible bread pudding will melt in your mouth. The sauce is also good with ice cream, pound cake, or just a spoon.

MAKES 10 TO 12 SERVINGS

1 (16-ounce) loaf French bread, sliced
1 (20-ounce) can crushed pineapple with juice
2 eggs
1 egg white
1 cup skim milk
¾ cup sugar
1 teaspoon vanilla extract
1 teaspoon butter extract
1 teaspoon ground cinnamon
Lemon Apricot Sauce (recipe follows)

Preheat the oven to 350°F.

Lay the French bread slices in a 2-quart oblong dish coated with nonstick cooking spray. Spread the crushed pineapple with juice evenly over the bread.

In a large bowl, beat together the eggs and egg white with the milk, sugar, vanilla and butter extracts, and cinnamon. Pour evenly over the pineapple. Bake for 45 minutes, or until set. Serve the hot bread pudding with the Lemon Apricot Sauce (see recipe at right).

LEMON APRICOT SAUCE

⅓ cup sugar
⅓ cup apricot nectar
1 teaspoon cornstarch
1 (5-ounce) can evaporated skimmed milk
1 tablespoon lemon juice

In a small saucepan, combine the sugar and nectar; bring to a boil. In a small bowl, combine the cornstarch and evaporated milk, and add to the nectar mixture. Return to a boil, and cook for 1 minute, or until thickened, stirring constantly. Remove from the heat; add the lemon juice.

Nutritional information per serving

Calories 240, Protein (g) 6, Carbohydrate (g) 48, Fat (g) 2, Calories from Fat (%) 8, Saturated Fat (g) 1, Dietary Fiber (g) 2, Cholesterol (mg) 36, Sodium (mg) 276, Diabetic Exchanges: 3 other carbohydrate

Sweet Potato Bread Pudding with Praline Sauce

If you enjoy sweet potatoes and cinnamon, "incredible," "fabulous," and "unbelievable" are adjectives you'll use to describe this melt-in-your-mouth dessert. The Praline Sauce is so delicious, you'll want to eat it by itself.

MAKES 10 TO 12 SERVINGS

1 (16-ounce) loaf French bread, cut into squares

1 (15-ounce) can sweet potatoes (yams), drained and mashed

1 (12-ounce) can evaporated skimmed milk

1½ cups skim milk

2 eggs

2 egg whites

2 tablespoons molasses

1 teaspoon ground cinnamon

½ teaspoon ground nutmeg

2 teaspoons vanilla extract

Praline Sauce (recipe follows)

Preheat the oven to 350°F.

Place the French bread squares in a 2-quart oblong casserole dish coated with non-stick cooking spray.

In a mixing bowl, beat the sweet potato, evaporated milk, milk, eggs, egg whites, molasses, cinnamon, nutmeg, and vanilla. Pour evenly over the bread, and press with your hands to submerge the bread in the liquid mixture. Bake 35 to 45 minutes, or until the pudding is set.

Top each serving with Praline Sauce (see recipe below), and serve immediately.

PRALINE SAUCE

2 cups sugar

3 tablespoons margarine

½ teaspoon baking soda

1 cup buttermilk

In a very large pot (mixture foams up while cooking), cook the sugar, margarine, baking soda, and buttermilk over medium heat, stirring frequently, until the sugar is dissolved. When the mixture foams, stir to beat down the foaming. The color will begin to caramelize. Cook until a slight brown color, about 20 to 30 minutes.

Nutritional information per serving

Calories 361, Protein (g) 10, Carbohydrate (g) 69, Fat (g) 5, Calories from Fat (%) 13, Saturated Fat (g) 1, Dietary Fiber (g) 2, Cholesterol (mg) 38, Sodium (mg) 430, Diabetic Exchanges: 0.5 skim milk, 4 other carbohydrate

DESSERTS & PIES

Chocolate Bread Pudding with Caramel Sauce

This light chocolate bread pudding with rich caramel sauce is an irresistible dessert right out of the oven.

MAKES 10 TO 12 SERVINGS

1 cup skim milk
2 cups evaporated skimmed milk
1¼ cups sugar
¼ cup cocoa
3 large eggs
3 large egg whites
1 tablespoon vanilla extract
1 (16-ounce) loaf egg bread, Hawaiian or sweet bread, cut into cubes
1 cup semisweet chocolate chips
Caramel Sauce (recipe follows)

Preheat oven to 350°F.

Combine milk, evaporated milk, sugar, and cocoa in a heavy saucepan over medium-high heat. Stir until sugar dissolves and mixture comes to a boil. Remove from heat.

In a large bowl, beat eggs, egg whites, and vanilla. Gradually whisk in chocolate mixture. Add bread cubes and chocolate chips. Transfer to a 3-quart casserole dish coated with non-stick cooking spray. Let stand until bread absorbs some of the custard, stirring occasionally, about 30 minutes. Cover with foil and bake until set in center, about 30 to 40 minutes. Serve warm or at room temperature with warm caramel sauce (See recipe at right).

CARAMEL SAUCE

MAKES 1 CUP

½ cup water
⅓ cup light brown sugar
2 teaspoons cornstarch
1 (5-ounce) can evaporated skimmed milk
1 teaspoon vanilla extract
½ cup chopped pecans, toasted, optional

In a small, heavy saucepan, heat the water and brown sugar over low heat until the sugar dissolves. Increase the heat and bring to a boil without stirring until the sugar mixture turns a deep golden brown, about 2 to 4 minutes. Combine the cornstarch and evaporated milk in a small bowl to make a thin paste and stir in to the pan. Cook until the sauce is slightly thickened. Remove from heat and stir in vanilla and pecans, if desired.

Nutritional information per serving
Calories 391, Protein (g) 13, Carbohydrate(g) 66, Fat (g) 9, Fat (%) 21, Saturated Fat (g) 4, Fiber (g) 3, Cholesterol (mg) 75, Sodium (mg) 291, Diabetic Exchanges: .5 skim milk, 4 other carbohydrate, 1.5 fat

Chocolate Bread Pudding with Caramel Sauce

Coffee Cheesecake

This rich, creamy cheesecake has just a touch of coffee. Leave out the coffee and you have a traditional cheesecake for purists.

MAKES 10 TO 12 SERVINGS

¾ cup graham cracker crumbs
1 tablespoon cocoa
¾ cup plus 2 tablespoons sugar, divided
2 tablespoons margarine, melted
1 (8-ounce) package reduced-fat cream cheese
1 (8-ounce) package fat-free cream cheese
⅓ cup all-purpose flour
1 tablespoon cornstarch
1 egg
2 tablespoons instant coffee dissolved in 1 teaspoon
    vanilla extract
⅓ cup fat-free sour cream
½ cup skim milk
4 egg whites

Preheat the oven to 325°F.

In a small bowl, combine the graham cracker crumbs, cocoa, 2 tablespoons sugar, and margarine. Press into the bottom of a 9-inch non-stick springform pan.

In a large mixing bowl, combine the cream cheeses, flour, cornstarch, ½ cup sugar, egg, and the coffee dissolved in vanilla, beating until well combined. Add the sour cream and milk, mixing well.

In a separate bowl, beat the egg whites until stiff, gradually adding the remaining sugar. Fold into the cream cheese mixture, and pour the mixture over the crust in the springform pan. Bake for 1 hour. Turn off the oven and leave the cheesecake in the oven with the door slightly open for 1 more hour. Refrigerate for at least 2 hours before serving.

Nutritional information per serving

Calories 212, Protein (g) 8, Carbohydrate (g) 28, Fat (g) 7, Calories from Fat (%) 31, Saturated Fat (g) 3, Dietary Fiber (g) 0, Cholesterol (mg) 33, Sodium (mg), 275, Diabetic Exchanges: 2 other carbohydrate, 1.5 fat

QUICK TIP:

When mixing cheesecake, use room temperature ingredients, don't overbeat, and mix at low speed to avoid whipping in excess air that will cause the cheesecake to rise and fall during baking. Do not overbake: cheesecake is done when the center is still wobbly and the edges are brown.

Cranberry Cheesecake

Everyone always loves cheesecake, and this recipe, laced and topped with cranberries, is a real holiday treat.

MAKES 8 TO 10 SERVINGS

½ cup graham cracker crumbs
1 tablespoon margarine, melted
1 (8-ounce) package reduced-fat cream cheese
1 (8-ounce) container part-skim Ricotta cheese
½ cup sugar
½ teaspoon almond extract
3 egg whites
Cranberry Topping (recipe follows)

Preheat the oven to 350°F. Coat a 9-inch non-stick pie plate with non-stick cooking spray.

In a small bowl, combine the graham crackers and margarine. Pat the mixture into the bottom of the pie plate.

In a large mixing bowl, combine the cream cheese and Ricotta until well blended. Add the sugar and almond extract, mixing well.

In another mixing bowl, beat the egg whites until soft peaks form. Fold the egg whites gradually into the cheese mixture until well combined. Pour half of the batter into the pie plate. Spread with ¾ cup of the Cranberry Topping (see recipe at right), and cover with the remaining cheesecake batter. Bake for 40 to 45 minutes, or until set. Remove from the oven, and cool on a rack. When cool, spread with the remaining Cranberry Topping. Refrigerate until chilled, about 2 hours.

CRANBERRY TOPPING

1 (16-ounce) can whole-berry cranberry sauce
¼ cup sugar
1 tablespoon cornstarch
¼ cup water

In a medium non-stick saucepan, cook the cranberry sauce and sugar over medium-low heat until the mixture is smooth, about 3 minutes.

In a small bowl, combine the cornstarch and water; add to the saucepan. Cook over medium heat, stirring constantly, until the mixture thickens. Refrigerate until lukewarm, 15 to 20 minutes, stirring in the refrigerator every 10 minutes.

Remove ¾ cup cranberry topping for the inside of the cheesecake. Refrigerate the remaining topping until well chilled.

Nutritional information per serving
Calories 261, Protein (g) 6, Carbohydrate (g) 38, Fat (g) 9, Calories from Fat (%) 31, Saturated Fat (g) 6, Dietary Fiber (g) 1, Cholesterol (mg) 27, Sodium (mg) 261, Diabetic Exchanges: 2.5 other carbohydrate, 2 fat

DESSERTS & PIES

Sweet Potato Cheesecake

Sweet Potato Cheesecake

This incredibly rich and velvety sweet potato cheesecake with a spiced crust is cheesecake at its best. For a shortcut, use a prepared reduced-fat 9-inch graham cracker crust. This is a wonderful dessert in the fall.

MAKES 10 TO 12 SERVINGS

1 cup graham cracker crumbs

2 tablespoons sugar

1 teaspoon ground cinnamon, divided

½ teaspoon ground allspice, divided

2 tablespoons margarine, melted

2 (8-ounce) packages reduced-fat cream cheese

1 cup nonfat plain yogurt

1 (15-ounce) can sweet potatoes (yams), drained and mashed, or 1 cup fresh, cooked and mashed

1⅓ cups dark brown sugar

1 egg

1 egg white

2 teaspoons vanilla extract

Preheat the oven to 350°F.

In a small bowl, combine the cracker crumbs, sugar, ½ teaspoon cinnamon, ¼ teaspoon all-spice, and the margarine. Pat into the bottom and up the sides of a 9-inch non-stick spring-form pan.

In a large bowl, beat the cream cheese and yogurt until creamy. Add the sweet potatoes, brown sugar, remaining cinnamon and allspice, beating until smooth. Add the egg and egg white one at a time, beating after each addition. Add the vanilla.

Spoon the mixture into the crust. Bake 50 to 60 minutes, or until set. Remove from the oven to cool. Refrigerate until chilled, about 2 hours.

Nutritional information per serving
Calories 308, Protein (g) 7, Carbohydrate (g) 44, Fat (g) 12, Calories from Fat (%) 34, Saturated Fat (g) 6, Dietary Fiber (g) 1, Cholesterol (mg) 45, Sodium (mg) 299 , Diabetic Exchanges: 3 other carbohydrate, 2.5 fat

DESSERTS & PIES

Chocolate Almond Cheesecake

Cheesecake lovers can indulge themselves with this rich-tasting version of an all-time favorite.

MAKES 10 TO 12 SERVINGS

½ cup chocolate wafer crumbs
1 (8-ounce) package fat-free cream cheese
1 (8-ounce) package reduced-fat cream cheese
1 cup sugar
1½ cups fat-free cottage cheese, pureéd in
   food processor until smooth
1 egg
1 teaspoon vanilla extract
¼ cup all-purpose flour
¼ cup cocoa
⅓ cup almond liqueur

Preheat the oven to 325°F.

Spread the chocolate crumbs on the bottom of a 9-inch non-stick springform pan; set aside.

In a large mixing bowl, beat together the cream cheeses, sugar, cottage cheese, egg, and vanilla.

In a small bowl, mix together the flour and cocoa; gradually add to the cream cheese mixture. Add the almond liqueur.

Pour the batter into the pan, and bake for 1 hour, or until set. Remove from the oven, cool to room temperature, and refrigerate until well chilled. Remove the sides of the pan, and serve.

Nutritional information per serving

Calories 216, Protein (g) 10, Carbohydrate (g) 29, Fat (g) 5, Calories from Fat (%) 22, Saturated Fat (g) 3, Dietary Fiber (g) 1, Cholesterol (mg) 36, Sodium (mg) 307, Diabetic Exchanges: 2 other carbohydrate, 1 fat

QUICK TIP:

A cheesecake shrinks in the pan as it cools, which can sometimes cause it to crack if the cheesecake sticks to the side of the pan. To help prevent it from cracking, run a knife around the edge of the pan after removing it from the oven.

DESSERTS & PIES

Strawberry Custard Brûlée

Brûlée is "burnt cream," a rich custard topped with a hard sugar crust. It's a restaurant quality dessert in the comfort of your own home. Raspberries can be substituted for strawberries.

MAKES 5 SERVINGS

1½ cups fresh strawberries, rinsed and sliced
2 tablespoons sugar
1½ tablespoons cornstarch
1 egg, lightly beaten
1 cup skim milk
2 tablespoons nonfat plain yogurt
½ teaspoon vanilla extract
2 tablespoons light brown sugar

Divide the strawberries among five 4- to 6-ounce ramekins or custard cups; set aside.

In a non-stick saucepan, combine the sugar and cornstarch; stir well. Add the egg, and gradually stir in the milk. Cook over low heat for 7 to 10 minutes or until thickened, stirring constantly. Remove from heat; cool 5 minutes. Fold in the yogurt and vanilla, mixing well.

Spoon the custard mixture evenly over the strawberries. Place the ramekins on a baking sheet. Sprinkle the tops with brown sugar. Broil 4 inches from heat for about 2 minutes, or until the sugar melts, or brown the tops with a miniature kitchen torch. Serve immediately, or refrigerate.

Nutritional information per serving

Calories 101, Protein (g) 4, Carbohydrate (g) 19, Fat (g) 1, Calories from Fat (%) 11, Saturated Fat (g) 0, Dietary Fiber (g) 1, Cholesterol (mg) 43, Sodium (mg) 45, Diabetic Exchanges: 1.5 other carbohydrate

DESSERTS & PIES

Orange Caramel Flan

This orange-flavored, creamy custard is light yet very satisfying. If you enjoy flan, this recipe is a wonderful choice.

MAKES 6 SERVINGS

½ cup sugar, divided
1 tablespoon water
3 eggs
¼ cup frozen orange juice concentrate, thawed
1 (12-ounce) can evaporated skimmed milk
½ cup skim milk
2 teaspoons vanilla extract
⅛ teaspoon almond extract

Preheat the oven to 300°F.

In a heavy, small non-stick saucepan, mix ¼ cup sugar with the water. Cook over medium-low heat until the sugar dissolves, stirring frequently. Increase the heat, and boil without stirring until the sugar turns deep golden brown, swirling the pan occasionally. Immediately pour the caramel into six 6-ounce custard cups. Carefully tilt the cups slightly, covering as much of the bottoms (but not the sides) as possible. Set the cups aside.

In a large bowl, whisk the eggs, orange juice concentrate, and remaining sugar. Gradually whisk in both the milks and the extracts. Divide the custard among the prepared cups.

Place the cups in a large baking pan. Add enough hot water to the pan to come halfway up the sides of the cups. Bake until the custards are set, about 80 minutes. Remove the cups from the water. Cover, and refrigerate overnight. Run a small, sharp knife around the custard sides to loosen. Invert a custard onto each plate, or eat inside the cup.

Nutritional information per serving

Calories 182, Protein (g) 9, Carbohydrate (g) 30, Fat (g) 3, Calories from Fat (%) 13, Saturated Fat (g) 1, Dietary Fiber (g) 0, Cholesterol (mg) 109, Sodium (mg) 116, Diabetic Exchanges: 0.5 skim milk, 0.5 fruit, 1 other carbohydrate

DESSERTS & PIES

Fantastic Trifle

Trifles serve a crowd and make a nice presentation. Of all my trifles, this is the most-requested recipe. It's easy to make and a guaranteed winner.

MAKES 16 SERVINGS

1 (16-ounce) angel food cake
⅔ cup sugar
3 tablespoons cocoa
1 tablespoon cornstarch
1 (5-ounce) can evaporated skimmed milk
¼ cup coffee liqueur
3 (1.4-ounce) chocolate-covered toffee candy bars, crushed
3 (4-serving) packages instant vanilla pudding mix
3 cups skim milk
2 bananas, peeled and sliced
1 (12-ounce) container fat-free frozen whipped topping, thawed

Cube the cake and place in a large bowl.

In a small non-stick pot, combine the sugar, cocoa, cornstarch, and evaporated milk. Cook over low heat until thickened, 7 to 10 minutes. Remove from heat; add the coffee liqueur, and cool. Pour the chocolate mixture over the cake in the bowl. Add the crushed candy to the cake mixture.

Beat or whisk the pudding mix and skim milk until thick. Pour over the angel food cake mixture.

In a trifle dish, layer the cake mixture, banana, and whipped topping. Repeat the layers, ending with the whipped topping. Refrigerate until serving.

Nutritional information per serving
Calories 299, Protein (g) 5, Carbohydrate (g) 61, Fat (g) 3, Calories from Fat (%) 9, Saturated Fat (g) 2, Dietary Fiber (g) 1, Cholesterol (mg) 5, Sodium (mg) 505, Diabetic Exchanges: 4 other carbohydrate, 0.5 fat

QUICK TIP:

Crush any extra toffee candy bars to sprinkle on top of the Trifle. It can also be garnished with strawberries.

Chocolate Trifle

When you need a show-stopping quick dessert to serve a crowd, here's your solution. No one can resist this dazzling series of chocolate layers. Make ahead of time, and refrigerate until ready to serve.

MAKES 16 SERVINGS

1 (18.25-ounce) package devil's food cake mix
1⅓ cups water
1 egg
2 egg whites
1 (4-serving) package instant chocolate pudding mix
3 cups cold skim milk
⅓ cup coffee liqueur
½ cup chopped chocolate-covered toffee candy bars,
    (two 1.4-ounce bars)
1 (8-ounce) container fat-free frozen whipped topping,
    thawed

Preheat the oven to 350°F. Coat two 9-inch non-stick round baking pans with non-stick cooking spray.

Combine the cake mix, water, egg, and egg whites in a mixing bowl, and beat for 2 minutes. Pour the batter evenly into the prepared pans. Bake for 25 to 30 minutes, or until a toothpick inserted in the center comes out clean. Let cool on a wire rack, and remove from the pans.

In a medium mixing bowl, combine the pudding mix and milk, and prepare according to the package directions. Chill in the refrigerator.

To assemble, place a cake layer in the bottom of a trifle dish or large glass bowl, then sprinkle with half the coffee liqueur, half the toffee candy, half the pudding, and half the whipped topping. Repeat the layers. Refrigerate until serving.

Nutritional information per serving
Calories 248, Protein (g) 5, Carbohydrate (g) 40, Fat (g) 6, Calories from Fat (%) 23, Saturated Fat (g) 3, Dietary Fiber (g) 1, Cholesterol (mg) 37, Sodium (mg) 411, Diabetic Exchanges: 2 other carbohydrate, 1 fat

QUICK TIP:

Try using chocolate fudge pudding in this recipe for more chocolate flavor, or milk chocolate pudding for a lighter version.

DESSERTS & PIES

Lemon Pineapple Trifle 🥕

When tart lemon custard is combined with pineapple-lemon filling, lemon lovers will not be able to contain themselves. Ladyfingers are available in most grocery stores in the bakery or frozen foods section.

MAKES 10 SERVINGS

¼ cup cornstarch
1 cup sugar
⅓ cup cold water
1 cup hot water
⅔ cup lemon juice
1 egg yolk, lightly beaten
4 ounces reduced-fat cream cheese
1 (8-ounce) can crushed pineapple, drained
1 (8-ounce) container fat-free frozen whipped topping, thawed, divided
24 ladyfingers

In a medium non-stick saucepan, mix the cornstarch and sugar. Gradually add the cold water, stirring to mix. Add the hot water and lemon juice, and bring to a boil over medium heat, stirring constantly. Cook until thickened, 7 to 10 minutes, then gradually pour 1 cup of the hot mixture into the egg yolk in a small bowl, stirring constantly. Return that mixture to the saucepan, and continue cooking for 1 minute. Transfer the custard to a large bowl, cover, and refrigerate until chilled.

Divide the custard in half; using a fork or whisk, blend half the custard with the cream cheese. Mix in the pineapple. Fold half the container of whipped topping into the pineapple custard mixture; set aside.

In a trifle bowl or a deep glass bowl, place a layer of the ladyfingers along the bottom and around the side of the dish. Next, spread the bottom with half the plain lemon custard. Spread with half the pineapple-lemon filling. Top with the remaining ladyfingers. Spread with the remaining plain lemon custard, and top with the rest of the pineapple-lemon filling. Top this with the remaining whipped topping. Refrigerate for at least 2 hours before serving.

Nutritional information per serving
Calories 273, Protein (g) 4, Carbohydrate (g) 51, Fat (g) 5, Calories from Fat (%) 18, Saturated Fat (g) 3, Dietary Fiber (g) 1, Cholesterol (mg) 126, Sodium (mg) 103, Diabetic Exchanges: 3.5 other carbohydrate, 1 fat

DESSERTS & PIES

Fruit Trifle

When summer fruit is in season, here's an out-standing choice for dessert—homemade custard layered with fresh fruit. Use whatever fruit you enjoy to prepare this quick-to-fix luscious creation. For a speedy approach, instant vanilla pudding may be substituted for the custard.

MAKES 16 SERVINGS

½ cup sugar

⅓ cup cornstarch

3 cups skim milk

2 egg yolks, slightly beaten

1 teaspoon vanilla extract

1 (16-ounce) angel food cake, cut into ½-inch slices

½ cup sherry, divided

1 pound fresh strawberries, stemmed and sliced

2 bananas, peeled and sliced

1 pint fresh blueberries

2 kiwis, peeled and sliced

1 (12-ounce) container fat-free frozen whipped topping, thawed

In a 2-quart non-stick saucepan, stir together the sugar and cornstarch. Gradually add the milk, stirring until smooth. Stir in the beaten egg yolks. Cook over medium heat, stirring constantly, until the mixture comes to a boil. Boil for 2 minutes, and remove from the heat. Stir in the vanilla. Transfer to a large bowl, cover with waxed paper, and refrigerate until chilled, about 30 minutes.

Arrange half the angel food cake slices in a single layer in a trifle dish or a deep glass bowl. Drizzle with ¼ cup of the sherry. Layer with half the fruit, half the custard, and half the whipped topping. Repeat the layers with the remaining ingredients, beginning with angel food cake and sherry and ending with the whipped topping. Refrigerate until ready to serve.

Nutritional information per serving

Calories 211, Protein (g) 4, Carbohydrate (g) 44, Fat (g) 1, Calories from Fat (%) 5, Saturated Fat (g) 0, Dietary Fiber (g) 2, Cholesterol (mg) 27, Sodium (mg) 251, Diabetic Exchanges: 3 other carbohydrate

Fruit Trifle

Pineapple Trifle

This effortless, elegant dessert will make a statement. Pineapple, cream cheese layers, and whipped topping will entice even chocoholics. For the height of indulgence, add fresh berries.

MAKES 8 TO 10 SERVINGS

12 ounces reduced-fat cream cheese
⅔ cup sugar
1 (5-ounce) can evaporated skimmed milk
1 (16-ounce) angel food cake, cubed
1 (20-ounce) can crushed pineapple, with juice
2 tablespoons cornstarch
1 (8-ounce) container fat-free frozen whipped topping, thawed

In a mixing bowl, beat the cream cheese, sugar, and evaporated milk until creamy. Fold in the cubed angel food cake.

In a small non-stick saucepan, combine the pineapple and cornstarch. Cook over low heat until thick, stirring constantly; set aside to cool 5 to 7 minutes.

In a trifle dish or a deep glass bowl, layer half the angel food cake mixture, half the pineapple mixture, and half the whipped topping. Repeat again, ending with whipped topping. Refrigerate until ready to serve.

Nutritional information per serving
Calories 343, Protein (g) 8, Carbohydrate (g) 59, Fat (g) 8, Calories from Fat (%) 21, Saturated Fat (g) 5, Dietary Fiber (g) 1, Cholesterol (mg) 25, Sodium (mg) 521, Diabetic Exchanges: 4 other carbohydrate, 1.5 fat

Glazed Bananas

Everyday ingredients turn into a dessert that makes a fabulous ending to a meal or a great anytime dessert snack. Serve over frozen vanilla yogurt or ice cream.

MAKES 6 SERVINGS

2 tablespoons margarine
¼ cup light brown sugar
⅛ teaspoon ground cinnamon
¼ cup fresh orange juice
3 firm bananas, peeled, split lengthwise, and halved

In a non-stick pan, heat the margarine, brown sugar, cinnamon, and orange juice until bubbly. Add the banana slices, and cook for 5 minutes, turning as needed. Serve immediately.

Nutritional information per serving
Calories 127, Protein (g) 1, Carbohydrate (g) 24, Fat (g) 4, Calories from Fat (%) 27, Saturated Fat (g) 1, Dietary Fiber (g) 1, Cholesterol (mg) 0, Sodium (mg) 49, Diabetic Exchanges: 1 fruit, 0.5 other carbohydrate, 1 fat

Ice Cream Pie

This quick dessert is loved by all ages. Keep it easy by using whatever chocolate cookies you have lying around for the crust—crush the cookies in a food processor or by hand.

MAKES 16 SERVINGS

1 cup chocolate wafer crumbs
1 cup graham cracker crumbs
¼ cup margarine, melted
½ gallon nonfat vanilla frozen yogurt, softened
Chocolate Sauce (recipe follows)

In a medium bowl, combine the chocolate wafer crumbs and graham cracker crumbs with the melted margarine, stirring until combined. Pat into the bottom of a 13 x 9 x 2-inch non-stick pan, and chill until firm.

Spread the frozen yogurt on top of the crust. Chill in the freezer for 20 to 30 minutes. Top with the Chocolate Sauce (see recipe at right), and return to the freezer until ready to serve.

CHOCOLATE SAUCE

⅔ cup sugar
3 tablespoons cocoa
1 tablespoon cornstarch
1 (5-ounce) can evaporated skimmed milk
1 tablespoon margarine
1 teaspoon vanilla extract

In a small non-stick saucepan, combine the sugar, cocoa, and cornstarch. Gradually add the evaporated milk. Cook over low heat, stirring, until the mixture thickens and boils, 7 to 10 minutes. Remove from heat. Add the margarine and vanilla. Cool slightly before spreading on top of the frozen pie.

Nutritional information per serving

Calories 238, Protein (g) 7, Carbohydrate (g) 41, Fat (g) 6, Calories from Fat (%) 21, Saturated Fat (g) 1, Dietary Fiber (g) 1, Cholesterol (mg) 3, Sodium (mg) 217, Diabetic Exchanges: 3.5 other carbohydrate, 1 fat

QUICK TIP:

Use your imagination with this recipe, and try different flavored frozen yogurts or low fat ice creams to satisfy your taste buds. Heavenly Hash low-fat ice cream was sooo good!

Mocha Fudge Mousse Pie

This pie was featured on the cover of Cooking Light *magazine and was one of their ten best recipes in their ten-year anniversary issue. A brownie mix and a pudding mix make this brownie decadence effortless to prepare. For flair, garnish with shaved chocolate.*

MAKES 8 TO 10 SERVINGS

⅓ cup warm water
1 teaspoon instant coffee
1 (19.85-ounce) box reduced-fat or regular
   fudge brownie mix
2 egg whites
1 teaspoon vanilla extract
⅓ cup chopped pecans
Mousse (recipe follows)

Preheat the oven to 350°F. Coat a 9-inch non-stick pie plate with non-stick cooking spray.

In a small cup, stir together the water and the coffee until dissolved.

In a large bowl, combine the brownie mix, coffee mixture, egg whites, and vanilla, stirring with a spoon until well mixed. Stir in the pecans. Pour the batter into the prepared pie plate. Bake for 25 minutes, or until the cake is set in the pan. Do not overbake.

Cool on a wire rack. Spread with the Chocolate Mousse (see recipe at right), and top with the coffee-flavored whipped topping. Refrigerate until serving.

CHOCOLATE MOUSSE

¾ cup skim milk
2 tablespoons coffee liqueur, divided
1 teaspoon instant coffee
1 (4-serving) package chocolate instant pudding mix
1 (8-ounce) container fat-free frozen whipped topping,
   thawed, divided

In a large bowl, stir together the milk, 1 tablespoon coffee liqueur, and coffee until the coffee is dissolved. Add the pudding mix, and beat at the high speed of a mixer for 1 minute, or until thick. Gently fold in half of the whipped topping. Spread the mixture evenly over the cooled brownie crust.

Combine the remaining coffee liqueur with the remaining whipped topping, mixing gently. Spread over the pudding mixture in the pie.

Nutritional information per serving

Calories 348, Protein (g) 5, Carbohydrate (g) 66, Fat (g) 7, Calories from Fat (%) 19, Saturated Fat (g) 2, Dietary Fiber (g) 2, Cholesterol (mg) 0, Sodium (mg) 361, Diabetic Exchanges: 4.5 other carbohydrate, 1.5 fat

Mocha Fudge Mousse Pie

Banana Eclair

Banana Éclair

This showpiece-quality dessert is a little time-consuming, but it's worth the effort. Make the shell ahead, and fill on the day of serving. Slice the éclair in half lengthwise, and then cut in slices down the middle to serve to a crowd.

MAKES 16 TO 18 SERVINGS

1 cup water
½ cup margarine
1 cup all-purpose flour
2 tablespoons sugar
2 eggs
3 egg whites
Banana Cream Filling (recipe follows)
Chocolate Glaze (recipe follows)

Preheat the oven to 400°F.

In a large non-stick saucepan over medium heat, bring the water and margarine to a boil, cooking until the margarine is melted. In a small bowl, combine the flour with the sugar, and add to the margarine mixture all at once, stirring vigor-

ously with a spoon until the dough forms a ball and leaves the sides of the pan. Remove the pan from the heat. Beat in the eggs and egg whites with a spoon, one at a time, and continue beating until the dough is stiff and glossy.

On a 15 x 10 x 1-inch non-stick jelly roll pan coated with non-stick cooking spray, form about two-thirds of the dough into one long oblong about 7 inches wide. Reserve a little extra dough to spoon into mounds along the top of the oblong. Bake for 20 to 25 minutes, or until golden brown. Remove from the oven, and with a sharp knife, make slits along the sides of the éclair about 2 inches apart to let the steam escape. Return to the oven, and continue baking for 10 minutes. Remove to a cooling rack.

Carefully slice off the top of the éclair. It may come off in pieces. Remove, and scoop out any soft dough inside the shell. Cool thoroughly.

Place the bottom on a serving platter. Fill the bottom éclair shell with half the Banana Cream Filling (see recipe on next page). Slice the remaining bananas over the topping. Cover with the remaining filling. Cover with the baked shell top (or pieces to form the top if not in a whole piece), and drizzle with the Chocolate Glaze (see recipe below). Refrigerate until serving time.

BANANA CREAM FILLING

2 envelopes whipped topping mix
1 cup cold skim milk
6 to 8 bananas, divided
¼ cup banana liqueur

In a large mixing bowl, combine both envelopes of the whipped topping with the milk, beating until the topping is very thick and forms a peak. Mash enough bananas to make 2 cups, and mix with the banana liqueur. Fold the banana mixture into the whipped topping.

CHOCOLATE GLAZE

1 tablespoon margarine, melted
2 tablespoons cocoa
1 teaspoon vanilla extract
⅔ cup confectioners' sugar
3 tablespoons boiling water

In a small bowl, combine the melted margarine, cocoa, vanilla, and confectioners' sugar. Stir in the boiling water to make a thin glaze. Refrigerate.

Nutritional information per serving
Calories 187, Protein (g) 3, Carbohydrate (g) 26, Fat (g) 8, Calories from Fat (%) 36, Saturated Fat (g) 2, Dietary Fiber (g) 1, Cholesterol (mg) 24, Sodium (mg) 96, Diabetic Exchanges: 1.5 other carbohydrate, 1.5 fat

Chocolate Fondue

Fondue is great for cocktail parties. Serve with fresh fruit, angel food cake, and marshmallows for an eye-appealing presentation.

MAKES 40 (2-TABLESPOON) SERVINGS

2 cups sugar
¾ cup unsweetened cocoa
2 tablespoons cornstarch
¼ teaspoon salt
4 cups cold skim milk
3 tablespoons margarine
1 teaspoon vanilla extract
¼ teaspoon butter extract

Mix the sugar, cocoa, cornstarch, and salt together in a non-stick saucepan. Add milk, stirring well. Over medium heat, bring to a boil. Lower the heat, and simmer 20 minutes. Remove from heat. Add the margarine, vanilla, and butter extract.

Nutritional information per serving
Calories 63, Protein (g) 1, Carbohydrate (g) 12, Fat (g) 1, Calories from Fat (%) 15, Saturated Fat (g) 0, Dietary Fiber (g) 0, Cholesterol (mg) 0, Sodium (mg) 37, Diabetic Exchanges: 1 other carbohydrate

QUICK TIP:

Reheat chocolate fondue in the microwave. Microwave for 1 minute, stir, and repeat until melted.

Tiramisu

Tiramisu

Simple to prepare and simply sensational to eat, this Tiramisu is a winner. Try it and you will see why! Espresso powder can be found in the coffee section at the grocery.

MAKES 16 SERVINGS

½ cup espresso or very strong coffee

1 tablespoon sugar

3 tablespoons coffee liqueur

1 (8-ounce) package reduced-fat cream cheese, softened

¾ cup confectioners' sugar

1 (8-ounce) container fat-free frozen whipped topping, thawed and divided

20 ladyfingers, split

Cocoa, for sprinkling

In a small bowl, combine the espresso, sugar, and the coffee liqueur; set aside.

In a mixing bowl, combine the cream cheese with the confectioners' sugar, beating until well blended. Fold in about 1½ cups whipped topping, reserving 1 cup for the topping.

In a 9 x 9 x 2-inch dish, place a layer of the split ladyfingers across the bottom of the dish. Drizzle with half of the espresso mixture, half of the cream cheese mixture, and repeat the layers, beginning with ladyfingers and ending with the cream cheese mixture. Spread with the remaining whipped topping in a thin layer on top of the dessert and sprinkle with cocoa. Refrigerate until well chilled.

Nutrition information per serving

Calories 141, Protein (g) 2, Carbohydrate (g) 23, Fat (g) 3, Calories from Fat (%) 23, Saturated Fat (g) 2, Dietary Fiber (g) 0, Cholesterol (mg) 12, Sodium (mg) 98, Diabetic Exchanges: 1.5 other carbohydrate, 0.5 fat

Peach Crisp

Frozen peaches make it possible to enjoy this dessert year-round. I admit I'm partial to the oatmeal crumbly topping, and it's likely you will be, too.

MAKES 10 TO 12 SERVINGS

2 (16-ounce) packages frozen peaches, thawed
2 tablespoons cornstarch
⅓ cup sugar
2 tablespoons lemon juice
5 tablespoons margarine
⅓ cup light brown sugar
1 tablespoon vanilla extract
¾ cup all-purpose flour
¼ teaspoon baking soda
1½ cups old-fashioned oatmeal

Preheat the oven to 350°F.

Lay the fruit in an oblong 2-quart casserole dish.

In a small bowl, mix the cornstarch and sugar. Toss the cornstarch mixture and lemon juice with the peaches in the casserole dish.

In a medium bowl, mix together the margarine, brown sugar, and vanilla. In a small bowl, stir together the flour and baking soda, and mix with the oatmeal and margarine mixture until crumbly. Sprinkle on top of the peaches.

Bake for 45 minutes, or until the topping is brown and the mixture is bubbly. Serve immediately.

Nutritional information per serving
Calories 195, Protein (g) 3, Carbohydrate (g) 32, Fat (g) 6, Calories from Fat (%) 27, Saturated Fat (g) 1, Dietary Fiber (g) 3, Cholesterol (mg) 0, Sodium (mg) 85, Diabetic Exchanges: 2 other carbohydrate, 1 fat

Berry Crisp

I had some frozen raspberries and whipped up this dessert to serve over frozen vanilla yogurt. Yummy! It works well substituting other berries, too.

MAKES 4 TO 6 SERVINGS

1 quart fresh raspberries or blueberries,
  or 1 (16-ounce) package frozen berries
3 tablespoons sugar
¼ cup margarine, softened
⅓ cup all-purpose flour
⅓ cup light brown sugar
¾ cup old-fashioned oatmeal

Preheat the oven to 350°F.

Place the fruit in the bottom of a 9-inch non-stick square baking pan coated with non-stick cooking spray. Sprinkle the sugar over the fruit.

In a medium bowl, mix the margarine, flour, brown sugar, and oatmeal until the mixture resembles a coarse meal. Sprinkle over the fruit. Bake for 30 minutes, or until lightly browned. Serve hot.

Nutritional information per serving

Calories 242, Protein (g) 3, Carbohydrate (g) 40, Fat (g) 9, Calories from Fat (%) 31, Saturated Fat (g) 1, Dietary Fiber (g) 7, Cholesterol (mg) 0, Sodium (mg) 94, Diabetic Exchanges: 0.5 fruit, 2 other carbohydrate, 2 fat

QUICK TIP:

Don't let winter months keep you from enjoying fruit. Fresh, frozen and canned fruit all work well.

Nectarine and Raspberry Crumble

Nectarines and raspberries are perfectly combined with a crumbly oatmeal topping to create a delicious treat. Frozen fruit may also be used; defrost first.

MAKES 6 TO 8 SERVINGS

6 tablespoons light brown sugar, divided
3 tablespoons all-purpose flour, divided
½ teaspoon ground cinnamon
4 ripe nectarines, peeled and sliced 2 inches thick
½ pint fresh raspberries
1 cup old-fashioned oatmeal
2 tablespoons margarine
2 tablespoons fresh orange juice

Preheat the oven to 425°F. Coat a 9-inch non-stick pie plate with non-stick cooking spray.

In a small bowl, combine 2 tablespoons brown sugar, 2 tablespoons flour, and the cinnamon. Toss with the nectarines. Gently toss in the raspberries. Place the fruit mixture in the prepared pie plate. Combine the remaining brown sugar, the oatmeal, and the remaining flour with the margarine and orange juice, mixing until crumbly. Crumble over the fruit.

Bake for 25 to 30 minutes, or until the fruit is bubbly. If the topping begins to brown too quickly, cover loosely with foil. Serve hot or reheated.

Nutritional information per serving

Calories 158, Protein (g) 3, Carbohydrate (g) 29, Fat (g) 4, Calories from Fat (%) 21, Saturated Fat (g) 1, Dietary Fiber (g) 3, Cholesterol (mg) 0, Sodium (mg) 38, Diabetic Exchanges: 2 other carbohydrate, 1 fat

DESSERTS & PIES

Blueberry Pineapple Crunch

So quick and easy, but unbelievably good. Lemon lovers will have a big smile while enjoying this cobbler-type dessert. It's great just out of the oven with frozen vanilla yogurt.

MAKES 16 SERVINGS

1 (20-ounce) can crushed pineapple in juice, undrained
2 cups fresh or frozen blueberries
1 (18.25-ounce) box lemon cake mix
⅔ cup light brown sugar
½ cup margarine, melted

Preheat the oven to 350°F.

In a 13 x 9 x 2-inch non-stick baking pan coated with non-stick cooking spray, spread the pineapple and blueberries along the bottom of the pan. Sprinkle evenly with the cake mix and brown sugar. Drizzle with the margarine. Bake for 45 to 50 minutes, or until bubbly. Serve hot.

Nutritional information per serving

Calories 246, Protein (g) 1, Carbohydrate (g) 43, Fat (g) 8, Calories from Fat (%) 30, Saturated Fat (g) 2, Dietary Fiber (g) 1, Cholesterol (mg) 0, Sodium (mg) 279, Diabetic Exchanges: 3 other carbohydrate, 1.5 fat

Blueberry Pineapple Crunch

DESSERTS & PIES

Apple Peanut Crumble

Baked apples with a peanut crumble topping hot out of the oven—sinfully good!

MAKES 8 SERVINGS

5 cooking apples, peeled, cored, and sliced (7 to 8 cups)
⅔ cup light brown sugar
½ cup all-purpose flour
½ cup old-fashioned oatmeal
½ teaspoon ground cinnamon
½ teaspoon ground nutmeg
⅓ cup margarine
2 tablespoons reduced-fat peanut butter

Preheat the oven to 350°F.

Coat a 2-quart oblong casserole dish with non-stick cooking spray. Lay the apples in the dish.

In a mixing bowl, combine the remaining ingredients. Mix until the consistency is crumb-like. Sprinkle over the top of the apples. Bake for 30 minutes, or until the apples are tender and the mixture is bubbly. Serve hot.

Nutritional information per serving

Calories 251, Protein (g) 3, Carbohydrate (g) 41, Fat (g) 10, Calories from Fat (%) 33, Saturated Fat (g) 2, Dietary Fiber (g) 3, Cholesterol (mg) 0, Sodium (mg) 118, Diabetic Exchanges: 1 fruit, 1.5 other carbohydrate, 2 fat

Coffee Toffee Dessert

This impressive, simple, make-ahead ice cream dessert is a perfect ending to any meal. The coffee liqueur may be omitted if you prefer.

MAKES 16 SERVINGS

1 (10-ounce) angel food cake
1 tablespoon instant coffee
1 tablespoon hot water
1 teaspoon vanilla extract
4 (1.4 ounce) bars chocolate-covered toffee candy bars
1 quart nonfat vanilla frozen yogurt, softened
1 (8-ounce) container fat-free frozen whipped topping, thawed
2 tablespoons coffee liqueur

Slice the angel food cake and lay it along the bottom of a 9-inch non-stick springform pan coated with non-stick cooking spray.

Dissolve the coffee in the hot water; cool. Add the vanilla to the coffee.

Crush the candy bars in a food processor or by pounding with a mallet. In a large bowl, combine the crushed candy and the dissolved coffee mixture with the softened frozen yogurt. Quickly spoon the mixture on top of the angel food cake.

Mix the whipped topping with the coffee liqueur, and spread over the yogurt layer. Freeze overnight, or until firm enough to cut.

Nutritional information per serving

Calories 180, Protein (g) 4, Carbohydrate (g) 31, Fat (g) 4, Calories from Fat (%) 18, Saturated Fat (g) 2, Dietary Fiber (g) 0, Cholesterol (mg) 6, Sodium (mg) 200, Diabetic Exchanges: 2 other carbohydrate, 1 fat

DESSERTS & PIES

Chocolate Chip Pie

This fast-to-fix crustless pie is like eating a thick chocolate chip cookie.

MAKES 8 SERVINGS

2 cups all-purpose flour

1 teaspoon baking powder

½ teaspoon baking soda

1¼ cups light brown sugar

4 tablespoons margarine, melted

2 eggs

1 tablespoon vanilla extract

⅔ cup semisweet chocolate chips

Preheat the oven to 350°F. Coat a 9-inch non-stick pie plate with non-stick cooking spray.

In a medium bowl, combine the flour, baking powder, and baking soda; set aside.

In a large bowl, combine the brown sugar, margarine, eggs, and vanilla. Stir in the dry mixture and the chocolate chips. Spoon into the prepared pie plate. Bake for 30 minutes, or until a knife inserted in the center comes out clean. Don't overbake. Let cool on a wire rack before serving.

Nutritional information per serving

Calories 307, Protein (g) 4, Carbohydrate (g) 53, Fat (g) 9, Calories from Fat (%) 26, Saturated Fat (g) 3, Dietary Fiber (g) 1, Cholesterol (mg) 43, Sodium (mg) 190, Diabetic Exchanges: 3.5 other carbohydrate, 2 fat

Chocolate Chess Pie

This effortless pie is truly outstanding—simple, sweet, and an indulgence to eat. Everyone always wants seconds.

MAKES 8 SERVINGS

2 tablespoons margarine, melted

1 cup sugar

1 tablespoon all-purpose flour

3 tablespoons cocoa

1 (5-ounce) can evaporated skimmed milk

2 eggs, beaten

1 teaspoon vanilla extract

1 unbaked (9-inch) pie shell

Preheat the oven to 350°F.

In a large mixing bowl, mix together the margarine, sugar, flour, cocoa, evaporated milk, eggs, and vanilla, beating well.

Pour the mixture into the pie shell. Bake for 30 minutes, or until firm. Cool and serve.

Nutritional information per serving

Calories 289, Protein (g) 5, Carbohydrate (g) 42, Fat (g) 11, Calories from Fat (%) 35, Saturated Fat (g) 4, Dietary Fiber (g) 1, Cholesterol (mg) 59, Sodium (mg,) 173, Diabetic Exchanges: 3 other carbohydrate, 2 fat

Custard Pie

A true custard lovers' delight—plain but palate-pleasing. To trim fat, use the crust recipe for the Apple Crumble Pie, page 452.

MAKES 8 SERVINGS

3 cups skim milk
1 cup sugar
½ cup all-purpose flour
2 eggs
1 teaspoon vanilla extract
1 unbaked (9-inch) pie shell

Preheat the oven to 350°F.

In a medium non-stick saucepan, heat the milk over low heat.

In a medium bowl, mix the sugar, flour, and eggs. Beat well and pour into the heated milk. Cook over medium heat until the mixture boils and thickens, 10 to 12 minutes. Remove from heat and add the vanilla. Pour the custard filling into the pie shell. Bake for 20 to 30 minutes, or until set. Cool and serve.

Nutritional information per serving

Calories 297, Protein (g) 7, Carbohydrate (g) 49, Fat (g) 8, Calories from Fat (%) 26, Saturated Fat (g) 4, Dietary Fiber (g) 0, Cholesterol (mg) 60, Sodium (mg) 164, Diabetic Exchanges: 3 other carbohydrate, 1.5 fat

DESSERTS & PIES

Apple Crumble Pie

Nothing beats a good apple pie—you'll love the crumbly topping with a light lemon glaze. For convenience, use a 9-inch unbaked pie crust from your grocery store.

MAKES 8 SLICES

1 cup plus 1 tablespoon all-purpose flour, divided

2 tablespoons cold water

2 tablespoons canola oil

1 teaspoon vanilla extract

1 teaspoon ground cinnamon

1 tablespoon water

⅓ cup sugar

4 cups peeled, sliced tart baking apples

Topping (recipe follows)

½ cup confectioners' sugar

2 tablespoons lemon juice

Preheat the oven to 350ºF.

In a small bowl, mix 1 cup flour and the cold water and oil together; press into a 9-inch non-stick pie plate.

In a large bowl, combine the vanilla, cinnamon, 1 tablespoon water, 1 tablespoon flour, sugar, and apples. Fill the crust with the filling. Sprinkle the filling with the Topping (see recipe at right).

Bake for 1 hour, or until the apples are done and the pie is bubbly.

In a small bowl mix the confectioners' sugar and lemon juice. Drizzle the glaze over the hot pie. Serve hot.

TOPPING

½ teaspoon ground cinnamon

½ cup crushed nonfat pretzels

¼ cup light brown sugar

¾ cup all-purpose flour

5 tablespoons margarine, chilled and cut into pieces

In a small bowl, combine the cinnamon, pretzels, brown sugar, and flour. Cut in the margarine until the mixture is crumbly.

Nutritional information per serving

Calories 341, Protein (g) 4, Carbohydrate (g) 58, Fat (g) 11, Calories from Fat (%) 29, Saturated Fat (g) 1, Dietary Fiber (g) 2, Cholesterol (mg) 0, Sodium (mg) 165, Diabetic Exchanges: 4 other carbohydrate, 2 fat

Apple Crumble Pie

Banana Cream Pie

Here's the ultimate combination for banana pudding fans. For a short cut, purchase a prepared graham cracker crust.

MAKES 8 SERVINGS

1 cup reduced-fat vanilla wafer crumbs
2 tablespoons margarine, melted
¼ cup plus ⅓ cup sugar
2 tablespoons cornstarch
1½ cups skim milk
1 egg, beaten
1 tablespoon vanilla extract
3 bananas, sliced
3 egg whites

Preheat the oven to 375°F.

In a non-stick pie plate, mix the vanilla wafer crumbs and margarine. Press the mixture into the bottom and up the sides of the pie plate, and bake for 5 to 7 minutes; set aside.

Increase the oven temperature to 400°F.

In a medium non-stick saucepan, combine ¼ cup of the sugar and the cornstarch. Gradually add the milk, stirring until blended. Cook over medium heat, stirring constantly, until the mixture thickens and comes to a boil, 10 to 15 minutes. Boil 1 minute longer, stirring constantly.

In a small bowl, gradually stir ⅓ of the hot mixture into the beaten egg. Return this to the remaining hot mixture, stirring constantly. Cook for another 2 minutes, stirring constantly. Remove from the heat, and add the vanilla. Spread the banana slices on the baked pie crust, and then cover with the custard.

With a mixer, beat the egg whites until soft peaks form. Gradually add the remaining sugar, beating until stiff peaks form. Spread the meringue over the filled pie, and bake for 4 to 5 minutes, until the meringue begins to turn golden. Watch closely. Serve immediately.

Nutritional information per serving

Calories 228, Protein (g) 5, Carbohydrate (g) 42, Fat (g) 5, Calories from Fat (%) 19, Saturated Fat (g) 1, Dietary Fiber (g) 1, Cholesterol (mg) 27, Sodium (mg) 141, Diabetic Exchanges: 3 other carbohydrate, 1 fat

QUICK TIP:

If a pie crust browns too quickly, cover the edges with strips of foil and continue baking.

Peanut Butter Banana Pie

Peanut Butter Banana Pie

A good old-fashioned banana pie with a touch of peanut butter is a hard combination to beat. Sprinkle with chopped peanuts, if desired.

MAKES 8 SERVINGS

1¼ cups reduced-fat vanilla wafer crumbs
2 tablespoons margarine, melted
⅔ cup sugar
3 tablespoons cornstarch
1½ cups skim milk
2 eggs, lightly beaten
2 tablespoons reduced-fat crunchy peanut butter
1 teaspoon vanilla extract
3 cups sliced banana
1½ cups fat-free frozen whipped topping, thawed

Preheat the oven to 375°F.

In a pie plate, mix together the vanilla wafer crumbs and margarine. Press into the bottom and sides of a 9-inch non-stick pie plate and bake for 5 to 7 minutes. In a small, heavy non-stick saucepan, combine the sugar and cornstarch. Gradually add the milk, stirring with a whisk until well blended. Cook over medium heat until the mixture comes to a boil; then cook for 1 minute more, stirring with a whisk. In a small bowl, gradually add about ⅓ cup hot custard to the beaten eggs, stirring constantly with a whisk. Return the egg mixture to the pot. Cook over medium heat until thick (about 1 minute), stirring constantly. Remove from heat, and stir in the peanut butter and vanilla. Cool slightly.

Arrange the banana slices in the bottom of the prepared crust; spoon the filling over the banana slices. Press plastic wrap onto the surface of the filling; chill for 4 hours. Remove the plastic wrap. Spread the whipped topping evenly over the filling. Refrigerate until well chilled, and serve.

Nutritional information per serving

Calories 310, Protein (g) 5, Carbohydrate (g) 56, Fat (g) 7, Calories from Fat (%) 20, Saturated Fat (g) 1, Dietary Fiber (g) 2, Cholesterol (mg) 54, Sodium (mg) 171, Diabetic Exchanges: 4 other carbohydrate, 1.5 fat

DESSERTS & PIES

Lemon Meringue Pie

Everyone loves an old-fashioned lemon meringue pie, especially one that's easy on the figure. It's best served on the day it's made, or the pie tends to get "weepy." Cheat by using an already prepared pie crust to save time.

MAKES 8 SERVINGS

1 cup all-purpose flour
1 tablespoon sugar
⅛ teaspoon baking powder
3 tablespoons margarine
2 tablespoons water
½ teaspoon vanilla extract
Lemon Filling (recipe follows)
Meringue (recipe follows)

Preheat the oven to 375°F.

In a medium bowl, combine the flour, sugar, and baking powder. Cut in the margarine until coarse crumbs form. Stir in the water and vanilla with a fork. Gather the dough into a small, flattened ball; on a floured surface, roll out to fit a 9-inch pie plate. If the dough is too stiff, add more water.

Transfer the dough to the pie plate, and pierce with a fork. Bake for 10 to 15 minutes, or until lightly browned. Remove from the oven and cool the pie crust slightly.

Lower the oven temperature to 350°F.

Fill the baked crust with the Lemon Filling (see recipe at right). Spread the Meringue (see recipe at right) over the pie filling, spreading it all the way to the edges. Bake the pie for 10 to 12 minutes, or until lightly brown. Cool, and then refrigerate until well chilled. Serve

LEMON FILLING

¼ cup cornstarch
1 cup sugar
⅓ cup cold water
1 cup hot water
½ cup lemon juice
1 teaspoon grated lemon rind
2 egg yolks, slightly beaten

In a large non-stick saucepan, combine the cornstarch and sugar. Blend in the cold water and then the hot water. Cook over medium-high heat, stirring constantly, until the mixture is thick and clear, about 10 minutes. Remove from the heat, and add the lemon juice and lemon rind. Return to the stove, and continue cooking for 2 minutes.

In a small bowl, blend about ½ cup of the hot mixture into the egg yolks. Return the yolk mixture to the saucepan, and continue cooking for 2 more minutes, stirring constantly.

MERINGUE

3 egg whites
¼ teaspoon cream of tartar
¼ cup sugar
½ teaspoon vanilla extract

In a mixing bowl, beat the egg whites with the cream of tartar at high speed until soft peaks form. Gradually add the sugar, beating well after each addition. Add the vanilla. Continue beating until the meringue again forms soft peaks.

Nutritional information per serving

Calories 264, Protein (g) 4, Carbohydrate (g) 50, Fat (g) 6, Calories from Fat (%) 19, Saturated Fat (g) 1, Dietary Fiber (g) 1, Cholesterol (mg) 53, Sodium (mg) 81, Diabetic Exchanges: 3.5 other carbohydrate, 1 fat

QUICK TIP:

To beat egg whites: Place the egg whites in a clean glass or metal (not plastic) bowl. Beat with a mixer until peaks form. Any bit of fat, oil, or yolk in the bowl will prevent the whites from whipping.

DESSERTS & PIES

Blueberry Meringue Pie

Use this easy, terrific crust with any pie. No rolling necessary—just pat into a pie dish.

MAKES 8 SERVINGS

1 cup all-purpose flour
1 tablespoon light brown sugar
3 tablespoons canola oil
2 tablespoons cold water
½ cup water
½ cup plus 3 tablespoons sugar, divided
2 tablespoons cornstarch
¼ teaspoon ground cinnamon
4 cups blueberries
1 tablespoon lemon juice
2 egg whites

Preheat the oven to 350°F.

In a medium bowl, combine the flour and brown sugar. Add the oil, stirring with a fork until crumbly. Add 2 tablespoons cold water, and stir until the ingredients are moistened. Press the dough evenly over the bottom and up the sides of a 9-inch non-stick pie plate. Bake for 10 to 15 minutes, or until lightly browned.

In a large saucepan, combine ½ cup water, ½ cup sugar, and the cornstarch, stirring well. Cook over medium heat, stirring constantly, until smooth, thickened, and transparent, about 3 minutes. Add the cinnamon and blueberries, and continue cooking over low heat for about 15 minutes. Remove from the heat; add the lemon juice. Pour the mixture into the baked crust.

In a mixer, beat the egg whites until stiff. Gradually add 3 tablespoons sugar, and continue beating until stiff, glossy peaks form. Spread the meringue over the blueberries in the pie. Bake for 10 to 12 minutes, or until well browned. Watch carefully. Cool and serve. Refrigerate the leftovers.

Nutritional information per serving

Calories 228, Protein (g) 3, Carbohydrate (g) 43, Fat (g) 6, Calories from Fat (%) 21, Saturated Fat (g) 0, Dietary Fiber (g) 2, Cholesterol (mg) 0, Sodium (mg) 19, Diabetic Exchanges: 3 other carbohydrate, 1 fat

QUICK TIP:

Never freeze custard or cream pies with meringue topping, but baked fruit pies freeze fine. Well-wrapped frozen baked fruit pies keep up to four months in the freezer.

DESSERTS & PIES

Sweet Potato Pecan Crumble Pie ▨ ❄

This is the ultimate pie! The crumbly topping with the crunchy bottom and the rich filling make this the most outstanding sweet potato pie you will ever eat! For a lower-fat version, use the crust from the Blueberry Meringue Pie on the previous page.

MAKES 8 TO 10 SERVINGS

¼ cup plus ⅓ cup light brown sugar

½ cup chopped pecans, divided

1 unbaked (9-inch) pie shell

1 (15-ounce) can sweet potatoes (yams), drained

⅓ cup sugar

2 eggs

1½ teaspoons ground cinnamon, divided

¼ teaspoon ground allspice

1 (12-ounce) can evaporated skimmed milk

2 teaspoons vanilla extract, divided

½ cup all-purpose flour

3 tablespoons margarine

Preheat the oven to 425°F.

In a small bowl, combine ¼ cup brown sugar and ¼ cup pecans. Sprinkle on the bottom of the pie shell.

In a mixing bowl, mix together the sweet potato, sugar, eggs, 1 teaspoon cinnamon, allspice, milk, and 1 teaspoon vanilla until creamy. Pour into the pie shell, and bake for 15 minutes.

Reduce the oven temperature to 350°F, and continue baking for another 25 minutes.

Meanwhile, in a small bowl, mix together the remaining brown sugar and vanilla, flour, and the margarine with a fork until crumbly. Stir in the remaining pecans. Sprinkle over the pie, and continue baking for another 20 minutes, or until done. Cool for 15 minutes, and serve.

Nutritional information per serving

Calories 351, Protein (g) 7, Carbohydrate (g) 49, Fat (g) 15, Calories from Fat (%) 37, Saturated Fat (g) 4, Dietary Fiber (g) 2, Cholesterol (mg) 48, Sodium (mg) 205, Diabetic Exchanges: 3.5 other carbohydrate, 3 fat

German Chocolate Angel Pie

This light meringue filled with a heavenly chocolate mixture can be made several days ahead and stored in the freezer for later serving. An all-age pleaser.

MAKES 8 SERVINGS

3 egg whites, room temperature
¼ teaspoon salt
¼ teaspoon cream of tartar
¾ cup sugar
1 tablespoon plus 1 teaspoon vanilla extract, divided
1 (4-ounce) bar German sweet chocolate
3 tablespoons water
1 (8-ounce) container fat-free frozen whipped topping, thawed

Preheat the oven to 300°F.

In a medium bowl, beat the egg whites with the salt and cream of tartar until foamy. Add the sugar, 2 tablespoons at a time, beating well after each addition. Continue beating until stiff peaks form. Fold in 1 tablespoon vanilla. Spoon into a 9-inch glass pie plate coated with non-stick cooking spray, forming a nestlike shell. Bake for 45 minutes or until set. Cool.

In a microwave-safe bowl, melt the chocolate in the water for 30 seconds, stirring in the microwave until melted; cool. Add 1 teaspoon vanilla. Fold the cooled chocolate into the whipped topping. Spoon into the baked meringue shell. Freeze. Thaw slightly to serve.

Nutritional information per serving

Calories 198, Protein (g) 2, Carbohydrate (g) 37, Fat (g) 4, Calories from Fat (%) 17, Saturated Fat (g) 2, Dietary Fiber (g) 1, Cholesterol (mg) 0, Sodium (mg) 109, Diabetic Exchanges: 2.5 other carbohydrate, 1 fat

Vanilla Sauce

This sauce is the perfect companion to fresh fruit. Layer fresh berries with the sauce, or fill crêpes with berries and top with the sauce.

MAKES 12 (2-TABLESPOON) SERVINGS

1½ cups skim milk
¼ cup sugar
1 tablespoon cornstarch
1 tablespoon cold water
1 egg yolk
1 tablespoon vanilla extract

In a medium non-stick saucepan over medium heat, scald the milk and sugar.

In a measuring cup, dissolve the cornstarch in the water; add to the hot milk, stirring in gradually.

In a small bowl, pour some of the hot milk mixture into the egg yolk, and transfer back to the saucepan. Cook, stirring constantly, for 5 minutes, or until the mixture thickens slightly and comes to a boil. Remove from the heat, and add the vanilla. Cool and refrigerate.

Nutritional information per serving

Calories 37, Protein (g) 1, Carbohydrate (g) 6, Fat (g) 1, Calories from Fat (%) 12, Saturated Fat (g) 0, Dietary Fiber (g) 0, Cholesterol (mg) 18, Sodium (mg) 17, Diabetic Exchanges: 0.5 other carbohydrate

DESSERTS & PIES

Ice Cream Cone Cupcakes

Kids in the Kitchen

Surprise Rolls

My youngest daughter makes these rolls for break-fast, and her friends all want the recipe. I keep these ingredients on hand to be ready at any time.

MAKES 8 ROLLS

3 tablespoons light brown sugar
½ teaspoon ground cinnamon
8 large marshmallows
2 tablespoons margarine, melted
1 (8-ounce) can reduced-fat crescent dinner rolls

Preheat the oven to 375°F. Coat 8 muffin cups in a non-stick muffin tin with non-stick cooking spray or line with paper liners.

Mix the brown sugar and cinnamon together in a small bowl. Dip each marshmallow in the melted margarine, and roll in the sugar mixture.

Separate the crescent dough into triangles. Wrap one triangle around each marshmallow, and pinch the dough together. Place each one in a muffin tin. If there is any extra margarine, drizzle over the top of the rolls. Bake for 8 to 12 minutes or until lightly browned.

Serve immediately.

Nutritional information per serving

Calories 168, Protein (g) 2, Carbohydrate (g) 23, Fat (g) 7, Calories from Fat (%) 40, Saturated Fat (g) 1, Dietary Fiber (g) 0, Cholesterol (mg) 0, Sodium (mg) 276, Diabetic Exchanges: 1 starch, 0.5 other carbohydrate, 1 fat

Cinnamon Rolls

When you have the urge for a wonderful cinnamon roll, make this quick recipe using canned biscuits and common pantry ingredients. These are as good as those found in a bakery.

MAKES 10 ROLLS

1 (10-biscuit) can refrigerated biscuits
4 tablespoons margarine, softened
2 tablespoons sugar
1 teaspoon ground cinnamon
¼ cup raisins, optional
¼ cup chopped pecans, optional

Preheat the oven to 425°F.

Flatten each biscuit with your hand or a rolling pin, and spread with margarine.

In a small bowl, combine the sugar and cinnamon. Sprinkle the cinnamon mixture on top of the margarine. Sprinkle with the raisins and pecans, if desired. Roll up each biscuit from one side to the other.

On an ungreased 15 x 10 x 1-inch non-stick baking sheet, arrange each biscuit roll to form an individual circle, touching one end of the roll to the other. Bake for 8 to 10 minutes or until lightly browned. Serve hot.

Nutritional information per serving

Calories 101, Protein (g) 1, Carbohydrate (g) 12, Fat (g) 5, Calories from Fat (%) 46, Saturated Fat (g) 1, Dietary Fiber (g) 0, Cholesterol (mg) 0, Sodium (mg) 233, Diabetic Exchanges: 1 starch, 1 fat

Sticky Honey Buns ❄

The combination of biscuits dipped in honey and rolled in coconut is hard to beat.

MAKES 10 BUNS

1 (10-biscuit) can refrigerated biscuits
½ cup honey
1 cup flaked coconut
⅓ cup chopped pecans, optional

Preheat the oven to 400°F. Coat 10 muffin cups in a non-stick muffin tin with non-stick cooking spray or paper liners.

Cut each biscuit round into three pieces. Pour the honey into a small bowl; in another small bowl or on a plate, mix together the coconut and pecans. Dip each biscuit piece into the honey; then coat lightly (roll) with the coconut-pecan mixture. Place three coated biscuit pieces into each muffin cup. Bake for 15 minutes, or until the biscuits are golden brown and done.

Nutritional information per serving
Calories 137, Protein (g) 2, Carbohydrate (g) 27, Fat (g) 3, Calories from Fat (%) 19, Saturated Fat (g) 2, Dietary Fiber (g) 1, Cholesterol (mg) 0, Sodium (mg) 200, Diabetic Exchanges: 1 starch, 1 other carbohydrate, 0.5 fat

Egg in the Bread

This timeless recipe has had a dozen different names. No matter what you call it, it's a great way to start the day.

MAKES 1 EGG IN THE BREAD

1 slice white or whole wheat bread
1 teaspoon margarine
1 egg
Salt and pepper to taste

Cut a 2-inch-square hole in the center of the bread.

In a small non-stick skillet, heat the margarine until melted and sizzling, and place the bread in the skillet. Break the egg into the hole. Place the cut square of bread in the pan, and cook it, too. Cook over a medium heat until the egg white is set, about 3 minutes. Turn over with a spatula, and cook on the other side until the egg is done and set. Season with the salt and pepper to taste.

Nutritional information per serving
Calories 188, Protein (g) 9, Carbohydrate (g) 16, Fat (g) 10, Calories from Fat (%) 48, Saturated Fat (g) 2, Dietary Fiber (g) 1, Cholesterol (mg) 213, Sodium (mg) 269, Diabetic Exchanges: 1 medium-fat egg, 1 starch, 1 fat

Easy Bunny Biscuits

These biscuits are lots of fun to make and to eat. They turn breakfast into an exciting meal. Great for Easter.

MAKES 5 BISCUITS

1 (10-biscuit) can refrigerated biscuits
10 raisins
5 maraschino cherry halves
20 slivered almonds

Preheat the oven to 450°F. Place five biscuits on an ungreased 15 x 10 x 1-inch non-stick baking sheet.

To assemble the bunny biscuits: Cut the remaining biscuits in half, and pull a little to form ears. Press 2 biscuit halves (ears) under the top of each whole biscuit to form the bunny head. In each whole biscuit, press in two raisins for the eyes, a cherry half for the nose and two slivered almonds on each side of cherry half for the whiskers. Bake for 10 minutes, or until the biscuits are done. Serve immediately.

Nutritional information per serving

Calories 116, Protein (g) 3, Carbohydrate (g) 21, Fat (g) 2, Calories from Fat (%) 16, Saturated Fat (g) 0, Dietary Fiber (g) 1, Cholesterol (mg) 0, Sodium (mg) 360, Diabetic Exchanges: 1.5 fruit

Easy Bunny Biscuits

KIDS IN
THE KITCHEN

Ham and Cheese Breakfast Bake

For those slumber parties, here's a simple breakfast casserole that feeds a group. Prepare ahead, and pop in the oven the morning after.

MAKES 8 TO 10 SERVINGS

12 slices white or whole wheat bread
6 slices reduced-fat American cheese
4 ounces lean sliced ham, cut into pieces
3 eggs
4 egg whites
2½ cups skim milk
1 teaspoon prepared mustard
1 teaspoon Worcestershire sauce
Salt and pepper to taste

Preheat the oven to 350°F. Coat a 3-quart oblong baking dish with non-stick cooking spray.

Trim the crusts off the slices of bread and throw away; line the bottom of the dish with six slices of bread. Place a slice of cheese on top of each slice of bread. Sprinkle with the pieces of ham. Top with the remaining six slices of bread.

In a large bowl, blend together the eggs, egg whites, milk, mustard, Worcestershire sauce, salt, and pepper until well mixed. Pour the egg mixture evenly over the layered bread. Cover with plastic wrap, and refrigerate overnight or leave out at room temperature for 1 hour.

Bake for 45 minutes to 1 hour, or until puffed up, lightly browned, and the egg is cooked inside. Serve immediately.

Nutritional information per serving

Calories 191, Protein (g) 13, Carbohydrate (g) 22, Fat (g) 5, Calories from Fat (%) 25, Saturated Fat (g) 2, Dietary Fiber (g) 1, Cholesterol (mg) 76, Sodium (mg), 620 Diabetic Exchanges: 1 lean meat, 1.5 starch

QUICK TIP:

Use whatever cheese you desire in this recipe—reduced fat shredded Cheddar works great, too. This dish is the perfect way to start the day with calcium and protein.

Funny Faces

This fun recipe makes one face. A 16-ounce can of peaches contains about six peach halves, so adjust the ingredients accordingly. If you're serving these at a party, have several bowls of different-colored coconut available for a variety of hair colors.

MAKES 1 FUNNY FACE

1 canned peach half
2 raisins
1 maraschino cherry half
2 tablespoons flaked coconut
Few drops of food coloring

Place peach half on a small plate. With a tooth-pick, scoop out two tiny holes in the peach half, and push in the raisins for eyes. Place a cherry half on the lower part of the peach for the mouth.

In a small bowl, toss the coconut with a few drops of food coloring to make the hair the color you want. Arrange the colored coconut on the top and sides of the peach to complete the funny face.

Nutritional information per serving

Calories 93, Protein (g) 1, Carbohydrate (g) 17, Fat (g) 3, Calories from Fat (%) 28, Saturated Fat (g) 3, Dietary Fiber (g) 1, Cholesterol (mg) 0, Sodium (mg) 29, Diabetic Exchanges: 1 fruit, 0.5 fat

Rah-Rahs

Lots of little girls want to be cheerleaders, and this recipe allows you to create one of your own. Kids are more willing to try all these foods when they're prepared in creative way.

MAKES 1 RAH-RAH

1 canned peach half
½ hard-boiled egg
4 raisins
¼ maraschino cherry
Ruffled lettuce leaf, washed and drained
2 (2- to 3-inch) carrot sticks
2 (2- to 3-inch) celery sticks
2 tablespoons shredded reduced-fat Cheddar cheese

Place the peach half, cut side down, on a plate to form the body of your Rah-Rah. Place the hard-boiled egg half, cut side down, on top of the peach half to form the head. Make two tiny holes in the egg for the eyes; push in 2 raisins. Place the cherry piece under the raisins for the mouth. Place the lettuce leaf on the bottom of the peach, tucking the leaf under a little, for the skirt. Place a carrot stick on each side of the peach for arms, and place two celery sticks below the lettuce leaf for legs. Place the shredded cheese around the top and sides of the egg for the hair, and place 2 more raisins on the peach for buttons.

Nutritional information per serving

Calories 133, Protein (g) 8, Carbohydrate (g) 15, Fat (g) 5, Calories from Fat (%) 34, Saturated Fat (g) 3, Dietary Fiber (g) 1, Cholesterol (mg) 114, Sodium (mg) 136, Diabetic Exchanges: 1 medium-fat meat, 1 fruit

Friendly Dog Salad

A good choice for animal lovers. Name your salad after your dog.

MAKES 5 FRIENDLY DOG SALADS

5 canned pear halves (about one 16-ounce can)
5 ruffled lettuce leaves, washed and drained
10 large pitted prunes
10 raisins
5 maraschino cherry halves

Place one pear half, cut side down, on each lettuce leaf. Place a pitted prune on each side of the large end of the pear half for the ears. (Use 2 prunes for each pear half.) Scoop out two tiny holes in each pear half for the eyes, and place 1 raisin in each hole. Place a cherry half at the top of the narrow end of the pear half for the nose.

Nutritional information per serving

Calories 85, Protein (g) 1, Carbohydrate (g) 22, Fat (g) 0, Calories from Fat (%) 0, Saturated Fat (g) 0, Dietary Fiber (g) 3, Cholesterol (mg) 0, Sodium (mg) 3, Diabetic Exchanges: 1.5 fruit

Special Apple Salad

Use a combination of red and green apples to enjoy this delicious salad. Remember, an apple a day keeps the doctor away!

MAKES 8 SERVINGS

6 cups chopped apples (peel left on)
2 tablespoons lemon juice
½ cup chopped celery
⅓ cup raisins
1 cup miniature marshmallows
¼ cup light mayonnaise

In a bowl, toss the apples with the lemon juice to coat evenly. Mix in the celery, raisins, and marshmallows.

Stir in the mayonnaise until all is well coated, and store, covered, in the refrigerator until serving.

Nutritional information per serving
Calories 113, Protein (g) 1, Carbohydrate (g) 24, Fat (g) 3, Calories from Fat (%) 21, Saturated Fat (g) 0, Dietary Fiber (g) 2, Cholesterol (mg) 3, Sodium (mg) 71, Diabetic Exchanges: 1 starch, 0.5 other carbohydrate, 0.5 fat

Pizza Rice

Rice and pizza combine to make a child's dream team. Use as a main or a side dish; either way, it's a hit. Omit the green pepper if desired.

MAKES 4 TO 6 SERVINGS

1 small green bell pepper, seeded and chopped, optional
1 (14.5 ounce) can diced tomatoes, with juice
1 (.7-ounce) package Italian salad dressing mix
4 cups cooked rice
1 cup shredded part-skim Mozzarella cheese

In a small non-stick skillet, sauté the green pepper until tender. Set aside.

In a large pot, combine the tomatoes with the Italian dressing, mixing over a low heat. Stir in the cooked rice, green pepper, and cheese. Cook over low heat until well heated and the cheese is melted, 3 to 5 minutes. Serve.

Nutritional information per serving
Calories 205, Protein (g) 8, Carbohydrate (g) 35, Fat (g) 3, Calories from Fat (%) 15, Saturated Fat (g) 2, Dietary Fiber (g) 2, Cholesterol (mg) 11, Sodium (mg) 599, Diabetic Exchanges: 0.5 lean meat, 2 starch, 1 vegetable

Burger Soup

This soup is a great way to get veggies into your children's diets.

MAKES 8 SERVINGS

1 pound ground sirloin
1 onion, chopped
1 teaspoon minced garlic
1 (15-ounce) can tomato sauce
1 (14.5-ounce) can chopped tomatoes
4 cups water
Salt and pepper to taste
1 tablespoon Worcestershire sauce
1 bay leaf
1 cup sliced, peeled carrots (in rings)
1 (11-ounce) can corn niblets, drained
⅓ cup rice, uncooked

In a large non-stick pot, cook the meat, onion, and garlic until the meat is done. Drain any excess liquid. Add the tomato sauce, tomatoes, water, salt, pepper, Worcestershire sauce, bay leaf, and carrots. Bring to a boil, lower heat, and cook for 10 minutes.

Add the corn and rice, and continue cooking over medium heat until the rice is done and the carrots are tender, about 30 to 40 minutes. Add more water if it's too thick. Serve.

Nutritional information per serving

Calories 160, Protein (g) 14, Carbohydrate (g) 21, Fat (g) 3, Calories from Fat (%) 16, Saturated Fat (g) 1, Dietary Fiber (g) 3, Cholesterol (mg) 30, Sodium (mg) 482, Diabetic Exchanges: 1.5 very lean meat, 1 starch, 1 vegetable

Burger Soup

Cheesy Broccoli Soup

Broccoli is disguised in this nutritious soup. If you want a cheesier soup, add more cheese.

MAKES 6 TO 8 SERVINGS

1 tablespoon margarine
1 onion, chopped
½ cup all-purpose flour
3 cups fat-free canned chicken broth
2 (10-ounce) packages frozen chopped broccoli, thawed and drained
1½ cups skim milk
4 ounces reduced-fat pasteurized processed cheese spread, cut into cubes
Salt and pepper to taste

In a large non-stick saucepan, melt the margarine and sauté the onion over medium heat until tender, about 5 minutes. Blend in the flour, stirring. Gradually add the chicken broth, mixing until blended with the flour. Add the broccoli, stirring to combine. Bring the mixture to a boil, stirring, and reduce the heat to low. Cover and cook for 15 to 20 minutes, or until the broccoli is done and the soup thickens.

Add the milk, stirring until heated and thickened. Add the cheese cubes to the soup, stirring and cooking over low heat until the cheese is melted and smooth. Season with salt and pepper. Serve immediately.

Nutritional information per serving

Calories 120, Protein (g) 9, Carbohydrate (g) 15, Fat (g) 3, Calories from Fat (%) 24, Saturated Fat (g) 1, Dietary Fiber (g) 3, Cholesterol (mg) 7, Sodium (mg) 515, Diabetic Exchanges: 1 lean meat, 0.5 starch, 1 vegetable

KIDS IN THE KITCHEN

Creepy Crawlers and Reindeer Sandwiches

Creepy Crawlers

Kids will have lots of fun making these sandwiches. They will even eat the carrot strip "legs."

MAKES 1 SANDWICH

2 slices bread
2 teaspoons peanut butter or enough to cover bread
1 carrot, peeled and sliced into 8 sticks
2 raisins

To make a sandwich, cut circles out of 2 slices of bread with a round cookie cutter or a glass. Spread the peanut butter on top of one circle. Place 8 carrot sticks for "legs" on the edge of the circle, sticking out on both sides. Top with the other circle of the bread, and put two raisins on top for the eyes.

Nutritional information per serving

Calories 217, Protein (g) 7, Carbohydrate (g) 32, Fat (g) 7, Calories from Fat (%) 29, Saturated Fat (g) 1, Dietary Fiber (g) 4, Cholesterol (mg) 0, Sodium (mg) 317, Diabetic Exchanges: 0.5 high-fat meat, 1.5 starch, 1.5 vegetable

KIDS IN THE KITCHEN

Reindeer Sandwiches

* See photo on page 473
Year after year, each of my children volunteered me to make their favorite reindeer sandwiches for their school Christmas party. Get your kids to help make these ahead; cover with damp paper towels, refrigerate, and you're ready in a flash.

MAKES 1 REINDEER SANDWICH

1 tablespoon creamy peanut butter or enough to cover bread
2 slices bread
2 twisted pretzels
2 raisins
1 maraschino cherry, halved

Spread the peanut butter on one slice of bread, and top with the other slice. Cut a triangular shape in the sandwich, discarding the ends and remainder of the sandwich. Place a twisted pretzel between the two slices of bread on two points of the triangle to form the reindeer's antlers. Place two raisins for the eyes and a cherry half on the remaining point for the nose.

Nutritional information per serving
Calories 297, Protein (g) 10, Carbohydrate (g) 41, Fat (g) 11, Calories from Fat (%) 32, Saturated Fat (g) 2, Dietary Fiber (g) 3, Cholesterol (mg) 1, Sodium (mg) 629, Diabetic Exchanges: 0.5 high-fat meat, 2.5 starch, 1 fat

Jack-O'-Lantern Sandwiches

Year-round this can be a grilled cheese "face" sandwich, and in the fall it becomes the ideal Halloween sandwich.

MAKES 1 JACK-O'-LANTERN SANDWICH

2 slices dark bread (pumpernickel or dark whole wheat)
1 slice reduced-fat American cheese

On one slice of bread, cut out a jack-o'-lantern face. Place a slice of cheese on an uncut slice of bread. Broil or toast in the oven until the cheese is melted. Remove from the oven, and top with the cut slice of bread.

Nutritional information per serving
Calories 181, Protein (g) 10, Carbohydrate (g) 27, Fat (g) 5, Calories from Fat (%) 22, Saturated Fat (g) 2, Dietary Fiber (g) 3, Cholesterol (mg) 10, Sodium (mg) 683, Diabetic Exchanges: 1 lean meat, 2 starch

Open-Face Tic-Tac-Toe Sandwiches

Definitely more exciting than a ham and cheese sandwich, this will appeal to kids who like to play games. With this tic-tac-toe board, you're sure to be a winner.

MAKES 1 SANDWICH

1 slice reduced-fat American cheese
1 slice bread
½ slice reduced-fat processed Swiss cheese
½ slice extra lean ham
Circular carrot slices

To make an open-face sandwich, place the slice of American cheese on top of the slice of bread. Cut the piece of Swiss cheese into four narrow strips. Arrange the Swiss cheese strips on top of the American cheese to form a tic-tac-toe board. Cut the strips of ham to form X's, and put on the tic-tac-toe board in the pattern you wish. Use the carrot circles for the O's. Toast in a toaster oven or broil under a hot broiler until the cheese bubbles. Serve immediately.

Nutritional information per serving

Calories 173, Protein (g) 13, Carbohydrate (g) 18, Fat (g) 6, Calories from Fat (%) 31, Saturated Fat (g) 3, Dietary Fiber (g) 1, Cholesterol (mg) 22, Sodium (mg) 854, Diabetic Exchanges: 1.5 lean meat, 1 starch

Cheese Quesadillas

These make a great snack or dinner. If you have leftover chicken, add with the cheese. Of course, include whatever ingredients you prefer.

2 (6- or 8-inch) flour tortillas
½ cup reduced-fat Cheddar or Monterey Jack cheese
Taco sauce, as desired

MAKES 3 SERVINGS

In a non-stick pan coated with non-stick cooking spray, on low heat, place one flour tortilla. Sprinkle with the cheese, and top with the other flour tortilla. Cook about 1 to 1½ minutes on each side, turning with a spatula, until the cheese is melted and the tortillas are light brown. Watch carefully. Cut into six wedges, and serve with taco sauce.

Nutritional information per serving

Calories 110, Protein (g) 7, Carbohydrate (g) 12, Fat (g) 3, Calories from Fat (%) 28, Saturated Fat (g) 2, Dietary Fiber (g) 1, Cholesterol (mg) 10, Sodium (mg) 294, Diabetic Exchanges: 0.5 lean meat, 1 starch

Mini Cheese Pizzas

Keep these ingredients around for a quick snack or lunch. Add pepperoni, if desired.

MAKES 10 PIZZAS

1 (10-biscuit) can flaky refrigerated biscuits
⅓ cup tomato sauce
½ teaspoon dried oregano leaves
½ cup shredded part-skim mozzarella cheese

Preheat the oven to 450°F.

Pat each biscuit into a 4-inch circle on a non-stick baking sheet coated with non-stick cooking spray.

In a small bowl, mix together the tomato sauce and oregano, and spoon the sauce on each biscuit round. Sprinkle the cheese over the tomato sauce, and bake for 8 to 10 minutes, or until the cheese is melted. Serve immediately.

Nutritional information per serving
Calories 67, Protein (g) 3, Carbohydrate (g) 10, Fat (g) 2, Calories from Fat (%) 21, Saturated Fat (g) 1, Dietary Fiber (g) 0, Cholesterol (mg) 3, Sodium (mg), 252, Diabetic Exchanges: 0.5 starch

KIDS IN THE KITCHEN

Mexican Pizza

My daughter Haley loves to have her friends over for parties, and their standard request is my home-made pizza. I tried this Mexican version, and not a piece was left.

MAKES 8 SERVINGS

½ pound ground sirloin
1 tablespoon chili powder
1 teaspoon ground cumin
1 (10-ounce) Boboli crust or pizza crust
1 cup salsa
1½ cups reduced-fat Monterey Jack cheese

Preheat the oven to 450°F.

In a small non-stick skillet, cook the meat until browned. Drain any excess grease. Add the chili powder and cumin. Cover the pizza crust with the salsa, cheese, and seasoned meat. Bake for 8 minutes, or until crisp. Slice, and serve.

Nutritional information per serving

Calories 201, Protein (g) 16, Carbohydrate (g) 17, Fat (g) 7, Calories from Fat (%) 33, Saturated Fat (g) 3, Dietary Fiber (g) 1, Cholesterol (mg) 27, Sodium (mg) 486, Diabetic Exchanges: 2 lean meat, 1 starch

Sweet Potato Pizza

Here's a fun way to introduce this nutritious veggie to the kids. A pizza always gets their attention. For a variation, sprinkle with marsh-mallows and cinnamon instead of sugar.

MAKES 6 TO 8 SERVINGS

4 to 5 cups thinly sliced fresh sweet potatoes (yams), peeled
¼ cup light brown sugar
1 teaspoon ground cinnamon
¼ teaspoon ground nutmeg

Preheat the oven to 400°F. Coat a 12-inch non-stick pizza pan with non-stick cooking spray.

Arrange the sweet potato slices to cover the pizza pan, overlapping the slices. Spray the slices with non-stick cooking spray. Bake 15 minutes or until tender.

In a small bowl, mix together the brown sugar, cinnamon, and nutmeg, and sprinkle evenly over the potato slices. Return to the oven, and continue baking until the potato slices are crispy, 5 to 10 minutes more. Slice, and serve immediately.

Nutritional information per serving

Calories 97, Protein (g) 1, Carbohydrate (g) 23, Fat (g) 0, Calories from Fat (%) 0, Saturated Fat (g) 0, Dietary Fiber (g) 2, Cholesterol (mg) 0, Sodium (mg) 11, Diabetic Exchanges: 1 starch, 0.5 other carbohydrate

Meatballs and Spaghetti ❄

Believe it or not, my mother turns to this basic but simple and delicious recipe for her meatballs and spaghetti. The younger ones will like the smooth sauce with no "green things" in it, yet grown-ups find there's plenty of flavor.

2 pounds ground sirloin
½ cup Italian bread crumbs
2 tablespoons grated Parmesan cheese
2 egg whites
1 tablespoon chopped parsley
½ teaspoon garlic powder
1 teaspoon dried oregano leaves
1 teaspoon dried basil leaves
Sauce (recipe follows)
1 (16-ounce) package spaghetti

MAKES 8 SERVINGS

Preheat the broiler.

In a large bowl, combine the meat, bread crumbs, Parmesan cheese, egg whites, parsley, garlic powder, oregano, and basil, mixing well to combine. With moistened hands, shape the meat mixture into balls. Place the meatballs on a non-stick baking sheet coated with non-stick cooking spray. Broil the meatballs for 5 to 7 minutes on each side; remove from the oven and add to the sauce (see recipe at right).

Bring sauce to a boil, reduce the heat, and continue cooking for about 30 minutes.

Meanwhile, prepare the spaghetti according to the package directions; drain. Serve the cooked spaghetti with the meatballs.

SAUCE

1 (28-ounce) can tomato purée
1 (8-ounce) can tomato sauce
1 teaspoon dried oregano leaves
1 teaspoon dried basil leaves

In a large non-stick pot, combine the tomato purée, tomato sauce, oregano, and basil. Cook over medium heat, stirring occasionally, until thoroughly heated, 4 to 6 minutes.

Nutritional information per serving

Calories 431, Protein (g) 34, Carbohydrate (g) 59, Fat (g) 7, Calories from Fat (%) 14, Saturated Fat (g) 2, Dietary Fiber (g) 4, Cholesterol (mg) 61, Sodium (mg) 774, Diabetic Exchanges: 3 lean meat, 3 starch, 2 vegetable

Sloppy Joes

This oldie-but-goodie is easy to throw together for a quick dinner—corn is a great addition.

MAKES 4 SLOPPY JOES

1 pound ground sirloin
1 small onion, chopped
1 (8-ounce) can tomato sauce
2 tablespoons light brown sugar
½ teaspoon paprika
Salt and pepper to taste
1 (7-ounce) can whole kernel corn, drained
4 hamburger buns, toasted

In a large non-stick skillet, cook the meat and onion until done, about 5 minutes; drain any excess liquid. Add the tomato sauce, brown sugar, paprika, salt, pepper, and corn. Cook over medium-low heat about 10 minutes, or until well heated and combined. To serve, spoon the meat mixture over the toasted buns.

Nutritional information per serving

Calories 335, Protein (g) 28, Carbohydrate (g) 42, Fat (g) 7, Calories from Fat (%) 19, Saturated Fat (g) 3, Dietary Fiber (g) 3, Cholesterol (mg) 60, Sodium (mg) 724, Diabetic Exchanges: 3 lean meat, 2.5 starch, 1 vegetable

Sloppy Joes

Baby Burgers

These are fun to make, and they look like real burgers. Mint lovers will love these.

MAKES 24 BURGERS

Few drops water
Few drops green food coloring
¼ cup flaked coconut
48 reduced-fat vanilla wafers
24 chocolate-covered peppermint patties, unwrapped
Water
½ to 1 teaspoon sesame seeds

Preheat the oven to 350°F.

In a small bowl, combine the water with the green food coloring. Add the coconut, and toss until all of the coconut is tinted green; set aside.

Place half the vanilla wafers, flat side up, on an ungreased non-stick baking sheet. Place one mint patty on each of the vanilla wafers. Place in the oven for about 1 minute, or just until the chocolate begins to soften. Remove from the oven, and sprinkle each with ½ teaspoon tinted coconut. Top with another vanilla wafer, flat side down, and press gently. Using your finger, dab the top of each vanilla wafer with just enough water to moisten, and sprinkle with a few sesame seeds.

Nutritional information per serving
Calories 89, Protein (g) 1, Carbohydrate (g) 18, Fat (g) 2, Calories from Fat (%) 18, Saturated Fat (g) 1, Dietary Fiber (g) 0, Cholesterol (mg) 0, Sodium (mg) 32, Diabetic Exchanges: 0.5 starch, 0.5 other carbohydrate

Popcorn Cake

Popcorn Cake 🥕

This colorful treat will tantalize your taste buds with sweet and salt in every bite.

MAKES ABOUT 20 POPCORN CAKES

½ cup unpopped plain popcorn
Dash salt, optional
4 cups miniature marshmallows
½ cup margarine
⅔ cup candy-coated milk chocolate candies

Pop the popcorn according to the package directions. Add salt if desired; set aside to cool.

In a medium pot, melt the marshmallows and margarine over low heat, stirring constantly, until smooth. Combine the candy coated milk chocolate candies with the popcorn. Remove the marshmallow mixture from the heat, and pour over the popcorn and candies. Mix gently. Spoon the mixture into a 13 x 9 x 2-inch non-stick pan or a 2-quart oblong pan coated with non-stick cooking spray. Refrigerate until the mixture until it hardens, so it's easier to cut.

Nutritional information per serving

Calories 126, Protein (g) 1, Carbohydrate (g) 16, Fat (g) 7, Calories from Fat (%) 46, Saturated Fat (g) 2, Dietary Fiber (g) 1, Cholesterol (mg) 1, Sodium (mg) 63, Diabetic Exchanges: 1 other carbohydrate, 1 fat

Ice Cream Cone Cupcakes

Ice Cream Cone Cupcakes

Be creative: use different-flavored cake mixes, and frostings, and top the icing with sprinkles. For a time-saver, use reduced-fat canned frosting.

MAKES 18 TO 24 CONE CUPCAKES

1 (18.25-ounce) box yellow cake mix
24 flat-bottomed wafer ice cream cones
6 tablespoons margarine
1 (16-ounce) box confectioners' sugar
3 to 4 tablespoons skim milk
1 teaspoon vanilla extract

Preheat the oven to 350°F.

Prepare the cake mix batter according to the package directions.

Spoon the batter into the cones, filling three-quarters full, and place the cones in muffin pans. Bake according to the package directions for cupcakes. Cool.

To prepare the icing, in a mixing bowl, beat together the margarine and confectioners' sugar, adding enough milk to reach spreading consistency. Add the vanilla. Ice each cone cupcake.

Nutritional information per serving

Calories 207, Protein (g) 1, Carbohydrate (g) 39, Fat (g) 5, Calories from Fat (%) 22, Saturated Fat (g) 1, Dietary Fiber (g) 1, Cholesterol (mg) 0, Sodium (mg) 176, Diabetic Exchanges: 2.5 other carbohydrate, 1 fat

KIDS IN THE KITCHEN

Clowns

Turn crispy rice treats into the head of your clown. Use different candies and colors to individualize your own clown.

MAKES 10 CLOWNS

4 cups miniature marshmallows
3 tablespoons margarine
6 cups crispy rice cereal
20 muffin paper cups
Reduced-fat creamy peanut butter, as needed
10 sugar ice cream cones
Small assorted gum drops, sliced crosswise in half
5 red jelly beans, sliced lengthwise in half

In a large, heavy non-stick pot, mix together the marshmallows and margarine over low heat, stirring constantly, until the marshmallows are melted and the mixture is smooth. Remove from the heat. Add the cereal, and stir gently to coat evenly. Cool the mixture about 5 minutes, or until it can be handled easily. Shape into ten balls (put margarine on your hands to keep the mixture from sticking to them). Place the balls on waxed paper, and let stand until firm (about 30 minutes).

Flatten 2 paper muffin cups for the base, and place a cereal ball on top for the head. For the hat, spread peanut butter (as your glue) on the edge of the open end of a sugar cone, and attach the cereal ball. Spread a tiny bit of peanut butter on 2 gum drop halves to make them stick to the cereal ball for the eyes. Spread a tiny bit of peanut butter on 3 gum drop halves to make them stick on the cone hat for the pom-poms. Spread peanut butter on a jelly bean half for the mouth on the cereal ball. Repeat with remaining cereal bars.

Nutritional information per serving
Calories 198, Protein (g) 2, Carbohydrate (g) 39, Fat (g) 4, Calories from Fat (%) 18, Saturated Fat (g) 1, Dietary Fiber (g) 0, Cholesterol (mg) 0, Sodium (mg) 204 Diabetic Exchanges: 1 starch, 1.5 other carbohydrate, 0.5 fat

Ooey Gooey Squares

My daughter Haley whips up these most requested squares for parties and friends all the time.

MAKES 48 SQUARES

1 (18.25-ounce) package yellow cake mix
½ cup margarine, melted
1 egg
1 tablespoon water
1 (8-ounce) package fat-free or reduced-fat cream cheese
1 (16-ounce) box confectioners' sugar
2 egg whites
1 teaspoon vanilla extract
1 cup semisweet chocolate chips

Preheat the oven to 350°F. Coat a 13 x 9 x 2-inch non-stick baking pan with non-stick cooking spray.

In a mixing bowl, beat together the cake mix, margarine, egg, and water until well mixed. Spread the batter into the bottom of the pre-pared pan.

In a mixing bowl, beat together the cream cheese, confectioners' sugar, egg whites, and vanilla. Stir in the chocolate chips. Pour this mixture over the batter in the pan. Bake for 40 to 50 minutes, or until the top is golden brown. Cool and cut into squares.

Nutritional information per serving

Calories 122, Protein (g) 2, Carbohydrate (g) 21, Fat (g) 4, Calories from Fat (%) 29, Saturated Fat (g) 1, Dietary Fiber (g) 0, Cholesterol (mg) 5, Sodium (mg) 117, Diabetic Exchanges: 1.5 other carbohy-drate, 1 fat

Ooey Gooey Squares

Double Chocolate Candy Pizza

This recipe has made me the most popular mom throughout all three of my kids' younger years of school. Now my daughters make it themselves, and it's requested by all their friends. Every time I make this for the kids, the adults are the first to grab a piece. Cut into small squares to please a crowd.

MAKES 12 TO 16 SLICES

½ cup margarine
1 cup sugar
1 egg
1 teaspoon vanilla extract
1½ cups all-purpose flour
¼ cup cocoa
½ teaspoon baking soda
1 cup candy-coated milk chocolate candies, divided
¼ cup flaked coconut
1½ cups miniature marshmallows
½ cup chopped pecans, optional

Preheat the oven to 350ºF. Coat a 12- to 14-inch non-stick pizza pan with non-stick cooking spray.

In a large mixing bowl, beat together the margarine and sugar until fluffy. Add the egg and vanilla, blending well.

In a small bowl, combine the flour, cocoa, and baking soda. Gradually add to the sugar mixture, blending until well mixed.

Spread the dough on the prepared pan, spreading the dough to within 1 inch of the edge of the pan. Sprinkle the dough with the candies, coconut, marshmallows, and pecans. Bake 18 to 20 minutes, or until the edges are set. Don't overbake. Cool, and cut into slices.

Nutritional information per serving

Calories 235, Protein (g) 3, Carbohydrate (g) 36, Fat (g) 9, Calories from Fat (%) 35, Saturated Fat (g) 3, Dietary Fiber (g) 1, Cholesterol (mg) 15, Sodium (mg) 123, Diabetic Exchanges: 2.5 other carbohydrate, 2 fat

QUICK TIP:

Use seasonal candies to keep in the holiday spirit on Halloween, Thanksgiving, Christmas, Valentine's Day, and Easter.

KIDS IN THE KITCHEN

Double Chocolate Candy Pizza

Double Chocolate Box Cookies

Start with a cake mix to make these outstanding cookies—even the finest baker won't suspect.

MAKES 36 TO 48 COOKIES

1 (18.25-ounce) box devil's food cake mix
3 tablespoons canola oil
1 egg
2 egg whites
¾ cup semisweet chocolate chips

Preheat the oven to 350°F. Coat a non-stick baking sheet with non-stick cooking spray.

In a mixing bowl, beat together the cake mix, oil, egg, and egg whites until creamy. Stir in the chocolate chips. Drop by rounded teaspoons onto the prepared baking sheet. Bake for 10 minutes, or until lightly browned.

Cool on a wire rack or waxed paper.

Nutritional information per serving
Calories 67, Protein (g) 1, Carbohydrate (g) 10, Fat (g) 3, Calories from Fat (%) 36, Saturated Fat (g) 1, Dietary Fiber (g) 0, Cholesterol (mg) 4, Sodium (mg) 87, Diabetic Exchanges: 0.5 other carbohydrate, 0.5 fat

Simple Sensational Chocolate Cake

This perfect beginner's cake uses four simple ingredients with simple instructions to create a mouthwatering chocolate cake with a moist, puddinglike texture.

MAKES 36 SERVINGS

1 (4-serving) package cook-and-serve chocolate pudding mix
2 cups skim milk
1 (18.25-ounce) package devil's food cake mix
⅔ cup semisweet chocolate chips

Coat a 13 x 9 x 2-inch non-stick baking pan with non-stick cooking spray.

Prepare the pudding mix according to the package directions, using the skim milk; cool to room temperature.

Preheat the oven to 350°F.

In a bowl, stir together the cake mix and the prepared chocolate pudding. Spread into the prepared pan. Sprinkle with the chocolate chips. Bake for 25 to 30 minutes, or until a toothpick inserted in the center comes out clean. Don't overbake. Cool, and cut into squares.

Nutritional information per serving
Calories 89, Protein (g) 1, Carbohydrate (g) 16, Fat (g) 2, Calories from Fat (%) 23, Saturated Fat (g) 1, Dietary Fiber (g) 1, Cholesterol (mg) 0, Sodium (mg) 129, Diabetic Exchanges: 1 other carbohydrate

Chelsea
Mint Brownies

This easy brownie recipe with mint filling and bitter chocolate glaze is impressive. With your eyes closed, you will think you are eating a delicious chocolate mint. This is a great holiday recipe—you can use food coloring to match your holiday theme.

MAKES 48 BROWNIES

1 (22.5-ounce) box reduced-fat or regular brownie mix
¾ teaspoon peppermint extract, divided
3 tablespoons reduced-fat cream cheese
3 tablespoons margarine, melted, divided
2 cups confectioners' sugar
Few drops green food coloring
1 tablespoon cocoa
1 tablespoon water

Preheat the oven to 350°F. Coat a 13 x 9 x 2-inch non-stick baking pan with non-stick cooking spray.

Prepare the brownie mix according to package directions, adding ¼ teaspoon of the peppermint extract. Pour the batter into the prepared pan. Bake according to the package directions. Do not overbake. Remove from the oven, and cool completely to room temperature.

In a mixing bowl, beat together the cream cheese, 1 tablespoon margarine, the confectioners' sugar, and ½ teaspoon peppermint extract until smooth. Add a few drops of green food coloring, mixing. Spread on the baked brownie layer.

In a small bowl, mix together the remaining margarine, cocoa, and water. Spread carefully over the cream cheese layer, and cool. Cut into squares.

Nutritional information per serving
Calories 83, Protein (g) 1, Carbohydrate (g) 16, Fat (g) 2, Calories from Fat (%) 20, Saturated Fat (g) 1, Dietary Fiber (g) 0, Cholesterol (mg) 1, Sodium (mg) 60, Diabetic Exchanges: 1 other carbohydrate, 0.5 fat

QUICK TIP:

If you're in a hurry to cool the brownie layer, place it in the refrigerator to cool it quickly. Make sure that you don't put the hot pan next to something that will be affected by its heat.

KIDS IN THE KITCHEN

All-American Crunch

Shhh! Cake mix and canned fillings are key ingredients for this rich tasting dessert.

MAKES 16 SERVINGS

1 (21-ounce) can cherry pie filling
1 (21-ounce) can blueberry pie filling
1 (18.25-ounce) package white cake mix
⅓ cup chopped pecans
⅓ cup flaked coconut
½ cup margarine, melted

Preheat the oven to 350°F.

In the bottom of a 13 x 9 x 2-inch non-stick baking pan, spread the cherry pie filling and blueberry pie filling in a striped pattern, making sure the bottom of the pan is completely covered. Keep each pie filling separate to form a flag design on the bottom. Sprinkle the dry cake mix evenly over the filling. Do not stir. Sprinkle the top with the pecans and coconut, and pour the melted margarine evenly over the top.

Bake for 30 minutes, or until browned. Serve immediately or at room temperature.

Nutritional information per serving
Calories 286, Protein (g) 2, Carbohydrate (g) 45, Fat (g) 11, Calories from Fat (%) 35, Saturated Fat (g) 2, Dietary Fiber (g) 1, Cholesterol (mg) 0, Sodium (mg) 276, Diabetic Exchanges: 3 other carbohydrate, 2 fat

Munch Mix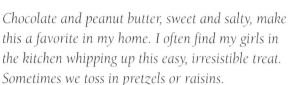

Chocolate and peanut butter, sweet and salty, make this a favorite in my home. I often find my girls in the kitchen whipping up this easy, irresistible treat. Sometimes we toss in pretzels or raisins.

MAKES 32 (¼-CUP) SERVINGS

1¼ cups reduced-fat peanut butter
1¼ cups semisweet chocolate chips
1 (15.2-ounce) box honey nut oven-toasted rice and corn cereal squares
1 cup confectioners' sugar

In a microwave-safe bowl or in a non-stick pan on the stovetop, melt the peanut butter and chocolate chips together. Mix with the cereal.

In a large, shallow container with a lid, place half the confectioners' sugar and all of the cereal mixture, then the remaining confectioners' sugar. Shake until evenly coated.

Nutritional information per serving
Calories 149, Protein (g) 4, Carbohydrate (g) 23, Fat (g) 6, Calories from Fat (%) 32, Saturated Fat (g) 2, Dietary Fiber (g) 1, Cholesterol (mg) 0, Sodium (mg) 157, Diabetic Exchanges: 1 starch, 0.5 other carbohydrate, 1 fat

Ghost Suckers

I can't even count the times I made these for Halloween favors at my kids' school parties when they were younger.

MAKES AS MANY AS YOU WANT

Sheet of white tissue paper
Round lollipop suckers
Black string licorice
Black marker

Place a sheet of white tissue paper over the top of each sucker. Gather under the candy, and tie the tissue with the black string licorice. With the black marker, make two dots on your ghost for eyes.

Nutritional information per serving
Calories 59, Protein (g) 0, Carbohydrate (g) 14, Fat (g) 0, Calories from Fat (%) 0, Saturated Fat (g) 0, Dietary Fiber (g) 0, Cholesterol (mg) 0, Sodium (mg) 17, Diabetic Exchanges: 1 other carbohydrate

Strawberry Smoothie

This makes a great snack, and my girls can whip these up themselves in the blender (or food processor). Refreshing, soothing, and delicious.

MAKES 3 SERVINGS

2 cups strawberries, fresh or frozen
2 tablespoons sugar
1 teaspoon lemon juice
1 cup low-fat vanilla yogurt

In a food processor or blender, mix together at high speed the strawberries, sugar, lemon juice, and yogurt until well blended. Serve immediately or refrigerate.

Nutritional information per serving
Calories 131, Protein (g) 5, Carbohydrate (g) 26, Fat (g) 1, Calories from Fat (%) 9, Saturated Fat (g) 1, Dietary Fiber (g) 2, Cholesterol (mg) 4, Sodium (mg) 55, Diabetic Exchanges: 1 skim milk, 0.5 fruit, 0.5 other carbohydrate

KIDS IN THE KITCHEN

Strawberry Heart Cake

This awesome cake is too good to save for just Valentine's Day. Turn it into a round layered cake year-round with 9-inch round pans. It begins with a cake mix and is easy to make.

MAKES 16 SERVINGS

1 (18.25-ounce) box white cake mix
¼ cup canola oil
2 eggs
2 egg whites
1 (3-ounce) package strawberry gelatin
½ (10-ounce) package frozen sliced strawberries (½ cup)
 (reserve extra for frosting)
½ cup skim milk
Strawberry Frosting (recipe follows)

Preheat the oven to 350°F. Coat one 9 x 9 x 2-inch non-stick square pan and one 9-inch non-stick round cake pan with non-stick cooking spray.

In a mixing bowl, combine the cake mix, oil, eggs, egg whites, strawberry gelatin, ½ cup strawberries, and milk, mixing until well blended. Divide the batter, and pour into the prepared pans. Bake for 25 to 30 minutes, or until a wooden toothpick inserted in the center comes out clean. Remove from the pans, and cool completely.

To form the heart: Place the square cake on a large platter. Cut the round cake in half, and place each half with the cut side next to the square side. You may need to trim corners. This now makes a heart. Turn the cakes so the square cake's pointed end is down and the round halves are at the top. Frost the heart cake with Strawberry Frosting (see recipe below).

STRAWBERRY FROSTING

3 tablespoons margarine
1 (16-ounce) box confectioners' sugar
½ (10-ounce) package frozen sliced strawberries (½ cup)

In a medium mixing bowl, mix together the margarine, confectioners' sugar, and remaining strawberries until well blended.

Nutritional information per serving
Calories 336, Protein (g) 3, Carbohydrate (g) 60, Fat (g) 9, Calories from Fat (%) 25, Saturated Fat (g) 2, Dietary Fiber (g) 1, Cholesterol (mg) 27, Sodium (mg) 262, Diabetic Exchanges: 4 other carbohydrate, 2 fat

Strawberry Heart Cake

Fruit Dip

Stock Your Pantry

One way to encourage nutritional meals and ease preparation is to have a stocked pantry. Many of the recipes in this book call for the following simple ingredients—keep these foods on hand, and you can have a quick and healthy meal every day!

Refrigerator Staples

Biscuits, refrigerated
Cheese, varieties and
   reduced fat
Cream Cheese, reduced fat
Eggs
Fruit, assorted
Garlic, chopped in a jar
Garlic, fresh
Green Onions (scallions)
Horseradish
Lemon juice
Lime juice
Margarine or Butter
Milk, skim and Buttermilk
Mixed greens
Onions, yellow and red
Peppers, green
Pie crust
Ricotta cheese, light
Sour cream, fat free or
   reduced fat
Vegetables, assorted
Yogurt, fat free or
   reduced fat

Pantry Staples

Barley
Bread, whole wheat or white
Bread crumbs, Italian or plain
Broth, canned, cubed,
   or powdered
Bulgur (yes, try using it!)
Couscous
Evaporated skimmed milk
Oil, canola, olive, sesame
Pasta, assorted shapes and
   flavors
Peanut butter, reduced fat
Pizza crusts, focaccia bread
   or Boboli
Potatoes, baking, red, sweet
Rice, white, wild, yellow, brown
Salsa
Tortillas, reduced fat
Tuna fish, white or salmon,
   canned

Baking Staples

Almond extract
Baking powder
Baking soda
Butter extract
Cake mix, assorted
Chocolate chips, semisweet
Cocoa
Coconut extract
Coconut, flaked
Cornstarch
Dried fruit, assorted
Flour, all purpose, self-rising
   whole wheat
German chocolate bar
Graham crackers
Instant pudding, assorted
Non-stick cooking spray
Nuts, assorted
Oatmeal
Sugar, brown
Sugar, confectioners'
Sugar, granulated
Sweetened condensed milk,
   fat free or reduced fat
Vanilla extract
White chocolate chips

Condiment Staples

Capers
Honey
Hot sauce
Ketchup
Mayonnaise, light
  or reduced fat
Mustard, Dijon or
  yellow
Roasted red peppers,
  jarred
Salad dressing, fat
  free or reduced fat
Salsa
Soy sauce
Spaghetti sauce,
  jarred
Vinegar, balsamic
  cider, distilled
Worcestershire sauce

Spice Pantry Staples

Basil leaves
Bay leaves
Chili powder
Cilantro (Coriander)
Cinnamon, ground
Cumin, ground
Curry
Dill weed leaves
Garlic powder
Ginger, ground
Mustard, ground
Nutmeg, ground
Oregano leaves
Paprika
Parsley flakes
Pepper, black
Pepper, coarse
  ground
Red pepper flakes
Rosemary leaves
Salt
Tarragon leaves
Thyme leaves

Canned Staples

Artichokes
Beans, assorted
Black olives
Broth, beef
Broth, chicken
Broth, vegetable
Corn
Creamed soups,
  reduced fat
Evaporated skim milk
Fruit, assorted
Green chilies, diced
Sweet Potatoes
  (yams)
Tomato paste
Tomato sauce
Tomatoes and green
  chilies, diced
Tomatoes, diced
Tuna and salmon

Frozen Staples

Chicken breasts
Pork tenders
Fish
Vegetables
Frozen yogurt
Ice cream, fat free
  or reduced fat
Shrimp
Sirloin, ground, roast
Turkey breast
Whipped topping,
  fat free

Back to Basics

Common Cooking Methods

Microwave

- Advantages: short cooking time, few nutrients lost, colors and flavors stay bright.
- Put a small amount of water in the dish; cover to create steam.
- Cook at 100% power. Halfway through, stir and rearrange food.

Boiling

- Advantages: Easy; good for tough vegetables.
- Disadvantages: Nutrients often leech out of food, vegetables become soggy, not crisp-tender (exceptions include potatoes, sweet potatoes, and corn).
- Immerse vegetables in enough water to cover.

Roasting

- Advantages: good for thick-skinned vegetables such as potatoes and winter squash.
- To roast vegetables, peel them and cut into large chunks. Toss with a little olive oil to avoid sticking.
- Roast vegetables in an oven at 350 to 400 degrees until tender.

Steaming

- Advantages: quick, and doesn't waterlog vegetables. A gentle way to cook.
- Watch your pot closely so it doesn't boil dry (no water).
- Use a steamer basket or platform to lift vegetables our of the water. Bring water to a boil, add vegetables, cover and reduce heat to cook until tender.
- The liquid should not touch the food; leave room for the steam to circulate.

Stir-Frying

- Advantages: efficient, since pieces have plenty or room to move in the pan, allowing surfaces constant exposure to heat. Reduces amount of fat needed to cook dense vegetables; brings out a great flavor.
- Cut vegetables into small, even pieces and stir over intensely high heat with small amount of fat and liquid.

Herbs

Common Herbs

Basil: Minty, clovelike flavor, and a key ingredient in Mediterranean and Italian cooking (pesto and tomato sauces), salads, stews, meats, and eggs. Basil is a summer herb, but during the winter it can be grown successfully inside in a sunny window. Available dried.

Bay leaf: This pungent, woodsy herb from the evergreen bay laurel tree, native to the Mediterranean, is mostly available dried. Bay leaves are used to flavor soups, stews, sauces, vegetables, and meats. They are removed before serving. Fresh bay leaves are seldom used in cooking.

Bouquet garni: A bunch of herbs (usually parsley, thyme, and bay leaf) that are tied together or placed in a cheesecloth bag and used to flavor soups, stews and broths. The tied bag is easily removed before the dish is served.

Chervil: A mild-flavored member of the parsley family with a distinctive anise tarragon flavor. Chervil can be used like parsley and is best fresh. Used with eggs, fish, salads, sauces, soups, and stuffing.

Chives: Mild onion flavor; available fresh year-round. Fresh chives can be snipped with scissors and will grow back after cutting. Best to add right before serving to retain their flavor. Chives are used to flavor appetizers, soups, eggs, and salads. Dried chives don't have the same flavor as fresh.

Cilantro: Also known as coriander or Chinese parsley, cilantro has a distinct aromatic flavor and is used in Asian, Caribbean, and Latin American cooking. Cilantro is available year-round and is sold in bunches. Season to taste—a little goes a long way.

Dill weed: A delicate, tangy, lemony taste. Use with fish, seafood, salads, egg dishes, breads, sauces, and vegetables. Fresh dill leaves are available in late summer and early fall. Available dried.

Marjoram: Also sweet marjoram. Marjoram belongs to the mint family and has a mild, sweet, oregano-like flavor. Most often found dried. Used to flavor lamb, veal, poultry, fish, stews, soups, and vegetables. Available dried.

Mint: Peppermint has a sharp and pungent flavor; spearmint is more delicate. Both have a sweet, refreshing flavor and a cool aftertaste. Mint is available year-round but is more plentiful in the summer months; dried mint flakes retain their flavor well. Mint is used in both sweet and savory dishes (like Mediterranean cooking) to flavor sauces, vegetables, jellies, fruit, alcoholic beverages, and as garnish for desserts.

Oregano: Belongs to the mint family and is related to marjoram and thyme. Oregano has a robust, pungent flavor and aroma. It makes an attractive small plant, and is an easy perennial to grow. Great with pizza or any Italian dish, soups, tomato-based dishes, sauces, vegetables, and chicken. Available dried.

Parsley: A slightly peppery-fresh-flavored herb, parsley is used as a garnish and a mild flavoring. The two varieties are curly leaf, which is used more as a garnish, and flat leaf or Italian, which has a stronger flavor and is used in cooking. Fresh curly parsley is available year-round, while Italian parsley is not always to be found.

Rosemary: Belonging to the mint family, this silver-green, needle-shaped leaf is highly aromatic and has a bold flavor with hints of both lemon and pine. Delicious sprinkled over any roasted meat, poultry, tomato-based dishes, seafood, stuffing, and soups. Easy to grow outside in hot, mild areas. Available dried.

Sage: Slightly bitter with a musty mint taste, sage is the primary herb in poultry seasoning. Dried sage (whole leaves or ground) is available. This powerful, assertive herb requires care in its use. Used in stuffing, sausages, and dressings, and compliments most vegetables.

Tarragon: Has a spicy, sharp flavor with licorice overtones. Tarragon is essential to classic French cooking and is available fresh in the summer and early fall. Use sparingly because of its dominant flavor. Available dried.

Thyme: Has a minty yet lemony aroma. It is the basic herb in French cuisine and integral to a bouquet garni (see page 505). Thyme is used to season poultry, meat, vegetables, fish, and soups. Fresh thyme is easily grown outdoors in pots. Available dried as leaves or ground.

Dry Herb Tips

- Dried or ground herbs begin to lose their flavor about 6 months after the container has been opened. Keep track by writing the purchase date on the bottom of the container.
- Dried herbs can be added early in the cooking process since they require longer exposure to hear and moisture to release their flavor.
- Store dried herbs in a tightly covered container in a cool, dark cupboard to maximize their shelf life.
- Crush dried herbs in your hand before adding to your food. This breaks down the leaves to better release their flavor.
- To substitute dry herbs for fresh, use this ratio: 1 teaspoon dried is equivalent to 1 tablespoon of fresh.

Fresh Herb Tips

- Most fresh herbs are added at the end of the cooking process so that the heat doesn't destroy their flavor and aroma.
- To store fresh herbs such as basil, chives, cilantro, parsley, and rosemary, snip off the stem ends and place in a glass or jar with the stems in about 1 inch of water. Seal with a plastic bag and refrigerate for up to a week.
- Oregano, tarragon, and thyme should last in a dry plastic bag in the refrigerator for four to six days.

Salad Greens

- 1 pound of salad greens creates about 6 cups torn pieces.
- To revive wilted greens, place them in ice water with 2 tablespoons of lemon juice; cover and refrigerate for 1 hour. Or, if time permits, wrap dried greens in dry paper towels and refrigerate up to 4 hours.

Common Salad Greens

Arugula: Intensely flavored and spicy. Best used as an accent with milder greens. Choose smaller leaves for less distinctive flavor. Use soon after purchase.

Bibb lettuce: Delicate, mild flavor and tender pliable leaves similar to those of Boston.

Butter or Boston lettuce: A tender, mild, and sweet staple lettuce. Delicious as a main green.

Curly endive (chicory): Slightly bitter with a fresh, crisp texture.

Escarole: Slightly bitter, mild flavor with pleasant, nutty undertones. Part of the endive family. Good as an accent green.

Green leaf and red leaf lettuce: Distinctive, buttery, fairly sweet. A versatile lettuce, good alone or in mixes. A staple lettuce.

Iceberg lettuce: Bland and mild flavor, crunchy texture. Makes an inexpensive, quick, and easy salad. Keeps in the refrigerator for 1 week. Choose solid, compact heads with tight leaves that range from medium green outer leaves to pale green inner leaves.

Mesclun: Not a type of lettuce or green, but a "chic" mix of greens of various textures and flavors (sweet, spicy, bitter, almost always includes arugula and a bit of herbs). The name means mixture. A year-round staple that is more expensive than other mixes.

Radicchio: Strong, bittersweet, and crunchy, this red-leafed green adds color to your mixtures. A member of the endive family, it lasts only a few days in the refrigerator and is expensive.

Romaine lettuce: Crisp, strongly flavored, somewhat bittersweet staple green. Mild enough as the main element of a salad or good for adding crunch and flavor to mixed green salads. Choice of lettuce for Caesar salad. Keeps in the refrigerator for up to 1 week.

Spinach: Not a lettuce, but used in salads. Strong, somewhat bitter. Great alone or mixed with other greens. Wash leaves thoroughly, as fresh spinach is usually sandy and dirty.

Watercress: With a strong, peppery flavor, watercress adds pep to other green mixtures. Also used as a garnish. Use soon after purchase.

Cooking Oils

When stored in a cool, dark place, most oils will keep for 1 year. If you live in a warm climate or want to keep oils for a longer time, refrigerate them.

Canola oil: This light, mildly flavored monosaturated oil will not dominate the food. Its high smoke point makes it great for high-heat cooking, such as deep frying. It is an all purpose oil: good for baking, cooking, and stir-frying.

Extra-virgin olive oil: Strong, slightly fruity flavor and good for salads, stir-fries, and most cooking. Monosaturated.

Peanut oil: Slightly heavy, nutty flavor, this monosaturated oil has a high smoke point making it great for high heat cooking like deep frying. It's also good for salads and stir-fries.

Safflower oil: With its light, bland flavor, safflower oil is all-purpose, but especially good for baking.

Sesame oil: For Asian cooking and for drizzling on stir-fries. The toasted varieties are rich in flavor, while the untoasted ones are lighter in taste. Polyunsaturated.

Roasting Chart

Beef	Weight (lbs.)	Oven Temp.	Minutes per pound	Doneness
Eye Round	2 to 3	325°F	20 to 22	medium rare
Rib Eye	4 to 6	350°F	18 to 20 20 to 22	medium rare medium
Sirloin Tip	4 to 6	325°F	25 to 30 30 to 35	medium rare medium
	8 to 10	325°F	18 to 22 23 to 25	medium rare medium
Tenderloin (whole) (half)	4 to 6 2 to 3	425°F 425°F	45 to 60 (total time) 35 to 45 (total time)	medium rare medium rare

Pork	Weight (lbs.)	Oven Temp.	Minutes per pound	
Crown Roast Ham, bone-in or Boneless, fully cooked	6 to 8 10 to 16	350°F 350°F	20 to 22 10 to 12	
Loin, bone-in	3 to 12	350°F	20 to 22	
Tenderloin	½ to 1	350°F	20 to 22	

Poultry	Weight (lbs.)	Oven Temp.	Minutes per pound	
Chicken Whole, unstuffed	3 to 3½ 4 to 10	350°F 350°F	20 to 22 20	
Duckling, unstuffed	4 to 5	400°F for 30 min then	15 to 18 at 350°F	
Capon, unstuffed	8 to 10	350°F	20 to 22	
Rock Cornish Hen, unstuffed	¾ to 1¼	350°F	45 to 75 (total cooking time)	

Turkey*	Weight (lbs.)	Oven Temp.	Total Cooking Time (hours)	
Unstuffed	6 to 8 8 to 12 12 to 16 16 to 20 20 to 24	325°F 325°F 325°F 325°F 325°F	2 ¼ to 3¼ 3 to 3½ 3½ to 4½ 4 to 5 4½ to 5½	
Stuffed	6 to 8 8 to 12 12 to 16 16 to 20 20 to 24	325°F 325°F 325°F 325°F 325°F	3 to 3½ 3 1/2 to 4½ 4 to 5 4½ to 5½ 5 to 6½	

* A turkey is done when it reaches 180°F at the inner thigh and the juices run clear, not reddish pink, when the thigh muscle is deeply pierced. If the turkey is stuffed, the temperature at the center of the stuffing should be 160°F. Begin checking turkey about 1 hour before the end of the recommended roasting time.

Tips and Tricks

Soups and Stews

- Too salty? Add 1 cup of chopped potatoes. Discard them after they have cooked. The potatoes will absorb the salt.
- Too sweet? Gradually add salt to fix the flavor.
- Slightly burnt? Add milk until the burnt flavor is gone.
- To remove fat: Drop ice cubes into the pot. The fat will cling to the cubes as you stir. Take out the cubes before they melt. Fat also clings to lettuce leaves.
- To thicken: add 1 tablespoon cornstarch to 1 cup liquid.
- When adding pasta or rice, remember: they expand to two or three times their original size.
- Don't boil soups with dairy products, they might separate. After adding milk, heat soup slowly.

Eggs

- If you can't remember if an egg is hard cooked or fresh, spin it. If it wobbles, it's raw. If it spins easily, it's cooked.
- A fresh egg will sink in water, but a stale one will float.

Produce

- To perk up soggy lettuce, add lemon juice to a bowl of cold water and soak the lettuce for 1 hour in the refrigerator.

- Store celery and lettuce in paper bags, not plastic. Leave the outside leaves and stalks alone until ready to use.
- Store tomatoes with their stems pointed down, and they will stay fresh longer.
- To get the most juice out of lemons or limes, bring them to room temperature or microwave on high for 30 seconds. Then roll them on the counter to burst the juice cells; slice and juice.
- To keep cut fruit from browning, gently mix the fruit with a small amount of honey to coat.
- Cut vegetables just before cooking—never let them sit in water. When they're exposed to air or soaked in water, they quickly lose much of their vitamin content and flavor.
- Never add baking soda to cooking vegetables; while it keeps them green, it destroys their vitamin content and will make them mushy.
- To preserve nutrients in your vegetables, cook them quickly in a covered pot.
- When buying vegetables, look for firmness, lots of green (or the primary color of the vegetable), and lack of damage with no soft spots or bruises.
- Vegetables are at the point of being fully cooked when you start smelling their aroma.

Sweets

- To soften rock-hard brown sugar, add a slice of soft bread to the package and close the bag tightly. In a few hours, the sugar will be soft again.

- Marshmallows won't dry out when frozen.
- To keep sticky ingredients (such as corn syrup, honey, and molasses) from sticking to your measuring cup, lightly oil the inside of the cup before using or coat with non-stick cooking spray.
- If a cake is stuck to the pan, try dipping the bottom of the pan in hot water to soften the ingredients (fat or sugar) causing the cake to adhere to the pan.
- To avoid cracks in cheesecakes, don't over beat the ingredients. Excess air can cause it to puff up in the oven, then collapse and crack. Bake the cheesecake longer, with lower temperatures. Once it's out of the oven, run a knife between the edge of the cheesecake and the pan. This allows the cheesecake to pull away from the pan as it cools.

Freezing Tips

- Food should be in an airtight container to retain maximum freshness.
- Liquids expand when frozen, so leave space in the container.
- Freeze in gallon-size freezer bags, squeeze out the air and stack flat.
- Refreezing: the general rule is that if food still has ice crystals, it can be refrozen.
- Label frozen food containers with contents, number of servings, and the date.
- Cream and custard fillings should not be frozen.
- Most baked goods, cakes, pies, and cookies freeze well.
- All soups can be frozen. Those that contain vegetable chunks that might get mushy can be pureed after thawing, then reheated with broth or milk.

General Tips

- If you overbrown garlic, throw it away and begin again.
- Begin your sautéing with a hot pan. If using a non-stick pan, put fat in it before heating.
- Toasting nuts intensifies their flavor, so you can use less.
- Pat chicken breasts dry before sautéing them.
- Freeze boneless, skinless chicken breasts, beef, and pork for 10 minutes before slicing for stir-fry: they'll slice more evenly and quickly.
- To remove skin from chicken easier, use a paper towel to grab the skin.
- After cutting onions or garlic, remove the odor on your hands by rubbing them on a stainless-steel utensil under cold running water.
- To peel garlic quickly, snip the pointy ends off individual cloves and microwave for 10 to 15 seconds.
- When sour cream or yogurt is added to a recipe, don't let it come to a boil; boiling will cause the sauce to separate. To prevent separation, the recipe should include about 2 tablespoons of flour or 1 tablespoon cornstarch for every cup of broth plus sour cream to be thickened. If sauce does separate, push the meat to one side and whisk the sauce vigorously to bring it back together.
- To keep fruit rinds from getting stuck in your grater, spray the grater with non-stick cooking spray. If you don't have time to grate, buy the dried version in the spice section of your grocery.
- When you burn something in a pan, add baking soda and water and the burn residue will come out.

- For easy food removal from a mold, spray it with non-stick cooking spray before adding the food.
- To counteract the acid in tomato and other acidic sauces, add a pinch of sugar.
- If available, use fresh ingredients, then frozen, then canned. Most importantly, use what is most convenient.

- Flour is most often used to thicken sauces.
- Cornstarch produces a more translucent mixture than flour and has twice the thickening power.
- Before adding thickeners to your sauces or soups, mix them well with a small amount of cold water to prevent lumps.

Cooking Terms

Bake: To cook food, covered or uncovered, using the indirect, dry heat of an oven. The term is normally used in reference to cakes, cookies, desserts, and casseroles.

Baste: To moisten foods during cooking with pan drippings or sauce to enhance the flavor and prevent the food from drying out.

Beat: To smooth a mixture by whipping it in a mixer or with a whisk.

Blanch: To plunge food into boiling water for a brief time. This preserves the food's color and nutritional value, loosens skins of tomatoes or peaches, and achieves crisp, tender vegetables.

Blend: To combine, using a mixer or by hand, two or more ingredients until smooth and uniform in texture, flavor, and color.

Boil: To heat a liquid until bubbles form continuously, rise in a steady pattern, and break the liquid's surface.

Braise: To cook food slowly in a small amount of liquid in a tightly covered pan on the stove top. Recommended for less tender cuts of meat.

Broil: To cook food a certain distance directly under dry heat. The indoor version of grilling.

Caramelize: To melt sugar slowly over low heat in a pot until it becomes a golden brown, caramel-flavored syrup.

Chop: To cut into coarse or fine irregular pieces, using a knife or food processor.

Coat: To cover food evenly.

Cream: To beat a mixture to a light, fluffy consistency. This process incorporates air into the mixture so baked products have a lighter texture.

Cube: To cut food into uniform pieces, usually half an inch or larger, using a knife.

Cut in: To work a solid fat into dry ingredients, usually with a pastry blender or two knives in a crisscross motion, until coarse crumbs form.

Dash: Less than one-eighth teaspoon.

Dice: To cut food into squares smaller than half an inch, using a knife.

Dissolve: To stir a dry ingredient into a liquid ingredient until the dry ingredient disappears.

Drizzle: To pour topping in thin lines in an uneven pattern over food.

Flake: To gently break a food into small pieces with a fork.

Fold: To gently combine, using a spatula, a lighter mixture with a heavier mixture by using a circular motion bringing the contents of a bowl to the top.

Glaze: A thin, glossy coasting on food.

Grate: To rub a hard-textured food against the small, rough, sharp-edged holes of a grater.

Grease: To coat a surface with a thin layer of fat or oil. Non-stick cooking spray may be substituted.

Julienne: To cut food into thin, matchlike sticks about two inches long.

Knead: To work dough with the heels of your hands in a pressing and folding motion until it becomes smooth and elastic.

Marinade: A savory liquid in which food is placed to add flavor and to tenderize.

Mash: To press or beat a food to remove lumps and create a smooth mixture.

Mince: To cut food into very fine pieces, smaller than "chopped."

Pare: To cut off the skin or outer covering of a fruit or vegetable using a small knife or vegetable peeler.

Partially set: A mixture that is chilled to the consistency of unbeaten egg whites. Other ingredients can be added and will stay evenly distributed and not sink to the bottom or float.

Peel: To cut off the outer covering or skin of a vegetable or fruit.

Poach: To cook in simmering liquid just below the boiling point.

Preheat: To heat an oven to a specific temperature before using it.

Purée: To change a solid food into a liquid or heavy paste, usually by using a blender or food processor.

Reconstitute: To bring a concentrate or condensed food to its original strength by adding liquid.

Reduce: To boil liquid rapidly, uncovered, so some of the liquid evaporates, and the flavor is intensified.

Rind: The skin or outer coating of a food (citrus fruits, watermelon, cheese).

Roast: To cook with a dry-heat cooking method (no liquid and uncovered in the oven). Used for meats, poultry, and vegetables.

Roux: A French term that refers to a mixture of flour and fat cooked to a golden or rich brown color and used to thicken sauces, soups, and gumbos.

Sauté: To cook or brown food in a small amount of hot fat with a frequent tossing or turning motion.

Scald: To heat a liquid to just below the boiling point. Tiny bubbles will form at the edge, and a thin skin will form on top of milk.

Score: To cut narrow grooves or slits partway through the outer surface of a food to tenderize or for appearance.

Sear: To brown a food quickly on all sides, using a high heat to seal in the juices.

Shred: To cut into long, thin pieces using the round, smooth holes of a shredder.

Simmer: To cook a food in liquid that is kept just below the boiling point. Bubbles will rise slowly and break just below the surface.

Skim: To remove a substance such as fat or foam from the surface of a liquid.

Slice: To cut food into uniform sized flat, thin pieces.

Soft peaks: To beat egg whites until peaks are rounded or curled when beaters are lifted from the bowl while the whites are still moist and glossy.

Soften: To let cold food stand at room temperature before using.

Steam: To cook food by placing it on a rack or in a steamer basket over a small amount of boiling water so that the vapor that rises cooks the food. Steaming helps retain flavor, shape, color, texture, and nutritional value.

Stew: To cook food in liquid in a covered pot for a long time until tender.

Stir: To mix ingredients with a spoon or utensil to combine, to prevent food from sticking during cooking, or to cool food after cooking.

Stiff peaks: To beat egg whites until peaks stand up straight when the beaters are lifted from the bowl while the whites are still moist and glossy.

Stir-fry: An Asian method of quickly cooking small pieces of food in hot oil over high heat, stirring constantly.

Strain: To pour a mixture or liquid through a fine sieve or strainer to remove large pieces.

Toss: To mix ingredients lightly by lifting and dropping them with two utensils.

Whip: To beat a food lightly and rapidly using a whisk or mixer, to incorporate air into the mixture and increase its volume.

Zest: The colored outer portion of citrus fruit peel that is often used as flavoring. Can be purchased dried.

Substitutions

If You Don't Have	Amount	Substitute
Balsamic vinegar	1 tablespoon	1 tablespoon sherry/cider vinegar or ¼ cup red wine
Buttermilk	1 cup	1 tablespoon lemon juice/vinegar + milk to make 1 cup; 1 cup plain fat-free/low-fat yogurt
Chocolate		
unsweetened	1 ounce block	3 tablespoons cocoa + 1 tablespoon margarine
semisweet	1 ounce	1 ounce unsweetened chocolate + 1 tablespoon sugar
semisweet chips	6 ounces	½ cup + 1 tablespoon cocoa + ¼ cup + 3 tablespoons sugar + 3 tablespoons margarine
semisweet chips	1 cup	16 ounces semisweet baking chocolate, chopped
Cornstarch	1 tablespoon	2 tablespoons all-purpose flour

If You Don't Have	Amount	Substitute
Flour		
all-purpose	1 cup	1 cup self-rising flour, omit any salt and baking powder from the recipe
self-rising	1 cup	1 cup all-purpose flour + 1½ teaspoons baking powder + ½ teaspoon salt
Pumpkin/Apple pie spice	1 teaspoon	½ teaspoon ground cinnamon, ¼ teaspoon ground ginger, ⅛ teaspoon ground allspice, ⅛ teaspoon ground nutmeg
Baking powder	1 teaspoon	1 teaspoon baking soda + ½ teaspoon cream of tartar
Garlic	1 medium clove	⅛ teaspoon garlic powder or ¼ teaspoon instant minced garlic
Milk	1 cup	½ cup evaporated milk + ½ cup water
Mustard, prepared	1 tablespoon	1 teaspoon dry ground mustard
Poultry seasoning	1 teaspoon	¼ teaspoon ground thyme + ¾ teaspoon ground sage
Ricotta cheese	1 cup	1 cup cottage cheese
Sour cream	1 cup	1 cup plain fat-free yogurt
Tomato juice	1 cup	½ cup tomato sauce + ½ cup water
Tomato paste	½ cup	1 cup tomato sauce cooked, uncovered, until reduced to ½ cup
Wine		
red	1 cup	1 cup apple cider, beef broth, tomato juice, or water
white	1 cup	1 cup apple juice, chicken broth, or water
Yogurt, plain	1 cup	1 cup sour cream

Yields at a Glance

Beans	1 15-ounce can	about 1¾ cups drained
	1 pound dried	about 2⅓ cups uncooked or 5 to 6 cups cooked
Garlic	1 medium clove fresh	½ teaspoon jarred minced garlic
Carrot	1 pound	3 cups chopped or sliced or 2½ cups shredded
Spinach	1 pound fresh leaves	10 to 12 cups torn pieces, about 1 cup cooked
	1 10-ounce package frozen	1½ cups
Rice, regular long grain	1 cup dry	3 cups cooked
Rice, wild	1 cup raw	3 cups cooked
Macaroni noodles	1 pound dry	about 9 cups cooked
Spaghetti noodles	1 pound dry	about 7 cups cooked
Tomato	8 small plum	1 pound
Sugar, brown	1 pound	2¼ cups, firmly packed
Sugar, confectioners'	1 (16-ounce) box	4 cups, unsifted

Conversion Tables

Generic Formulas for Metric Conversion

Ounces to grams	multiply ounces by 28.35
Pounds to grams	multiply pounds by 453.5
Cups to liters	multiply cups by .24
Fahrenheit to Centigrade	subtract 32 from Fahrenheit, multiply by five and divide by 9

Metric Equivalents for Volume

U.S.	Imperial	Metric
⅛ tsp.	—	0.6 ml
½ tsp.	—	2.5 ml
¾ tsp.	—	4.0 ml
1 tsp.	—	5.0 ml
1½ tsp.	—	7.0 ml
2 tsp.	—	10.0 ml
3 tsp.	—	15.0 ml
4 tsp.	—	20.0 ml
1 Tbsp.	—	15.0 ml
1½ Tbsp.	—	22.0 ml
2 Tbsp. (⅛ cup)	1 fl. oz	30.0 ml
2½ Tbsp.	—	37.0 ml
3 Tbsp.	—	44.0 ml
⅓ cup	—	57.0 ml
4 Tbsp. (¼ cup)	2 fl. oz	59.0 ml
5 Tbsp.	—	74.0 ml
6 Tbsp.	—	89.0 ml
8 Tbsp. (½ cup)	4 fl. oz	120.0 ml
¾ cup	6 fl. oz	178.0 ml
1 cup	8 fl. oz	237.0 ml
1½ cups	—	354.0 ml
1¾ cups	—	414.0 ml
2 cups (1 pint)	16 fl. oz	473.0 ml
4 cups (1 quart)	32 fl. oz	.95 liters
5 cups	—	1.183 liters
16 cups (1 gallon)	128 fl. oz	3.8 liters

Oven Temperatures

Degrees Fahrenheit	Degrees Centigrade	British Gas Marks
200°	93°	—
250°	120°	—
275°	140°	1
300°	150°	2
325°	165°	3
350°	175°	4
375°	190°	5
400°	200°	6
450°	230°	8

Metric Equivalents for Weight

U.S.	Metric
1 oz	28 g
2 oz	58 g
3 oz	85 g
4 oz (¼ lb.)	113 g
5 oz	142 g
6 oz	170 g
7 oz	199 g
8 oz (½ lb.)	227 g
10 oz	284 g
12 oz (¾ lb.)	340 g
14 oz	397 g
16 oz (1 lb.)	454 g

Metric Equivalents for Butter

U.S.	Metric
2 tsp.	10.0 g
1 Tbsp.	15.0 g
1½ Tbsp.	22.5 g
2 Tbsp. (1 oz)	55.0 g
3 Tbsp.	70.0 g
¼ lb. (1 stick)	110.0 g
½ lb. (2 sticks)	220.0 g

Metric Equivalents for Length
(use also for pan sizes)

U.S.	Metric
¼ inch	.65 cm
½ inch	1.25 cm
1 inch	2.50 cm
2 inches	5.00 cm
3 inches	6.00 cm
4 inches	8.00 cm
5 inches	11.00 cm
6 inches	15.00 cm
7 inches	18.00 cm
8 inches	20.00 cm
9 inches	23.00 cm
12 inches	30.50 cm
15 inches	38.00 cm

Cookware Tips

Preparing delicious, healthy meals often starts with cookware. I recommend using cookware with Teflon® non-stick coating. It is convenient, easy to clean and limits the amount of cooking fats needed so meals are healthy and you can stay Trim & Terrific.

It is also important to properly use and care for any type of cookware so you get the most flavor out of your meals and to help prevent kitchen accidents or fires.

Here are some important things to keep in mind about kitchen safety and cookware care:

Never leave any heated cookware unattended.

- Unattended cooking is the number one contributor to cooking fires—the leading cause of fires in homes across America.

Don't let your pans get too hot.

- Temperatures can rise very quickly in an empty pan left on high heat. High temperatures can lead to intense spattering when food is added, which can be a burn hazard.
- Avoid preheating empty cookware on high heat. Low or medium heat is sufficient.

Learn how to tell when your pan is properly preheated.

- If you are using a non-stick or empty pan, flick a few drops of water onto the pan from your wetted hand. Once the water droplets begin to sizzle and dance in the pan, it is sufficiently preheated.
- If the pan has a small quantity of oil or fat in it, place a small crouton or piece of onion in the pan. When the food is browning on the edges, the pan is ready for cooking.
- Never flick water into hot oil—it will spatter intensely and be a burn hazard!
- Always turn on the exhaust fan or open a window before cooking.
- If accidentally overheated, usually by leaving a preheating pan unattended, some types of cookware, including non-stick, can emit fumes that are harmful to pet birds. Always move your birds out of the kitchen before cooking.

Prolong the life of non-stick cookware through proper care and handling.

- Properly clean non-stick cookware by simply washing with hot, soapy water after each use. A sponge or dishcloth is usually all it takes to get the surface thoroughly clean.
- Try not to use abrasive cleaners or scouring pads. If you've got stubborn food residue, use a non-abrasive cleaner such as soft scrub.
- Generally, using plastic, nylon, or wooden utensils is best since they prevent marring. Avoid using knives and cutting food in the pan to prevent scratching.
- For best performance use cookware that isn't scratched. But non-stick coatings are pretty resilient and cooking with scratched cookware won't affect the safety of your food. And, even if you do ingest any particles, they are not harmful to your health.

Brought to you by DuPont™ Teflon® non-stick coatings

Index

REFERENCE